EGYPTIAN AMERICAN JOURNEYS

EGYPTIAN AMERICAN JOURNEYS

Edited by
Fikry F. Andrawes and
Mahmoud A. Elshazly

OLIVE
BRANCH
PRESS

An imprint of Interlink Publishing Group, Inc.
www.interlinkbooks.com

First published in 2022 by

Olive Branch Press
An imprint of Interlink Publishing Group, Inc.
46 Crosby Street, Northampton, MA 01060
www.interlinkbooks.com

Library of Congress Cataloging-in-Publication data available:
ISBN-13: 978-1-62371-898-5

Printed and bound in the United States of America

CONTENTS

Introduction 1

In Sha'allah Aroosa: Finding My Way as a Jewish Egyptian American Woman
Joyce Zonana 4

What Is Home?
Hesham Issawi 14

Breaking Walls and Building Bridges
Maysaa Barakat 21

Illegal Immigrant
Gamal Omar 31

Fragments of the Story of My Passage from Alexandria to New York
Marlène Barsoum 44

My Story "Without Why"
Naeem Mady 53

The Ghoneims' Egyptian American Story of Three Generations
Annie Whitney 65

Recollections from a New World
Fekri A. Hassan. 74

Egypt's Ballerina
Magda Saleh 91

My Journey from Birth until Retirement
Mahmoud F. Agha 108

We Are the Sum
Souheir Eldefrawy Elmasry 120

The Story of a Long Life
Lofty Basta. 137

Navigating Life between Three Continents
Samia I. Spencer. 151

How I Came to Manage Billions
Sherif Abou Sabh. 162

An Incomplete Journey from the Middle East to the New World
Mostafa El Khashab. 169

An Egyptian Pioneer in Aerospace Engineering
Awatef Hamed 178

My Journey in Brief
Mohamed Elgamal. 187

Between Egypt and America
Mona Mobarak. 201

My Intellectual, Social, Professional, and Cultural Journey in the United States
Sherif Nasr. 214

From Cairo to New York: The Challenges
Mona Mikhail. 223

Me an Engineer? Dealing in Banking? I Love It!
Samir Ansary. 229

My Life in Two Cities
Sylvia Iskander. 243

From Egypt's Farmland to Nagasaki and Everywhere in between
Tarek Nazir Saadawi 253

Work in Progress
Dina Samir. 266

Seeing the World While Working
Fayek Andrawes. 280

From Egypt to England to America
Giselle Hakki 291

A Common Life with Uncommon Blessings
Norm Toma 304

Excerpts from My Life in Egypt and the States
Rawia El Wassimy-Agha. 311

Two Deviations Converged to Correct My Path
Reda Athanasios. 326

From Egypt to America and Back to Egypt
Nahla Bakry. 340

From a Nile Delta Village to the Long Island Sound
Mahmoud Elshazly 357

Saba, Gameela, and Me
Nimet Habachy. 375

The Many Journeys between Egypt and America
Fikry Andrawes 384

INTRODUCTION

Egyptians are relative newcomers to the United States. For thousands of years, ruling powers came and went, but the inhabitants of the Nile valley tended to stay in the land of their birth. They rarely emigrated from Egypt. Instead of losing population, the Nile and its fertile flood-plain attracted foreign settlers from outside its borders and became a true melting pot. Nomadic people, traders, foreign bureaucrats, and even former prisoners of war were absorbed into the native popula-tion, creating a unique culture that exists to the present day.

Modern times have seen a notable reversal of the pattern. Successive waves of emigration from Egypt started after the Second World War. Independence from colonial rule and the creation of the state of Israel caused increased political instability in the region. Small numbers of Egyptians, as well as resident foreigners, began to leave the country. This trend accelerated with the 1956 war against England, France, and Israel. But after the 1967 war with Israel, the trickle became a flood. Many Egyptians became disillusioned with the governmental system and decided to emigrate. They were further encouraged because a promising destination had become available.

A few years earlier, the passing of the Immigration and Nationality Act of 1965 (the Hart-Caller Act) in the United States opened the door to educated and professional Egyptians. This Act, which did away with the prior racially-based quota system, was a result of the civil rights movement and was one of President Lyndon Johnson's Great Society programs. As a result, a wave of Egyptian immigration to the United States began. Members of this cohort tended to be well-educated and many had advanced degrees.[1]

Why did they leave Egypt? How did they adjust to and integrate into their new lives in the United States? How did they relate to their motherland? The answers to these questions are, of course, highly individual.

The autobiographical essays in this book touch on these themes in a variety of ways. Although the editors made a deliberate attempt to include contributors from diverse backgrounds, this collection does not claim to be representative of a larger population of Egyptians, or to constitute a scientific study. Rather, these are the personal reflections of thirty-three Egyptian–Americans, living in cities and towns across the United States. They include engineers, medical doctors, taxi drivers, businesspeople, scientists, housewives, Egyptologists, artists, teachers, and university professors, among others. The authors are equally divided between men and women. They include Jews, Christians, and Muslims, as well as non-believers.

As we shall see, Egyptians emigrated for a variety of reasons: educational, political, religious, and economic. Some were pushed out of Egypt by adverse circumstances; others were pulled toward the United States seeking new opportunities. Often, it was a combination of both.

The poet Ahmed Fouad Nigm expressed this yearning in words that were set to music in a popular song:

Forbidden from leaving
Forbidden from singing
Forbidden from talking
Forbidden from smiling
Forbidden from complaining

---

1   The US census of 2016 estimated the number of residents claiming Egyptian ancestry to be about 256,000, and the number of Egyptian-born to be about 181,677. Of the wave of immigrants who came to the United States from Egypt after 1967, 58% were scientists and engineers and 70% had graduate degrees.

Forbidden from even being silent
A detective in every alley
Soldiers in each harbor
Even though my love for you increases
God knows what else will be forbidden.

The writer Yousif Idris put it this way: "In the Arab world there isn't enough oxygen to produce one writer! Oxygen is needed not only for writers, but for everyone to be able to excel in their jobs. Without oxygen, society will suffocate."

IN SHA'ALLAH AROOSA:
FINDING MY WAY AS A
JEWISH EGYPTIAN AMERICAN WOMAN

Joyce Zonana

Because my family immigrated from Cairo to the United States in 1951, when I was under two years old, I never really lived in Egypt. Instead, Egypt lived in me. Our home in Brooklyn was drenched in the life my parents had reluctantly left behind in Cairo: we listened to the music, ate the food, spoke the language, and followed the customs of the "old country." I was raised to be a dutiful Egyptian daughter—reverencing my mother, obeying my father, deferring to my brother, and preparing to marry at an early age. "In sha'allah aroosa, ان شاء الله عروسة" my relatives all said whenever they greeted me as a child: "May you be a bride, God willing!"

We were Egyptian; that was obvious. But we were also Jewish. In early 1950s New York—and even, unfortunately, to some still today—that combination struck people as an oxymoron. Our crowded apartment was in a neighborhood populated by Irish and Italian Catholics and Eastern European Jews. In some ways, our customs were closest to the Mediterranean Catholics with whom we lived side by side. Eastern European Jews refused to believe we were Jewish: "You mean you don't eat gefilte fish? You don't speak Yiddish?" Try as I might to explain, I was stymied—confused—myself. When I said we were Jews from Egypt, the retort from my young companions was always, "But I thought all the Jews left Egypt with Moses. Isn't that what Passover is about?"

What my parents told me was confusing, but the Old Testament story of the Exodus was even more so. In Biblical times, the Jews were said to have been slaves in Egypt. Yet my parents had lived comfortable middle-class lives in Cairo, and they sorely missed their homeland. The biblical Exodus was a deliverance. Our exodus was something else entirely. Why then did we leave? Vague hints about rising anti-Semitism led me to understand that somehow things had gotten complicated. But still the story remained murky, and my identity remained puzzling.

When I insisted on the Egyptian part, my little friends ogled me with wonder: "Does that mean you're related to Cleopatra? Did you ride a camel? Did you climb the pyramids?" Americans were fascinated with ancient Egypt, unable to grasp the fact that I was born in a modern nation-state with a cosmopolitan, multi-religious, multi-ethnic population. But I'm not sure I understood that either.

We had a handful of relatives who had immigrated to the United States before us, but the majority of my parents' families remained behind, until the Egyptian government's response to the tripartite invasion forced them out. After 1956, most of my mother's family—her parents, a sister, two brothers—immigrated to Brazil, unable to obtain visas for the United States. My father's older brother and his family, including my paternal grandmother, eventually joined us in New York. But even though we spent time with our relatives, I never felt as if we were part of a real community. For much of my childhood, I felt oddly isolated.

Once a month or so, we drove to the Arab stores on Atlantic Avenue to buy the ingredients for the Middle Eastern dishes we loved: ful muddamas, ba'lawa, amardin, wara' anab, kobeba, kofta, and more. During those magical outings, my father would speak Arabic with shopkeepers, and I would watch delightedly as both my parents relaxed into the rhythms and gestures of home. This seemed to be where we belonged, and yet we never cultivated relationships with other Egyptians or other Arabs. Although I asked why, my parents evaded my questions.

When relatives gathered, they also often spoke Arabic, enthusiastically and volubly, but most of the time, the language in our household was French—the language, my parents assured me, of educated people in Egypt. Again, I wondered why. My father—who had a French law degree—had served as a French-Arab interpreter in the mixed tribunals in Cairo; in the United States, he sometimes took on translating jobs to supplement his income as a bookkeeper. I was fascinated by the Arab language and begged my parents to teach it to me. They never did, and aside from some common expressions and curse words, I never learned it, despite several efforts when I grew older. Not knowing Arabic remains one of my greatest regrets.

Throughout my childhood, two impulses competed for mastery over me: one was the desire to fully know and understand the Egypt my parents had been devastated to leave; the other was to free myself from my family's grip and to become, somehow, truly American. Egypt, like the United States, glimmered like an unattainable mystery—the one behind me, the other before me. My parents rarely spoke in detail about the homeland they had lost, and as the political climate there for Jews worsened, it seemed less and less likely we would ever return, even if only for a visit. And so, I threw myself into becoming American: I strove to master English, longing for independence and autonomy.

My parents still hoped I would be an aroosa, but as a would-be-American adolescent growing up in the 1950s and 1960s, I did not at all want to be a bride, rebelling against the conventional feminine roles my mother tried to instill in me. I refused to cook or to learn any of the domestic arts, and—to the family's horror—ached to attend an Ivy League school away from home. My high school teachers encouraged me, and I moved into a dorm at seventeen, only to find my first year at college overwhelming and terrifying.

I'd chosen to go to the place that most symbolized patrician, privileged "America" to me—Harvard/Radcliffe—and the results were predictably disastrous. What was I doing there, a poor Jewish-Egyptian immigrant girl from Brooklyn? Unable to find peers, to discover any reflections of myself, I dropped out and returned home, only to move out again within a few months and rent an apartment alone, truly scandalizing the family. The year was 1968, and although still deeply conflicted, I threw myself into the youth culture of the day.

After many fits and starts—including a stint working in publishing and some time as a housepainter—I managed to earn an undergraduate degree and eventually a PhD in English literature. My goal was to become blandly American, as I strove to put both my Egyptianness and my Jewishness behind me.

In 1986, my first full-time college teaching job took me to Norman, Oklahoma, where I was hired as an assistant professor of Victorian literature in the English Department at the University of Oklahoma. A more alien environment for me could not have been imagined, and yet, again, that was precisely what appealed to me about it: the challenge of mid-America. In my passion to fit in, I tried to embrace this new world: I learned to drive a car, bought a ranch-style house with an attached garage, planted tulips in my backyard, chose appliances from Sears, drove out into the prairie to commune with the buffalos. One year, I even threw a Christmas tree trimming party for colleagues and friends—a tree-trimming party, replete with Christmas carols, home-baked German cookies, eggnog, and mulled cider! I could not have gotten further from my roots.

That party was the turning point. Somewhere in the middle of that evening, I found myself gripped: What was I doing? Who did I think I was? A Jewish Egyptian immigrant, adrift in America's heartland, playacting at belonging.

Among my colleagues in Oklahoma was a Native American scholar and writer, Geary Hobson. Early during my time in Norman, he invited me to a pow-wow deep in the countryside west of Oklahoma City. I spent that evening watching in wonder as native men, women, and children danced and sang and talked and laughed. When I asked Geary how I, as a white woman, could help redress the wrongs done to the indigenous peoples of this land, his answer was simple: "Embrace your heritage. Learn about your ancestors."

Another colleague, Nicholas Howe—son of Irving Howe, the prominent Jewish intellectual, and Thalia Phillies, a Greek-born classical scholar—helped me to accept my own Mediterranean Jewish heritage. Along with Nick's wife, Georgina, we shopped in Oklahoma City's well-stocked Middle Eastern grocery and celebrated Jewish holidays. New Yorkers exiled on the prairie, we were out of our element, but together we found a way both to be ourselves and to participate in this strange new world.

My teaching of Victorian literature, coupled with my commitment to feminism, led me to a line of research that also allowed me to explore and embrace my own identity. In graduate school, I'd read Edward Said's groundbreaking *Orientalism*, a book that shows how the Orient has been constructed—and dominated—by the West. Said's arguments made sense to me, especially as I considered how most Americans I met simultaneously exoticized and demonized Eastern individuals—including, of course, Egyptians.

As I intensively read and taught about nineteenth-century British women writers, I began to notice another insidious aspect of Orientalism, what I eventually termed *feminist orientalism* in an article I published in *Signs: Journal of Women in Culture and Society* in 1993 ("'The Sultan and the Slave': Feminist Orientalism and the Structure of *Jane Eyre*"). What I saw again and again was the use of the figure of a purportedly oppressed Middle Eastern woman to articulate their critiques of the oppression of women in the West. Starting with Mary Wollstonecraft and moving through her daughter Mary Shelley and culminating with Charlotte Bronte, the British and American writers I studied all framed their arguments for women's rights in the West as the *removal* of Eastern despotism and oppression. Thus, they could be seen as arguing not for a radical restructuring of Western society, but rather for making the West more like itself: more enlightened, egalitarian, democratic, etc. Feminist orientalism allowed Western feminists to make their arguments palatable to their Western audience.

Immersing myself in the research for this article made me think more and more about my own experience as an Oriental woman in Western society. And I realized that what I was doing as I researched and wrote my scholarly articles was in fact studying my own experience of seeing and being seen "under Western eyes." It was time to decolonize my own mind, to stop claiming objectivity and to speak from my own perspective—as, indeed, an Egyptian Jewish immigrant from Brooklyn.

The first thing I did was to turn away from traditional scholarship toward a more personal, intimate style of writing. I wrote one transitional essay, focusing on my relationship with a novel by Dickens. And in 1997, I began a memoir, eventually published in 2008 as *Dream Homes: From Cairo to Katrina, an Exile's Journey*. Part of the work for the memoir was gathering more specific information about my parents' lives in Egypt, as well as learning much more about Egypt in general and Egyptian Jews in particular. I intensively interviewed my parents and other family members; I talked with other Egyptian Jews; I read books and articles that allowed me to understand more fully what had happened in Egypt in the first half of the twentieth century that ultimately led to what one writer has called the "dispersion" of Egyptian Jewry.

The facts that emerged intrigued me. I discovered that, while some Jews had lived in Egypt since antiquity, many others had migrated from other parts of the Ottoman Empire during the nineteenth century, drawn by favorable living conditions and business opportunities. My father's side of the family had come to Egypt from Syria, settling in Heliopolis. My mother's ancestors were from Syria and Iraq, and they had lived in Cairo's elegant downtown.

The Jews of Egypt were a varied lot—some identifying with the British occupiers and aspiring to a European identity (hence the French-speaking), others joining in with communist and Egyptian nationalist movements to liberate Egypt from foreign dominance. Within my own family, there was a range: one of my father's brothers was a Zionist who had moved to Palestine in the mid-1940s; a maternal great-uncle had been an Egyptian nationalist; most of the other members of the family simply hoped to live their lives peacefully in Egypt, staying out of politics.

But politics came for them, no matter how much they tried to avoid it. In the 1940s, pent-up resentment against the British occupiers fostered demonstrations and violence against Jews, who were cast as foreign oppressors despite their full engagement in Egyptian society. In 1945, a demonstration on the anniversary of the Balfour Declaration led to the looting of Jewish stores and the burning of several synagogues. That's when my father—who also worked for the grand rabbi of Cairo, Nahum Effendi—made his decision to emigrate to the United States. He applied for a visa and waited five years for approval. We left in the early spring of 1951.

I'd been born in 1949—my parents' long-awaited first child—a year after the establishment of the state of Israel. During my mother's pregnancy, there had been more anti-Semitic (or, more properly, anti-Zionist) rioting and propaganda. My mild-mannered father was arrested under the suspicion that he was plotting to build a bomb in his kitchen. My mother's pregnancy was a difficult one, and she had to remain in bed for the full nine months. I've always felt that, in the womb, I absorbed her anxiety and sense of vulnerability during that difficult time—a vulnerability and anxiety that have remained with me ever since.

More and more, as I learned more about my family's past, I longed to visit Cairo, to see for myself the place that had shaped my parents and therefore me. My parents continued to discourage me: "There's nothing there for us anymore." But I felt there was indeed something for me, and the visit felt like an existential imperative.

Through my writing and research, I'd met the Egyptian-American, Muslim political scientist Mervat Hatem. I'd read her work on Egyptian feminists' interactions with Western feminists; she'd read my article on feminist orientalism. When we met, she said she'd wondered how a Western woman could write such an essay. When I told her I was born in Egypt, she said, "Oh, then we must be cousins." When I sheepishly admitted I was Jewish, she concluded, "Then we are sisters."

I told Mervat about my desire to visit Cairo; she assigned me more reading: Amitav Ghosh's *In an Antique Land*, a wonderful book about medieval Egypt and the deep interconnections among Jews, Muslims, and Christians. This, along with Ammiel Alcalay's *After Jews and Arabs:*

Remaking Levantine Culture, introduced me to a new way of thinking about the lives of Jews in Egypt and throughout the Middle East. Both Ghosh and Alcalay worked to undercut both the Arab and Jewish nationalist narratives, showing that Arabs and Jews belonged together—that, in fact, many Middle Eastern Jews *were* Arabs, as I came to believe myself to be.

Mervat and I arranged to visit Egypt together, early in the winter of 1999, during Ramadan—which I decided to observe by fasting along with everyone else. Mervat would be staying in her family's apartment near the Saad Zaghloul Metro station; I took a room at the Windsor Hotel. I wanted to be near the old downtown, where my parents had lived, not far from the former Rue Soleiman Pasha (now Tala'at Harb), near the central synagogue, Char Hashamayim on Adly Street, close to Groppi's, the pastry shop everyone in the family still raved about.

The moment I stepped off the plane, I knew I was home. Men had unrolled prayer rugs beside the baggage claim area; I was tempted to bow down to the ground with them. All around me, I saw dark skin and dark eyes that reflected back my own; when I entered the taxi the hotel had arranged for me, the driver's greeting, "Ahlan wa sahlan"—"Welcome to your homeland," he repeated in English—brought tears to my eyes.

Mervat had worried about how to introduce me to people. Should we tell them I was Jewish? I decided, yes, of course, I wanted everyone to know I was Jewish, born in Cairo, returned to see the city for myself: "Ana Yahudiya Masriya," I learned to say. People's faces invariably lit up, "Ahlan wa sahlan," I heard again and again: "We miss the Jews of Egypt."

During that first trip to Cairo, I visited many old synagogues and Jewish neighborhoods. I met the president of the Jewish Community of Cairo, Carmen Weinstein, a woman who was valiantly fighting to preserve the Jewish heritage and presence in Egypt (her efforts have been admirably furthered by the current president, Magda Haroun). I also spent time exploring Coptic Cairo, and the area around Al Azhar. The week went by astonishingly quickly, and by the time I returned home, I knew quite clearly that Egypt was a deep part of me, and that I would be back again and again.

Indeed, in the next few years, I did return several more times, often in the company of a Muslim man I had met, an African American law professor who ran a study program in Cairo. Bernard led me more deeply into Egyptian life—he arranged for me to meet Naguib Mahfouz, for example—and I am grateful for the experiences we shared there together.

After my memoir came out in 2008, I continued to read widely about Egypt and its Jews. I read works by other Egyptian Jewish writers and found myself especially attracted to the works of writers who acknowledged and explored the connections between Jews and Arabs. Unfortunately, many Egyptian Jews—while remaining nostalgically attached to their homeland—have turned their backs on these connections.

I've been especially inspired by the mid-twentieth-century writer Jacqueline Kahanoff, whose essays on Levantinism and novel *Jacob's Ladder* offer a profound model for integrating Arab and Jewish identities. More recently, the works of Egyptian Jewish French writers Paula Jacques and Tobie Nathan struck me as breaking new ground. I've translated one novel by Tobie Nathan, *Ce pays qui te ressemble*, coming out in 2020 as *A Land Like You*, and I am hoping to translate several novels by Paula Jacques.

These days, I live in Bay Ridge, a bustling Brooklyn neighborhood with many other Egyptians and Arab Americans (along with Russians, Greeks, Irish, Koreans, and Italians). Just down the street is the owner of Sahadi's, the Lebanese grocery on Atlantic Avenue my family frequented when I was a child. I shop at Balady Market, a wonderful store on Fifth Avenue nearby, where I buy their homemade torshi and halawa. Every day, I hear Arabic on the street, and its mellifluous tones comfort me. I find myself meeting more and more Egyptian and Egyptian American friends, and when I use the local car service, I'm always delighted when the driver turns out to be Egyptian. I recognize them by the warmth of their smiles and the depth of their eyes. It feels as if, at long last, I've found my community. And not too long ago, I married for the first time, becoming, indeed, an aroosa.

Americans need to know that Jews lived happily in Egypt for many centuries. They need to understand that Islam and Judaism are sister religions; they need to grasp that it is competing nationalisms and false stereotypes that have created the tragic split between peoples who truly belong together. As I continue to read and write, I am committed to helping make that new understanding possible.

———

JOYCE ZONANA, a professor emerita at the City University of New York, is a writer and literary translator. Her memoir *Dream Homes: From Cairo to Katrina, an Exile's Journey* was published by Feminist Press. Her most recent translation, Tobie Nathan's *A Land Like You* is published by Seagull Books and offers a portrait of Egypt's Jews during the first five decades of the twentieth century.

WHAT IS HOME?

Hesham Issawi

What defines *home*? Is it people, a specific place, or the memories made during a certain period of time?

Like many other fresh immigrants, I worried that I'd never feel at home in the United States. I was going to college with my Egyptian accent, not knowing anyone, not belonging to any ethnic group. I was an alien. And I was afraid I would always be an alien.

Little did I know, the US Citizenship and Immigration Services would call me an alien, because I'm not an American citizen. It was strange reading the word *alien* in my application, but in the United States, you get used to it, and even laugh about it. Which I did. Things can feel strange when you are in a foreign country at twenty years old. Everything is new, and therefore everything is exciting. Missing the bus is exciting. Slipping in the snow doesn't hurt as much. Watching the same people riding the bus with you on a daily basis, at the same time, in the early morning, you end up getting to know those people, even though you never uttered a word to them. Just by looking, staring, and making eye contact, you know them. And yes, you can find a beautiful lady and fall for her every morning on your ride, and then forget about her until the next morning, when you fall again for her. It is those silent, unspoken moments that make everything worth it.

Oak Street is the name of the street in Evanston, Illinois where I lived when I moved to the States from Egypt. I took the bus every morning for an hour to reach my school. It was exciting because it was new and fresh. That street was full of big oak trees. You couldn't see the end of the street because of the trees. They reminded me of streets in Maadi, Egypt, a nice neighborhood on the outskirts of Cairo. In our youth, we used to call the area the American Colony because many foreigners lived there. The American School was and still is there. But Chicago was freezing cold and windy in a way Egypt never was. Nevertheless, it was new and exciting.

One of the issues new immigrants struggle with most is identity, and the sense of belonging. It's a difficult process to feel part of a place and melt into it. But the United States is the easiest place to do that; I found it to be a welcoming country and the American people are the most welcoming. Sure, there are exceptions: the racists, the bigots, and the anti-immigrants. But I would say the majority are not like that. In my personal experience, I was more welcomed than pushed away. Maybe that was because I lived in an academic environment—I'm not sure— but during my first years in the States, I felt very much supported and encouraged by Americans, who helped me to assimilate.

I arrived in the United States in 1990, when US troops were sent to Kuwait during the first Gulf war. It was a tumultuous time for many Americans, and there were many cultural and political discussions in classrooms about the war, Islam, the Middle East, Arabism, the Palestinian issue, the conflict with Israel, and many other related topics. I was in the middle of this because I was from this part of the world. I was not into politics or cultural issues when I was in Egypt, so I wasn't prepared for this wave of questioning: "Who are you? What do you guys mean by Arabism? Who are the Palestinians? Why do you hate Israel? Why is Islam so violent? Who built the pyramids? The Jews built the pyramids? Oh, no, noooo, Black Africans built the pyramids." In my mind, I always thought Egyptians built the pyramids. I was bombarded with all these questions and curiosity, which wasn't bad because it was stimulating.

I was always in a defensive position and had to move to an offensive position by reading, researching, and arming myself with the truth about who I was and where I came from. It was a time of self-discovery and reflection about my native culture. It made me special among my American peers in the classroom.

This led me to art. I discovered that art was what I needed; it was the language I could use to explain and define myself. Americans were eager to learn, and I was eager to tell them, so I had to find and dig deep into my history and myself. It was a win-win situation.

I changed my major to study photography, the language of light and shadows. I stood in the darkroom, printed my photos, exhibited them to others, and got comments and criticisms. It was an inspirational time that motivated me to move to the next level, which was motion picture.

I took a class on the aesthetics of film and studied the visual language of cinema. I was in love with the process. Translating an image in my head to a visual language and sharing it with everyone was just magical. I studied filmmaking for four years at Columbia College in Chicago. I was introduced to personal filmmaking. If you put yourself in movies, you could say something personal. When I discovered that, I started another journey—this time in the world of cinema. It's an amazing world, because you travel while you're sitting wherever you are; you don't go anywhere physically, but emotionally, you're flying. It's a visceral experience. The beauty of cinema is that it opens the door to diversity because you can watch movies from all over the globe and cross any borders and language barriers. Cinema has a universal language and grammar—the visual language of cinema.

In Chicago, I learned about myself, and got my first job, and had my first marriage. It was home for a while, where both good and bad memories happened. After graduation, I worked at a TV channel and in the documentary field. I started to make indie documentary films, and because I'm Egyptian, I used Egypt as my story. I did historical documentaries about ancient Egypt with the Learning Channel, and then other films for the History Channel. But again, I was not telling my story; I was telling other people's stories. That led me to narrative filmmaking. So, I decided to move to Los Angeles, California, to Hollywood.

The move to Los Angeles was not complicated, because the United States is a very mobile country. You pack your bag and drive away; it's a typical American story. This is exactly what I did. As I drove to California from Chicago, I got to see and experience the vastness of the States.

By the year 2000, I was in Los Angeles, looking for a job. The economy was good and it was easy to find jobs. Then 2001 came, and 9/11 changed everything. The day the two towers fell in New York, my ex-wife woke me up at 9 am, Los Angeles time, to tell me. I was in shock.

Then the news came that the suspects were from the Middle East. *Oh my God*, I thought, *here we go*. I had a job interview in the following days. It was very awkward. Everyone was in shock, and I was walking into an interview. It seemed like bad timing.

The first question was, "Hmm, I notice an accent. So where are you from?"

I thought, *Oh shit…what should I say? Should I lie?* Then I answered, mumbling, "Egypt… I am Egyptian, originally."

Then came that look. It might have been an innocent look, meaning nothing. But my subconscious reacted, and I interpreted the look in many ways. Ultimately, I didn't get the job, but I figured it was time to make a movie. As strange as it sounds, it was actually a good time to tell our story and expose ourselves. Instead of hiding, it was time to get out my camera and speak the language I love—the language of cinema.

I ended up making a couple of short films, which gave me the confidence to make a feature film. Of course, I had to find financing and producers and deal with the business of filmmaking. I love the art of filmmaking, but the business side of it is tough.

Luckily, things worked out, and I finished my first film by 2008. The movie was entitled *AmericanEast*. I put my story, from Chicago and Los Angeles, along with other stories from friends, into the movie. In fact,

9/11 was one of the reasons we were able to make *AmericanEast*. I was introduced to Tony Shalhoub, a famous American TV actor, known for the TV series *Monk*. His background is Lebanese, and after 9/11, he wanted to know more about his cultural roots. We met in this moment of awakening. He liked the script and became part of the film. His name was attached to the project, which helped move things forward and get the movie made. We were able to get the financing in place, and then we got the green light to shoot the film.

AmericanEast was a hard film to make. We tried to be balanced in how we presented its political and social views. Some people in the Arab community in the United States criticized the film because we were critical of our own culture. However, for us, the film was about digging deeper into our culture and breaking taboos. One of our influences was Spike Lee, the African American filmmaker.

AmericanEast took me to Egypt after all those years in the States. I had left Egypt in 1990 and I returned in 2005 for a documentary job, and then went back again in 2009 for the Cairo Film Festival, where *AmericanEast* was screened.

I felt tarnished by criticism from reporters and journalists in Cairo, who didn't get what life was like for Arabs and Muslims in the United States. I couldn't express myself in Arabic at that time because my Arabic was rusty. In the press conference, one of the reporters called me a Zionist. I tried to explain to the audience that our lives as Middle Easterners in the United States are different from the lives of people in the Middle East. We must assimilate into a different culture, and therefore we develop different habits, traditions, and ways of thinking.

Then we screened the film at the Dubai Film Festival, and the audience was more receptive. They got it, and we had productive discussions.

After I returned to Los Angeles, the images and smells of Cairo's streets—the noise, the small alleyways, the Nile—stuck with me. I felt I needed to make a movie about Cairo. By 2009, I had finished writing the movie *Cairo Exit*, and we started filming it in Cairo the following year. The film is a *Romeo and Juliet* inspired story set in the ghettos of Cairo. Love doesn't have boundaries; it doesn't care about poverty or religious differences. This is the kernel of the film.

But in Egypt, every script must pass through the censorship office. I wasn't aware of this and didn't know that, without approval from the government, I wouldn't be able to make the film. The censorship rejected the script because one of the characters is a Coptic Christian Egyptian, and she falls in love with a Muslim man. They said the story was too sensitive to tell. They gave me many comments on the script and said I had to make the changes if I wanted to make the film.

I said, "No way."

Luckily, my producer was crazy enough to let me start filming without a permit. We started shooting in Cairo with actors who weren't well-known at the time. Now, they are stars in Egypt. I was arrested many times. I had a very good production manager, whom I called the Maradona of Egyptian Streets, and he was able to get us out. He used many techniques to soften the attitude of the policemen.

The movie screened at the Dubai Film Festival at the end of 2010. The Egyptian censorship office found out about it and banned the film from ever being released in Egypt.

By 2011, the Arab Spring had started. A sudden wave of protests took place in the streets of Egypt, demanding a change of regime. Somehow, *Cairo Exit* became part of this movement. The story includes many of the elements that caused the revolt, and shows the struggle of the youth to find jobs and start new lives, and all the other obstacles they faced.

I joined the protests and believed in what the Western media labeled the Arab Spring. Suddenly, my life took a totally different and unexpected turn. There was hope in Egypt! I could take my camera and film anywhere without being harassed, or afraid of the internal security service. There was an explosion of self-expression by young musicians; there was an explosion of underground music and independent cinema. Art in general became accessible and was used to express the nation's wounds.

I struggled with whether to stay in Egypt or head back to my chosen home in Los Angeles. Egypt would always be part of my upbringing, but the United States had shaped my identity; it had influenced my thinking and my attitude toward life. A teacher in my film school once told me, "All we want from you is to be." This became my slogan—to be who I am and be true to myself. I want to be committed to living the truth, rather than just understanding it. I believe we can use the visual medium to bring cultures together and create a better understanding of our humanity.

Unfortunately, the dream of the Arab Spring faded. It was naïve to believe that a society can change because of protests and massive demonstrations. It's more complicated than that. Some things are so deeply rooted in society that they can't change quickly.

I found myself caught between the United States and Egypt. It's like a tug of war. When I am in Egypt, I long for the States; once I return to the States, I long for Egypt. The idea of choosing between these two countries and my two identities feels impossible. Somehow, I need to find a bridge between them. I believe that bridge is cinema and making films. It could be called escapism, but it helps bring out my ideas and feelings and make them more real, more tangible, more visible.

———◆———

HESHAM ISSAWI is a movie director in Egypt and the United States. Oh, East is East, and West is West, and never the twain shall meet/Till Earth and Sky stand presently at God's great Judgment Seat/But there is neither East nor West, Border, nor Breed, nor Birth/When two strong men stand face to face, tho' they come from the ends of the earth!

BREAKING WALLS AND BUILDING BRIDGES

Maysaa Barakat

I was born and raised in the Cairo suburb of Heliopolis. As my first and foremost significant role model, my mother was but one of a series of strong women who have had a positive impact on my life. My father, a mechanical engineer and a general in the Egyptian army, together with my brother, my husband, and my two daughters, are my main anchors and support group. Born in the mid-1960s, going to school in the 1970s, and attending college in the 1980s, I shared the middle-class values of my generation: education, hard work, fairness, and most importantly, level-headedness. To these values, my parents added empathy. While weaving the fabric of this chapter, I will reflect on the influence my background has had on my career choices, and how it has led me to focus on the importance of cultural competence and its crucial impact on future generations.

In the 1960s, Heliopolis was developing into an upper-middle class neighborhood, with Indian laurel and royal poinciana trees on both sides of the streets, high-rise residential buildings, and a pleasing architectural environment. Heliopolis residents were generally well-educated professionals, whose lifestyles were a happy medium between modernity and tradition. The English school I attended for twelve years mirrored our Heliopolis culture. Secular, co-educational, and private, it was unique among a myriad of public and Catholic schools and single-sex and private language institutions. My schoolmates and I had similar family backgrounds; our parents looked and dressed alike and shared the progressive values of their era: open-mindedness, common sense, and a healthy appreciation for responsible freedom, as well as respect for cultural traditions and moral standards.

Sheltered in the magnificent school campus and its majestic buildings, rumored to have been standing since the early years of the British occupation, I spent my formative years engaging in classroom debates, attending gatherings in the assembly hall, singing in the choir, proudly displaying my art creations, and most of all, playing basketball on the outdoor courts. I was among the highest achievers and a permanent fixture of the elite class A group; however, I did not stand out. During those years, I blended in nicely with most of my peers and was clearly visible only to a few good friends.

An incident stands out as I remember my adolescent years. On the eve of the final exam of the year, my parents were peacefully enjoying the pleasant breeze of a May evening on the balcony of our seventh-floor apartment, which was in a beautiful and tall building. From there, I could see my entire world; my school stood majestically two blocks away, and in the turnabout was the metro train that took me to the club where I played basketball. Relieved that the academic year was coming to an end, I asked my parents for permission to go out with my school friends after the final. My father casually asked if we would be accompanied by a teacher. "No," I replied, thinking that we were in tenth grade and did not need a chaperone. My parents exchanged one of their familiar looks. Then, my dad firmly ended the conversation by saying I could not go in the absence of an adult, adding, "What do you think? We're not in America!" Little did he, or I, know that I would be spending more than half my adult life striving to bridge the cultures of Heliopolis and the United States.

In contrast with the homogeneous nature of my school and neighborhood, my parents' family backgrounds were quite different. My maternal grandparents had settled in the prestigious suburb of Zizinia, in Alexandria, after years of traveling throughout Upper Egypt, where my grandfather was a judge. He held my grandmother in very high regard, only referring to her as "El Hanem," a title reserved for female members of high-ranking families. Indeed, she was a sophisticated and charismatic community leader, who contributed to multiple charities and organizations. She spoke French fluently, was very creative, and had an impeccable sense of fashion and an exquisite taste in home furnishings. She was an important member of a long line of strong women who influenced my life. Competing with her for the title of "alpha female of the household" was Amma Zeinab, the housekeeper and nanny who helped raise my mom and her two brothers—hence the qualifier "Amma," a familiar way to address an older person in Upper Egypt. Amma Zeinab was a single, illiterate woman who refused to ever get married, rejecting the authority of a husband. She was the matriarch of her extended family and the breadwinner for her many nieces and nephews. My mom and uncles loved and respected her, and yes, also feared her. Even though Amma would never allow herself to sit down in the presence of my grandmother—implicitly acknowledging their class status—the power struggle between the two was real, and all of us learned to stay clear whenever a face-off was looming on the horizon. These two distinct, yet similarly strong and outspoken, women were in vivid contrast with my kind, timid, and soft-spoken paternal grandmother, Teta.

On my father's side, my grandparents lived in Shamshira, a beautiful small village on the Rosetta branch of the Nile. Our family gatherings during the Eid holidays included six uncles, two aunts, and many cousins. Teta would try to hide us and instruct us not to be seen, for fear of the evil eye. As children, we had the best time fishing, riding donkeys, and getting in small rowboats on the Nile. We were treated like celebrities because my grandfather was the omda, who was the most important person in the village, the equivalent of a mayor. We were also special because we were urbanites who came from the capital city of Cairo and dressed and spoke differently. I was always fascinated watching my dad switch to his rural dialect whenever he met with his siblings and cousins, who all did likewise; it was as if they were bilingual within the same language. As I grew older, the patriarchal nature of the mentalities in Shamshira became obvious to me, as well as the subtle sexist comments and gender roles. However, even in the 1950s in Shamshira, there were enlightened people, and my grandfather, the omda, was among the most progressive. He fully supported the education of women; thus, his eldest daughter, my aunt, became the first woman in the family to receive a university degree.

Embraced by my family on both sides, I developed an early awareness and sharp sensitivity for cultural differences, norms, behaviors, and expectations. Proud of my heritage, I used to share my knowledge of life in Egypt's villages with my big city friends. I showed off my skills by imitating my dad's and uncles' rural dialect and bragged about our family roots. My interest in diversity and fascination with cultures were encouraged by my mom, who took after her own mother. A polished and refined graduate of the elite school Notre Dame de Sion in Alexandria, she was able to reach out and relate to people from all walks of life. It was pure pleasure to hear her quote and comment on the innumerable Egyptian proverbs that accurately mirrored Egyptian life and mentalities.

When I received a bachelor's degree in architecture from the Faculty of Engineering at Ein Shams University in Cairo, my dad was boasting with pride. While considering employment opportunities, I had concerns about working in the field, and expressed a definite preference for more sheltered environments. My dad was disappointed in my attitude and encouraged me to pursue the most challenging positions, confident I could do anything. I applied for a job at the National Authority for Tunnels (NAT), created in 1983 to carry out the construction of the first underground metro line in Cairo, in collaboration with the French government.

In 1987, I was the youngest architect in the Department of Technical Studies, which was headed by a small-framed woman who was nonetheless a giant in her field, Shoushou El Bedeiwy. She was a competent and strong engineer who had broken the glass ceiling in her male-dominated profession. During my years at NAT, she was a role model who afforded me countless learning opportunities, including collaboration with the international architects of the Société Française d'Études et de Réalisations de Transports Urbains (SOFRETU), the French consulting firm in charge of the project's development. I also worked with iconic Egyptian artists, especially Dr. Salah Abdel Karim, who coordinated the selection and acquisition of numerous art pieces to decorate the underground metro stations. I was selected to represent my department in the ribbon-cutting ceremony celebrating the inauguration of the very first Cairo metro line, and presented the scissors to French President François Mitterrand, who was present for the momentous occasion.

For three years, I enjoyed my short and exciting career as an architect, until I fell head over heels in love with a tall and handsome engineer, Essam Abou Zeida. We married in 1990 and moved to Columbus, Ohio, where he pursued doctoral studies. In our new environment, not blending with ordinary people, I stood out. Overnight, I found myself in the spotlight, out of my comfort zone. Eventually, I accepted the situation and used my new status as an exotic person to advocate for my country and promote a better understanding of its people and their culture. I felt like a living version of the proverbs my mom loved to quote, which carry the wisdom of centuries of human experience. They reflect the inherent patience and deep rooted faith in God shared by Coptic and Muslim Egyptians alike.

Soon after moving to the United States, we had two beautiful daughters: Farida and Aliah. Through them, I became even more sensitive to cultures, constantly reflecting on the embedded values they carry. In an effort to help my children integrate into American society and ease their transition into school, I applied for a job as a teacher in the Learning Center of Westerville (LCW), a private preschool where they were enrolled. I was hired and, surprisingly, loved being a teacher. Actually, an architect and an educator have more in common than most people might think. Both professions require creativity, critical thinking, problem-solving skills, the ability to focus on the big picture while tending to details, and taking culture and context into account.

I attended many professional development sessions to better prepare myself for my newfound passion and started thinking about education as a second career, not just a temporary job. During my time at LCW, I was able to combine my personal and professional experiences to educate my colleagues and my daughters' classmates about Egyptian culture. The girls knew that, as a family, we were somewhat different: we spoke Arabic at home and had no relatives in the United States. They were not allowed to eat the red slices of meat on pizza and learned to say, "We are Muslims, we don't eat pork." It was also beneficial for my daughters to learn and talk about their Egyptian roots. I worked at LCW for four years, during which I became head teacher and was assigned some administrative responsibilities. By then, Essam had successfully completed his PhD, and it was time to go back to our native country.

Upon returning to Egypt in 1996, I accepted the offer to be in charge of establishing a preschool program replicating the LCW model in one of Cairo's new and fast-growing private schools. The principal, a powerful woman, gave me the authority to (1) design and supervise the preparation of the physical space of the Child Development Center; (2) create and execute a marketing campaign for the Center; (3) to hire qualified teachers: (4) develop the curriculum and needed technology and order textbooks and learning materials; and (5) to interview parents and enroll their children. It was both the best and the most testing of times. I appreciated the autonomy and challenge, as well as the opportunity to sharpen my knowledge and skills, both as an architect and an educational administrator. Essam and I enjoyed the novel situation of having a village of parents, family, and friends to help care for Farida and Aliah, and I was able to commit heart, mind, and soul to bringing the Child Development Center to fruition. I ran the program for about three years, filled with many successes and a few frustrations; overall, however, it was a fulfilling learning experience.

Based on my work at the Child Development Center and my experience in the United States, I was offered the position of assistant principal at the new American division at the school. In addition to the skills I applied in developing the Center, this job required effective communication, conflict resolution, and sound advocacy, since I also served as liaison between the Egyptian school administration and the American principal and teachers. The school principal, Dr. Gary Kenny, and I collaborated on the launching and development of the procedures needed to obtain accreditation of the school. Navigating through many layers of cross-cultural bumps and conflicts, as well as administrative and educational challenges, I emerged as a more seasoned and competent school manager. For twelve years, I assumed leadership positions and served as a consultant for several prestigious international schools, spearheading improvement projects, self-study programs, and accreditation efforts. For my role as head of the International General Certificate of Secondary Education (IGCSE) in one of the schools, I was honored by the British Council in Cairo with the Beacon Award for Coordinators, from the Cambridge International Examination.

By 2008, I had hit the glass ceiling of school leadership in Egypt, and the time had come for a new venture. We returned to the United States, where Essam was appointed visiting scholar at Auburn University in Alabama. Farida started college, Aliah entered high school, and I tagged along with no real plan, but confident that good things would happen. Shortly thereafter, I met Dr. Samia Spencer, a compatriot, an old friend and neighbor of my mom, and an accomplished and well-respected member of the Auburn University faculty and community. She became a mentor who inspired and guided me as I embarked on a journey toward my third career, as a university professor. Based on her advice and invaluable recommendation, I was admitted to the master's program in educational leadership at Auburn University and awarded a teaching assistantship. In May 2010, I completed the degree, and I received the PhD four years later.

Being a graduate student was a different and invigorating experience, highlighted by the vivifying level of maturity and experience that my professors and colleagues brought to the table. We were immersed in theory, dialogue, debate, and self-reflection. These stimulating exercises allowed me to acquire and assimilate the theoretical foundation I was lacking. When I integrated this newly gained knowledge with my extensive experience as a practitioner, my thoughts gradually started to align and make sense. Thus, I was able to excel in my studies and earned many honors from the department, the College, the University, and various professional organizations. I was appointed graduate student ambassador and was recognized as a David L. Clark Scholar, in addition to receiving the Outstanding International Graduate Student Award, and another from the Alma Holladay Endowment for Academic Excellence. Thanks to institutional travel funds, I presented papers on cultural competence and educational leadership at state, national, and international conferences. Clearly, Auburn University appreciated the unique and valuable perspective I brought to its programs as a mature and experienced international student.

I will forever be indebted to my professors and the members of my dissertation committee for their impact on my professional development and their invaluable advice while I was preparing for the job market. However, I must single out Dr. Fran Kochan—professor, dean, and mentor—whose influence on my life remains quintessential. An educator, scholar, and pioneer in her field, she was instrumental in breaking the glass ceiling in her profession, thus paving the way for other women to follow in her footsteps. Like my mother, she was strong in a gentle way, leading with competence and empathy. As a professor at Florida Atlantic University, I aspire to follow the example of Dr. Kochan and apply the principles and values she taught me as I mentor my own students.

Sailing between countries and careers, my personal life and professional experience continued to merge, providing a deeper and broader understanding of humanity. In this present day and age, perhaps more than ever before, and in a world where conflict, violence, mistrust, and misunderstanding are widespread, there is an urgent need to reverse the trend and reject prejudice, discrimination, and hatred. Through my teaching, research, and collaborative work, I seek to promote enlightenment, understanding, acceptance, and tolerance. In short, in light of my multicultural background, my interdisciplinary education, and my vast experience crossing two centuries on two continents, I am unconditionally committed to breaking barriers, fighting ignorance, advancing dialogue, and building bridges. And even though the bridges are sometimes abused, nevertheless they are an important and much-needed asset. As I view it, this process starts as an intrapersonal endeavor that engages the self in reflection and that challenges deeply rooted beliefs.

During my journey, I drew wisdom and strength from the lessons I learned from many powerful women who surrounded me as I was growing up, starting with my mother, grandmothers, and mother-like figures. I also owe much to my two daughters, who have shown strength as they morphed from being culture-conflicted kids to mature and confident global citizens. My role models also include women I was fortunate enough to encounter along the way: acquaintances, lifelong friends, mentors, teachers, supervisors, and colleagues, from all walks of life. There were homemakers, politicians, educators, engineers, ambassadors, TV directors, and writers; some were highly educated, others barely literate. Among those who influenced me, some were Egyptians; others were not, which leads me to conclude that strong women are not necessarily from the East or the West, and do not follow principles associated with a particular culture or country. The extraordinary personalities who stand out in my mind were individuals who believed in basic human rights and acknowledged that everyone, regardless of gender, must enjoy the freedom to make choices for themselves, for there are no books or movements that provide a mold that fits us all.

In short, to my daughters, and to all the young women in Egypt and beyond, I say: be true to yourself, make decisions wisely, while weighing their consequences, and surround yourself with enlightened individuals who know you, appreciate you, and are committed to helping you spread your wings and reach your goals.

Boca Raton, Florida.

Previously published in 2016 in *Daughters of the Nile*, edited by Samia I Spenser

———•———

MAYSAA BARAKAT is Associate Professor in the Department of Educational Leadership and Research Methodology at Florida Atlantic University (FAU). She received her PhD in educational leadership from Auburn University, Alabama in 2014.

ILLEGAL IMMIGRANT

Gamal Omar

The muezzin called for the sunset prayer, declaring the completion of another day of fasting, on February 3, in the month of Ramadan. My family gathered around the *tablea* to eat. My father was a 54-year-old farmer, but his face made him seem twenty years older than that. The sun had burned his skin. It had become like an over-roasted peanut. And smoking had taken a lot from his lungs. It was as if he were expelling some of his lung cells every time he coughed into his handkerchief.

My mother, full of activity and pretty, was like a bee going around the flowers, extracting pollen to feed her five children—two boys and three girls, one of whom was married and on her own. I was the eldest.

Around the tablea, we were having our "break fast," the words between us very rare. Each of us was watching the others' words. I was on one side of the tablea, and they were on the other. Something had happened. We all knew what it was. But we were afraid to face it. It was like a fetus: we knew it was coming, we even knew it was a boy, we knew what month it was coming but we didn't know what it was going to look like, its color, or what its crying was like.

I waited until we had finished our meal. I don't remember what it was. I chewed it, but I was in another world, feeling the heavy burden of telling my family. I'd carried that burden within me for the last three months, but now was the time to tell them. Tonight. I didn't know where I would start. I had always thought I had a kind heart, one influenced by feeling, especially toward my family. But I was surprised to now find myself another person, with another heart. It was as if I were an actor in a play, with no relationship between my role in the play and my role in life. I looked around at my brother and sisters and I couldn't meet my mom's eye. In plain, unfaltering words I told them, "I'm leaving tonight, and no one is going to come with me to see me off. I don't want anyone from the town to know, even our relatives—only a small number of my family and some friends."

I didn't wait to hear their answers or reactions to the news, which, like an anchor on TV, I'd just delivered, and I ran to my room.

My brother, ten years younger than I, didn't know how to express his feelings. Suddenly, he felt he had become a man, responsible for a family, and a heavy weight had fallen on his shoulders—all between the beginning and end of one meal. He was happy and sad. He wanted to listen to what I was saying and do what I wanted, but at the same time, he didn't want to. I asked him to tell four of my friends that I wanted to see them for something urgent tonight. My youngest sister went to bring my married sister from her house. All of this happened minutes after we broke the fast in Ramadan.

In my room, I prepared a small bag to carry on my shoulder, like someone traveling for a couple of days. I didn't want to attract anyone's attention and wanted to be light in my movement. Sneaking into America or a European country happened in secret, like a military invasion—the fewer people who knew about it, the better. We had to keep it secret to succeed.

Interactions between families and relatives in our town bred the fire of jealousy among us. We reveled and rejoiced in each other's failures. That was why I left stealthily— as if I were sacrificing myself for the nation. The land surrounding us loved us and kept us safe, but when she threw us out, she did it without mercy. It was a one-way street; you couldn't return unless you succeeded in your mission. When we left, we left as secretly and silently as we could, so no one would get upset and fight back.

The minutes after I told my family I was leaving were very difficult. I was in my room, acting like I was preparing my bag. No one came near the room. The only thing that broke this silence was the arrival of my four friends. I told them about my leaving tonight, and that we were going to say goodbye in this room because I didn't want any neighbors to know what I was doing. But my friends insisted on going to the airport, and I failed to persuade them not to. I regretted telling them. You control a secret until the words come out of your lips; the moment those words come out, it's as if their hands encircle your neck and your destiny is in other people's hands. In the end, I asked them to meet me on the road leading out of the town. I asked my brother to carry my bag and go alone, meeting me on the road out of the town too. One by one, they said goodbye and left.

My father was a simple farmer. He tried all of his life to take care of his children as best he could. He didn't make you feel his love. Even with his candid heart, no words came out of his mouth to express that love. His facial expression showed that he was strong and tough. People feared him, not because of his strong body, but because of his courage and honor, which some took as foolishness. His loud voice represented toughness. The first time I saw his eyes tear up was when I came down the steps to our house as I left home. Every step was like a hammer hitting his heart. He hugged me tightly. I had looked for that warmth in our relationship all those years, but he was like our land: you had to hoe it to produce the goodness out of it. In that moment, I saw his kind heart and the flow of his compassion—the feelings he had hidden from us. He took himself out of my arms and disappeared into his room.

If kindness is concentrated in a person, my mom would be that person. With her kindness and sweetness, I found her strong, solid. She hugged me, but her eyes didn't shed a tear. She showered me with prayers and advice on how to be careful on my journey. I found her stronger than my father. I hugged my sisters, who were thrilled about something they had long waited for. Traveling and leaving the country was our town's life. We grew up with it. Every street had a family with someone overseas.

In the 1970s and 1980s, the Gulf countries got a big share of Egyptian immigrants, but in the 1990s, Italy and the United States got a flood through their borders. Neither my father nor my uncle went to the Gulf, as many others had done when we were children. Yet we saw what the migrants brought back: electric machines and clothes for their children and families. We didn't have those machines or clothes. At that time, I wished to have a relative of mine living overseas; when you had a father or a brother or son working in a European country—or even more so, in the United States—it was a sign of class status. Working in the United States meant a person had the highest status in my town. The name "America" was like a drum in our land. Even with the thousands of miles between us and the United States, I was going there. The wave of leaving for the West had been going on for a few years and had begun to produce a lot of changes in my town. And now, I was following the caravan. My sisters were excited about my leaving. My departure was long overdue, by our town's standards.

One last time, I looked at our home's walls, at my mom's face and my sisters' expressions. None of us knew if or when we would meet again.

I met my brother, who was carrying my bag, on the road out of the town. Saying goodbye to him gave me the strength to face the unknown waiting for me, because I knew he would be taking care of the family. He would become a young man who was strong in body and kind to his parents. I insisted we say goodbye on the road and that there was no need for him to come to the airport.

I wanted to take public transportation from Benha City to the new Cairo airport, so I could save my money for the unknown awaiting me, but one of my friends hailed a Suzuki taxi, which were famous in Benha. It looked like a small duck running in the streets. He caught it at the bank of the Nile, from where it would take us to the airport. My friends were engaged in a conversation from which I was far removed, due to the worry and the thoughts in my head. What if I went to the airport and there was a problem with my army service certificate; what if it wasn't clear enough? Or perhaps something was wrong with my passport, which had been issued a few months ago; maybe it was on a blacklist or a red list or a brown list for some reason. And the ticket to Ecuador itself—what sort of person would travel to Ecuador? Where was Ecuador on the map? The state bureaucracy always hurt us. It was as if we'd been created to serve the system, rather than the other way around.

I also thought about my experience of taking leave without pay from my work in Shobra. I had written a request of just two lines on a long piece of paper. The director of the school signed and stamped it, as did the manager, who referred it to his superior in the region. I went to see that man at another school. He signed it without agreeing or disagreeing, just referred it to his superior. The regional education board signed and stamped it and referred it to the provincial board. The first page became so full of signatures and stamps, which we moved to the back of the paper. The provincial education board had three offices, all of which added signatures and stamps. Finally, I arrived at the chairman of the board, whom I could only see on one day of the week. When I entered, he looked at the request and he said, "No, we don't have enough of your specialty." I went through this cycle three times; each time, I got the same signature, same stamps, and the same result. Then a friend told me, "Finish the request in Shobra. When you come to the province board in Benha, there is someone I know who can finish this request if you give him some money." And it happened. The request was done in minutes, thanks to my friend and the mysterious power of the Egyptian pound.

Even the contract that I brought with me to prove I had work in Ecuador was fake. But the mysterious power of money made the bureaucracy move with the speed of light. I requested a one-year unpaid leave from work and received the approval at home; I didn't even have to go to the offices of the provinces for it.

The little Suzuki took the road between Benha and Cairo at a magnificent speed. I always thought this car only ran on the small inner streets in Benha, but I was surprised at its capability on the freeway too. This was the first time I had been to an airport, old or new. I hadn't met anybody or seen anybody off.

We arrived around 11:00 p.m. When I got close to the building's entrance, I saw an X-ray machine for the bags. I didn't know whether my friends could enter with me, so we stood in front of the door exchanging our goodbyes. The words between us were inadequate in their meaning, even if full of feeling.

Wael was the one among us who knew what to do, at least practically speaking. He had friends who'd left the country, and he had traveled to Jordan to work one summer. This was not his first time at the airport. And he had been thinking about making the journey himself. We had talked about it, but in the end, he had told me he couldn't do it for lack of money.

I hugged my friends and said they didn't have to wait. I said, "I'll go in to finish the process."

Wael said, "We'll wait out here for twenty minutes. If you don't need anything from us, we'll leave."

I took my bag and I stood in a short line, which moved very fast. I put my bag on the conveyor belt to put it through the X-ray machine. It went through very fast, without setting off an alarm. Inside the terminal, I went to the Spanish airline, Iberia. No Egyptian or Arab airline flew Ecuador. I checked my bag and went to the departure gate, holding my passport, the first I'd owned in my life, in my hand. The line moved slowly to the window. I handed the passport to the officer, who opened it and looked at the picture, looked at my face, and raised his hand, and then lowered it onto the passport, stamping it, and permitting me to leave. The whole process took only five minutes. Oh my God, five minutes! If I'd known that, I would have talked to my friends a little longer. I had an hour and a half now before the plane would leave. What would I do with this time?

I went upstairs to the waiting area. The shops were clean and flashy for foreigners. In this building, the European and Western airlines arrived and left. I heard Oum Kalthoum singing Ibrahim Nagi's poem, and the music of Riad Al-Sunbahti, in the last part of her song "Al-Atlahl." Like a villager leaving home for the first time, I saw everything around me that I had never given attention to as suddenly important and necessary. My feet took me to a worker inside the shop where Oum Kalthoum's song was playing. I approached him and said, "I'm leaving Egypt tonight. I don't know when I will come back. Can Thouma's voice be the last thing I say goodbye to in Egypt?"

He looked at me and smiled. And he said, "As you like."

Oum Kalthoum's voice began after the musical introduction: "Oh my heart, don't ask where love is. It was a tower of imagination which fell. Give me a drink and have a drink. And it's ruined. And tell me about life as the tears told before."

While I was waiting and listening, I saw a young man who was a bit tall, with a wide chest and dark skin. He had a lot of gel in his hair, making it shiny, as if it were dripping onto his shoulders. He was almost my age and carried a small bag on his shoulder. He sat near me. We exchanged a look, and after saying hello, he introduced himself. His name was Mohammed Al Kafrawi. I asked him, "Where are you going?"

His answer was, "I'm going to Ecuador."

The words stung my ears. Was it possible Mohammed was from my town, and was my age, and I didn't know him? Impossible! At least I would know his face. The whole thing couldn't be just by chance. Were there other people who knew the route to sneak into the United States? I said, "Where are you from, Mohammed?"

His answer was, "From Benha."

After finding out that Mohammed was from a small village near us, I was less surprised. We fell into laughter when we knew we were from neighboring towns and enjoyed the surprise of having a companion on the journey. Mohammed was from a small kafr near our village, and there were marriage relationships between the two towns. My village was closer to the city and its level of education was higher; Mohammed's kafr was named after a big landowner's family from before the free officers' regime. The people in my town always laughed when his kafr tried to change its name to Kafr of the Free.

Oum Kalthoum's voice rose, saying, "Has love ever seen drunken people like us?" Two young men came through the entrance and walked toward us. Mohammed and I knew them both. Adnan was one year younger than me. He hadn't completed his education; he left primary school and worked as a farmer on his family's land. He was raising cattle and selling them. He was of medium height and medium weight and had foxy eyes. The other was Rashid, who was seventeen years old, and was very tall and skinny. He was from my extended family and was Adnan's nephew. They were on their way to Ecuador too.

The funny thing was that, after breaking the fast, Mohammed had gone to Adnan's house to say goodbye and tell him he was leaving for the United States. He made a point of doing that especially since Adnan had two brothers and cousins in the United States. But Adnan hadn't told Mohammed he was leaving too. And now, here they were, meeting each other at the airport.

Mohammed asked him, "Why didn't you tell me you were leaving too?"

Adnan laughed and told him, "Oh, I thought you were leaving on the Italian airline. And I had a lot on my mind at that time, so I forgot."

Adnan was confident his brother and cousin would support him and follow his and his nephew's journey. Mohammed had no brother in the United States, but he was proud that he had a brother in Saudi Arabia who was willing to pay for everything. I didn't know either Adnan or Rashid well. But now we were a traveling group, gathered in a waiting room in the Cairo airport, without having planned to travel together. Oum Kalthoum's voice rose, singing the last part of "The Ruins:" "And each one of us went his way, not saying we wanted it, but luck wanted it."

The announcer announced that our flight was delayed fifteen minutes. We went to the gate and walked down a passageway from the terminal onto the plane. It was different from what I had seen in Arabic movies. In the movies, there were stairs to go on and off the plane. How, I wondered, dare the Arabic movies not prepare us for changes in life? I always assumed I would do the same thing that happened in the movies.

The airplane was small. My seat was beside a young Egyptian man. His name was Ass'ad. He was going directly to the United States, not to Ecuador. He worked in the United States and was on a visit to his family in Egypt. I felt jealous of him. I wished my trip were direct like his. I felt I was going to a world I wasn't prepared for.

The airplane began to move. I did everything Ass'ad did. As the airplane began to run down the Cairo Airport runway, I felt shaking. I felt as if my soul were being taken away. The plane was flying away from the surface of the earth, and the lights of the runway were farther and farther away. Cairo's lights seemed shiny in the distance. The Spanish airplane was taking us away from our friends, family, and home. In my head, I heard Oum Kalthoum's voice: "Don't say we wanted it. Luck wanted it."

The airplane entered a sea of black night, with nothing to see.

My jealousy of Ass'ad going directly to the United States, and my feeling of weakness and helplessness, shamed me into telling him that I was on my way to sneak into the States. I couldn't tell him I was on my way to Ecuador because it was the only country in the region that didn't require a visa for entry. Mexican visas were denied to people in my region due to pressure from the American authorities. The same restrictions applied to Guatemala, El Salvador, Honduras, and Panama. We had no other way but through Ecuador.

I looked at my watch, which was still on Cairo time, to end my day of fasting for Ramadan. I was not going to follow the religious scholars' permission to abstain from fasting if one were a traveler, because I was hoping to get closer to Allah, and therefore to be successful in spite of my illegal conduct. We were nice people; we weren't looking to do bad things to anybody. But we were pushed to do that. None of that was by our hand; rather, it was imposed on us.

I didn't leave my seat. I don't know why. Maybe it was because I was afraid of doing something wrong. Or maybe I was shy and thought I would do something foolish, giving a bad impression about our people and our country. We had to be civilized, especially if we were among Westerners, let alone on one of their airlines. Mohammed did the same. He tried to show that he was a gentleman and not a commoner. Rashid stayed in his seat too. The only one who was free from all that, and didn't care about the reaction of other people, was Adnan. He moved between my place in the front of the plane and Mohammed's seat in the back.

We, the educated people, looked down on Adnan, who had not finished his primary education and was illiterate. But in truth, I wished I could be free like Adnan, not caring what the Westerners thought of our behavior. Why couldn't we be ourselves, as the Westerners were when they came to our land? It was our "Westerner complex." We grew up with it: civilization and forward movement belonged to the West, and we had to copy them to be modern like them. I wished to be free from that feeling, but I was glued to my seat.

After a short period in the air, Ass'ad fell deeply asleep. I couldn't sleep. I had a bad habit of not being able to sleep when I was away from home. I needed at least two nights to get used to the new place. In the quarter of a century I had lived in my town, I had slept outside our home two times: when I went to a camp in Alexandria for one week, and another time in Al Ismailia on the Suez Canal, during college.

We arrived at Madrid Airport in Spain. I waived at Ass'ad and called for Mohammed, Adnan, and Rashid to get ready. There was heavy rain outside the airplane window. We weren't used to heavy rain in our town. As I stood in the passenger line exiting the airplane, an airline employee asked me for my passport. He asked the four of us for our passports, but he didn't ask for Ass'ad's passport. Maybe a jealous person had phoned the Spanish authorities and told them about our plan to sneak in. I'm joking of course, but it has happened before. Some people from my town got out of Madrid Airport under the guise of needing to make connecting flights and snuck into Spain, and from Spain, they went to either Italy or the Netherlands. This is probably why they asked for our passports. But was it only those from my village and the kafr nearby, and not from everyone who carried an Egyptian passport? Was our town that famous in Spain?

I was full of shame. All the passengers, especially the Egyptians, looked at us like we were dirt. Or like we were a terrorist cell being captured. We walked down the stairs from the plane. They didn't have the modern technology we had at the Cairo Airport. Or if they did, they used it for different people, not us. In Egypt, we used modern technology, and spent money on it, to please the Westerners, whereas here they used the old stuff on us. And they took our passports—only ours.

We rode on the bus from the plane to the airport, and an official went with us, carrying our passports. He asked us to wait. All the other passengers entered the terminal, but we waited by the door. After ten minutes, he came out and gave one of us his passport. After that, every five minutes, another passport came out, until they had allowed the four of us to enter the waiting room on the second floor. This was how Europe welcomed me the first time I stepped onto its land.

We had to wait about six hours for the flight that would take us across the Atlantic to Ecuador. It was a huge terminal, bigger than the airport in Cairo, and full of movement and faces from everywhere on earth. What a place to be during Ramadan! We couldn't look at all the fashionable dresses women were wearing. It wasn't cold or rainy weather, so their dresses were very short. And they got shorter as the temperature rose inside the hall. O Allah, I'm fasting!

A bunch of young people from my town had tickets to Columbia, and on their way back from Columbia to Cairo, they snuck into Italy. Now they were in Milan, because they didn't have the means to purchase tickets to the United States, which were more costly than tickets to Italy. This determined the class structure in my town now. The US economy was much better and stronger than the others, so those who went to the United States would make more money than those who went to Italy and were in the top class. The people who went to Italy were in the second class, and the people who went to Arab Gulf countries were in the third. Even the son of the pasha, who got his father's land back after the reform laws in Nasser's era, divided it into a wide street and a less-wide street—all according to a plan he knew and we knew and the whole town knew, but the authorities could not see it. So, two areas emerged. One was for the people who worked in the United States. They bought land next to each other; it was the best and the most expensive land, and it increased in value more than the land of the people who worked in Italy's area, which wasn't as expensive. That was how the Italian neighborhood and the American area in our town had developed. Ten years later, the Egyptian minister of housing made a similar plan for all Egyptian land so the state could control and organize building on the agricultural land.

I went inside the waiting room and looked for the entrance and exit, just in case I needed to escape. I had heard stories in my town, like the story of the son of Abu Tish, who succeeded in escaping from this place. I had to consider what would happen if I failed my journey to the United States. Maybe one day I would need to escape from this place. Then what could I do? Anything I could do would be much better than going back to my town. Going back was death itself.

I looked for the airline office in the airport to ask about our next flight—what gate and what time. Then I looked for the bathroom. Inside the clean and beautiful bathroom, I shut the door behind me and slowly began to take off my belt. I touched the secret place where I had hidden around thirty-four hundred dollars, part of my journey's cost, until Allah or some of my friends or relatives in the United States helped me with the rest. I felt shaking in my body when I thought, "What if no one is able or wants to help me? What will I do? How will I continue the journey?" I hadn't told anyone in the States that I was coming or asked them to pay for the rest of my trip. I had only tried to get the phone number of my cousin who lived in the States from his mother. But she had told me she had no new number for him after he had moved.

I could feel my temperature rising in the bathroom. My head was boiling. So, I ran out.

Editor's note.

Gamal Omar's account covers only the beginning of the longer story of his trip to the United States. The full account can be found in his book مهاجر غير شرعي (*Illegal Immigrant*), in which he describes how he was smuggled through six countries to reach the States. It shows the dangers some Egyptians were willing to risk to go to the US. The trip took about two months, using semi-professional smugglers who specialized in various legs of the journey through different countries. Some lost their lives on this trip. Omar arrived in New York virtually penniless. He took odd jobs and become a taxi driver. Eventually, he met and married an American, settled his problems with the Immigration Service, and became a US citizen. Omar has now been in the United States for twenty years. He lives in Brooklyn, with his wife and their ten-year-old son.

Omar has a college degree from Egypt, where he taught mathematics. In addition to his Egyptian formal education, he has educated himself on a wide range of subjects. He is an authority on Nasr Hamid Abuzaid and is known for his work on modernizing Islamic thinking. Since coming to the United States, he has authored six books, published in Egypt, one of which carries the title of this chapter.

———•———

GAMAL OMAR is an Egyptian American writer who has been living in Brooklyn, New York for the past two decades. His first published Arabic work is called *Sneaking In* (مهاجر غير شرعي), a story of an illegal immigrant's journey through six countries to the borders of the U.S. He is also a researcher specializing in studying, critiquing, and writing about Arabic and Islamic thought in modern and contemporary times. He published six books.

FRAGMENTS OF THE STORY OF MY PASSAGE FROM ALEXANDRIA TO NEW YORK

Marlène Barsoum

All those who have left their home behind are in a position to think of home in a new way, while trying to skillfully negotiate a relationship with the host country. I have chosen the fragment to structure the story of my passage from Alexandria to New York in order to mirror the workings of memory, which is fragmentary and ephemeral. I will alternate between my personal narrative of uprooting and an interpretation of the repercussions of the experience. I will dwell less on my personal story in order to give more space to the exploration of the complex phenomenon of displacement, which has become a norm in our times. I hope the fragments that follow will not only provide a glimpse into my journey but, more importantly, will open a window onto the trials and triumphs of those who summoned the courage to leave the shores of their homelands.[1]

Fragment 1. *"The past is a foreign country: they do things differently there."* (L. P. Hartley, *The Go-Between*)[2]

---

1   The theoretical passages included in this essay appear in my article "Nostalgia and Beyond: The Cases of Andrée Chedid and Emile Ollivier," *Dalhousie French Studies,* Vol. 99 (summer 2012): 89–104.

2   L.P. Hartley, *The Go-Between*. (New York: Stein & Day, 1967), 3.

I was born in Alexandria to an Egyptian-born Italian mother, Liliana Simi, and an Egyptian Coptic Christian father, Barsoum Elias Barsoum. I was gifted with a golden childhood: happily married parents, a beautiful home, and many wonderful friends. I also attended a school I loved—The English Girls' College, later renamed El Nasr Girls' College. We took vacations in Agami and Marsa Matrouh in the summer and in an oasis in Mariout in an incongruous Swiss-styled chalet named The Desert Home in the winter. Alexandria was a cosmopolitan city, where people of different ethnicities and religions all lived in harmony. British, Greeks, and Italians, attracted especially by the very active commercial harbor of Alexandria, resided there. Armenians, French, Maltese, Syrians, and Lebanese were also numbered among its inhabitants. This cosmopolitan landscape continued well into the 1960s.

Our life was shattered with my family's uprooting in 1966, when I was still an adolescent. Why such a departure? Primarily because of the nationalization of my father's cotton brokerage firm under Nasser, as the country was becoming increasingly socialist. Furthermore, freedoms were being curtailed during that period. In fact, we were part of a wave of Christian Egyptians, who were starting to feel insecure in Egypt in the late 1960s and immigrated primarily to the United States, Canada, and Australia. The 1965 Immigration and Nationality Act, which opened the doors of the United States to peoples from non-Western countries, no doubt facilitated this migratory movement. Leaving Egypt was wrenching, mostly for my Italian mother, who considered Egypt to be her beloved country, my brother, Bruno, my sister, Caroline, and me. We headed first to Canada, where we spent fourteen months in Montreal while waiting for our US visa to come. We arrived in New York in June 1967.

Fragment 2. *"Memory takes a lot of poetic license. It omits some details; others are exaggerated, according to the emotional value of the articles it touches, for memory is seated predominantly in the heart. The interior is rather dim and poetic."* (Tennessee Williams, *The Glass Menagerie*)[3]

For the purpose of this essay, the "article" mentioned by Tennessee Williams would be the land forsaken. Memory, as we know, does not simply reproduce the past, it reinvents and fictionalizes it. One may ask: what are the uses of memory? Does it bind or liberate? What of the gulf that separates memory from truth? After all, as Williams states, memory has to do with feelings; it is therefore subjective and often flawed.

With cultural identity becoming increasingly diffuse in our globalized world, nostalgia for a past, fixed and comprehensible, is perhaps both a response and a defense—doubly so in the case of the deracinated individual. Eva Hoffman eloquently describes, in her memoir, the workings of nostalgia: "Nostalgia—that most lyrical of feelings—crystallizes around these images like amber. Arrested within it, the house, the past, is clear, vivid, made more beautiful by the medium in which it is held and by its stillness."[4] Other writers have picked up on the theme of the frozen state caused by nostalgia. Tara Bahrampour elaborates upon this in an article titled "Persia on the Pacific." She relates the story of a generation of young Iranians living in Los Angeles, yearning for a country they have never seen. They are, for the most part, the offspring of an elite, who was wrenched from a life of privilege in Iran, living a "shadow existence" in Los Angeles that will never live up to the charmed life their parents remember. She comments that "the outdated styles seem to reflect a deeper inertia among the exiles—an inability to move beyond the political and social mindset of the Shah's era."[5] She quotes an Iranian producer and actor,

---

3   Tennessee Williams, *The Glass Menagerie.* (1945; rpt. New York: The New York Classics. A New Directions Book, 1970), 21.

4   Eva Hoffman, *Lost in Translation: A Life in a New Language* (New York: Penguin, 1989), 115.

5   Tara Bahrampour, "Persia on the Pacific," *The New Yorker,* November 10, 2003, 52–60, 58.

now living in Los Angeles, as saying: "I've read somewhere that this is typical—the home country moves forward but migrant groups don't."[6] This resulted in the boys' identification with an anachronistic Iran, a country and era now vanished, that belonged to their grandparents. I have discovered that it takes years to fully comprehend the impact of dislocation. Border-crossing is not merely physical and geographical. The displaced person moves from the transparency of the homeland, where the frame of reference is clear, to the opacity of the host country, where cultural codes are not yet understood. Emotional and psychological adaptation to a new culture is the other challenge to be faced.

One can sketch several developmental stages before reaching a point of relative harmony in the host country. The first stage is tinged with a sense of loss, which makes one slip into nostalgia, coloring one's memory of the homeland. Although the first impulse during that stage is to create a simulacrum of the forsaken home, and to withdraw into cultural ghettos, with their promise of safety nets to newcomers, we did not give in to that. For that matter, there was no Egyptian community in New York in the 1960s. Moreover, coming from a cosmopolitan city, such as Alexandria, it was not an impulse we had. We integrated quite quickly. But our idealization of Alexandria (with the exception of my father, who could not indulge in nostalgia because he was the family's sole provider and had to remain clear-headed) persisted for some years. And yet, New Yorkers welcomed us. They were friendly and hospitable. The situation was different before 9/11. At the time, most people had never met an Egyptian, and many were fascinated by ancient Egypt, as well as by the depiction of Egypt in literature. A question I was often asked was "Have you read Lawrence Durrell's *The Alexandria Quartet*?", which gave way to "Have you read Naguib Mahfouz?", after he was awarded the Nobel Prize in 1988. People I met also wanted to discuss, of course, the then-recent Arab-Israeli war of 1967.

The second stage starts after one has been in the host country for a decade or two and has been more or less freed from the grip

6   Bahrampour, 58.

of the struggle for survival. Now able to experience the host country on its own terms, the urge to compare it with the homeland is less insistent. A period of reflection then opens up for some, which can lead to the possibility of making something new of oneself. This occurs with the negotiation of a fresh multiple identity, which is tantamount to a translation of the self. We find Salman Rushdie, for example, broaching the subject of the translated self, highlighting the losses and gains that result when he makes the narrator of *Shame*, perhaps the author's persona, say, "I have been *borne across*. It is generally believed that something is always lost in translation. I cling to the notion… that something can also be gained."[7] We cannot help but notice the word-play in the expression "borne across." On the one hand, it makes one refer to the etymology of the word *translation*—"a carrying or bringing across." On the other hand, usage of the past tense of *to bear* evokes, quite clearly, the notion of birth. The meaning conveyed, therefore, is that self-translation is a form of rebirth. With one's new bi-, or tri-, cultural identity, one benefits from what both Michael Ondaatje and Salman Rushdie call "a double vision," which helps one straddle two worlds without feeling pulled by either one.

*Fragment 3. *"Discontinuity and nostalgia are most profound if, in growing up, we leave or lose the place where we were born and spent our childhood, if we become expatriates or exiles, if the place, or the life, we were brought up in is changed beyond recognition or destroyed. All of us, finally, are exiles from the past."* (Oliver Sacks, "The Neurologist's Notebook")[8]

Severed from both past and birthplace, the deracinated person is called upon, according to Oliver Sacks, to go through quite an arduous intellectual process if harmony is to be reached. He writes, "Those whose lives have been broken across and who achieve harmony and unity (if they achieve it at all) only much later, by an extraordinary

7   Salman Rushdie, *Shame* (New York: Vintage Books, 1989), 24.
8   Oliver Sacks, "A Neurologist's Notebook: The Landscape of His Dreams," *The New Yorker*, vol. 68 (July 27, 1992): 56–66, 60-61.

act of self-integration and transformation—an act depending on an intense, difficult, but healing recollection, which serves (in Freud's word) to 'retranscribe' memory, to replace fantasy memories with genuine ones."[9] To see oneself in the present anew is a way of reclaiming oneself. This new status releases fresh energies, which allow one to live meaningfully in the host country.

Separation from one's place of birth seems to sharpen the need to recollect in order to bridge, reconcile, and integrate discontinuities caused by uprooting. The urgency to create surges forth in some—we have witnessed a proliferation of diasporic memoirs and autobiographies as well as works in the visual arts in the last few decades—since art strives to give coherence to experience. Such an urgency is sharpest, it seems, for those whose birthplace is either off-limits or has been destroyed because of the disturbance of old patterns and mores frequently caused by political upheaval. That community of deracinated artists / writers, after years of creative incubation, has made its artistic work a territory for the exploration of the phenomenon of displacement. Not only in order to mine the meaning of theirown past experiences and weave it into an intelligible whole, but also to fulfill what Oliver Sacks believes is the wish to transcend the personal "by the cultural need to remember the past, to preserve its meaning, or give it a new meaning, in a world that has forgotten it."[10] By universalizing their personal story, these artists / writers provide a door of entry for the viewer / reader, who can then identify, and perhaps experience, a sort of catharsis.

Fragment 4. *"If you cannot revisit your own origins—reach out and touch them from time to time—you are forever in some crucial sense untethered."* (Penelope Lively, *Oleander Jacaranda*)[11]

Having always been studious, I was happy to be able to go to college soon after my arrival in New York. I majored in literature, a subject

---

9   Oliver Sacks, 66.
10   Sacks, 61.
11   Penelope Lively, *Oleander Jacaranda*. (New York: Harper Collins, 1994), 129.

I loved, and later earned a PhD from Columbia University, which led me to a life in academia. I have had, for some years now, the good fortune of teaching courses on exile, immigration, and nomadism, among other subjects. Many of my students are immigrants, to whom these courses speak in an immediate way. For some, it has given them the vocabulary to express their own experience of uprooting. Moreover, for many years, my research has focused on the works of Andrée Chedid, a writer born in Egypt, of Lebanese origin, who explores subjects that are close to my heart: exile, identity, and the envisioning of peace in the context of war. This was my way of relinking with Egypt and of deepening my understanding of the experience of uprooting. Unable to return to Egypt with any regularity, I have managed to journey back on the intellectual level. Both my teaching and writing have been gratifying in that they allowed me to create an inner home in some respects. While I agree with the Egyptian-born British writer Penelope Lively, quoted here, that the return to origins is necessary, I have discovered that the journey back does not need to be physical.

Fragment 5. *"Art creates a past that is constantly renewed."* (Hilary Mantel, "A Past Recaptured")[12]

The past does not remain static, as the above epigraph suggests, if the workings of memory continue unabated in probing the nature and meaning of recalled experiences, measuring both their impact and the distance that exists between truth and recollection. Furthermore, one might ask in the case of the deracinated subject's relationship to the past, is that individual exiled from a certain moment in time or from a place? Would a return to the homeland necessarily provide a solution? The return may be difficult because it may reveal that one has become a stranger in a strange land. With the realization, however, that one's birthplace is no longer a familiar site of belonging, the return can also arrest nostalgia. The journey back home can therefore help one move

---

12   Hilary Mantel. "A Past Recaptured" *The New York Review of Books,* November 29, Vol.48, No.19, 2001, 51.

forward by catalyzing the embrace of one's hybrid identity and the recognition that one has several homes.

I did return to Egypt. Both trips were poignant, as it was the encounter of a transformed person with a land that had changed. I had indeed become a stranger in a strange land. And yet, it was not painful, because certain things had remained unaltered: the great warmth and hospitality of the people, the sparkling beautiful sea and sky of Alexandria, the marvelous monuments. I was struck how people, waiters at restaurants and taxi drivers, who work so hard yet make a meager living, insisted on not accepting payment when they discovered we were Egyptians who were visiting Egypt (we, of course, insisted on paying). What gracious hospitality!

Final Fragment. *"Home is where one starts from. As we grow older/The world becomes stranger, the pattern more complicated."* (T. S. Eliot, "East Coker, *Four Quartets*)[13]

Uprooting, as has been suggested, involves losses and gains. Successful mourning, as Freud observed, involves the introjection of the deceased. I have tried to internalize my roots, thus incorporating inwardly the Egypt I had lost in reality. I was eventually also able to negotiate three worlds (Egypt, Italy, New York), to offer hospitality to my plural identity. This suppleness toward the notion of identity and toward eventually adapting to a new country and culture may have been facilitated, in part, by the cosmopolitan atmosphere that existed in the Alexandria in which I was raised. Moreover, while growing up in Egypt, my father often spoke of the richness of being bicultural to my brother, sister, and me. He tried to underscore that hybridity was a gift, not a wound, as it is sometimes depicted in immigration or diasporic literature. He used to take my little brother (who was sometimes kicking and screaming), sister, and me to the museum in Cairo and playfully referred to the Egyptian mummies and statues as our great-great aunts and uncles. He wanted to give us a sense of the rich history of Egypt that was

13   T.S. Eliot. *Four Quartets.* (New York: Harcourt, Brace & Co., 1943).

our heritage. He gave equal time to discussing Roman history and Romans, my mother's forebears. My father's discussions, I believe, helped me develop certain cultural sensibilities, which have allowed me to easefully embrace a plural identity and to move across diverse cultural spaces. With time, I grasped and enacted the notion of inner roots. This has freed me from the paralyzing forces of nostalgia and alienation, thus opening up a space for new possibilities.

I now live contentedly in New York, an international city, which allows me to keep my triple identity intact. I feel comfortable in this other home, where I meet people who hail from all four corners of the world, enriching the city with their unique talents and worldviews. I no longer harken back to the halcyon days in Alexandria. I have a healthier relationship to Egypt that is no longer based on a sense of loss. And yet Egypt remains, in my mind, my beloved country, where I enjoyed such a happy childhood. I am relieved, however, to have shed the yoke of nostalgia. It would have hindered my journey in this new land.

I am grateful to the practices of reading (many texts by displaced writers) and writing, which have helped me make sense of my displacement. They allowed me to gain insight into both the losses and gains of dislocation, the lure and pitfalls of nostalgia, and the (im) possibility of return. Reading and writing became, for me, an instrument in a liberating process of transformative self-knowledge. The adventure continues!

MARLÈNE BARSOUM was born in Alexandria and has been living in New York since 1967. She is Professor of French at Hunter College and at the Graduate Center (The City University of New York). She is the author of two books: *Les Voies de la paix dans les récits d'Andrée Chedid* (Editions Karthala, 2017) and *Théophile Gautier's Mademoiselle de Maupin: Toward a Definition of the "Androgynous Discourse"* (Peter Lang Publishing, Inc., 2001). A number of her articles on travel writing have also appeared in different academic journals.

MY STORY "WITHOUT WHY"

Naeem Mady

It was the summer of 1969—specifically June 26, at 2:00 pm. My plane from Amsterdam had just landed at John F. Kennedy Airport (JFK) in New York, one of largest airports in the United States. It was my first time in the States, as they call the country here. It was my first time outside Egypt, or as we call it, Misr. I had flown for ten hours, followed by a two-hour process to get through customs. Now, I was standing in middle of the arrival lobby, looking for my close friend Wadid, who was supposed to be waiting for me. To my surprise, he was not there. I waited in the same spot for a few hours in disbelief: Wadid, my only connection to this new world, was nowhere in sight.

For the first time, the magnitude of what I had done hit me. What did I do? I had left everything! I left Egypt, my wife, family, friends, my job as a chemist, and my other job as a folklore-dancing choreographer.

Three days before I left for the United States, I had married the love of my life, Lily. We met during our first year at Asyut University in Upper Egypt and fell in love. I knew Lily was the one I wanted to spend the rest of my life with, so we made a decision to get married quickly, before I left, which would make it easier to have the needed paperwork for Lily to join me later, as my wife.

I had a reasonably easy life in Egypt, as most college graduates did in those days. I was in my early twenties, and life was okay in

Alexandria. Unfortunately, my father, who worked as an engineer in the Army, had passed away, but I had a great family. My mother took care of the whole family: my sister Lila was in college, my oldest brother, Nabil, was an agricultural engineer, and my younger brother, Mounir, was a dentist. I had a lot of friends, including my two closest friends, Hisham and Kahil. We were so close that we used to spend every single day together in high school and college. I was financially okay, not because of my monthly salary of 20 Egyptian pounds from the textile company in Alexandria, where I worked as a chemist, but from money I earned as a choreographer.

You might ask why in world I would leave such an easy life and move across the world to a country where I didn't know anyone (except Wadid, who was not there), a country I did not know much about. And without a job awaiting me. All I had was $200 and two suitcases with limited clothing. Looking back, I wish I'd had a cell phone, internet, Google, and Facebook.

The truth is, I didn't have a good answer to why I had come. For me, immigrating to the United States was not about making more money or seeking a better life. Rather, it was my nature to seek challenge, excitement, adventure, and the freedom to do what I wanted to do. It was to hope, to dream without limitation and only imagination. That is what I believed the United States offered: no limitation to what you can do and what you can accomplish, the freedom to choose, and the opportunity to plan the course of your life and future. And that is what I have enjoyed most in the last fifty years of living here.

When people hear my story, they say, "God, you faced a lot of problems and suffered so much when you first came here." Somehow, I never felt that way. To me, those problems were challenging opportunities, and with my optimistic nature, failure was never an option. What drives some of us as immigrants is our sense of success and accomplishment. When I lived in Egypt, I never thought people judged you based on your religion. And when I lived in the States, I never thought people judged you based on how you look or where you came from. I now realize some people do judge you for different reasons; they do this everywhere in the world. In one country, you could be discriminated against because of your religion, and in another country, based on your nationality or appearance. However, I never thought about it back then, and it never really affected my life, one way or another.

So, back in June 1969, there I stood, all alone at JFK Airport. I knew I had landed in New York, but I had no idea where to go. I didn't know how far I was from New York City. It took me another twelve hours of traveling by bus and walking, while carrying my two bags (no bags with wheels in those days) to reach New Jersey. "Why New Jersey?" you ask. That's where my missing friend Wadid lived, and I was determined to find his house. He was the only person I knew in this country, and thankfully, I had his address. After 36 hours of traveling, I finally found myself knocking on Wadid's door at 3:00am, in the middle of nowhere, in a small town in New Jersey.

His brother answered the door and gave me the shocking news: "Wadid isn't here. He was drafted by the US Army and sent to Vietnam."

I froze at the door, in disbelief. I told his brother I was exhausted. I'd just come all the way from Egypt, I'd been traveling for two days and had no place to go. I was tired, hungry, and about to faint.

Reluctantly, he let me in. He took me to a room they rented upstairs in this small house, which was owned by an elderly woman who lived downstairs. The room was very small, with one tiny bed and a chair. I sat on the chair, and he sat on the bed.

He started our conversation by saying, "You can only stay here till morning and then you need to leave." He asked why I'd come to this country. He said it was very difficult here, and I should go back to Egypt."

He continued talking, but I only heard the first few sentences before I fainted into a deep sleep. And I was glad I did. This was not what I wanted to hear on my first day in the United States.

He woke me up at 6:00am and put me on a bus to New York City.

For every day of my first month in the United States, I knocked on the doors of employment agencies in New York City. For 30 days, I put on my only three-piece suit, picked up my only briefcase, and hit the road from 8:00am till the last office closed at 6:00pm. Although I was desperate to find a job because I was running out of money, this process was interesting to me. I practiced my English (very important to get a job), I practiced my interview skills, and most importantly, I learned what companies expected from me as a chemist. My knowledge as a chemist, who had graduated from Alexandria University, although limited, was good enough to allow me to do a reasonable interview.

When I had finished with most of the New York City agencies, I crossed the river to New Jersey. The first interview I was able to get with a company was not for a chemist, but for a worker to pack boxes for the sewing machine company Singer. To get there, I had to walk, on one of July's hottest days, in my three-piece suit, carrying my briefcase, for three hours. When I got there, I was told all the jobs had been filled. I was disappointed because I needed a job—any job—to survive. I was down to my last $20; I had no relatives to lean on, and the few Egyptian friends I'd made were all in the same situation. However, I was excited that at least I had my first interview at an American company.

Toward the middle of July 1969, an agency in New Jersey got me an interview at a PVC plastic company in Patterson. This was it for me: my English was somewhat better, my interview skills were developed, and I knew I had to get this job.

The laboratory manager, a Chinese chemist, asked me, "Do you have experience in the lab?"

I said, "No, but I am a chemist and I studied in labs for years."

He asked, "Do you know what a PVC is?"

I had read as much as I could about PVC in the library to prepare for the interview, so I said, "Yes, it is a vinyl chloride polymer."

"Where do you live?"

"New York City."

"Do you have a car to come to New Jersey?"

"No, but I could move here tomorrow."

"How will you get to work?"

"I will move close to the company and walk."

He said, "Okay. We will let you know."

I said, "I need a job. I don't care if it's as a chemist, a technician, or even cleaning the lab."

He paused, smiled, and asked, "When can you start?"

I said, "Now."

That was my big breakthrough. And a breakthrough is what you need as an immigrant, with any degree. Your first job is what will give you an American experience in your field. It will give you the opportunity to succeed and to further develop your career. My job was as a chemist and lab technician in the PVC quality-control lab.

I moved into a room at the YMCA in Passaic, New Jersey. It was very small room, with one tiny bed that wasn't big enough for more than one person to sleep. All the residents on that floor used one bathroom down the corridor from my room. My brother, Dr. Mounir Mady, arrived in the United States the same week I got my first job. He stayed with me in that YMCA room. I worked night shifts in the lab to allow Mounir to sleep in the bed at night. He went out in the day to look for a job as a dental technician, while I slept in the daytime.

September 1996, on the long Labor Day weekend, I worked sixteen hours a day for three days, doing double shifts with overtime. This earned me enough money to rent an apartment in Garfield, New Jersey. It was a big triumph for me to have my own place in the United States. My brother and I moved in with only our bags. We slept on the floor, using our clothes as a mattress, with no furniture or utilities. We were so happy to have our own place, where we could make hot tea using hot water from the tap water because we did not have gas to cook.

The apartment was an hour's walking distance to work. The shortest route was to walk along the train tracks. To keep myself occupied during my walk, I either counted the tracks or sang Egyptian songs.

Although I was content with my job, I kept in contact with some employment agencies I'd used during my job hunt. Why? Because I knew I wanted to get a better job. This is what differentiates successful Egyptians in the United States from others who have a college degree and are content to stay with their first job. As long as the latter are making money, they think it's fine. The successful ones, however, don't only think about money; they seek challenges to better themselves, develop their knowledge, gain experience, and advance in an environment that rewards and encourages achievers, and that doesn't limit what you can achieve.

It only took three months before an employment agency got me an interview with one of the largest consulting companies in the United States. The company was the testing arm for Booz Allen Hamilton. As a result of my better interview skills, and everything I'd learned during my few months of working at an American company, the lab manager offered me the job. It was a dream job, working for a global company, with an amazing salary.

One small issue was the fact that the company was in Florham Park, in the middle of nowhere. You could only reach this company by car, and I had no car. The lab manager was so interested in hiring me that he took me for lunch that day, and on the way back, we stopped at a house down the street from the company. He introduced me to the elderly woman who lived in this large, historic house and who sometimes rented a room—not for the money but to help people like me. Mrs. Baldwin was a gift from God. She treated me like a son for the little money I paid for the room I rented. I was allowed to use the whole house. She made me breakfast and dinner, washed my clothes, and cleaned my room. She was over 70, but she worked as if she were 30 years old. She volunteered every day at hospitals and other charities, cleaned the whole house, and took care of the whole yard. This inspired me because it confirmed my belief that not everyone works only for money; some work because it gives them a sense of value. As they say, some people work to live and some live to work. I enjoy both.

In January 1970, my wife came to the United States. I brought all of my friends with me to JFK Airport to welcome her. It was so exciting to have Lily finally join me, so we could be together and share our life challenges.

After Lily arrived, we were finally able to take our honeymoon. We spent a week at the Waldorf Astoria. You are probably wondering: after only six months in the United States, how were we able to afford a week at the most expensive hotel in New York City? We were able to because Lily and I stayed at Mrs. Baldwin's home. Then, in the next few months, she got a job at the same company where I worked. Our next major accomplishment was purchasing our first car: a 1956 white convertible Impala. After that, we moved to our own apartment in Madison, New Jersey.

Among the most important feelings an immigrant has are loneliness and a sense that one doesn't belong. Family and friends play a big role in your life when you are far from your native country. They give you a sense of security and support and also minimize any homesickness. Having my wife by my side to build our life made everything much easier. Lily was a fighter with endless energy, and that was a big factor in our success story. A few years later, my mother and my sister Lila joined us in the United States. This made my family feel more complete, and I no longer felt guilty or worried about leaving them behind alone in Egypt.

On October 6, 1971, our first child, Eddie, was born. As I left the hospital, all of a sudden, I thought, "I have to drive more carefully; I have a responsibility for another life now!" On July 27, 1975, our second child, Michelle, was born. She came with a big smile on her face. So now we had two children, a brand-new car, our first house, and a dog named Happy. That completed, as they say, the American dream.

I had always known my chemistry degree from Alexandria University would not be enough for the career development I wanted. A college education in Egypt was based only on memorization and not on understudying the subject matter. Therefore, I enrolled in Farleigh Dickenson University to get a master's degree in chemistry. I never really liked chemistry in high school or when I was at Alexandria University. I would have preferred to become a choreographer, dancer, or stage manager. However, my father advised me that a college degree was essential for a meaningful career in the United States. I received my master's degree in chemistry in two years, with the highest score of 4.0 out 4.0. I enjoyed the learning experience so much that, although I had two young children, and Lily and I both worked full time, I decided to enroll in a PhD program at Rutgers University. It was not easy to manage a full-time job, family, house, and school, but continuing my education served as a catchup process for not growing up in this country; it allowed me to melt into the society, understand the culture, and be more competitive in my career development. One thing I learned is so true: "Education is information given to you; learning is information you take in yourself."

In the mid-1970s, we moved to Connecticut, where I took a job as a laboratory manager at Philip Morris. We lived in a great house with a pool and garden, where we entertained our family every weekend. Those years were the best years. Lily did not have to work for some time, and I enjoyed my job.

Unfortunately, in 1980, Philip Morris closed that office and offered me a general manager position in Greenville, South Carolina. I did not want to move to the South. Searching for a job ten years after settling in the United State was much easier. I got amazing offers from three large companies, and accepted the one from Ciba-Geigy, managing big state-of-the-art analytical laboratories in New York. While it turned out to be a good job, it was too structured and not as challenging as my job at Phillip Morris. After a few years at Ciba, I went back to night school and completed a business degree from Long Island University. I learned more about marketing and business, which I really enjoyed.

Although I had a very good salary at Ciba, living in New York was a lot more expensive than Connecticut. So, I decided to start a video production company. It would keep me challenged, as well as use my interest in art, theater, and production. Video production was new in 1983. I bought the first video camera for consumers and named the company Universal Video System (later renamed Universal Video Production). I really started this company to make more money, and then start a company in my chemical field. It did not work that way. The video company grew; I was good at video production and editing. I bought better equipment and expanded the business. My first employee was my son Eddie, when he was thirteen years old. He was smart, a fast learner, and good at anything he did. I worked at my full-time job and Eddie went to school, and at night, we were editing and developing the company. The business grew, and we moved to one of the largest houses in Pomona, New York. The house was so large. We had room for our family to live in the seven bedrooms and seven bathrooms on one floor, and plenty of space to run the video production company from another floor. It had a large swimming pool and tennis courts. In addition, I bought my dream car: a 500 SL Mercedes Benz. I don't mean to brag about what we had, but in our world, all that was the measure of success.

Our biggest video production contract was with Con Edison, to develop a series of engineering video training tapes. By the mid-1980s, the company had grown so much that my oldest brother, Nabil, decided it would better for his children if their family joined us in the United States. Nabil was in his late forties and the general manager of large perfume company in Egypt. He was a lot of fun to work with when he started working at the video company.

When I met Wahid Boctor, he did not know too much about production, but he was a pioneer in broadcasting and had founded the first one-hour Arabic TV show in California. The program was called AATV, and the Arabic community loved it because there was nothing like it in the United States. I partnered with Wahid and produced a show in the Northeast based on his show. We expanded in New York and New Jersey, and he in California. AATV was nonpolitical and gave the Arabic community a window into Middle East news and entertainment. The show was expensive to produce every week, and although it was somewhat supported by advertisements, it was losing money. I kept it up in spite of that because I enjoyed the celebrity status it gave me in our small Arabic/Egyptian community; although I was not really looking for such fame, I did like the feeling of accomplishment.

I started a company that produced Arabic audiotapes and CDs. We were the first company to market all Arabic stars from the Middle East. I mean all top stars: Amr Diab, Kazem el-Saher, Walid Toufic, Ragheb Alama, Majida el-Roumi, Najwa Karam, Mohamed Mounir, Sabah, and more. Then we started to sponsor concerts and produced a

US tour for some of the stars. Some were profitable, such as Amr Diab and Kazem el-Saher; others I lost money on. In general, although I loved the Arabic TV and concerts, they were financial losses; however, the video production company was so successful that it could support my fun with the TV and concerts.

In addition to all of this, I started another company, called Media East, to promote tourism in Egypt, with a focus on scuba diving. The Red Sea is one of the best areas in the world for scuba diving, and I thought it would be a great business opportunity, as well as a way to give back to the country I love: Egypt. We opened an office within an existing travel agency in New York City; unfortunately, the Egyptian Tourism Agency and Ministry of Tourism did not show any interest in the marketing campaign our video production company prepared. Although we had a powerful program to promote tourism in Egypt, we could not get the support we needed in Egypt for our tours.

We expanded the company from New York to other states, and Eddie moved to Florida and established a new office, which became the headquarters. In 1996, Michelle got married to Pete and had our first granddaughter, Samantha. Their family moved to Florida to join Eddie at the expanding business. We also opened a new company based on the concept of a party showcase, with office space in Boca Raton. It provided all you needed for events: video production, photography, bands, DJs, flowers, decorators, invitations, and event planners. It was a unique concept and the first of its kind at that time.

In 1998, we moved to a house in New Jersey, with a stunning view of Manhattan. Eddie was expanding the company into the entrainment market, Michelle was managing the office, and Pete was managing the production staff. I was still at my full-time job at Ciba, where I was promoted to director of regulatory affairs, while still managing the video production company. Lily was still working at Ciba as a senior analytical research scientist, and I had a very good salary from both Ciba and the video and entertainment companies. We were making a good level of income. I would not say I enjoyed having a lot of money; rather, I liked the feeling of financial security for my family. As an immigrant, with no one to lean on for support, the biggest concern you have is financial security.

In 2000, the millennium year, Lily retired, and I was promoted to vice president of regulatory services, managing a group I founded called Ciba Expert Services. I subsequently launched a symposium under the auspices of this group that addressed global food packaging safety and regulations. It included presenters from around the world and was one of my most accomplished projects in my career. The concept was so successful that it has become a standard in the industry, and several organizations around the world offer the same program.

Lily and I moved to Florida in 2005 to be close to our children and grandchildren. Three years later, Eddie got married to Ashely, who was a native Floridian. She met Eddie when she was at college, finishing her art degree. Our family was melting pot in American society, with both our children born in the United States and married to spouses from American families. This made me happy because, although they are proud of their Egyptian heritage, they are not foreigners in this country.

In 2010, Ciba, a two-hundred-year-old company, was sold to BASF. It is interesting that, just as we as humans are born and we die, companies are formed and then disappear. Ciba Expert Services was sold to a large consultant company based in England. My group fit perfectly into that company. Although I was sixty-five—the average retirement age—at the time, working as vice president of regulatory services for this company was interesting and challenging to me, so I continued working. Helping the largest global companies to introduce their products into the market safely, and in compliance with government agency regulations, was one of my major accomplishments.

My belief is that if you decide to leave your home country and immigrate to a new world, you need to be ready to accept the challenge. If you only think about making money, you will most likely fail, or have limited success. If instead you focus on working hard, developing yourself, and learning, you will have a chance to succeed. And, yes, money comes with success. You need education, but education is something given to you; learning is something you need to actively participate in. You need to accept your new environment and its challenges, because that is what will ignite your imagination and drive you to succeed.

There are so many successful and accomplished Egyptians—way beyond me and my limited success. Most of them started like me, with next to nothing. Some achieved considerable financial success and became some of the richest people in the United States. Some achieved major professional success, in fields such as engineering, medicine, and technology. I like to say my modest accomplishments were a small part of both. And most importantly, I believe I was a good representative of Egypt, while I also contributed to the development technology and regulations in the United States.

———

NAEEM MADY was born in Alexandria, Egypt and moved to the USA in1969. He is married to Lily Mady and they have 2 children and three grandchildren. With over 50 years of professional experience as a chemist and business manager, he has published and presented numerous papers in the field of Analytical Chemistry and Regulatory Compliance. Mr. Mady was included in Marquis Who's Who in America. His work took him to countries around the world. He was socially active in the New York community he lived in as he is in Florida where he now lives with his family.

THE GHONEIMS' EGYPTIAN AMERICAN STORY OF THREE GENERATIONS

Annie Whitney

When I was six years old, my grandmother, Judith (Judy) Stone Ghoneim, gifted me a gold ring for Christmas. Far too big for my fingers at the time, and representing a legacy far too great for me to process, I put it away until I grew into both the piece and the story behind it. My name is Anne Stone Whitney—or Annie, as I prefer—and I am from Charlotte, North Carolina.

My story starts a good while before my time. My grandmother, whom I called Gran, grew up in a Jewish family in New York City. She was born in 1933, at the height of the Great Depression, and was raised during the Second World War. She had lived at home throughout her university studies, and was itching for an adventure, so in September 1959, she embarked upon one.

Long before the days of the single-currency Eurozone and intra-European railroads, she backpacked and hitchhiked her way across the continent. It was, of all things, a chance encounter with two women at the Lion Gate in Mycenae, Greece, that oriented her life forever toward Egypt. These two women, also tourists, had just returned from Egypt. Still reeling from the wonders they had seen, they encouraged her to seize the opportunity and visit.

Though she had no plans to go to Egypt, Judy heeded their advice and caught a ferry from Athens to Alexandria a few days later. In an age before cell phones, her family had no idea where she was, and she had no clue how to make her way from Alexandria to Cairo. On the boat, she met a colonel from the Egyptian army, who explained where and how to reserve a bus ticket, which she did upon arrival. When she boarded the bus, there was a single seat remaining: one next to a young Egyptian man reading *Time* magazine. He could tell the young lady seated next to him, Judy, was an American, and asked to practice his English with her.

They spoke for the next three and a half hours, and with no plans for accommodations nor any contacts in Cairo, my grandmother accepted an offer to stay at his family's home in Heliopolis. Many years later, she half-jokingly remarked to me that trusting this stranger in a faraway land was a "dumb thing" for a young woman like herself to do. But that decision changed her life forever, and it is the reason I am here today. The stranger, Nabil Abdel Rahim Ghoneim, would become my grandfather.

Over the next week, Nabil took Judy to Luxor and then toured with her around the classic Cairo sights—the mosques, the pyramids—before she was due to catch her return ferry. Over the next months, she remained in Europe, picking up odd jobs and all the while corresponding with Nabil by post. Judy returned to Egypt by boat, this time departing from Genoa, and on December 27, 1959, the two married in secret. The following September, they held a formal ceremony in Cairo jointly with Nabil's brother, Adel, and his new wife, Makaram, at the Semiramis in Tahrir Square. Judy's parents joined from New York and met Nabil's family for the first time, the unlikely union of an American Jewish family and an Egyptian Muslim one. Despite their families' religious traditions, what united the bride and groom was their common (and a bit scandalous) atheism.

Judy and Nabil had every intention of staying in Egypt. Judy began to build her life there and secured a job at the American College for Girls. Nabil, a new doctor, opened a gynecological clinic. The couple gave birth to a girl, Jilan Catherine Ghoneim (my mother), delivered at the Italian hospital.

However, as life grew more difficult for the young family, they looked for a way to leave. My then-toddler mother had been born a dual citizen, so my grandmother had no problem leaving Egypt with her. But she, of course, refused to leave my grandfather behind. Egyptian exit visas for nationals were increasingly hard to come by, rendering a typical American marriage visa impossible to obtain, so Judy and Nabil concocted an elaborate, creative—and secret—plan to secure their exit.

That's where my gold ring comes in. Worried that leaving Egypt without state permission could lead to the freezing of his bank account, Nabil began to convert his savings to gold he could liquidate upon arrival in the United States. The last of this gold was in the form of coins, 1911 British sovereigns adorned with face of King George. Our family saved them and eventually mounted them on rings for my sister and me. They serve as daily reminders of both the courage Nabil had to start anew, and the strong ties that link us back to Um El-Dunya.

Rather than dodging the government, Nabil decided to hide his escape in plain sight. He applied for a job as a doctor with Egypt's foreign aid agency and was posted to the Congo. Judy and their baby moved with him to the post. By day, he provided medical aid, and by night, worked with Judy as they continued to chart the next steps in their journey to the United States.

My grandmother and mother left the Congo shortly thereafter for New York City, where Judy leveraged every contact she had in hopes of securing a visa for her husband. The difficulties were compounded by the fact that Nabil would be entering the United States without a valid Egyptian exit visa. Eventually, she made contact with a congress-man from Alabama, a state to which our family had no connection whatsoever, who offered to push an emergency bill through Congress, permitting Nabil's entrance without proper documentation. The bill passed, and he scheduled his departure from the Congo quite literally in the dark of night—and during a long weekend, so an extra day would pass before anyone noticed his absence—to join his wife and young daughter in New York City.

Thankfully, Judy came from a large and loving American family, whose loud Thanksgiving dinners are not unlike Egyptian *iftars*, and who welcomed and supported Nabil. Together, he, his wife, and his daughter began to build a new life. To practice as a foreign doctor in the United States, Nabil completed a second residency, this time at Yale University in New Haven, Connecticut, and with a specialization in radiology rather than gynecology. The new specialty led him to a job in Fayetteville, North Carolina, where he became chief of radiology at the Veterans Affairs Hospital. Needless to say, a move from the hustle and bustle of Cairo to a sleepy military town in eastern North Carolina was not without its challenges; my grandparents would drive at times upwards of an hour to track down pita and yogurt to bring the flavors of Egypt to their new home in the American South.

That move is also the reason I am here today. My mom spent much of her childhood in North Carolina, completed her university studies here, and has lived in the state almost continuously since. She met my father in Charlotte, which is also where my sister and I were born and raised.

***

Enter my story. With the exception of the occasional Egyptian dish on the dinner table, my childhood was marked far more by the culture of the American South than by that of Egypt. It was not until our first family trip—and my mother's first trip in over two decades—to Cairo in 2008 that I gave due credence to this dual aspect of my family's identity. At the time, I was twelve years old, and my sister ten. The trip was as much about us meeting our family for the first time as it was absorbing the sights, sounds, and smells of this homeland of ours so far from the land we called home.

My first encounter with Egypt was simultaneously my first with the Middle East, Africa, and more broadly, the desert. A disoriented feeling came over me as I peered out the airplane window during our final descent into Cairo. *Someone forgot to plant grass,* I wanted to say. *Where is it?* wondered my North American eyes, trained to see green color schemes. Expanses of beige stretched as far as I could see in every direction: sand, buildings, sun baked roads. Taken aback, my mind began to open for the first time to a world so far from the one I knew.

It didn't take long, however, to see past the difference in landscape and toward the similarity in manner. When we arrived at my Aunt Mona's apartment in Heliopolis, which she had kindly lent us for the trip, we found a house full of Nabil's brothers and sisters-in-law, and a kitchen counter covered with all sorts of Egyptian sweets. One of our great uncles asked if we would like lamb or beef kufta for our first dinner in Egypt, and then quickly corrected himself to say he would be bringing both. This was family—family I had never met, yet who immediately treated me as if I had grown up alongside them. The Egyptian way.

Over the next two weeks, we mixed tourism with family visits. We spent our days at the Sakara and Giza Pyramids, and in the evenings, shared meals with many different branches of the extended family. We celebrated Christmas on the Nile, tried *taameya* from street vendors, and prayed that food poisoning would evade us (it did not). It felt crazy to me—there I was, half a world away, with cousins who looked not at all unlike my sister and me. I was devastated to leave and hoped to return soon. However, the global financial crash of 2008, and the fallout from the revolutions in Egypt in 2011 and 2013, prevented our family from doing so.

Sometime after that trip, I finally grew into the ring my grandfather left behind. I wore, and still wear, it each day as a reminder of where I came from and as a promise to return. This promise first manifested not in a physical return, but in a linguistic one. Although my family only spoke English growing up, I began studying Modern Standard Arabic during my first semester of university and eventually added Egyptian Colloquial Arabic.

As a non-native speaker, I will always be an outsider to the language—the ع and خ will forever stump me—but even just beginning to learn Arabic brought me closer to the grandfather I never knew. I took a term off from my studies in 2017 and moved to Cairo. I was twenty at the time and felt strongly that I needed to return to my roots, get to know my many cousins still there, and immerse myself in the language and culture, rather than study it from afar. Most everyone around me thought I was nuts for disrupting my education and uprooting my life, and frankly, I probably was.

In fact, I even questioned it myself. In the moments before the plane landed at Cairo International Airport, I shocked myself by audibly uttering, "What the f*** am I doing?!" I was a young woman, who had taken leave from university to move to Egypt alone, found an Arabic school online and roommates over WhatsApp, and done little in the way of planning. The final moments of the flight were full of panic as my obsessive American organizational instincts kicked in. One of the great lessons the months ahead in Egypt would teach me was the IBM mentality: *inshallah, bukra, malesh* (God willing, tomorrow, never mind). "Everything will be fine," and it was.

The months that followed were very sweet, filled with Arabic classes during the week and visits with my grandfather's brothers and their children and families on the weekends. I made dear friends from Egypt and across the world, and I built the relationships with my cousins that I'd hoped to build. I traveled the country, visiting Abu Simbel, Ain Sokhna, Alexandria, Aswan, the Black Desert, Edfu, Fayoum, Luxor, the White Desert, and more. I grew to love the food so much that I obsessively checked Zooba's Instagram account for the announcement of their first American location, which opened, to my delight, in New York City in 2019. My time in Egypt taught me to enjoy the freedom that comes with sitting around chatting over a cup of tea for six hours, with no urgency to rush off to the next appointment, as well as to wholly embrace a "the more, the merrier" mentality.

I spent long evenings on Nile feluccas, took calligraphy classes in Maadi, attended an Egyptian American fusion concert at the Citadel hosted by the United States Embassy, and volunteered with St. Andrew's Refugee Services. I experienced an Egyptian wedding, grew to love the smell of *taameya* and *shisha* wafting through the streets, lost myself in the maze that is Khan el-Khalili, and tried (and hated) *fesikh*. I celebrated Sham el-Nesim in my cousins' backyard, camped out in Land Rovers in the White Desert, sand-dune surfed (and failed) down the hills of Fayoum, rode horseback through the open desert, and grabbed drinks at Horeya—the bar where much of the 2011 Revolution was planned, still marked by the scars of bullet holes. And so, so much more.

That said, I also learned a lot about the more trying sides of life in Egypt—the sides that perhaps encouraged my family and others to emigrate. I was not looked upon favorably as a young woman living on my own. I shared an apartment with an Austrian and a German, both females. Even though we paid our rent on time each month and caused few problems, the landlord refused to interact with us directly and insisted that our household be headed by a male. Our building's *bawab* (doorman) believed the only possible explanation for such an all-female roommate configuration was that we were running a brothel, which I can assure you we were not. Street harassment was also an ever-present issue.

I was in Egypt during an economically and politically unstable time. I arrived two months following the unpegging of the currency. It was a great time, frankly, to be a foreigner in Egypt, because prices had dropped, and the buying power of the dollar had more than doubled. But I was aware while every meal I bought for the equivalent of just a few American cents, millions of Egyptians could no longer afford their most basic necessities. Tensions began to simmer, and bread riots broke out in some parts of the country.

I arrived a few days before the sixth anniversary of the 2011 Revolution, and a little less than a year after the disappearance of Giulio Regeni. An Egyptian professor of mine warned me to be cautious, to not engage politically, and to not attract attention as a foreigner. In the lead-up to the anniversary, an officer showed up at my apartment to "investigate," with neither a warrant nor an explanation. My roommates and I assumed they were trying to keep tabs on foreigners.

My second day of Arabic classes, located in Tahrir Square, was to fall on the anniversary of the revolution. A cousin warned me not to leave the house that day in case of an uprising, but I didn't want to miss any class so soon after my arrival. Nothing went terribly wrong, but I will never stop wondering why I saw a trail of blood through Tahrir Square that day. I also grew wary of accessing independent news websites after two friends of mine, who worked with a foreign government, became concerned they were being followed, electronically and in-person, by the authorities.

I went to Alexandria with some friends for Easter weekend. Without a doubt, it was my favorite place in Egypt. It felt as if two of my favorite cities, Nice and Cairo, had morphed into one. The seafood was fresh, the water blue, the people in the streets happy. On Good Friday, which was April 7, 2017, my friends and I went to visit St. Mark's Coptic Orthodox Cathedral. It was beautiful, so we sat in the pews to rest and chat for half an hour, before resuming our tour of Alexandria by foot. Two days later, on Easter Sunday, the church was attacked by suicide bombers with ties to ISIS, killing seventeen and injuring at least another four dozen. I know that attacks happen all over the world—in the United States, as well—but my physical and temporal proximity to this one left me particularly saddened and uneasy.

***

Egypt, I learned, is a state of mind. It's about letting go, living in the moment, laughing when plans fall through, embracing the fact that a ten-minute taxi ride on paper is often an hour-long ride in practice, ordering one thing and receiving another, and welcoming the presence of others at all times.

From time to time, I ask myself, "What am I?" My mother was born a dual citizen in Egypt and later moved to the United States. She never had to acquire American nationality, but she did experience the world through the eyes of an immigrant child. Does that make her a first- or second-generation immigrant? I would say a "1.5 generation" immigrant, which makes my sister and me "2.5 generation" immigrants—or as I prefer, simply beneficiaries of immigration, like most Americans.

My time in Egypt and my own discovery (or rediscovery) of my heritage and my family's story groomed an interest in immigration law, which I am now pursuing. The many times a day the sun bounces off this ring my grandfather left behind and catches my eye, I am reminded that I am who I am both because of the opportunities my family's move offered me and because of the unique mix of cultures that underpins our family.

———•———

ANNIE WHITNEY is a student at Harvard Law School who credits her desire to pursue immigration law to her Egyptian American background. She has worked in refugee camps in the Mediterranean region and on the United States-Mexico border.

RECOLLECTIONS FROM A NEW WORLD

Fekri A. Hassan

Much has happened since I, then twenty-five years old, went, in the stealth of night, to the dark, shadowy surroundings of Khufu's Great Pyramid of Giza and Sphinx that has watched over Egypt from its perch on this high desert plateau overlooking the Nile for millennia. It was quiet and serene, with only the sound of grains of sand whisked by a subtle breeze. I had come—as Native Americans traditionally do—looking for a vision. I was planning to leave Egypt, and I alone had to make this life-changing decision. Out of the dark surroundings, an officer in his white uniform asked me what I was doing there. A few months later, I was on a plane to Lovefield Airport in Dallas, Texas, to study archaeology at Southern Methodist University (SMU).

I had received my bachelor's degree (BSc) in geology and chemistry from the Faculty of Sciences at Ain Shams University five years earlier. Among others who graduated with honors, I was commissioned (تكليف) to serve as a teaching assistant/demonstrator (معيد) in the Department of Geology. The position guaranteed, as was then common in Egypt, I would be employed permanently as a university academic and begin a career that led to earning a PhD and becoming a lecturer, with routine promotions to higher academic ranks.

I entered the Faculty of Sciences in 1959, with the firm belief that science was the key to understanding the world, and that it was impossible for anyone who was not familiar with the methods and accomplishments of modern science to fathom how this world works, and how it can be improved. I was extremely fond of reading to the extent that my mother worried I would lose my eyesight. I ended up literally reading "undercover," beneath the bedsheet, to avoid being reprimanded. I have not lost my passion for reading and returned to Egypt in 2008 with six tons of books. It was only natural for me, immersed in a world of books, to think I would want to continue to be able to read, and eventually to be able to write.

My first readings were of magazines and adventure novels. I opened my eyes on the issues of *The World on Monday* (الأثنين والدنيا) and the *al-Mosawwar* illustrated magazine that my maternal uncle Ali (خالي علي), who lived with us, brought home. I was fond of him and his welcoming smile and sparkling eyes, a gift he shared with my mother. To him I owe my fascination with learning and reading, as to my mother I owe my faith in education and dedication to make it possible to all—as she did with her two sons and five daughters. The gentleness, dignity, and sense of humor of my father were a lesson in humane living, self-reliance, and kindness.

Reading was the means by which I began to construct the larger world around me—a world that extended well beyond my daily journey to school and beyond the confines of family life. Through the magazines, I began to realize the horrors of British occupation. In the Battle of Ismailia, seven thousand^ British army soldiers surrounded the building of the Ismailia governorate to force its 140^ Egyptian police officers and soldiers to surrender so they could occupy the building. The Egyptian police force resisted, and fifty were killed. The remaining eighty were wounded. This was on January 25, 1952. In a suburb of Suez, Kafr Abdou, 156 houses were demolished on December 8, 1951, by a force consisting of ten thousand British troops; five hundred tanks and armed vehicles were deployed to overcome the resistance by the three hundred families who resided there, together with the Egyptian police force that came to their aid. Only now do I know these statistics; then I was eight years old. I do not know if this was what drove me to dress in an officer's uniform and to make wooden swords so I could duel with our neighbor's son, who was slightly older than I was. My fascination then with the military may have been a result of witnessing as a six-year-old the Egyptian army officers returning in their tanks in February 1949, to the cheers of thousands of Egyptians, after having fought to the bitter end, encircled in a small pocket at Faluja الفلوجة, thirty kilometers northeast of Gaza City, by Israeli armed forces after the 1948 armistice. They were led by a fearsome dark-skinned leader who was called for his bravery the Black Hyena الضبع الأسود (perhaps more fitting in English to call him a Black Panther). Among the returning officers, unknown to me then, was one officer, who a few years later, led a revolution to liberate Egypt from British colonialism, Colonel Gamal Abdel Nasser.

I am not sure if it was during the Arab-Israeli 1948 war or during 1956 that my family was crowded in a shelter during air raids. We heard a frightening explosion of an armaments depot in the Citadel. When I was thirteen years old, I walked to Attaba Square to buy a dagger to arm myself, stationed on the roof of our house, to defend my family against Israeli paratroopers, who were reported to have been dropped from attacking airplanes.

I was born on August 11, 1943. The Battle of Alamein, with the defeat of the German army, had stopped Rommel's march into Cairo a year earlier (November 11, 1942). Germany faced serious setbacks in 1943, which included a series of German defeats on the Eastern Front, the Allied invasions of Sicily and Italy, and Allied offensives in the Pacific—which cost the Axis its initiative and forced it into strategic retreat on all fronts. Two years later, just before my second birthday, the United States dropped atomic bombs on Hiroshima and Nagasaki. I grew up with the threat of a nuclear holocaust in the arms race between the United States and the USSR.

By 1943, Egypt had been under British occupation for sixty-one years. While Egypt remained neutral in the war between the Allied forces, which included England, Egyptians were forced to contribute to the war effort. Many Egyptians, in their zeal to end the British occupation, sympathized with Germany. In February 1942, the British government, through its ambassador, Sir Miles Lampson, pressed King Farouk to have a Wafd or Wafd-coalition government. On the night of February 4, 1942, British troops and tanks surrounded the king's Abdeen Palace in Cairo, and Lampson presented Farouk with an ultimatum. Farouk capitulated, but Egyptian Army officers were outraged at this humiliation and vowed to end British rule, which they did on July 23, 1952. I was nine years old then. Ordinary people were dancing in the street. I was too young to understand the significance or the circumstances of the revolution, but I heard many stories about the king's avarice, his corrupt Italian entourage, and his ferocious appetite.

My father was an ardent supporter of the Wafd political party, but I was too young to follow political issues. But by the time I was in my teens, political parties were banned, and Egypt was ruled by the revolutionary army officers. At any rate, I was consumed with other more interesting issues: I was reading adventure novels and the stories of Sherlock Holmes, and I was totally taken by the antics of the honorable and smart gentleman thief, (اللص الظريف) Arsène Lupin (ارسين لوبين). Holmes, the detective, stirred my intellect and made me attentive to how our mind works. Lupin, on the other hand, captivated me with his wit, made me sympathetic with his concern for the poor, and perhaps made me more aware of social issues than of politics.

But one day, still in my early teens, I went to the Azbakia second-hand-book market, as was my habit, to get my stock of novels, only to be told by the bookseller, who did not have the appearance of an intellectual in his *galabyia*, that I was now old enough to start reading more serious books. He handed me an Arabic translation by Hana Khabaz of *Plato's Republic* and swapped it for all the money I had, which I naively handed to him. Little did I know that my life, as a result of this, would never be the same again. Not that I understood much of what was in the book; the translation was awful, and the text was too deep for me, but I realized the value of questioning what appears to be, on the face of it, reasonable. I later read literary novels and plays, discovering Hemingway, Steinbeck, and Ibsen, among many others. By the time

I was in college, where science was taught in English, I had begun to augment my reading of Arabic translations with books in English. To improve my standing in English, I enrolled in a course offered by the American cultural center in Cairo. After an orientation exam, I was placed in the last tier of the courses. My American teacher was the first American I had met. She introduced me to Faulkner. She was probably from the Midwest, in her early thirties, clean and proper, encouraging and decent. I passed the Michigan University examination in the proficiency of English (ECPE), which, I was overjoyed to discover, allowed me to teach English. It is still the certificate I value most, perhaps because it was a result of self-learning.

No one in my generation escaped Hollywood movies. As a boy, I enjoyed the films of dueling, and one of my favorite actors was Tony Curtis. Was it the *Purple Mask* that I saw in Cinema Realto in Shoubra? Another actor who revealed the psychology of growing up in the United States was James Dean in *Rebel without a Cause*.

I was in a crowded bus in Cairo when I learned about the assassination of President John F. Kennedy, on November 22, 1963, in Dallas, Texas. I did not know then that five years later I would be in Dallas at the spot where he was shot. I graduated in 1963 and joined the Faculty of Science as a teaching assistant. I enjoyed teaching geology, as well as the company of the other teaching assistants, and made long-life friends, who were added to my friends from high school. Between 1963 and 1968, I was becoming my own person and developing the main elements of my personality. I was still dedicated to reading, expanding my horizons, and being enriched by books translated from many languages. These books were offered at affordable prices by the Ministry of Culture, largely due to the vision of an enlightened intellectual who happened to be one of the Free Officers of the 1952 revolution, Tharwat Okasha (1921–2012). He was the minister of culture from 1958 to 1962 and 1968 to 1970. My debt to him is incalculable. He opened up a window to all forms of culture. Not only did I benefit from the books but I also became a regular visitor to the Cairo Opera House, where I listened to classical music and reveled in the operas and ballet performances by international groups, including the Bolshoi.

Egypt under Nasser (1918–1970), who ruled from 1954 to 1970, struggled to gain its national identity, and to find its place in a world struggling with the rivalry between the United States and the USSR, and with post-WWII economic developments. Nasser's rule was what now seems like a tragic Greek drama. He came from Upper Egypt and witnessed the poverty suffered by Egyptian farmers. He then lived in Cairo and Alexandria, where he was engaged in the daily life of simple, ordinary people. In his youth, he joined the army and fought in the 1948 Arab-Israeli war, but he was neither a practicing politician nor an ideologue. He was evidently dissatisfied with the political parties because they were looking out for their own interests, as he saw it. Such debates and political maneuvering were clearly not in tune with his military perspective on how to get things done as a commander. He thought he could do it all alone, but this opened him up to severe criticism and hostility. Nevertheless, he was the first native Egyptian ruler since the end of Pharaonic times; he had distinctive Egyptian features and was tall and charismatic. He became immensely popular, having awakened a sense of pride and defiance not only in Egypt, but in the entire Arab world. But he was not favored by the Muslim Brothers, who were keen on putting him under their thumb. He was also disliked by the Arab monarchs, who were shaken by his revolutionary rhetoric, and he was definitely the target of anger and dismay by the Israeli, British, and French governments for his anti-colonial and pro-Palestinian policies. Moreover, he dared to nationalize the Suez Canal in July 1956. In October of the same year, Israeli, British, and French forces invaded Egypt.

When Nasser came to power, the Americans thought he could be their man in the Middle East. They were engaged in the fight against communism, and on their way to becoming the greatest world power, displacing the traditional imperialist powers of Europe. Accordingly, the United States sided with Nasser against the British-French-Israeli attack on Egypt in 1956, but failed to bring him to yield to their will in the Middle East. He was strongly opposed in 1958 by Foster Dulles, who prevented Nasser from building the Aswan High Dam. This policy allowed the Soviet Union to gain influence in Egypt and forced Nasser to turn to the Soviets for constructing the dam.

In the early sixties, I read George Orwell's *Animal Farm*, and in 1984, I read Aldus Huxley's *Brave New World*. I was still disinclined to devote myself to any political ideology. Instead, I was drawn to the sciences, and when I joined the Faculty of Sciences, I realized that the main references to our scientific topics were by American scientists. It became clear that if I were to advance in my studies, I had to go to the source. In addition, my outlook on life was broad and free, and it became apparent that it was risky to have your own voice.

A year after I earned my master's degree in geology from Ain Shams University, Egypt suffered a humiliating defeat, in 1967. I walked from Heliopolis to Abbasia soon after Nasser went on the radio and with a voice full of sorrow and sadness, declared defeat and said he would step down. I walked at night. It was quiet and eerie. The shock to Egyptians was unbearable, and as soon as people realized what had happened, they poured into the streets and demanded he remain in office.

Nasser died in 1970. It was not until 1973, under President Anwar el-Sadat, when Egyptian army troops breached the formidable 150 kilometer long, 20 to 25 meters high Bar-Lev line along the Suez Canal, allowing Egyptian army divisions to start the liberation of occupied Sinai, that a sense of honor was restored.

In that same year, I earned my PhD in anthropology from SMU. I arrived there at the invitation of Professor Fred Wendorf, an American archaeologist who graduated from Harvard after being injured in Italy in World War II. He was on the US team in charge of rescuing the monuments threatened by the construction of the Aswan High Dam. He was a prehistorian who realized how much of Egypt's prehistory was still unknown. Equipped with the broad perspectives of archaeological methods in the 1960s, he began a systematic survey of Nubian prehistoric sites, producing two landmark volumes on the prehistory of Nubia. By the end of the Nubia campaign, he decided to extend his work to the north, along the banks of the Nile River and subsequently into the Egyptian Sahara (Western Desert). He collaborated with and was given great assistance in securing permits by Professor Rushdi Said, who was the director of the geological survey of Egypt. Rushdi had been to Harvard and knew Fred at that time; he became a professor of geology at Cairo University, before assuming the task of directing Egypt's effort in search of rocks and minerals. I was introduced to Fred by Rushdi to serve as a field geologist in Fred's survey of the Qena-Sohaj region. My fate as an archaeologist was sealed when Fred secured for me a scholarship to study Egyptian prehistory with him in Dallas.

So, there I was in Smith Hall, where Fred had founded a department of anthropology, trying my first taste of American coffee offered to students and faculty from a centrally located dispenser, a testimonial to American ingenuity and collegiality. I was introduced to the Student Union, where students retreated for food and refreshments, and to attend student-sponsored events. I was truly intrigued by the money changing machine at the entrance of Union Hall and began to appreciate the American way. There was more than films, Hemingway, and filtered coffee to the American way, to be discovered in and beyond Dallas—"from the redwood forest to the Gulf Stream waters." The immensity and diversity of the United States is amazing, to say the least—from the sleepy little towns in the South to the hustle and bustle of Chicago and New York, from Taos way up high in eagle snow-capped mountains, to the barns and wheat fields of eastern Washington state, from the forest of the Olympic Peninsula and its woodsmen, to the beaches of Miami. Bars, ranches, parking lots, malls, and 7/11 twenty-four-hour convenience stores—all these places were symptomatic of a deeper organizational structure, efficiency, convenience, and order.

The population mix was equally diverse—from well-to-do middle-class White Americans in Dallas Highland Park, to people in the slums of Harlem, to the man I saw in Chicago picking food from a garbage can. Americans lived in parallel worlds that were nevertheless linked in a mysterious way; perhaps the binding thread was the dream of becoming, and the opportunity to become someone someday. The path for many was not easy, but the American way was about overcoming adversity. American history, as Yousef Idris, socialist Egyptian writer remarked, is full of thousands and thousands of inventions made by individuals who contribute to the making of a better life for themselves and society. It is perhaps, as he remarked, also due to the freedom of speech, and the support for research.[1]

For me, the United States has always been an ongoing human experiment, the youngest human enterprise to liberate a nation, as much as possible, from traditional European political bonds. The United States could not rid itself totally from some darker spots in the European past, such as the racist beliefs of some Whites, and could not escape from the tyranny of top industrialists and financial institutions, preventing the country from becoming fully aware of the social and economic benefits of social justice, equity, and diversity. In this context, I could easily understand what was behind the assassination of Dr. Martin Luther King Jr. (April 4, 1968), who was an African American minister and activist, and became the most visible proponent and leader in the civil rights movement, from 1955 until his assassination. A short time later, Robert Kennedy, brother of President John F. Kennedy, was assassinated (June 6, 1968). Robert Kennedy was US attorney general and a senator from New York. He was opposed to racial discrimination and the US involvement in the Vietnam War, and was an advocate for issues related to human rights and social justice, and formed a working relationship with Dr. King.

The assassination of Dr. King sparked rioting and looting, with people flooding onto the streets of major cities. Soon riots began primarily in Black urban areas. Over a hundred major US cities experienced disturbances, but the riots in Chicago were extremely serious. The 1968 Democratic National Convention was held in Chicago in late August to select the party's candidates for the presidential election. Prior to and during the convention—which took place at the International Amphitheatre—rallies, demonstrations, marches, and attempted

---

1   يوسف إدريس1977 Yousef Idris, *Notes-Will* مفكرة- الإرادة، مكتبة غريب
(Cairo: Ghareeb Publisher, 1977).

marches took place on the streets and in the lakefront parks. These activities were primarily in protest of President Lyndon B. Johnson's policies for the Vietnam War. It was then that I arrived in Dallas,

Years after the official end of slavery, racial discrimination and prejudice were still emotionally explosive issues. The descendants of the sons from Black Africa, who were shipped from their homeland to serve in cotton plantations, were actively seeking an end to discrimination, coinciding with worldwide movements for independence from colonialism. The 1960s were a vibrant time of protest and liberation movements, of hope and creativity. The feminist movement, with roots in industrialization and World War II, became a strong current, with significant consequences for American society and the rest of the world. I was intoxicated by all these developments, which revealed the vitality, the self-renewing, and the transformational potential of the United States.

This era was also marked by an outpouring of protest folk songs by Bob Dylan, Joan Baez, and Pete Seeger. To my baby daughter, Mona, realizing this was to be her land and she had to know it, I hummed lines from Woodie Guthrie's song, written in 1940, "This Land is Your Land":

This land is your land, this land is my land
From California to the New York island,
From the Redwood forest, to the Gulf Stream waters

This land was made for you and me.

Mona did well. Bright and talented, she excelled in her studies and graduated from Rutgers University *cum laude*, to be the valedictorian of her class. She was given the choice of a full scholarship to do her PhD by Harvard, Chicago, and Princeton. She chose Princeton and is now an associate professor at Duke University.

Mona was born in Pullman, Washington, where I got my first job as an assistant professor at Washington State University. To get there, I had first to complete my PhD at SMU in the sleepy University Park neighborhood. I was sheltered from the world and barely touched by the election of Nixon in 1969 and his impeachment in 1974. A year after I was granted my PhD, I started teaching for a short term in Chicago, with its windy streets and museums, at the University of Illinois, Chicago Circle, and after that at Wayne State University for a year (witnessing my first snow blizzard!) before I joined Washington State University, Pullman, Washington in 1975 where I became full professor in 1983.

Anthropology widened my horizons and nurtured my interest in finding out more about the human condition, after I discovered Darwin's theory about the origin of the species. Exploration of the social dynamics that led to what we are today was my passion and the reason for expanding my reading in almost all fields of knowledge. While geology gave me a sense of the incredible antiquity of the Earth and made me aware of five hundred million years of organic evolution, anthropology opened the door for learning about the five to six million years of human evolution that ultimately led to our own human ancestors 200,000 years ago. Not only did I see Egypt and the United States on this vast evolutionary journey, but I also was made aware of the intricate web of relations between cultures. This was a different perspective on current world affairs, which are typically viewed with relatively little historical depth. It gives me hope and it reveals the strength of the American way, which welcomes innovations and is enriched and constantly renewed by cultural diversity, as well as revitalized by the willpower of millions who struggle against poverty, marginalization, and social injustice, and who are inspired by their search for knowledge and the dream of self-actualization. These were the individual Americans who made a great country in record time; it was not made by some misinformed bigots who tried to drag the country back to its darkest moments, when it was still overpowered by ruthless landowners who resorted to slavery and discrimination. The great technological and scientific achievements of Americans became manifest one year after the Chicago riots of 1968, when Apollo 11 was launched, sending man for the first time to the moon.

My faith in the transformational potential of American culture was renewed when many universities, including WSU, where I was teaching, began to teach courses in cultural studies, Afro-American studies, Hispanic-American/Chicano/Latino studies, as well as world history. I am extremely happy that the Department of History at WSU now has a World History program in which all PhD students receive training in the historiography and methodology, as well as the teaching of, world history. The program is led by professors with thematic expertise in imperialism, war and society, gender and sexuality, race and ethnicity, religion, environment, labor systems, public history, and cultural memory. The department still offers a first-year undergraduate core requirement in a course called Roots of Contemporary Issues, noted for its pioneering impact on pedagogy, thematic approach, and the use of student-driven inquiry into transnational trends and issues. I was fortunate to be involved in this course when it was first initiated.

The United States would not be that great if academics did not have as much freedom as they do to innovate and keep up with a changing world, as well as the freedom to contribute to its betterment. During the 1990 Gulf War, I proposed and was given the green light to teach a course on Middle Eastern peoples and cultures. No such course was being offered at the university on this topic. It was important for US students to learn about the Arab world, which has since become of major concern to US international politics. It was amazing to learn how little they knew about that part of the world. Universities have a major role to play in preparing young Americans for their new world. Some politicians would clearly benefit from a course on world history, and another on Middle Eastern peoples and cultures.

In Dallas, I got to know a few other Egyptian students and a few more from other Arab countries. They were all university graduates, and we had our occasional gatherings over Egyptian food. Religion was never an issue, and it never was when we were university students in Egypt. You can imagine my surprise when I discovered a mosque frequented by Saudi-backed preachers in the small university town of Pullman. It was clear Saudi Arabia was on an unholy mission to radicalize Muslim students from Pakistan, Afghanistan, and the Arab countries, even in the smallest of US towns. This coincided with the reign of President Anwar el-Sadat, who courted Islamists to strengthen his position against Nasserites and socialists. Little did he know, he was digging his own grave and plunging Egypt into an age of terror. He was assassinated by Islamic jihadists in 1981. The satanic powers of hatred and blinding fanaticism by extremist Islamic jihadists became manifest on September 11, 2001, with the attack on the twin towers of the World Trade Center in New York City that left nearly 3000 people dead.

In Abdeen Square, on a trip back to Cairo from London, while passing by a juice bar, I glanced at a TV screen and saw the smoke from the collapsing buildings. Egypt was under President Hosni Mubarak, who came to power after Sadat's assassination. By that time, Egypt had become closely allied with the United States, thanks to Sadat.

In 1994, I became Sir Flinders Petrie Chair of Archaeology at the Institute of Archaeology, University College London. London brought me closer to Cairo, and the Institute of Archaeology provided a wonderful opportunity to work with internationally renowned archaeologists in all disciplines of archaeology, archaeological sciences, and cultural heritage studies.

I returned to Cairo in 2008 and in January 2011 and witnessed the revolution that ended Mubarak's rule. Shortly thereafter, Mohamed Morsi, a member of the Muslim Brothers, was elected president. Morsi studied at California State University and taught from 1982 to 1985 at California State University, Northridge. He was born in 1951, a year after, Sayyed Qutb, who became a leading figure, invested the Muslim Brotherhood with extremist ideological rhetoric. Qutb too was in the United States, where he studied English from 1948 to 1950. A promising intellectual and literary critic, Qutb underwent a psychological transformation in the States. One of his attacks on American life centered on what he perceived as the overt sexuality of women. It seemed that sex was one of the issues that preoccupied the minds of Islamic radicals, who succeeded in the 1970s to make the head cover (hijab) a marker of virtuous Islamic girls and women—who otherwise would not be judged as virtuous. The hijab was not known when I grew up in Egypt. I was saddened to see how Islamists had succeeded in penetrating Egyptian society not only on the organizational and institutional levels, but also by introducing religious phrases into everyday life. The scepter of religious fanaticism and prejudice that we thought was a thing of the past after the 1919 revolution, when all segments of the nation were united, had returned to subdivide and terrorize. Islamists are not the only threat that Egypt and the world face today; the reactionary political movements in Europe have been ongoing for some time. The rise of such reactionary forces, reviving the terrifying memories of intolerance, chauvinistic nationalism, and racism, adds to the deep woes of our current times.

As an open society, the United States encompasses different pursuits, practices, and communicative styles. I was fortunate to have come to the States to study archaeology, with its distinct anthropological perspective, and to have been taught by US professors from different cultural origins, who emphasized the universality of scholarship. My horizons widened beyond the scope of becoming a professional archaeologist, which I had to be, to embrace a humanistic perspective, with a concern for how the present is shaped by a much deeper past than meets the eye. Most of our world problems are the result of a parochial outlook, dating back to the setback from the ideals of the Enlightenment in favor of the interests of a profit-making economy as the ultimate objective, regardless of the means. I was privileged to be one of the scholars who participated in an international symposium held at the Smithsonian in 1981 called How Humans Adapt (the same title as the book),[2] drawing on a variety of disciplines to speculate on how future adaptations may ensure the continued survival of humanity. This kind of opportunity for scholars to discuss and debate ensures the vitality and resilience of the American culture, not necessarily through the immediate adoption of policies based on the outcomes of scholarly symposia but through the long-term, diffuse,

─────────────

2   Donald J. Ortner, *How Humans Adapt: A Biocultural Odyssey* (Washington, DC: Smithsonian Institution, 1983).

and widespread dissemination of ideas in a free academic and social environment.

Woodrow Wilson—who spent twenty-five years as a professor, writer about politics and history, and president of Princeton University—became the leading academic political scientist of his time and left his mark on the development of American higher education. His academic career served as preparation for his entrance into politics in 1910, which led swiftly to the governorship of New Jersey and the presidency of the United States. In one of America's finest moments, President Wilson made a speech in 1918 that spelled out what America wanted the post-World War I world to be:

> *"What we demand in this war, therefore, is nothing peculiar to ourselves. It is that the world be made fit and safe to live in; and particularly that it be made safe for every peace-loving nation which, like our own, wishes to live its own life, determine its own institutions, be assured of justice and fair dealing by the other peoples of the world as against force and selfish aggression. All the peoples of the world are in effect partners in this interest, and for our own part we see very clearly that unless justice be done to others it will not be done to us. The program of the world's peace, therefore, is our program..."*

This segment of his speech is worth quoting because of what it meant to Egyptians, who, suffering from British imperialism, saw in it a call for action. In 1919, Egypt witnessed a revolutionary uprising that fueled and escalated not only the struggle against British colonialism but also the course of a cultural revolution that still reverberates in all the cultural circles of contemporary Egypt. I and others are the grandchildren of this revolution.

The United States, for me, as shown by the words of Woodrow Wilson, was founded as an outcome of the spirit of the Enlightenment— that shining moment in the history of humankind during the seventeenth and eighteenth centuries when reason was celebrated as the power by which humans understand the universe and improve their own condition. The United States is, in fact, not as much a country as it is an ideal. It is a kaleidoscope of individuals who are not unified by the land where they were born (immigrants still contribute significantly to the making of the country), or a common mother tongue, or an ethnic bond with their fellow citizens. Instead, Americans are united by their quest for freedom, knowledge, and progress. From the beginning, Americans succeeded in putting aside religious differences. The founding fathers were painfully aware of the misuse of religion during medieval times, and the religious wars and persecutions that tormented and divided Europe, compelling many individuals and families to seek refuge in a new land. It became constitutional that "Congress shall make no law respecting an establishment of religion, or prohibiting the free exercise thereof." The United States did not adopt a national religion; it championed the cause of tolerance and reason, leading to unprecedented advancements in all fields of knowledge and the arts. From 1775 to 1783, Americans fought again monarchical regimes and drafted a Declaration of Independence, the pronouncement adopted by the Second Continental Congress meeting at the Pennsylvania State House in Philadelphia, Pennsylvania, on July 4, 1776.

Gazing at the imposing statue of Abraham Lincoln in Washington, D.C.—a man who made the Declaration of Independence the center piece of his policies for the abolishment of slavery in his Gettysburg Address in 1863—one has to reflect upon the power of ideas and words, and on the sound foundation of American principles, which eventually defeated slavery and placed a Black man as the head of the state. True, discrimination and racial prejudice are resurging among some reactionary politicians, but there are also demonstrations and opposition decrying their policies. The fight against racism is grounded in the rock on which the United States rests: "We hold these truths to be self-evident, that all men are created equal, that they are endowed by their Creator with certain unalienable Rights, that among these are Life, Liberty and the pursuit of Happiness."

The United States has also been shown to be a viable alternative to totalitarian and fascist regimes and has inched its way to center stage in world politics. Yet it has to maintain its footing and recall the principles on which it has been founded, and that what is good for Americans has to be good for everyone on this planet. Woodrow Wilson put it eloquently: "We see very clearly that unless justice be done to others it will not be done to us."

———•———

FEKRI HASSAN is Emeritus Petrie Professor of Archaeology at the Institute of Archaeology, University College London and currently Director of the Cultural Heritage Program at the French University in Egypt. He taught at Washington State University and has led archaeological expeditions to Egypt since 1974. He is the author of more than 250 publications on Archaeological theory, Egyptian prehistory and climate change.

EGYPT'S BALLERINA

Magda Saleh

My name is Magda Saleh. I am an Egyptian ballerina, Egypt's first prima ballerina. Only a coincidence of time, place, and circumstance—and one man, Egypt's first and greatest minister of culture, Dr. Sarwat Okasha—made it possible for me, an Egyptian girl born of an Egyptian father, Dr. Ahmed Abdel Ghaffar Saleh, and a Scottish mother, Florence Farmer, to turn a fantasy into a dream into an unimaginable reality.

Egyptians were no strangers to the art of ballet, although we did not have our own national ballet company until 1966. Ballet was first performed in Egypt at the opera house built upon the command of Ismail, the khedive of Egypt, for the lavish festivities celebrating the inauguration of the Suez Canal in 1869. There were many ballet studios in Cairo and Alexandria. Ballet training was considered beneficial to girls, its strict technique conducive to good posture, elegant deportment, poise and grace, but definitely with no thought of those girls turning professional. My father had no objection to my taking up the benign activity of a once-weekly class.

Mother first enrolled me at age six in a class at the British school in Heliopolis. In the mid-1950s, my father was named dean of the Faculty of Agriculture at Alexandria University. My family moved there, and my mother enrolled me in ballet classes offered at the Conservatoire de Musique d'Alexandrie. My teachers were certified by the British

Royal Academy of Dance (RAD). Overcoming my father's grave misgivings, I was next enrolled at the Arts Educational School (AES) at Tring Park in Hertfordshire, England. My stay at AES was cut short by the 1956 Suez crisis. Returning to Alexandria, I resumed classes at the Conservatoire, now taught by a local teacher. Life changed in many challenging ways in Egypt in the aftermath of the tripartite aggression by Britain, France, and Israel. Rebuffed by the West, Egypt allied with the Soviet Union and embraced socialism.

In 1958, President Gamal Abdel Nasser charged Sarwat Okasha, his fellow free officer in Egypt's 1952 revolution, with founding a ministry of culture. Dr. Okasha, a man of exceptional refinement and erudition, and a true son of Egypt, conceived and established the enduring cornerstones of far-reaching cultural policy in post-revolutionary Egypt. He was the founder of the many institutions upon which the bedrock of cultural life rests, and from which its activities devolve to this day, the vagaries of the domestic political and cultural climates of the past decades notwithstanding. He considered the Academy of Arts, a unique major institution, the cornerstone of his long-term plan for the ministry of culture he envisioned. The Academy was formally established by presidential decree in 1959. Dr. Okasha's introduction of classical ballet into Egyptian culture under the auspices of the state was controversial, but he prevailed, and a Higher Institute of Ballet was among the seven founding institutes of the Academy, along with institutes for Arabic music, art criticism and aesthetics, cinema, music, folklore, and theater.

The creation of the Egyptian National Ballet began as part of the very active cultural exchange programs between the USSR and Egypt. The future institute was established in October 1958 as a modest ballet school under the administration of the Opera House.

At that time, I was still attending the Conservatoire in Alexandria. One day, a distinguished visitor was invited to observe class—none other than Igor Moiseyev, the founder, choreographer, and artistic director of the Moiseyev Folkdance Troupe, in Egypt on tour. After class, he called me over and informed me that the following year, a teacher from the Bolshoi Academy in Moscow would be coming to

Cairo to establish a ballet school. He advised me to apply. Word later reached us in Alexandria that the Russian teacher had arrived, and auditions were taking place. The family was moving back to Cairo, as my father had been transferred to Ain Shams University, where he subsequently became dean of the Faculty of Agriculture. I auditioned and was accepted, and began my career as a real ballerina.

Our fledgling school was located in two borrowed studios at the Higher Institute of Physical Education for Girls in Gezira, beneath the landmark Cairo Tower. At the end of our first school year, we performed a class concert at the Opera House, arranged by our teacher, Mr. Alexei Zhukov, in which I was given the only solo of the evening. The event was very successful. Every year thereafter, a new batch of hopefuls auditioned. The Soviet staff was increased yearly, until the full complement was reached for the nine-year program of the Russian Academic Classical Ballet curriculum.

In 1963, the expanding ballet school moved into its own impressive four-story building dedicated to classical ballet on the campus of the new Academy of the Arts in Giza. Alongside the dance curriculum, the institute offered regular schooling, in accordance with the Ministry of Education syllabus, for all the pupils, who started training at age nine. An entire floor was dedicated to music studies, including piano and solfege. An undergraduate division was created, offering a BA degree in dance, which was later followed by graduate studies for the MA and PhD degrees. There were workshops for scenery, costumes, accessories, and ballet shoes, staffed by Egyptian artisans trained by Soviet experts, a physical therapy center, a fully equipped kitchen that provided meals, and bus transportation. All of this was provided by the state, free of charge.

I began to speak of concentrating on my dance career. My parents would have none of it. We compromised. I would be allowed to pursue this fierce passion on the condition I complete my schooling. Once that was achieved, it was university. No university, no ballet, period. I obtained my BA in English Language and Literature in 1968 at Ain Shams University, where my father was now vice rector. I also completed the undergraduate course at the Higher Institute of Ballet, earning a diploma in 1966. I was top of my class in both, and scandalized the rector of Ain Shams University by declining to join the English Department as a junior faculty member in order to dedicate myself to my art. My father warned me against this single-minded determination to pursue a dance career. Both as a father and a distinguished academic, he would incur a grave social risk in allowing his daughter to become a professional dancer—a métier viewed with opprobrium in our largely conservative society. He also pointed out that dance, like sport, was a high-risk occupation, and injury might bring a career to an abrupt and untimely end. Another realistic consideration was the brevity of such a career, lasting at best into one's late thirties or early forties.

By our fifth year, in 1963, we had progressed so far as to perform, for our annual concert, an ambitious program that included *Swan Lake*, Act II, followed by a variety of both classical and character dances. I was assigned a duet, *The Blind Girl*, which I performed with fourteen-year-old Yehia Abdel Tawwab. It became our exclusive signature dance, repeated to great acclaim over the years. That same year, an event occurred that fixed the future course of my life. The Soviet Ministry of Culture announced that five scholarships had been awarded to pupils at the Egyptian Ballet Institute to study at the fabled Bolshoi Academy of Ballet in Moscow. Five lucky girls of my class were chosen: Diana Hakak, Maya Selim, Wadoud Faizy, Aleya Abdel Razek, and myself. After much bureaucratic delay on both sides, we finally arrived in Moscow on December 6, 1963. We were the first single girls to be sent from Egypt to study in the USSR, which caused much anxiety at the Egyptian Cultural Bureau. We spent two years in Moscow, both personally challenging and artistically enriching, and had the most exceptional and privileged experience any aspiring ballerina might hope for. We graduated in 1965 and were awarded our diplomas. From sheltered young girls, we had become self-reliant, strong young women. We had managed our daily lives, had held our own with our Soviet compeers, and were ready, upon our return to Cairo, to assume our role as the Bolshoi Five, the pioneers of Egyptian ballet.

Our return home coincided with the most fortuitous return of Dr. Okasha for a second term as minister. As a result of our earnest and persistent representations, the Egyptian Ballet Institute embarked upon an impressive and challenging project: to present for the first time a full-length ballet on the stage of the Cairo Opera House. Our Soviet experts made an apt choice for this enterprise: a ballet within the capabilities of the dancers, all of whom, with the exception of the five newly minted professionals, were still students at various levels at the Institute. The ballet was *The Fountain of Bakhchisarai*, the tragic tale of the Crimean Tatar Khan Girei.

Preparations involved several months of intensive rehearsals, which started in the summer of 1966. The Soviet Ministry of Culture dispatched celebrated choreographer Leonid Lavrovsky, former artistic director of both the Bolshoi Ballet and the Bolshoi Academy of Ballet, to oversee the production. The premiere on December 4, 1966, was a triumph and a sensation beyond our wildest dreams. The audience accorded us an uproarious ovation. The press was exuberant. Naysayers who had scoffed at the idea that Egyptians could master the art of ballet were silenced at last. Backstage to commend us after the performance, Dr. Okasha announced that he had, during an intermission, invited President Nasser to attend, and the president was coming the following night. I had the honor of performing the role of Maria for President Nasser and his spouse, Mme. Tahia Kazem. What a memorable coming out of the Egyptian national ballet, to be known as the Cairo Ballet Company! Shortly thereafter, the president bestowed upon the principals involved an unprecedented honor. For the first time in our history, dancers were honored by the state. The Bolshoi Five received the Order of Merit; the male principals, still students, were awarded the Certificate of Merit. The Order of the Republic was conferred upon the dean of the Higher Institute of Ballet, Mme. Enayat Azmi, and the Soviet experts and Maestro Shaaban Aboul Saad, who conducted the Cairo Symphony Orchestra.

Scarcely had all the excitement died down when the Ministry of Culture made an astonishing announcement: we were being sent to

Aswan in January 1967 to participate in the celebrations marking the completion of a phase in the construction of the High Dam. Aswan? How would we be received in the conservative far south of Upper Egypt, by a public that had never seen a ballet? We performed under very rudimentary conditions in a makeshift theater. Contrary to our expectations—as I have recounted in the 2016 documentary film *A Footnote in Ballet History?*—we were rapturously received by our audiences, who had no problem at all following the unfolding drama and appeared neither shocked nor offended by the novelty and daring of the art form itself. The dramatic entrance of Khan Girei at the end of the Act I battle scene was hailed with excited shouts of "Allahu Akbar!" Our performances were extended, and we were greeted with adulation by the population wherever we went. A humble old peasant, following a performance, found his way onto the stage to tell me, "This is so beautiful, ya sitt!" It was the most treasured compliment of my career.

Later the same year, 1967, the year of our "mad experiment" in Aswan, the nation, the region, and the world were stunned by an event whose repercussions reverberate to this day. The disastrous Six-Day War with Israel ended in a triumph for the Jewish state, an unfathomable, crushing defeat for Egypt after years of the glorification of our armed forces. There followed a protracted War of Attrition (1969–1971) over the Suez Canal. From our perspective, the future looked very bleak. But the Egyptians are nothing if not survivors, so the nation collectively picked itself up, dusted itself off, and carried on. Where arts and culture were concerned, Dr. Okasha viewed the activities of his ministry as essential at this challenging time, and no current or planned undertaking was curtailed, including his ongoing global campaign to salvage the monuments of Nubia.

With the Egyptian Ballet Institute off to a meteoric rise, we zealously carried on, to do our part in the national recovery, dancers on a mission. Following the triumph of *The Fountain of Bakhchisarai*, our Soviet artistic directors staged a new ballet yearly, in which, between 1968 and 1971, I was assigned leading roles: *Giselle*, the grand pas de deux from *La Bayadère* in a variety program, *Nutcracker*, *Don Juan*,

Daphnis and Chloe staged for us by celebrated Ukrainian-French dancer and choreographer Serge Lifar at the invitation of Dr. Okasha, *Paquita, Don Quixote*, in which the part of Kitri turned out to be my final role with the Cairo Ballet Company. Following the performances of *Don Quixote* in May 1971, my partner Abdel Moneim Kamel and I received the highest accolade any ballet dancer can dream of. We were invited as guest artists to perform the lead roles in the ballets *Giselle* and *Don Quixote*, with two of the greatest ballet companies in the world in their home theaters (the Bolshoi Ballet in Moscow, and the Kirov Ballet in Leningrad), on a tour that also took us to state theaters in Tashkent, Uzbekistan, and Novosibirsk in Western Siberia. Such invitations are rare indeed. This was both a tremendous, unprecedented honor and a daunting prospect. Moneim and I made ballet history.

Even as the Egyptian Ballet Institute seemed in an unstoppable ascendant, storm clouds were gathering over our prospects, and over Egypt. President Nasser died suddenly on September 28, 1970. The same year, Dr. Okasha's tenure as minister of culture was terminated by President Anwar Sadat. Then the unimaginable happened: our home, the Cairo Opera House, was consumed by a massive fire on October 28. It was a devastating blow to the arts and culture in Egypt, and its effects were felt for years. Many promising and many flourishing careers abruptly ended or were lengthily paused. Years before, I had exclaimed in anguish to my parents that "If I could not dance, I would only be half alive." I was trying to put into words my feeling of only really existing while performing, to express the ineffable transfiguration I experienced when stepping from the wings onto stage, but now the time had come to give up dancing. A vital part of my being was stilled, as I sought to divert this passion into another channel. My mother, always my life guide, urgently advised me to pursue another course: the academic option. There was increasing demand for Egyptian ballet to be "Egyptian."

Seeking new experiences, and to broaden my horizons in the field of dance, I applied for a scholarship to study modern dance in the United States. I thought to eventually join the ranks of those among my colleagues who were exploring the potential for choreographies based on Egyptian history, mythology, and culture, for which there was untold wealth of material. The instant success that had greeted the Reda Folkloric Troupe in 1959 was the theatrical precedent for this development. Dancer and choreographer Mahmoud Reda, who had attended classes during the first year of our school in 1958, had created a colorful program of dances and vignettes, in which he starred with his leading dancer, the entrancing Farida Fahmy. From their premiere, they were propelled to national acclaim and international fame.

I submitted my application essay to The American Friends of the Middle East (AMIDEAST), and still reeling from the loss of the Opera House, set off on the Soviet tour in December 1971. My parents traveled to Moscow and Leningrad to witness the crowning of their daughter's dance career, with what mixed emotions I can hardly imagine. I was touching the heights and plumbing the depths at one time. My father's prescient misgivings over my physical fitness were premonitory. I had been troubled by muscle pain and cramping in my lower legs since the second year of my studies, which had disrupted my training and plagued my performing, but I was determined to master my body and bend it to my will, so I persevered despite the warning signs. Performing the taxing role of Kitri in *Don Quixote* for thirteen consecutive nights, a feat worthy of the *Guinness Book of Records*, proved the breaking point. Not for the first time, I was sent to recover at the Black Sea resort of Sochi by the Soviet Ministry of Culture, and work resumed in the fall in preparation for the tour.

The stress was immense, compounded by the agonizing loss of the Opera House, and the physical problems resumed. There was, however, no turning back. I was going to perform on those hallowed stages if it killed me. I can proudly claim that the final performance of my career was dancing *Giselle* at the Bolshoi Theater with the Bolshoi Ballet, but I had reached the end of endurance. My mother telegraphed me from Cairo that the US scholarship had come through, and I accepted. The die was cast. I was making a leap from East to West, much to the dismay of our Soviet patrons.

In August 1972, leaving everything behind, I headed out to start over as a graduate student. The international scholarship was awarded by the American Association of University Women (AAUW). AAUW selected the Dance Department at the University of California at Los Angeles, one of the most well-regarded in the United States. I must have been quite a novelty to faculty and students alike—an Egyptian prima ballerina in their midst, nothing like what they had anticipated, given their misconceptions about women from my part of the world. I cannot claim that my introduction to student life or to modern dance was plain sailing at the outset, but I was accorded wholehearted support, and I acclimated. Entire new vistas opened up before me. It was another transformative experience, akin to yet radically different from my time in the Soviet Union.

I obtained my MA in 1974. My thesis was entitled *An Exploration in Modern Idiom of Egyptian Themes*. A PhD was the last step necessary to ensure my place in academe, and again, I was fortunate to secure the Anderson Fellowship from the School of Education at New York University. The topic I chose for my dissertation, *A Documentation of the Ethnic Dance Traditions of the Arab Republic of Egypt*, entailed making a documentary film of a broad sampling of dance in diverse cultural areas of Egypt: urban and rural, Nile Valley, deserts, and littoral. With the subsidy and technical support of the Egyptian Cinema Organization, and the cooperation of the Center of Folk Arts, I embarked upon a series of field trips that turned out to be a voyage of eye-opening discovery of my own country. Storied Egypt and her people! The resulting film, *Egypt Dances* (1978), remains an ethnographic classic, and both my film and dissertation are sought-after resources by researchers worldwide to this day. It was a grueling five years, but with the unfailing support of my mother, I became Dr. Saleh in 1979.

My unwavering focus throughout those years of study was Egypt, the Academy, and my future role in furthering the cause of Egyptian ballet, but the situation in Egypt was changing in troubling ways. During my visits to Egypt in the 1970s, I could not but be aware that all was not well. The nation was undergoing severe socioeconomic trauma, a jarring result of the imposition of new policies. I have often viewed the deteriorating conditions at the Academy and the Higher Institute of Ballet as a microcosm of the state of the nation. Suffering unwarranted neglect and abuse, our handsome Institute, once the envy of touring dance companies and the showcase on proud display for visiting delegations, was wrecked. These conditions were mirrored by the breakdown of discipline at all levels among students, staff, faculty, and employees. The Soviet experts were expelled following the Soviet invasion of Afghanistan in 1979. With hardly any Egyptian fully trained in pedagogy to step into the void, the Institute finally imploded.

Witnessing this disintegration over the years, I hesitated between Egypt and the United States. Sadly, it was the state of my mother's health that decided my future course. I undertook her care, and soon I had both my ailing parents in my charge. Following my return to Cairo in 1983, Dr. Samha El Kholy, the president of the Academy, invited me to rejoin the Egyptian Ballet Institute to help restore it. I was promoted to full professor and dean, the first of the Institute's graduates to assume that position. Conditions were by now appalling. My partner and colleague Yehia Abdel Tawwab, returning from studies in Moscow at the same time as I came from the United States, put it succinctly: "I feel I have been struck by amnesia. My past has been wiped out!"

This was the beginning of the darkest decade of my life. With grim determination, I threw myself wholly into the task of restoring order and discipline, and the situation soon turned around. The building might be in ruinous dilapidation, but it was clean and quiet, and everyone was at their station, performing their duties. Standards improved, and the ballet pupils and senior students presented a very creditable class concert at the end of the 1984–1985 school year. Dr. Okasha honored us with his presence and offered praise for "his dream revived." Five Egyptian dancers participated in the Fifth International Ballet Competition, in 1985, in Moscow, and one pair made it to the semifinals. This progress was noticed and received favorable media and public attention.

While this might seem very positive and hopeful, I almost imme-diately had to come to grips with a baffling phenomenon. Some among the five-hundred-plus souls housed in the Institute had extremes in outlook, attitude, and behavior in dealing with the endeavor. To my dismay, where I had expected wholehearted cooperation, I found some people were actively, overtly, or covertly bent on obstructing and un-dermining all accomplishments and thwarting every endeavor, even though these improvements were for the benefit of all. At the core of this clique were three of the most senior faculty members, colleagues, and fellow artists. Within the Academy, resentment about unfavorable comparisons with the resurgent Ballet Institute spread among the leadership of the other institutes. The media coined a name for the pernicious behavior of such individuals: "the enemies of success."

The relentless pressure of exertions—domestic and professional—left me beleaguered, frustrated, and exhausted. I decided upon a drastic step that I hoped would, by exposing the whole ugly mess, provoke a strong corrective response from the higher authorities. I abruptly handed in my resignation from the Academy—both dean-ship and professorship—and waited. If I was ever under any illusion that this cry in the wilderness would achieve my goal, it was instantly dispelled. My resignation was accepted. One of the clique was imme-diately appointed dean in my stead, and without missing a step, life and activities at the Institute reverted to past practices. I should have known that, if I wanted to trigger an official inquiry into the circum-stances that provoked such a resignation, I should have submitted my resignation "with cause," in tedious detail.

To me, the most egregious, unforgivable betrayal of our mission, and of the young lives entrusted to our care, was the brazen exploita-tion of our vulnerable charges by the very state that heretofore had nurtured the arts, for the purposes of tawdry propaganda, and worse still, by members of the faculty raiding with impunity the human and material resources of the Institute for personal gain in commercial and private activities. The high standing the Egyptian ballet had achieved was diminished and cheapened and has never recovered.

I would like to close my account of this episode by making a comparison. The Egyptian and Chinese ballets were founded by Soviet experts at nearly the same time in 1958. Following Mao Zedong's calamitous decade-long Cultural Revolution (1966–1976), Chinese ballet personnel, who had been subjected to horrifying persecution, were able to regroup, and the Chinese ballet was revived. Currently, China produces some of the finest ballet dancers of both genders to be found anywhere. Our tale in Egypt falls woefully short of such an example. But today, the renovated Institute is a state-of-the-art facility, and decades on, the Egyptian Ballet still exists, at both the Academy and Opera, against daunting odds. I will cling to hope.

I remained at home for fourteen months, caring for my parents, as their lives gradually ebbed. It was a profound grief to my brothers and me to witness the slow decline of two such vibrant, brilliant people. I was engaged in this task and its many cares and responsibilities when, out of the blue, an undreamed-of opportunity presented itself. There was a cabinet reshuffle in late 1987, and an artist, Farouk Hosni, was nominated minister of culture. The appointment caused a bit of a furor, as his seniors were bypassed by the prime minister in his favor. We were slightly acquainted, and the connection, if not close, was cordial. Delighted that we would finally have an artist at the helm of the ministry consecrated to the service of the arts, I sent him a congratulatory telegram, and thought no more of it. To my utter amazement, two weeks later, I received a phone call from the new minister, offering me the position of director of the New Cairo Opera House. I could scarcely credit my ears! We agreed to meet and discuss. Our views were in accord, and I accepted the position, with one caveat: "No committees." Hosni wholeheartedly concurred— though his promise was immediately broken, to my chagrin. The surprise report of my appointment met with widespread approbation and stunned more than the several candidates vying for the honor. There was outraged disbelief in some quarters. The single negative note was sounded by my former professor, Dr. Janice Gorn, a titled "Great Teacher" at New York University. She warned, "Don't do it.

Remember what happened to you at the Ballet Institute. It'll happen again." Prescient words.

The New Opera House, supported by a generous $50 million outright grant from the nation of Japan to the people of Egypt, was actually a multipurpose facility, termed by the donors a "culture and education center." Despite President Sadat's proclamation at the time of the disaster in 1971, the Egyptian government had failed for seventeen years to rebuild or replace the old Opera House, though several foundation stones had been laid in various locations. Evidently, culture was no longer a high priority. The gift offered the Ministry of Culture a facile solution, and the recipients promptly dubbed the center a new opera house. A prime location was allotted to the project, on the Nile at the southern tip of Gezira Island. I had attended the laying of the foundation stone by President Mubarak in 1985. The New Opera House construction phase was nearing completion.

To recount in detail my experiences as the first, or founding, director of the new complex would require a tome, not several paragraphs. Let me state at the outset that being selected for the post was an exceptional privilege, and I remain sincerely grateful for this unique opportunity. I believe I might be the first woman in opera history to head a national opera theater. It was both an awesome challenge and a weighty responsibility. The hopes of all my fellow artists were pinned on me, with the eyes of the nation and the world looking on in anticipation of a celebration worthy of Khedive Ismail.

I was assigned an office in a tumbledown shack on the construction site. To my good fortune, I secured Abdallah Al Ayyouti, the technical director of the old Opera House, and Aida Hussein, formerly of the General Organization for Information, to assist me in my work. This team was rounded off by a secretary, Manal Mahmoud, loaned to my office by the onsite opera construction project. Those three were the best collaborators I could hope for: unswervingly loyal, tireless, enthusiastic, dedicated, determined, and undeterred by the adversity we would confront as we labored at a Herculean and ultimately thankless task. So much to be done, so little time. We were into December

1987, with construction completion by Kajima Corporation scheduled for March 1988, and the inauguration decided for October 10, 1988, to coincide with the annual celebrations marking the 1973 October War—the Suez Canal Crossing. I was starting from scratch: no preparations—administrative or artistic—undertaken in the past years, no budget allotted, nothing. We hit the ground running. My feverish campaign was like opening fifty fronts simultaneously. In the hectic months that followed, working with the Japanese—including the embassy, the cultural bureau, Kajima Corporation, Nikken Sekkei (the architectural firm), and the Japan International Cooperation Agency—was a uniformly outstanding and rewarding experience. Regretfully, I cannot say the same for the Egyptian Ministry of Culture.

The first sign of something amiss was the immediate formation of a committee for the inauguration of the opera, headed by the first under-secretary of the ministry, Fouad al Orabi. Simultaneously, access to the minister who had given me his word we would work "hand in hand" was cut off. The committee did not convene, and I received no communication or direction from any quarter, so, left to my own devices, I unilaterally took every initiative I deemed necessary to get everything launched. I consulted with Dr. Hussein Kazem, director of the General Authority for Organization and Administration, on the formulation of a temporary decree establishing the opera administration, pending a presidential decree creating a general authority for the new National Cultural Center. I outlined a detailed plan for a festive three-day celebration, culminating in the inauguration and the program for the gala night itself, followed by a week of Egyptian-Japanese programs. I invited the corps of ambassadors to petition their governments for contributions to the inaugural season. Rallied by my friend and ally, US Ambassador Frank Wisner, there ensued a collegial diplomatic competition, and the schedule filled. I solicited support from the business community for contributions to an independent fund managed by the Friends of the Opera Association. I obtained a Japanese grant of nearly one million Egyptian pounds to purchase pianos and other instruments. I requested and received gifts for the opera, such as a Bosendorfer grand piano from the government of Austria. With Egypt's foremost IT experts, I explored systems to ensure the most streamlined, up-to-date, and efficient management achievable within a hidebound bureaucracy, and so on—all the way to pursuing the creation of a logo, and the issuance of a commemorative stamp with the postal service. Media-whiz Ms. Hussein worked her vast network of contacts on a daily basis, creating mounting anticipation for the inauguration, while Ayyouti organized the purchase of matériel necessary to furnish his backstage domain. I proceeded at a frantic pace to deliver, knowing all too well that success would be the minister's, failure would be mine.

While I was focused on achieving this goal, I soon became aware of trouble brewing. I began to receive calls from concerned artists, pleading with me to "hold firm and persevere," a sure sign something nefarious was afoot. Well-informed of my activities, the ministry seemed content to allow me to proceed. The completion of construction and handing over of the opera to the ministry marked a sudden change. Obstruction of my work and efforts to take control of my activities became a daily provocation in an increasingly toxic atmosphere. Tension and pressure mounted relentlessly. In June, I delivered to Gamal Hamza, the undersecretary for financial affairs at the ministry, the decree creating a "temporary central administration," prepared by Dr. Kazem, and requested the minister finally appoint me to the post he had promised. Days later, the decree was signed, appointing opera singer Ratiba el-Hefni the new director of the opera. I was named artistic director, her subordinate. The news caused a sensation. The Japanese were thunderstruck, and astounded confusion reigned at home and reverberated abroad. Withdrawal was not an option. I had resigned once in protest and would not do it again, as was evidently expected, and be labeled a quitter. The schemers at the ministry should do their own dirty work. My team and I hung on in our shack for a month while I made a show of performing my new duties. El-Hefni demanded my files, and I discovered what it was to become a non-person overnight. Any mention of me, even as artistic director, was banned in the media, while my work was attributed to my supplanter.

In August, I was summarily fired on the trumped-up charge of hampering an important national project. The manner was viciously punitive, designed to impugn my character and integrity. Ayyouti was asked to remain but refused. Aida was shown the door, and Manal was transferred to an obscure corner of the ministry. Excitement over a national milestone was extinguished. A lackluster inauguration marked the messy, improvised debut of our eagerly awaited new opera. The Japanese ambassador invited me to the gala as his special guest. I was much struck in the aftermath of all this tribulation by the number of people who somehow obtained my phone number and called, not to commiserate, but to share with me their own devastating experiences of hard work and commitment being rewarded with base maltreatment. I have often been asked why, and what happened? I have asked myself the same and can only conjecture, since I received no explanation from the man who placed me in this position. I served at the pleasure of the minister. If I had at any stage lost his confidence, why not just summon me to his office, and as a common courtesy, inform me of the fact?

After twenty-three years in office, Hosni was by far the longest-serving minister in the history of the Ministry of Culture, cannily navigating the shoals and evading the pitfalls threatening his ascent, as he ingratiated himself to his superiors all the way to the top. I believe he early on made a conscious choice to serve power rather than culture. He was no Sarwat Okasha. I know his animus against me has lasted well beyond my departure from the scene. There is no reference or record of my service in the archives of the opera. He ordered the removal of my portrait, commissioned by opera chairman Dr. Samir Farag (2000–2004) for the new portrait gallery of former directors.

My prospects appeared blighted beyond recovery. Much against the grain, I rejoined the Academy, to which I had been reinstated in order to be seconded to the opera. Grief was followed by immeasurably greater loss. My parents passed away—first my father, in 1989, and my mother in 1991. I moved for a final time to the United States in 1992. A year later, I met and married my husband, Egyptologist Jack Josephson, with whom I revived my earlier interest in the history of ancient Egypt. I continued to serve the cause of Egyptian art and culture in my new home, albeit in a much more modest manner than my earlier ambition had envisaged.

The eminent Egyptian lawyer Ali el Shalaqani had sued the minister and ministry pro bono on my behalf. Five years after my removal to New York, I received word from Shalaqani's office that the Council of State had found in my favor, declaring the minister's action wrongful and punitory, while stating that the time elapsed precluded reinstatement, so that was a hollow victory.

On my most recent visit to Egypt, at the end of 2019, I discovered, much to my bemusement, that thirty-two years after the events I have recorded here, I was now an icon, a legend, named among Egypt's most noteworthy women, and a living symbol for a growing nostalgia wistfully hearkening back to a near-mythic golden age. I am humbled, but my deepest, enduring regret remains that I was not able to serve my country as I had hoped. And I am far from alone.

———•———

MAGDA SALEH is a graduate of the Bolshoi Academy of Ballet in Moscow. She was prima ballerina with the first Egyptian national ballet, the Cairo Ballet Company, since its inception in 1966 until 1971, when the old Cairo Opera House was destroyed by fire. She has danced as a guest artist at two of the world's most prestigious ballet companies, the Bolshoi Ballet in Moscow and the Kirov Ballet in Leningrad, starring in "Giselle" and "Don Quixote." She was the first dean from among its graduates of the Higher Institute of Ballet at Egypt's Academy of the Arts, and the founding director of the New Cairo Opera House, the National Cultural Center. Currently, Magda lives in New York with her husband, the eminent Egyptologist Jack Josephson.

MY JOURNEY FROM BIRTH UNTIL RETIREMENT

Mahmoud F. Agha

I was born in Cairo, Egypt, on the afternoon of July 18, 1941, to Kadria Mahmoud Gendia and Fikry Hassan Agha. My father was a lawyer and worked with my maternal grandfather, Mahmoud Fahmy Gendia "Bey" (a title given by the king to important people), and my mother was a homemaker who dedicated her life to taking care of her family. When she was ten years old, she lost her mother to breast cancer, so she took on the responsibility of being in charge of the house and taking care of her three younger siblings. The youngest was only a few months old at the time.

Both my father and grandfather (geddo) held leadership positions in the Egyptian Bar Association, and Geddo was also involved in local politics, including being a member of parliament in 1950 and a member of the Al-Wafd Party. My parental grandfather, Hassan Ibrahim Agha, was a high school Arabic teacher.

I was the first grandchild for both grandparents, so naturally I was showered with love, affection, and attention from an early age. I was especially close to my geddo and spent a lot of time with him. I would accompany him to work at the court, and to the Egyptian Bar building, and went shopping with him. Geddo's office was in downtown Cairo on Sherif Pasha Street, and he took me shopping twice a year at a department store called Cicurel. Cicurel was famous for having the latest things from Europe. During the winter, Geddo lived in Helwan, a town south of Cairo, (Helwan is now considered part of greater Cairo) famous for its natural hot sulfur springs. During the summer, he lived in his country estate in the village of Meet Halfa, north of Cairo. Until I was roughly eight years old, I went with him to Helwan almost every Thursday and spent the weekend with him. During these weekends, we went to the Japanese botanical garden, and the hot springs, and paid social visits to his friends. During the summer, Geddo stayed at his country estate, and the entire family spent a few months with him. Since Meet Halfa was close to the city, the working men of the family went to Cairo in the morning for work and returned in the afternoon. We children had fun playing in the garden, picking plums and apricots, and having fresh bread baked in a conventional brick oven. Everything was fresh from the fields, including the poultry. Since my geddo was the head of the Gendia family, we had family gatherings at his home almost every night. Meet Halfa and the Gendia family were almost one thing. Geddo was also there for many milestones of my childhood, such as when he bought me my first bicycle at age seven.

From the day I was born until 1959, we lived in the family house in Shobra. It was a big house, comprising three apartments on three floors, with a big garden in the back. My mother's brother, Ismail, and his family lived on the ground floor, we lived on the first floor, and my mother's sister, Soad (Tante Susu), lived on the second floor. My mother's other brother, Ibrahim, and his family lived in Helwan. Since my aunt's apartment was the smallest, her children, Mohamed and Shaden, lived with us, which made us more like siblings than cousins. This seemed only natural, considering that my mother and Tante Susu were inseparable and always shared everything. Their special relationship shaped and affected our lives and showed us the meaning of truly selfless love. Tante Susu was a second mother to me, my sister Mona, and my brother Hassan. During the Shobra years, we gathered every summer evening in the huge north-facing terrace of our apartment. Carpets and cushions were spread on the floor, and we sat listening to the radio, talking, and eating; family time was different than it is today, with TVs and cell phones.

When the time came for us to move from Shobra to Mohandessin, a new residential area in Dokki, developed by the Syndicate of Engineering Professions, Tante Susu told her husband, Uncle Tawfik (who was an architect), to design a building that both of our families could live in, otherwise she would not move. Uncle Tawfik complied and designed a building that had separate apartments, with a few common shared areas, including a garden and a dining room on the roof, where we ate lunch together every day. This house became our family's home base until 2015 and grew with us as the family grew and we had to build additional floors. It was where my wife Rawya and I had our first home together, before moving to the United States; it was where my daughter Jehan lived when she decided to move to Egypt, and where she and her husband Ahmed eventually lived when they first got married. This home on Shehab Street was where we celebrated birthdays, holidays, such as Ramadan and Eid, and the births of children and grandchildren. It was also where we mourned the deaths of loved ones, including my parents, who both passed away there.

When we moved to Mohandessin, it consisted of villas and small buildings surrounded by fields and greenery. We even had a clear view of the pyramids in the distance. Sadly, as the years went by, the villas and fields were replaced by high-rise buildings and congested streets. Our home met its fate in 2016, when we sold it and the new owner tore it down to build a taller building that could accommodate more tenants. Now, our family is scattered across Cairo, and even across different continents.

My early schooling was at Shobra Preparatory School, where I obtained my preparatory school certificate in 1952, the year of the army coup d'état, which permanently changed the social life and structure of the country. It was the start of military rule in Egypt, which, in my opinion, sadly continues until today.

After finishing preparatory school, I was transferred to Tawfikia Secondary School, across the street from my preparatory school. It was one of the oldest and best-known public schools in Cairo. It had a swimming pool, which was not found in other public schools in Cairo, where I had my first swimming lesson and found my love for water. Although we never lived in Maadi, I persuaded my father, who was the lawyer for the Maadi Development Company, to get me a membership at the Maadi Club so I could pursue swimming competitively. I was on the swimming and water polo teams, and my coach was Sobhy Badr, a former water polo player with the Egyptian national team. We had a sports day every year at Alexandria Sporting Club, so my friends and I traveled to Alexandria by bus and stayed for a couple of fun nights. We had a talent variety show every Monday, presented by the club members. Since club members were of different nationalities, various national dances were performed, including American Western dances and German folkloric dances. We had many parties at the club swimming pool, where I learned to dance.

In school, I was involved in different activities, such as the Boy Scouts. We went camping in the desert in Helwan, where it was so cold at night that we sat around the campfire to keep warm. I also joined the school's fencing team for one year. We trained at the Egyptian fencing club in Azbakia Park.

During my high school years, I had my first trip abroad in the summer of 1956, to Lebanon and Syria. The trip was organized by the Ministry of Education. For a fifteen-year-old high school student, it was exciting to experience another country. My father always encouraged me to travel, especially abroad, to gain experience and learn to be independent.

I finished high school in 1957 and was accepted at Faculty of Engineering, Ain Shams University, where I decided to major in architecture. That major was more rigorous than other programs and required us to spend some days away from our homes, eating and sleeping in the school, while working on projects. During these days, we cultivated a strong friendship with each other because of our common experience and became almost like family. My bond with many of my classmates continues to this day.

During my years at Ain Shams University, I traveled to Germany twice (in 1960 and 1961) for summer trainings. Besides work, these trips prepared me to live and support myself without the help of my family. I had the opportunity to visit many cities in Germany, Italy, Switzerland, and Belgium. Germany was where I had my first girlfriend.

When I graduated, in 1962, the laws at that time mandated that every engineer and architect must first work for the government for at least two years, renewable for another two years. Accordingly, I was assigned a job at the Ministry of Housing, Public Building Establishment, which later became the Arabic Bureau of Engineering Design. My uncle Tawfik was the director of Projects and Design there, so he became my mentor.

It was normal in those days to work two shifts. The first shift was with the government from morning until early afternoon. The second shift from 6:00 to 9:00 or 10:00 pm was in a private practice. My first afternoon job was at the office of one of my former professors, Wadid Pharaon. Then I moved to the office of Professor Mahmoud El Hakim, who was chairman of the Architectural Department at Ain Shams University. Finally, in 1964, I moved to the office of Mahmoud Riad and stayed there until I went to the United States in 1970. Mr. Riad was a pioneer in the field in Egypt and designed many buildings, including the headquarters of the Arab League. During my tenure at his office, I learned a lot and developed a strong friendship with Hassan Mansour, who was another mentor to me and became one of my best friends.

In 1965, I responded to an ad for teaching assistants at the newly established Faculty of Engineering at Al Azhar University. I was accepted and began a new job. The chairman of the department was Dr. Erfan Samy, who became my advisor for my Master's of Architecture thesis. Since my new working hours could be combined in three days, I had plenty of time for a private practice. I started my private practice with two friends, Moheb Ibrahim and Yousry Foad, and also continued my work at the offices of Mahmoud Riad and Sayed Elkomy. Since my MA was from Al Azhar University, an Islamic university, I had to study religious subjects and pass an exam before submitting my thesis. I received my master's degree in early 1969.

In July 1967, I met Rawya for the first time at the Ahly (National) Club. She was studying at the Faculty of Economics and Political Science at Cairo University. My father and her uncle, the Honorable Judge Aly Abaza, were classmates in law school and had the idea to set us up. When I saw Rawya, I knew she was the one I wanted to spend the rest of my life with. At this social gathering were her older sister, Gazbeya and her fiancé, Mokhtar Abaza (Uncle Aly's son), and Tante Laila, Uncle Aly's wife. Mokhtar and I hit it off as we had a lot in common, including age and mutual friends. Based on the customs of those days, to go out, Rawya and I had to have a chaperone. Our chaperones were Gazbeya and Mokhtar, or Rawya's younger two sisters Tahany (Toutou) and Azima (Mimi). Rawya and I got officially engaged on September 10, 1967 and married on July 6, 1969. Between 1967 and 1969, I was working on my MA, building our apartment, and enjoying time with the love of my life.

In October 1969, I was nominated by Al Azhar University for a scholarship in East Germany, but I rejected it because I strongly believed the best place for architectural graduate studies was the United States. I was already in contact with the University of Pennsylvania (UPenn) in Philadelphia, one of the few universities with a PhD program in architecture. I was accepted into the program, and after making it through many hurdles—including demonstrating my ability to pay the tuition (my cousin who was working in Saudi Arabia wrote a letter of support) and getting all the necessary approvals for leave without pay from Al Azhar University—all that was left was to get a security clearance from the government. My passport passed from employee to employee until it reached the last officer, who needed to stamp it as a seal of approval. But instead of stamping it, he threw another hurdle my way: I had to get approval to study abroad from the Ministry of Higher Education's Study Abroad Administration. I followed his instructions and went to the director's office with my papers. As soon as he reviewed them, he made a big "X" on the first page and said no travel to the United States was permitted at this time, based on guidance from the Intelligence Services. This guidance was reflective of the politics of the time, as Egypt's president, Gamal Abdel Nasser, was taking a stand against the United States and other Western countries after the 1967 Arab-Israeli war.

I was in total shock and disbelief. I went back to my job at Al Azhar University, heartbroken. My boss, Dr. Erfan Samy, advised me to do what others had done before: apply for a visa to go on vacation in Lebanon or another Arab country and then travel from there to the United States. I followed his advice and applied for a vacation in Kuwait to visit my cousin. However, my dear friend Ahmed El Ezaby suggested I speak with his brother-in-law, who was a high-ranking police officer with strong connections to other departments in the Ministry of Interior. In Egypt, many things need connections (wasta) to get done, and Ahmed's brother-in-law was the very wasta I needed. After I met with him and left my passport, he called a few hours later to congratulate me on getting approval for an exit visa to visit Kuwait and other countries. The "other countries" clause is what allowed me to obtain an entry visa to the United States.

There were no direct flights from Egypt to the United States, as relations between the two countries were strained, so I had to take another route. On January 24, 1970, I boarded an Egypt Air flight to London, with $200 in my pocket, and left behind my bride of six months so she could finish her last year in college. I stayed in London for a few days with my cousin Mohamed (Tante Susu's son), who was working on his PhD at University of Liverpool. On January 27, I landed at JFK Airport, and my dream came true: I was finally on US soil.

My friend and mentor from the days of Mahmoud Riad's office, Hassan Mansour, had traveled before me, so he picked me up from the airport. I spent four days in New York City, and it was love at first sight (similar to how I felt when I saw Rawya for the first time). I was thrilled walking in the streets of Manhattan, between all the buildings I used to see in architectural magazines and movies. The night of my arrival, I had dinner with Hassan, his wife, Monique, Dr. Hussein Shahine and his wife, Nanou. Hussein, who had just been made a junior partner at a New York office specializing in hospital design, tried to persuade me to pursue my career in the United States. The idea seemed absurd to me, so I laughed and told him I planned to go back to Egypt after finishing my PhD. Little did I know that, almost forty-nine years later, I would still be living in New York City. After three days of sightseeing, I took the Metro line to Philadelphia.

At the 30th Street station, a friend of my father, Dr. Salah Soliman, picked me up and took me to the UPenn dorm, where I would stay for a few months. The dorm was a motel on the banks of the Schuylkill River, which had been converted into temporary student housing. The receptionist who checked me in asked where I was from, and when I said Egypt, she responded by saying she was Jewish. I was confused by her response and I responded by saying, "So what?" She apparently liked my response because she went on to introduce me to Philip Khoury, a Lebanese doctoral student in medical research. We were the only two who spoke Arabic and we became good friends. He made my adjustment to life in the United States easier.

At my first meeting with Dean Perkins, the chairman of the PhD group, I had a huge confession to make. I shared with him that the cousin who had written my letter of support could not really support me financially, that I only had $200 with me, that I had left my wife in Cairo; and that I left Egypt illegally, so I could not go back in the near future. Dean Perkins was shocked and told me that I put him in a difficult position because the student visa required that I be a full-time student. I could have a part-time job, but that would not pay for my tuition or living expenses. He said he needed time to think about what our options were. After reviewing my master's thesis, he decided to give me eight credits toward the twenty credits required for the PhD, which reduced the cost of tuition and living expenses. He also told me to see Mr. Kar at the Office of International Students so he could help me further.

After I shared my story with Mr. Kar, he gave me a contact at the Immigration Services Office and said to request an application for permanent residency. He advised that, if asked why I wanted to do so, I should say that I fell in love with the country. Once my application had been submitted, my status would be permanent resident pending, which meant I could be a part-time student and have a full-time job. I went to see Mr. Kar's contact, and he explained the different forms of sponsorship and said I needed to find an employer who would sponsor me.

After two weeks of searching for a job at architectural firms, I almost gave up, especially considering that my money was evaporating as every minute passed. Finally, I found an ad for a position in a firm in Camden, New Jersey, across the Delaware River from Philadelphia. I went in for an interview and was hired on the spot. They signed my sponsorship papers, and I submitted the papers to the Immigration Services Office. After a year and a half of working for the Camden firm, they laid me off, which meant I had to think of a plan B for my sponsorship. Luck was on my side, because three days later, I found an opening at Vincent G. Kling Architects, the biggest office in Philadelphia. I had a great time working there because of the professional and friendly environment. I gained a lot of experience in running and organizing big projects. I was assigned to the team working on the AT&T (195 Corporation) office complex in New Jersey.

In June 1970, Rawya finished her studies at Cairo University and she traveled to New York City soon after. It was her first time leaving home, and traveling alone, so as you can imagine, she was very nervous. I met her at JFK, and we spent a couple of days in New York City before going to Philadelphia. I tried my best to comfort Rawya and help her to adjust to the big transition. We moved to a one-bedroom apartment in the newly completed University of Pennsylvania Graduate Towers.

I continued to work full time and took two courses each semester. I would come home from work, eat dinner, sleep, then wake up at 5:00 am to study every day. I was able to pay my tuition through short-term loans from the University, which made the financial burden easier. Rawya found a job in the Physics Department, so we had two incomes. Life was not easy, especially because we were alone, without our families and support system, but we made it work, and I believe it made us stronger as a couple.

I reapplied for the permanent residency so I could continue to manage both my studies and work, but this time, I applied for self-sponsorship for the two of us. Shortly after that, we received our green cards. The entire process took almost a year and half, which is hard to imagine, given the politics around citizenship in the United States now—especially under the pervious Trump administration.

Every year while at UPenn, I applied for financial aid; however, I always received the same letter of rejection indicating a shortage of funds. After the October 1973 war and the start of Kissinger's shuttle diplomacy, I received the same rejection letter; however, two weeks later, I received another letter from the architectural department granting me $1,500 to assist me in preparing my dissertation. All Egyptian students who enrolled in the program after me were granted financial assistance easily. It seems that politics influenced the decision.

My field of specialization was the natural means of environmental control, which was in response to the oil embargo and energy crises in the mid-1970s. My dissertation title was *The Concern of Microclimate and Comfort Zone as Generator for the Courtyard House Design with Particular Emphasis on the Hot-Arid Zone*. I developed a computer program to test courtyard houses during the design phase, so a comfort zone could be achieved without the use of mechanical equipment.

The pressure of working full time, going to school, and smoking caught up with me, and led to a heart attack. I was hospitalized for three weeks. I begged the doctor to postpone my admission to the hospital until after I submitted my dissertation, but he refused and told me I had to go immediately, unless I wanted to die. I asked Rawya to call Dean Perkins and inform him of the situation, and he was very supportive and said to focus on getting healthy and not to worry about the dissertation submission or graduation. After I was released from the hospital, I spent four weeks at home, during which I finished writing, typing, printing, and binding my dissertation. I submitted it to Dean Perkins and was still able to graduate in December 1975, as I had hoped.

During the years from 1970 to 1976, I experienced and appreciated the opportunities that were given to me in the United States. After my heart attack, however, I was depressed and wanted to return to Egypt, because I wanted to die there. Rawya had grown used to living in the United States and was pursuing a master's degree; however, she missed Egypt and her family. It seemed that Egypt was calling us. But then I received a call from Hussein Shahine, who asked me to come to his office in New York City. He and Hassan Mansour talked me out of going back to Egypt, and Hussein offered me a job with his firm, Rogers, Butler and Burgun (which later became, and to this day is, Rogers, Burgun, Shahine, and Deschler, RBSD). The firm wanted to break into the market in the Middle East, so I was made responsible for overseeing projects there. Rawya and I moved to the City, and a year later, we got our citizenship. My professional career at RBSD spans forty-two years. I started as project manager of As Salam International Hospital and was a principal for the last twenty years.

In 1978, we were blessed with the arrival of our daughter Jehan, followed in 1986 by our son Mostafa. Both our children went to the United Nations International School because we wanted to make sure they were in a school where they could be proud of being Egyptian Americans. Jehan went to college at Tufts University and got her master's degree at Georgetown University. Mostafa went to Curry College. Jehan married Ahmed Akel in 2012 and gave birth to their daughter, Sherifa, in 2015. They live in Cairo, where Jehan works at the Institute of International Education, and Ahmed works at British Petroleum. Mostafa proposed to his long-time girlfriend, Wiebke Reile, in 2017, and they live in Brooklyn, New York. Mostafa works in the hospitality business at the Ink48 Hotel in midtown, and Wiebke is currently pursuing her PhD.

Throughout our life in the United States, it was always very important for us to remain connected to Egypt. Remember, we moved here thinking it was temporary and we would eventually return to Egypt. Rawya dedicated her life to raising our children to be proud of their identity. She made it a point to teach them Arabic and to take them to Egypt every year. It has also been important to us to be active in the Egyptian American community. Our social interactions with the Egyptian communities in New York started with the Egyptians Americans Professional Society (EAPS), which was established in 1974. As the name implies, membership was limited to any Egyptian professional and their family. We met monthly to listen to a guest speaker, followed by a potluck dinner. Once a year, we organized a two-day symposium with topics that were of concern to the Egyptian American community. The organization started with about five families, and the monthly meetings rotated among the families' homes. When the number of members increased, the monthly meetings were held at a rented space, with a volunteer host designated to organize the dinner dishes brought by the members. EAPS was a great way for our children to meet other Egyptian Americans and for them to form a support system with others who shared the experience of being born in the United States to Egyptian immigrant parents.

Now, I am nearing retirement and am looking back at almost forty-nine years in the United States. I do not regret a moment of it and am proud of what I have achieved. Despite the ups and downs, I think the best decision Rawya and I made was to stay in this country and raise our children here.

———•———

MAHMOUD F. AGHA graduated from Ain Shams University in 1962 with a degree in architecture engineering. He obtained a masters degree from Al Azhar University in 1969 and a PhD in Architecture from the University of Pennsylvania in 1975. He is a registered architect in the State of New York, New Jersey, Pennsylvania, and in Egypt. He is married to Rawya M. Agha and has two children: Jehan, who resides in Egypt, and Mostafa, who resides in New York.

WE ARE THE SUM

Souheir Eldefrawy Elmasry

From where I stand now, I look at what I was and what I came to be, and I realize that I have had a rich, varied life. Although, by nature, I like to keep a personal space not easily accessible to others, I am also aware of how my life and my experiences can benefit others. So, this personal history is the result of a compromise between these two forces, concentrating on the experience I gained when I traveled from Egypt to the United States, how I applied what I gained when I returned to Egypt, how Egypt has changed, and what I think can be done to redress what has changed.

I was born in Cairo, Egypt, to a middle-class couple. My father came from a relatively well-to-do family in Menoufiya Governorate. His father started the company that manufactured Eldefrawy Cigarettes, a business he bequeathed to his oldest son. To his other sons, he gave education.

My father lost his mother while still a child, left Menouf and the family for high school in Tanta, and later studied agriculture at King Fouad University, renamed Cairo University. He never returned to live with the family in Menouf. It was expected that, like his cousins, he would marry an Eldefrawy. But he had studied genetics and believed one should not marry relatives. He married my mother from outside the family, and this added to his feeling of being an outsider. All of this kindled his nostalgia for his roots and was expressed in the family stories he told my sister and me.

My father was a storyteller. He also was interested in popular science. He passed on these interests to my sister and me. I recall when I was ten years old, arguing with my teacher about the origin of the moon. She told the class it was formed, like the earth, of vapor condensing; I told her my father had shown me pictures, showing it was formed from a part of the earth.

My mother was a housewife. Her father was an illiterate businessman with a fantastic intellect, who could not only manage his business, but also calculate the complex calculations he needed when he started investing in building apartments. In the 1920s, he built the apartment building at 82 Eldzaher Street. On the ground floor was a mandara, which served as his personal office and salon. My uncle Hussein recounted that there, every Thursday evening, my grandfather congregated with his friends. Zaki Mourad, father of the singer Laila Mourad, played the oud, and my grandmother supplied a huge tray of bassboussa. Uncle Hussein was there in 1928, when the older brother of the singer Mohamed Abdel Wahab came to my grandfather in the mandara to ask for his advice: his younger brother had made three thousand pounds from his first hit song, "Kollena Neheb el-Amar wel Amar Beyheb Meen?" ("We all love the moon and the moon loves whom?"),[1] and he wanted to know if he should buy an apartment building in Faggalah.

One day, when I was four or five years old, my grandmother was in the kitchen and pointed at the new maid. She said to the man who supplied maids, "Take her back to the village, she is not resourceful." That must have sunk into my psyche: if you're not resourceful, they will send you back to the village! This is probably why I have a continued need to be resourceful and don't give up easily. At other times, I saw two of my grandmother's maids pull out the tableyya from behind the kitchen door and eat before they served us. My grandmother used to say, "They should not serve us while they're hungry *Illi mas-ool*

---

1   https://www.youtube.com/watch?v=VTTJ7W7JBM0

minnak yeegy abl mennak (He who depends on you comes before you). I still apply this rule when I return home after a workday and put my driver's dinner into the microwave before I put mine. Many of my grandmother's stories and my personal stories form the basis of the Ana wa Nahnoo (AwN) Program I created when I returned to Egypt.

From the nineteenth into the early twentieth century, Cairo was a cosmopolitan place. Greeks, Italians, Jews, and Armenians flocked to it. Jobs and businesses were plentiful. There were Greek grocers, Armenian dentists and seamstresses, etc. My grandfather's building was inhabited by Jews and Greeks. There were still Jews left when I enrolled in the lycée, but many started leaving in the 1950s and 1960s. When I was three or four, my grandmother would say to me, "Elatho." For many years I thought it was Arabic, never knowing it was Greek for "come here."

In the 1950s in Cairo, we ate real Italian pizzas, with anchovies and boiled eggs, not the Americanized version. This is in contrast with the Midwest in the 1960s when my husband and I arrived: Americans didn't eat yogurt or ducks or pizza. They mainly ate beef, chicken, and potatoes. One day, as a student, I walked into a pizzeria next to the University Hospital in Minneapolis. A tall man with a tweed jacket and suede elbow patches, probably a Minnesotan farmer who was bringing his wife for treatment at the hospital, asked: "What is pizza?"

My education was in French, mainly at St. Joseph de L'Apparition, a nuns' school, and at the Lycée Français du Caire in Bab el Looq. The nuns' school had a swimming pool, tennis courts, and a skating ring. There was order, discipline, and an emphasis on ethics. I read a lot—an average of three or four books per week. I also played chess and could beat my older cousins. The police stories, the chess, and my kind of intellect directed me toward science, and that meant leaving the nuns' school and enrolling in the lycée, which was against my mother's vision for my sister and me. Her vision for our education was to teach us French, how to play the piano, how to paint, and after high school, we would either get married or study French at the university then get married, but not work. It was a strange vision coming from my mother, who, after high school, was unhappy her father didn't allow her to go to London like her classmates and continue her education. When she was a teenager, she wanted to be a writer and translate the novel *Little Women* by Louisa May Alcott. She kept a decent-sized library at home. When my father's eyes started failing him, she read to him aloud.

My father's vision for his daughters was different. He wanted us to have careers and be independent. His vision prevailed. What I gained from the nuns' school, in addition to the French language, was an excellent command of Arabic, good writing skills, and a sense of ethics. Although we sometimes joked about what the nuns taught us in ethics class ("If a man looks at you with lust, pray for his soul!"), it crept under our skin. When an anthropologist friend told me, "You are fueled by a sense of fairness," I recalled the nuns' teaching about ethics and the different recommendations my father gave us, such as "Never side with your sister when she is wrong." Fifty years later, when I returned to Egypt and was shocked by the change in culture and ethics, I used this background to create the AwN Program for children.

At the lycée, I liked the sciences and the Arabic and English languages, but not history or geography. My Arabic teacher, Monsieur Fouhil, thought I was a budding writer. He offered to give me free lessons to hone my writing skills. I told him I didn't want to be a writer; I wanted to be a scientist. Forty or fifty years later, after having been a successful scientist, I started writing.

The main events during high school were the burning of Cairo, and the July revolution in 1952. We were not a political family. During my schooling years, I was intellectually not much different from girls my age in the West. However, socially and emotionally, I was an underdeveloped creature. Our family did not join social clubs, lest my sister and I meet and befriend young men! We weren't allowed to read the novels of Ihsan Abdel Koddous because they had too many love scenes.

After high school, I studied pharmacy at Cairo University. In my second year, I became engaged to Dr. Fouad Hetta, a highly connected, much older pharmacist and laboratory analyst in the army. It was an arranged marriage, and we were married the next year. In the daytime,

I was a pharmacy student with two long pigtails. In the evening, I hid my pigtails in a bun and dressed like a much older married lady, with black suits and diamonds. I switched my cologne from the light, young Antilope to the more mature Arpege and Ma Griffe. I had gone through life with an ignorance that is unbelievable by our standards today. My sister and I were not allowed to ride bikes. We had to ride them in the secluded suburb of Maadi. If my mother read a novel (e.g., *Forever Amber*), she burned it, lest my sister or I read it. My mother took pride in delivering to her older, well-established son-in-law a "closed-eyed kitten" he could mold to his habits. Boy, have we come a long way! Nahla was born right after I took my final pharmacy exams. Fouad was traveling a good deal of the time we were married. Two years later, the marriage was no more.

After graduation, I studied for a degree in drug analysis and bio-logical standardization, worked for a couple of years in pharmaceutical laboratories, and applied for a scholarship to the University of Utah in the United States. During Nasser's time in the early 1960s, Egypt sent out hundreds of thousands of graduates on scholarships to many countries. I wanted out of Egypt, but my mother—who was always eager to see me married—said that since I was a divorcee, it was not proper for me to live alone abroad. At the scholarship office in the Mogama building, I met an old colleague, Dr. Ahmed Elmasry, who was on vacation from Moscow. Before he returned to Moscow, he asked for my hand. We got married by proxy after he left. I left for the United States in January 1962. Ahmed soon joined me, and Hassan was born at the end of the year. Tarek was born as I was finishing my PhD in 1967.

After a year at the University of Utah, Ahmed and I moved to the University of Minnesota. I studied pharmacology at the medical school; he studied medicinal chemistry at the pharmacy school. We led an exceedingly fast-paced life, which was all work and study. I had never taken a multiple-choice test. I laughed at a multiple-choice question showing a graph of a blood pressure tracing, where we had to guess which drugs were applied at specific points in time to cause the observed changes in blood pressure. Once, in a physiology test at the University of Minnesota, I was surprised by the large number of multiple-choice questions, which needed much more time than what was given to solve them. I made this observation to the instructor, who said, "It's done on purpose. Our students are future physicians. We don't want them, when they score 100 percent, to think they know it all." I compared this with high schools in Egypt, where students can have a final score of more than 100 percent.

It was easier to get jobs and scholarships in my field of study than in Ahmed's. I asked my advisor, Dr. Mannering, to write me a recommendation for a postdoctoral position that was open. He refused, saying I should wait until my husband found a position and follow him there, because I would have no problem finding a position. I obediently accepted, although in the 1960s, my sister was in Algeria on a teaching assignment, and no one questioned why she should be in Algeria and her husband in Egypt. At the time, some segments of US society were more closed minded than some segments of Egyptian society.

After graduation, both Ahmed and I did postdoctoral research at the University of Pittsburgh and then at the University of Michigan. In the fall of 1970, we returned to Egypt to teach for two years at the College of Pharmacy, Cairo University. I adjusted to my new life and enjoyed, in particular, living in Maadi, halfway between the two sets of grandparents—Elmasry in Helwan and Eldefrawy in Abbassieh. I had missed having family close by. However, just weeks after returning to Egypt, Ahmed wanted to go back to the United States. His homesickness had been satisfied.

Two years later, when I was with Nahla in San Francisco to present a paper and chair a session at the International Congress on Pharmacology, I received a telegram from Ahmed asking me not to return to Cairo. A professor we knew at the University of Michigan wanted both of us to work with him. Ahmed was bringing the boys. I knew we weren't coming back to Egypt. In 1975, he joined Abbott Laboratories, and I soon followed him. Ahmed's stay at Abbott Laboratories was miserable; there was too much change in his department. We were there when he passed away in 1979. Hassan was a teenager, and Tarek was a preteen. I was lucky to have a job and to be able to support the family.

When I was a senior pharmacologist at Abbott Laboratories, I was offered a director's position at G.D. Searle, which was a couple of steps above my position. Abbott wanted to keep me, so they offered me a project manager position, but Jim—who supported the Project Management Department—was not happy. He said, "You scientists don't fit here. You are always looking for the truth. There is no truth. There is just a perception of the truth." I had been programmed to think of truth, truth in ethics, truth in science—albeit, relative truth—and continuously worked at refining this truth, but I would not confuse it with a perception of it.

Another time, a director in the Licensing Department approached me. He was looking for a pharmacologist, who was both steeped in the different aspects of pharmacology and comfortable with French culture (not just the language), to help him deal with some finnicky small French pharmaceutical companies when he went on licensing trips. I happened to be one of the rare people who fit these conditions and I was very excited about the position. A week later, he bluntly retracted the offer, saying, "I was told we can't have an attractive single woman as part of the traveling licensing team!" I was shocked and furious. I wasn't going to be a woman; I was going to be the only pharmacologist among a bunch of businessmen. I could help them evaluate opportunities on the spot so they wouldn't have to wait to bring them back to us to evaluate. I could be the bridge in culture. But no, I was a woman and that trumped everything. It was the early 1980s, some fourteen years after I had obediently accepted Dr. Mannering's refusal to give me a recommendation and instead wait until my husband found a job and follow him. The world had changed, but not enough. There was talk of gender discrimination, but the old guard felt no need to change their blunt talk. I considered a lawsuit and spoke to a woman attorney, but eventually shelved the idea.

After Ahmed passed away, it was not easy going from the sheltered life I had to a new life. Ahmed had kept the finances and managed all operations. We didn't have a supportive social network and

I was under psychological pressure. One time, when I was flying in a propeller plane from Atlantic City to Washington D.C., I panicked and thought, "Oh my God! What would happen to my children if the plane fell and I died? Their schools? They can't go back to Egypt!" Now, looking back at the years when I was newly widowed and the only breadwinner in the family, I ask myself, "Was I a strong woman?" I think of myself not as strong but just as "shock absorbent." On some days, I would leave the lab and go out on the grounds of Abbott Park, where I could cry and nobody could see me. I longed not to have all of those responsibilities, for the day I could come home, open the door, and smell food somebody had cooked for me.

After Ahmed passed away, my mother and father stayed with us for six months. Upon her arrival, my mother looked at a small statue of the Buddha at the top of the stairs and asked me to take it down. I reminded her, "Mom, this is my home." I also had to remind her not to give the children their dinner when they returned from school, because we are used to all having dinner together. When she started saying that, as a single woman, I shouldn't live abroad alone and I had to go back to Egypt, I stood my ground. I made it clear I was not uprooting my children.

A new chapter in my life was starting. We couldn't afford cleaning help, so on weekends, we cleaned the house together. I think working together makes you closer to your children than having fun together. I have always kept close relationships with my children and their friends, to whom I was Mama Egypt, and we still have meaningful discussions and share books and thoughts. Both Hassan and Tarek went to college at the University of Chicago and stayed close by. Nahla once dreamt that I was swimming in a pool surrounded by my children. I kept my distance from them but watched over them out of the corner of my eye. I guess this is how I viewed our relationships: a good deal of caring, but also room for growth.

Less than a year after Ahmed passed away, my cousin Dr. Ahmed Eldefrawy, his wife Rafiah, and their two sons (Ayman and Ashraf) moved from Kentucky to Chicago. We became very close. My cousin recommended that I become the secretary of the Egyptian American Club. This thrusted me into the local, then national, social work of the Arab American community. I became involved in the nascent American-Arab Anti-Discrimination Committee (ADC).

In the 1980s, the FBI had conducted a sting operation code named ABSCAM, short for Arab Scam. It was a public corruption investigation that used a convicted con man, Melvin Weinberg, to pose as a wealthy Arab and videotape several public officials accepting bribes. Six congressmen and one senator were indicted. There was no justification for the choice of "Arab" identity in the operation since no wealthy Arab had been involved in public corruption bribes. Senator James Abourezk, who for years had been fighting for the rights of Native Americans in South Dakota, was incensed that "they would have never called it JEWSCAM." Senator Abourezk founded ADC as a rallying call for Arab Americans to stand up for their dignity and rights. Chapters were formed. Being a woman and the secretary of the Egyptian American Club landed me a seat on the board of the Chicago ADC chapter. Three years later, I was elected as its chair, moving me more into social work and away from my science background. This increased with my involvement with the Islamic Cultural Center (ICC) of Greater Chicago.

When we first moved to the Chicago area, we sent Hassan and Tarek to Sunday school at the ICC. The ICC was built at the beginning of the twentieth century by the Bosnian community in Chicago, in cooperation with some Arabs and other non-Bosnians. It was a melting pot for ethnically different Muslims: Turks, Albanians, Anglo-Saxon converts, Pakistanis, Indians, Egyptians, etc. The Women's Group of the ICC regularly raised funds to support the education of young Bosnians to study at Al-Azhar University in Cairo, on condition that after graduation, they would serve as imams at the Center. It supported several consecutive imams, including young Mustafa Ceric, who, while serving as imam of the Center, studied for his PhD at the University of Chicago. He returned to Bosnia and later became the grand mufti of Bosnia and Herzegovina.

Volunteering at the ICC was an eye-opening experience. Bosnians have an acute sense of self, which was sharpened by the fact that they were the only Muslim country in Europe. The mosque held a special place in their lives. Because they did not speak Arabic, their imam, who spoke Arabic and could read the Qur'an, held a place somewhat equivalent to that of a priest. Marriages and engagements were held in the social halls of the ICC. A mother leaving the hospital with her newborn baby would first stop at the ICC to have the imam say the shehada in the baby's ears.

When Jim Edgar became governor of Illinois, he appointed me to the board of directors of the Illinois Humanities Council (IHC). This was when I came to appreciate the humanities, history, and geography, and this eye-opening experience influenced much of what I did when I returned to Egypt.

One day, the governor's assistant for ethnic affairs, Pat Michaelski, called me and said, "Does your mosque have a museum or an archive department? The governor [a devout Christian] wants to meet the representatives of the different legitimate religious groups, and in order to exclude the many non-legit organizations, we have put the condition that each must have a museum or archive department. Churches, synagogues, and temples have them, but the mosques on the South Side and on Elston Street [built by Arabs and Pakistanis, respectively, and frequented by thousands of worshippers every week] don't have them. I know these mosques are legitimate organizations, but they don't satisfy the conditions."

I showed her the museum of the ICC. It presented the history and the identity of the Center, including a prototype of the first building and the addition to the building, photos of the different imams and chairs of the board, and photos of visits to the Center by VIPs, such as Chicago's cardinal. Because Bosnians cared about their identity, and the Center was part of who they were, they cared to have a museum. I could not forget this incident and the importance of cultivating a sense of identity and self-value in children and youth. I built on it further in the lecture series we developed at the ICC, which became one of the bases of the AwN Program.

Ten years after Ahmed passed away, I met Talat Othman, a recently widowed, successful Palestinian American businessman, and a major supporter of the ICC. He proposed to me. I took a leave of absence from Abbott, and we were married. A year later, I took an early retirement from my position as manager of technology licensing.

For the following nine years, Talat and I—either singly or together—went full throttle helping the Arab American and Islamic American communities in Chicago and in the United States. Earlier, when Jim Edgar was secretary of state and I was chair of the local ADC board, I had developed a good relationship with him. So, when he ran for governor, we enlisted the mainly Democratic Arab American community to support him although he was a Republican. He won and asked me to serve as one of his two appointees on the board of directors of IHC. Later, I was asked by Marjorie Benton to join her, Nancy Stevenson, and Maggie Daley (late wife of Mayor Daley) on the Child, Youth, and Family Advisory Committee of the Chicago Community Trust. In 1994, we brought to the Chicago Cultural Center the exhibition "Forces of Change: Artists of the Arab World." I was told that the famous Chicagoan Lester Crown said this exhibition shook the City. Nobody envisioned Arab women artists to be so talented. The mayor of Chicago decreed that November, the month of the exhibition, was to be Arab American month in Chicago.

My involvement with the IHC changed views I had held for years. I had put science on a pedestal and looked somewhat down on the soft sciences of history and the humanities in general. My research on thrombolysis had strengthened this view. During my last years in pharmacology at Abbott, I had developed an animal model to test for thrombolytic drugs, which dissolve blood clots and save lives. In the experiment, as the blood clot dissolved, my heart would skip a beat. It was a dizzying feeling. We could save lives! At the IHC, I learned that changing people's thinking was as important as saving their lives. I was made aware of the importance of having youth hold onto their identity. Communities where members had a sense of who they were, and were at peace with it, stayed away from wrongdoing. A study comparing different immigrant communities found that a group's sense of identity was preserved when the group met regularly, every week, in the same place, and interacted during those meetings, and when the group developed a self-reflective literature, such as by writing personal stories or memoirs.

I returned to Egypt in 1999–2000 and started a completely different chapter in my life. Before this, science and pharmaceuticals were my main concern, and social work was my hobby. Now, my hobby became my main concern. After a short period of pro bono work in pharmaceutical consulting, and a good deal of reflection and comparison between the Egypt I had left and the Egypt I returned to, I came to the conclusion that what ailed us was the loss of a sense of self-value. We did not value ourselves. I wasn't interested in the why this happened; I wanted to help correct it, and I wanted to do something for children, who were the future of this country. How would I do this?

Over a period of three to four years, I created a program to instill in children a sense of self-value—the four parts of the AwN Program. I first thought the problem was in the individual, so I created a first book (*Ana*) to focus on boosting a sense of self-value. In it, children developed a sense of self-value by learning to be organized, always having goals, delaying reward, showing emotional intelligence, collecting family stories, and creating their personal history. Children learned to discuss, reflect, and express themselves.

I later realized the issue was not just with the individual, but also the relation of the individual to their surroundings, so in the second book (*Assasseyat we Maharat*), I laid out the basis for the relationship of the individual (ana) to the us (nahnoo). The third book (*Ikhtelafoona we Tawasooloona*) explored our differences and how not accepting our differences was hurting us. The fourth book (*Mojtama'oona*) addressed the resultant community of healthy ana dealing in a healthy nahnoo, where there was respect, democracy, rule of law, trust, etc.

I relied on many observations I had collected in the States of the immigrant communities that held onto their identities, meeting regularly every week, in the same place, interacting during those meetings, and developing a self-reflective literature. Based on Pat Michalsky's observation—that mosques in the Chicago area, with the exception of the ICC, did not have museums or decent archive departments—the AwN Program asked children to create their personal histories. I also relied on many personal observations from my family and my previous life in Egypt.

I included many simplified explanations of concepts that were usually taught to much older individuals. I felt that if these concepts were simplified, children could grasp them and benefit from them. So, I presented Howard Gardner's multiple intelligence theory, Erich Fromm's definition of true love as respect, caring, responsibility, and knowing, and Edward Banfield's observation that societies where families selfishly turn inward on themselves develop amoral familism and stay poor. I included stories about the tribal conflicts in Rwanda and Kenya in order to have children value the rule of law and realize the limitations of the tribal system. I included the story of my technician at the University of Michigan, who, at the end of his first day at work, refused to work beyond 5pm, saying, "I am not an animal to keep on working." When he understood that animals don't work, but toil, and can't relate to what they produce or take pride in it, and that only humans can work, he gave his work what it needed, and excelled in it. I included discussions of cultural vignettes, such as, "I am with my brother against my cousin and with my cousin against the stranger," to teach children critical thinking.

I was disappointed, however, to discover that Egyptian children didn't like to read. Books were rarely gift items. So, we created from the four AwN books a four-semester program wherein children met regularly, every week, interacted and reflected, and put down their thoughts on papers. The cultural department of the US embassy appreciated the program and supported it; the assistant cultural affairs officer said, "Egypt needs this program."

Whenever funds were available, we presented the AwN Program in schools and youth centers. We presented it in twelve governorates.

A study on the effects of AwN concluded that it changed not only the children, but also the facilitators and the teachers who taught it. We had observed this informally, but the study proved that the children learned to work with goals, be more organized, and show emotional intelligence, among other things. It also showed that the teachers and facilitators learned to stay in the background and give the children room to grow, and they themselves learned the same concepts. Over the years, children have often commented that they felt respected in the program. Respect was a recurrent observation. I also noticed that our children often lacked love and attention and responded beautifully when they received them. I was on a mission. I had seen a different Egypt and I was slowly discovering how to bring back parts of what I had seen. I did not have a name for what we taught. It was not just ethics. It was much more.

From children, we moved to youth. I wrote books and developed the Ana wa Nahnoo El-Shabab Program, which teaches youth that development involves give and take. The youth learned to give as much as they took. Then I wrote books and developed programs for mothers, including a book on the danger of excessive TV viewing and a video program teaching mothers how to raise their children and solve problems they encountered in the process.

Understanding what ailed Egypt and what I could do to change it became my utmost interest. During my many trips to the United States, I brought back dozens of books on education, psychology, and development. I read Jean Piaget, Maria Montessori, their precursor, the Russian Lev Vygotsky, and the famous psychologist who built on their work, Reuven Feuerstein. I was fascinated by Feuerstein's work on the cultural rehabilitation of Moroccan Jewish immigrants to fit into Israeli society, and how this could help us to rehabilitate culturally deprived Egyptian youth. Through my readings, I discovered Lawrence Harrison's work on culture. He headed the United States Agency for International Development (USAID) in several South American countries and noticed that some communities benefited from the application of their projects and developed, while others did not.

He related this to cultural elements in a community that help make it susceptible to development. At Harvard University, he set up the Culture Matters Project, which studied the cultural conditions associated with development. I discovered that 90 percent of the concepts AwN instilled in children were associated with development-prone societies. AwN did not just teach ethics, it helped recreate conditions (e.g., order, punctuality, frugality, honesty, work ethics, responsibility, achievement, respect of others, and rule of law) that used to prevail in Egypt and made it like other development-prone societies. I came to the conclusion that the issue was culture. We had not preserved our culture.

Over the years, we presented our work on AwN and the Culture and Education for the Child and Family Foundation (CECF) we had set up at five international meetings. Applying the CECF programs in Egypt was no easy task. Unfortunately, what prevails in Egypt is not quality, or how to best help the country, but simply wasta, which overrules what is best for the country. Anybody in a position of power feels they can copycat quality work and give it to the "trusted ones" to do the work. The trusted ones congregate in cohesive tribes no outsider can access. When I was in the United States, every time I did good work I was recommended for a position. When I served on the board of the Egyptian American Club, I was recommended for the board of ADC, which led me to serve on the board of the American Muslim Council, and the governor of Illinois then recommended me to the board of directors of the IHC, which in turn had me recommended to serve with the wife of the mayor of Chicago on the advisory committee of the Chicago Community Trust, and so forth. Not so in Egypt.

When I reflect on where I was and where I am now, and where Egypt was and where it is now, and on the different factors that have affected me and those that have affected Egypt, I see we are all the sum of what we have gone through. I am lucky to have benefited from the several situations I was in. Egypt is unlucky to have wasted the opportunities it had. From my reflection on myself and of Egypt, I go to reflecting on the postcolonial eras of many countries. When people say, "We wish Egypt gets its own Mahathir Mohamad," they don't realize Mahathir Mohamad was the product of his environment, the British system. So was Lee Kuan Yew. They have been to the other side of the mountain. Colonialism may extract the wealth of the colonized countries, but it gives them a system conducive to development. It lets them go to the other side of the mountain, where there is respect, hard work, discipline, and order.

Nasser planned for Egypt to go to the other side of the mountain. Thousands of youth were given scholarships to the United States, USSR, England, etc. Both my husband and I received one of these scholarships. India also did the same. Hundreds of thousands of Indian scientists came to the United States for studies. Some returned, others stayed, but both helped build a bridge between India and the United States. The Gulf countries, in their own way, visited the other side of the mountain—they built skyscrapers and shopping malls and brought the colonizers as consultants and businessmen. Even Iran, a few years back, had six ministers holding PhD degrees from the United States. It genuinely worked at educating and building the individual. That was part of its religious mandate. But in Egypt, Sadat—while opening the country to the West—discontinued the scholarships. Egypt, in its poverty, compensated by having a tsunami of locally produced degrees, supported by abstracts, not by original papers, since the latter were exorbitantly expensive to obtain. Education took a nosedive.

Presently, there is an effort in Egypt to rebuild the educational system. It is a good start but an uphill battle. I hope the next effort is to target culture, which I feel is the real issue. I continue working with CECF to effect the change I can affect, my effort being largely the result of having been on the other side of the mountain.

———

SOUHEIR ELDEFRAWY ELMASRY received her PhD from the University of Minnesota Medical School. She was the manager of Technology Licensing at Abbott Laboratories in North Chicago and contributed effectively to the social, educational, and cultural activities of her community. After 30 years in the US, Eldefrawy returned to Egypt and focused her attention on children's education. She wrote about the risk of television on the development of children brains and in 2005 she wrote a book on the subject in Arabic. She also published a series on the same topic titled *Ana Wa Nahnoo*. Souheir has a daughter who lives in Cairo and two sons who work between the UK and the US. As a result, she lives between three continents.

THE STORY OF A LONG LIFE
Lofty Basta

I am eighty-eight years old and I've been asked to share my story with you, which requires me to use "I" as events are recited. That should not be interpreted as representing arrogance, or a boisterous streak in me. I promise to try to be honest enough not to gloss over my shortcomings while I highlight my triumphs. I confess that I see the world through my own eyes, colored by my traditions, beliefs, culture, upbringing, and experiences—many of which controlled my judgment and shaped my conduct. Although I will strive to be as objective as my memory allows me to be, my recollection of certain events may be at variance from the truth in certain respects. These variances are unintentional, and if they happen, I ask for forgiveness. My mentors include many people who never acquired fame nor even have recognizable names, but my encounter with each has influenced my thinking and behavior throughout my life. I confess that initially I was not a good team player, but I learned the hard way to be one; any of us are only as good as the others who work with us, and the ultimate success of a leader represents the sum of achievements of the many.

My Childhood and Adolescence

I grew up in a middle-class religious environment. My father was the headmaster of Iman High School. Among its most famous students was Nazier Gayed, who subsequently became Pope Shenouda III. My father was known to be firm, disciplined, reliable, and a fair and even-handed man. After the death of his father, his two brothers, three sisters, and mother moved in to live with us while I was still young. My mother was the daughter of a senior priest—a dominant figure who visited twice a year. I had three brothers and two sisters. All in all, fourteen individuals lived in the same house permanently. My mother never complained about this big crowd. She always said, "God will provide." In retrospect, I admire her for coping. To be honest, I would not have been able to emulate what she was doing.

In my early life, I learned to compete for first place. At home, I viewed myself as the neglected second child (my older brother was always the center of attention), and in Iman's preparatory school, I jumped ahead two grades because of academic excellence—from being a first grader to being a fourth grader the following year. This had its downside as well as its obvious upside. I lacked social maturity, even as I excelled academically. I was two years younger than my peers until graduation. At Iman's junior high, I continued to be at the top of my class. I was punished by one of the teachers unfairly when he alleged that my score on a math test was 29 out of 40. When I went home, I found out that he failed to include the 9 out of 10 that I scored on the first question; my total score should have been 38 out of 40. When I showed this to the teacher, he did not apologize or show any remorse. I pretended to be sick to avoid attending his class after this incident.

I talked to my dad and insisted that I would never go to Iman's high school because he might be accused of being partial to me. My dad agreed. I attended Shubra High School instead.

I continued to thrive academically at high school, but my social immaturity became more obvious. Starting high school at the age of twelve, while others were older than fourteen, translated into being smaller in stature and having weaker muscles. My voice was still high pitched, while others had started to have sonorous voices and hair in their arm pits, as well as smelly sweat. I was considered a nerd interested in homework, while my peers dwelled in talk about sex and physical prowess. In other words, my interests were still those of a child, while my peers were on their way to adulthood, albeit with bad hormones. Otherwise, high school was a place for real learning and maturation. Students were taught by knowledgeable teachers, such as Mr. Davis, who taught us English and who called me "the dictionary of the class," Mr. Choulet, who taught us French, and Mr. Ibrahim, who was a master of biology. No wonder our graduating class contained three (I was one of them) among the top ten of fifty-five thousand taking the national high school graduation exam.

At Ain Shams University

I started medical school in 1948. As usual, I was consistently first in my class. I spent the preparatory year with the others in Kasr El Eini. When Ain Shams University started the next year, in 1949, I transferred with the Shubra and Heliopolis students to the new campus. I studied hard, read the books, and was taught by giants in their fields, such as Professor Heinz, who taught anatomy, and Derry, who taught physiology. I played several sports, among which were basketball, football (soccer), tennis, and badminton. But I never excelled in any. I studied classical music and played chess, in which I excelled. I spent most evenings in the school helping others grasp various scientific concepts. In our final year exam, I ranked only fourth among my peers because I was given a passing grade in gynecology and obstetrics after I completed my oral exam, although I obtained the highest score on the written test. I viewed this as evidence of unfair bias, and it caused me a lot of bitterness and grief.

I graduated from Ain Shams University in Cairo in January 1955, at the age of twenty-one, and served as "Rotating Intern" for one year. At its conclusion, the military officer in charge of the university hospital further reduced my grade, making me twentieth in my class. There were only nineteen places for residency at the university hospital. Luckily for me, Laila Zaki Khaled, who ranked first in my class, decided not to pursue a clinical specialty and opted to become "Instructor of Histology" instead. Furthermore, Dr. Ali Eissa, the new head of the Cardiology Department welcomed me as the first resident in his department. The role of my classmates, Drs. Hassan Hosny Yousef and Yusri Robin Ghattas, in ensuring that none of my other classmates applied for the position of resident in cardiology and left it to me can't be underestimated.

During my two years of residency, I obtained a diploma in internal medicine, after which I became "Instructor of Clinical Medicine" and was recognized as a gifted teacher and clinician. My teaching clinical rounds were attended by many students. I applied to further my studies in Britain, as twenty-four other fellows in my class did. After lots of effort, I was granted permission to go abroad for three months to attend the fall postgraduate medical course in Edinburgh. By contrast, the rest of my colleagues were each granted four years of study leave.

In Britain

I trained at the Royal Infirmary (Western General Hospital) in Scotland, where Dr. Logan was starting his work on the intensive cardiac care unit in Edinburgh, and Dr. Gilchrist was injecting digitalis into the heart. I visited Dr. Pantridge in Belfast, Ireland, where he started his work on heart attacks. After obtaining MRCPE (Member of the Royal College of Physicians of Edinburgh) in less than three months, I moved to London at the behest of Dr. Hamdy El-Sayed, who was the registrar in cardiac surgery to Drs. Cleland and Melrose. At Hammersmith Hospital (the postgraduate medical school of London), I was trained by Drs. Goodwin and Hollman in the Cardiology Department and took care of patients born with malformations of the heart, as well as published scientific papers in the field. Also, I attended the weekly conferences of Dr. Paul Wood and other medical conferences in radiology and neurology. It is notable that I was approved to travel to Britain to attend the six-week course in cardiology held in October. In the span of three months, I obtained two doctorate degrees (MRCPE from Edinburgh in December and MRCP London in January); thereby, I became the first Egyptian to accomplish this feat. As expected, I was subsequently elected "Fellow" not just "Member" of both Royal Colleges, which was routine and was based upon conduct and contributions. In return, I received a letter from Dr. Mohammed Attia informing me I would no longer receive my monthly salary from the University until I returned to Egypt, citing that I had completed my studies and there was an urgent need for my services.

I returned to Egypt in April 1960, at the age of twenty-six. Upon return to Ain Shams University, I became "Lecturer in Cardiology." To be further appointed "Assistant Professor of Medicine" at the University should have been a no-brainer. Instead, Dr. Zaki Swaydan, the "Chairman of Medicine" at that time, denied me a position twice and offered those positions to whom I thought to be much inferior outsiders (Drs. Abou-El-Maati Nabih and Yehia Mahran). I complained.

Eventually, I was appointed to the third position. In addition, I practiced medicine and cardiology at my clinic in the heart of Cairo and achieved fame and success. I was married in 1961 to Laila Yousef Estafan, and we had three children (two boys and a girl). I wanted to start the first cardiac intensive care unit in Egypt to replace the fever unit in the Italian Hospital. The administrators of the hospital agreed to my plans. I met for dinner with Dr. Ismail Salam, who was at that time connected to Nasser's government, and I shared my plans with him. He informed me that it was impossible to convince the president to approve the intensive care unit, since it would cost the patients more than he allowed.

I had to convince my wife to leave the country. She was reluctant to move. Not unjustifiably, she reasoned that I would achieve fame and fortune in Egypt. We lived by the Nile and were served by five people. We had it made!

In the United States

It took me ten years to convince my wife to relocate to the United States. I resented the despotism of Nasser, the president of Egypt, and the direction the medical school was taking. I became obsessed with having my children grow up in a free society. Because I was not allowed to travel to the United States, I arranged with Dr. Peter Nixon of Charring

Cross Hospital in London to write me a letter, which I promised never to honor, stating I would fill his role at the hospital for a few months during his summer vacation. I obtained a visa to London. At the same time, my wife applied for immigration to the United States, using her maiden name. She got a visa to the United States from the London Embassy, which was issued sooner than expected, due to the help of friends in Iowa. She and our children were able to join me in October, four months after my arrival in Iowa, in June 1971.

In many ways, I was lucky to come first to the University of Iowa, where I met great people, such as Dr. Lewis January, a prior president of the American Heart Association, and Dr. Ernie Theilen, who was a professor at the time. The chief of cardiology, Dr. Frank Abboud, was previously a classmate of mine. His father lived in Cairo and was one of my patients. I was appointed "Research Fellow" in the section of cardiology at the University of Iowa.

A few months later, I was asked to cover for some of the Iowa professors when they took vacation. I made the clinical rounds in their place. This opened the floodgates for me: I proved my clinical and teaching abilities and mixed with the students. Some students invited me and my wife to several picnics, and we invited several students to our house. Subsequently, when some junior class students were stressed and wanted to kill themselves, the chief of medicine asked me to act as their counselor. I encouraged them and was considered their newfound friend. Also, I became "Fellow of the American Heart Association, Council in Clinical Cardiology." I was very happy in Iowa.

I started in Iowa in July, obtained a basic science degree in September, a license to practice medicine degree in December, and sat for the FACP (Fellow of the American College of Physicians) examination the following June. Usually foreign graduates wait three years before applying, but thanks to Dr. January, I was treated as an exception. The following year, I took the written exam in cardiology, and in 1973, completed the FACC (Fellow of the American College of Cardiology). Also, I was elected fellow of the College of Chest Physicians, in recognition of my research. In addition, I won the Best Teacher Award from the senior class and was nominated for it by the junior class. I also received the 1972–1974 Distinguished Academic Leadership Award by the fellows. Teaching and humanitarian awards have been showered on my career since then. Whatever university I taught in, I won teaching awards.

Later in my career, I was chosen as chairman of a committee to establish a permanent Abboud's Chair in Medicine, in recognition of Dr. Abboud's contributions to the excellence of medicine at the University of Iowa. My wife and I contributed generously to this effort.

My tenure in Oklahoma lasted twenty years. It began in 1974, when I became "Chairman of the Cardiology Department and Professor of Medicine" at the Oklahoma Health Sciences Center. The good will that I had accumulated in three years in Iowa, I was about to squander in three months in Oklahoma. Initially, I was perceived as overconfident, opinionated, hardheaded, and unwilling to listen. Luckily for me, I learned my lesson quickly and started to treat everyone with due respect. I concentrated on improving education and services, and was able to recruit good people.

In 1976, a delegation from Tulsa offered me the position of "Director of Cardiology" at its largest new hospital, with a ten-year contract that guaranteed that I would double my Oklahoma City income, with no ceiling. I accepted the offer. I gave well-attended lectures weekly, was voted "Chairman of Cardiology" at the Tulsa branch of the University of Oklahoma, participated in multi-center research trials, and established a thriving multi-person practice in cardiology. I was voted the most influential physician in the state, founded the nonprofit organization "Growing Healthy in Oklahoma," and made numerous presentations to schools that involved the dissection of the heart. I was given awards by the American College of Chest Physicians and cofounded the American Society of Nuclear Cardiology. In addition, my wife and I established scholarships for medical students in various disciplines at the Oklahoma Health Sciences Center, Oklahoma State University, and the Tulsa University. Also, I was asked to chair a committee to establish a chair for Middle Eastern Studies at the University of Oklahoma, but I moved to Florida before I could fulfill that task.

In 1993, I got tired from my very demanding private practice, especially after I developed some health issues. I completed the Wyeth-Ayerst APM Executive Management Development Program at the Wharton School at the University in Pennsylvania and moved to the University of South Florida as "Professor of Medicine." Soon thereafter, I became chairman of the Cardiology Department there. While in Florida, I taught, saw patients, and participated in research, as expected. Also, I got involved in many other projects. My wife and I established a nonprofit organization named PROJECT GRACE (which stood for Guidelines for Resuscitation and Care at the End-of-life). My activity in end-of-life medical treatment issues became widely known. I gave many lectures on the subject, launched a partnership between the American College of Cardiology and PROJECT GRACE, lectured copiously on the subject, served on the boards of Tampa Bay Hospice and Clearwater Hospice organizations, and published three books on the subject.

My involvement with the American College of Cardiology became widely recognized. In addition, I served on the University Medical Services board, which oversaw the financial issues of medical practice of University of South Florida physicians. Also, I served in many capacities and chaired several task forces at Tampa General Hospital. I participated in the Bay Area Ethics Council and chaired the Ethics Committee at Morton Plant Hospital in Clearwater. My wife and I were among the million dollar donors to Ruth Eckert Music Hall to educate underprivileged youth how to play classical music, so they could become good team players, acquire leadership skills, and excel. Subsequently, I joined the practice of wonderful colleagues at Clearwater Cardiovascular Consultants at the start of 2000. I enjoyed seeing patients and continued my nonprofit projects.

In 2002, I suffered a severe bout of multiple sclerosis that sent me to the Mayo Clinic in Rochester, Minnesota. I underwent seven brain biopsies before they confirmed the diagnosis. I became unable to walk and I saw double. My personality changed, and I became angry at the slightest provocation. I had to retire and wrote to my patients (whom I loved dearly) that I couldn't take care of them anymore. With perseverance, determination, and lots of physical therapy, as well as encouragement, I was able to walk again. After several months, I achieved a substantial recovery and wanted to resume my work. But I was never the same again.

In 2005, my son in California asked me to move there to help in the care of our newborn granddaughter. I joined the faculty of the University of California San Francisco as Clinical Professor of Medicine and taught as a volunteer professor.

During my long service in academic medicine and private practice settings, I gave hundreds (possibly thousands) of lectures in cardiology and medical ethics to several societies, continued to receive service awards (nineteen major ones), and served on several boards of the American College of Cardiology and its ethics and geriatrics committees. I participated in the Bethesda Conference about end-of-life medical treatment challenges, chaired a conference on the subject matter for the American College of Geriatric Cardiology, and was active in American College of Cardiology national and international societies. I published more than 140 scientific peer-reviewed papers in many distinguished medical journals, was a section editor of medical ethics for the *Journal of Geriatric Cardiology*, and a member of the editorial board of many US medical journals. I authored three books: *Cardiology for the Primary Care Physician, Graceful Exit*, and *Life and Death on Your Own Terms*, as well as numerous medical textbook chapters on end-of-life medical care and ethics. Chief among the latter are: *Braunwald Textbook of Cardiology*, two textbooks on geriatric cardiology (one by Dr. Michel Rich), two books on current diagnosis, two books on current therapy, and a nursing textbook edited by Lin Weeks.

In My Retirement

I'm trying to stay somewhat active in my retirement. I continue to be connected to the American College of Cardiology, albeit not as much as before. I was invited by Dr. Brian Olshansky to write a chapter on medical ethics for electrophysiologists and the use of implantable devices, which was published by the Self-Assessment Program of the American College of Cardiology in 2019. As before, my interests have been varied and ever-changing. I gave lectures on global warming, gene editing, Egyptian antiquities, and the world rankings of the United States. I also continued to be active in lecturing about end-of-life medical issues. I was invited to give the keynote address to the master's degree graduating class of 2019 at St. Antonius and St. Cyril Theological School, held at the Nixon Library in Los Angeles, California.

Recent Relationship with Egypt

When I left Egypt, I thought my relationship with my native country was over. In 1974, however, I received an invitation from President Sadat to attend a conference in Cairo with other Egyptian American scholars and to meet with him in El-Kanater, where he announced his decision to improve Egypt's relationship with the United States, distance Egypt from Russia, and improve Egypt's relationship with Israel. Jeehan Sadat shared her autographed photograph with my wife Laila. During that visit, I noticed that many aspects of Egyptian life had deteriorated immensely. I remained skeptical about the future of Egypt.

In the late 1980s, I was invited to give lectures in various cities in Egypt and other Middle Eastern cities (e.g., Riad, Dammam, and Gidda), and to participate in Middle Eastern cardiology conferences. I performed heart catheterizations, and made demonstrations at Ain Shams University, and was invited to give lectures at Azhar Medical School and at Embaba Heart Center.

I was especially touched when I visited Dr. Ali Eissa while he was undergoing renal dialysis in Abbassia. While I was holding his hand, he said, "Do you see what is happening to me?" He went on to say, "My wife is dying of cancer and my only son, Khaled, was killed in Spain. Why don't you return to Cairo and take my practice and live in my apartment, which we will vacate soon, and which is by the River Nile?"

Fighting my tears, I said I had gotten used to life in the United States, but would consider this generous offer. He was a great man, as well as being my first cardiology mentor. I have rarely met people with such selflessness and generosity of spirit. This encounter will live forever in my memory.

After moving to California, I revived my connections and love for Egypt. I became very interested in it and continued to read avidly about Egypt's history and politics. Also, I befriended many wonderful diplomats who visited or lived and worked in our area. Fueled by my closeness to some influential Egyptians, I became devoted to aiding the plight of minorities in the Middle East and have been in contact with religious leaders, heads of parties, and ministers in Egypt. My only political book is *Let There Be Spring: Trump is Not the Future of Egypt*. The book won the third prize for books on politics and public policies. Still, I believe in my core that only Egyptians will be able to write the new chapter of Egypt's revival. The United States can help only if needed.

My Relationship with Religious Leaders

My relationship with religious leaders deserves special mention. I have been active in the Coptic Church since a young age. I was a Sunday school teacher, then a physician to His Holiness Pope Kyrillos and Pope Shenouda, and many bishops and clergy. I was given a special medallion of recognition by Pope Kyrillos when he had a heart attack in 1970. Also, I was blessed that H. H. Pope Shenouda, accompanied by fourteen bishops and priests, stayed in my house in Tulsa during the Pope's first visit to the United States in 1977. I visited with him several times after that, in various places in Ohio, Florida, and California. I served on the board of trustees of the Coptic Cultural Center in Cairo. The board was committed to building a state-of-the-art building to house the history of Coptic dialects, artifacts from the monasteries, treatises about different Popes, children's books and games about religion, and dresses of the Orthodox monks. It would hold meetings and seminars on orthodox faith and comprised a cafeteria, gift shop, and recreational and meeting facilities.

Recently, I became close to Pope Tawadros and met with him several times in Egypt and the United States. I visited him and the Grand

Imam, as well as several ministers and heads of political parties in Egypt. I served on the board of deacons of several Coptic churches in Tampa and Clearwater, Florida, and in Hayward, California, and was involved in its ancillary and educational programs. In Hayward, my family and I helped in completing the Coptic Youth Center. My wife and I decided to honor the memory of my father by contributing generously to this project. This 16,400-foot landmark was built to further a healthy lifestyle and the pursuit of knowledge in a virtuous environment by Coptic youth, and to help assimilate Coptic newcomers in American society. This elegant building became a Hayward landmark.

I served on the board of directors of the American Jewish Committee's San Francisco chapter, and on the AJC's Leadership Council for two years. My philosophy has always been that equality and justice have to become the mantra and guiding principle for every recognized religion. I always held that religions should bring us closer to our God and to make us better persons, and not be used to justify our hate of others since all of us have equal intrinsic human worth. I wrote a book and tens of articles on the subject. My writings were disseminated throughout the United States, Canada, Europe, and Egypt. They were mailed to senior officials as well as the public at large. I believe that cooperation between Egypt and its neighbors, including Israel, will help to promote peace and deliver tranquility and much-needed progress to the area. My wife and I continue to care about the poor, the needy, the newcomers, the youth, and those in need of aid to learn. We should never differentiate between people based upon religion, gender, and skin color, country of origin, sexual orientation, family name, or method of upbringing.

Was It All Worth It?

We make our decisions in life based upon the imperatives of the time, not knowing what the future holds, and hope for the best. To quote Shakespeare, in *Julius Cesar*, "There is a tide in the affairs of men, which taken to the flood, leads on to fortune; omitted all the voyage of their life is bound in shallows and in miseries." After a long journey on

Earth, one looks into the rearview mirror and asks the question "Was it all worth it?" Yes, one can't edit one's past as an author can, but the question begs for an answer. Overall, was the journey on this planet worthwhile?

I have few worries and I am content with what I achieved. God provided light to guide my decisions, which were more correct than not. My wife and partner, while being an ophthalmologist, walked by my side for sixty years, cared for us, and was our chief comforter and my advisor. My three children are thriving. Victor, my oldest son, was respectively co-president then president-founder of European mergers and acquisition firms. He is well-known—was invited to the Queen's palace—and has three successful sons. Steven, my second son, has been the CEO of three successive companies, was among a small select group called upon to meet with the president of the United States in the White House, and has three wonderful young daughters. Mona, my daughter, lives with her dogs in Reno Nevada; she obtained her PhD in social work from the University of Pennsylvania.

The one thing I regret more than anything else is that I didn't spend more time with my kids when they were growing up. But this problem would have been worse had I stayed in Egypt. I was wired to work and compete since childhood. Luckily for our family, my wife gave priority to the well-being of me and our children. Overall, I am very content with my life's journey. Contentment is to like what you have, not to have what you like.

Conclusion

To tell my story is not to recite my accomplishments only. I had my share of failures that I regret, and I wish I could have done a better job to quell them. Initially, I was not a good team player and had a chip on my shoulder. I learned the hard way that others deserve to be complimented and acknowledged for their contributions. After all, a leader is only good because of the unique contributions by others on the team. Also, I learned that silence has many voices; it doesn't help to beat one's chest. Let others see your good deeds and judge you.

I learned also that the new generation will be much better than us. They need from us the mentoring and encouragement to excel.

It is fitting to conclude by reciting the prayer I delivered in the one-year commemoration of the massacre at the Pittsburg Tree of Life Synagogue:

"Dear Lord, Heavenly Father, as we commemorate this heinous act of ending the lives of innocent worshippers in Pittsburg Synagogue, while praising your name, we are reminded that all of us are brothers and sisters representing Your handiwork and are commanded to love and cherish each other as equals. When asked "Who is Your friend?", You chose the Good Samaritan—someone with a different religion from yours, who harbored love, caring, and compassion in his heart, which he dispensed generously for a fellow human in need without expecting a return. Each passing day, numerous good deeds and numberless acts of kindness are done in Your name by some of us. On the other hand, Jews, Christians, and Muslims, as well as others, are slaughtered throughout the world because of their beliefs, gender, color of their skin, sexual orientation, or ethnic heritage. Let us remember that we belong to the same species and that a multicolor tapestry of humankind woven in unity is much more beautiful than a pale one composed of one color and defined by uniformity or unanimity. May Your love for us guide our actions. Amen!"

———◆———

LOFTY BASTA MD, FRCP, FACC is a physician, a family man, a gifted leader, teacher, clinician, scientist, ethicist and philanthropist. Over the last three decades, he renewed his love for Egypt, its history and potential.

NAVIGATING LIFE
BETWEEN THREE CONTINENTS
Samia I. Spencer

Writing about one's life raises many questions and requires immersion in the past, but where does that past begin, and what should be included or left out of it? As one ages, it seems that the early years become more and more important, at least for this writer—a little girl born and raised in cosmopolitan Alexandria, to parents whose families were deeply rooted in Upper Egypt, who finds herself later in life navigating between three continents while touring the world. Clearly, all cannot be told in a few pages, a selection must be made. I will focus mostly on the early part and the later years. This will make it possible to measure the distance traveled between the two ends, including serendipitous goals achieved and dreams unfulfilled.

The peace, quiet, and stability of my childhood and adolescence are probably the reasons for the strength and fortitude that allowed me to weather the storms of adulthood and welcome the serenity of the twilight. To this end, I give my parents credit for securing the early sound conditions, and for instilling in me the values that have guided me all along. My father, Dr. Samuel Iskander, was born in 1907, in Sanabo, a small village near Assiut; he had only an older half-brother. When he was at a very young age, his family moved to Alexandria, where he was educated in an American mission school and an Egyptian school, before going to Cairo University for medical studies—the only

Egyptian institution of higher education at that time. After completing the required government service in a small town in Upper Egypt, he opened his private practice in Alexandria in a popular neighborhood near the main train station, not far from where his parents lived. My father was my idol. As a family man, he was loving, caring, and affectionate. Socially, he enjoyed people, was a bon vivant, and had a good sense of humor. As a doctor, he was passionate about his profession and treated his patients like friends, regardless of their social standing or educational backgrounds.

On my mother's side, the family was much larger. She was the sixth of a brood of eight, whose fifteen descendants are spread across Germany, Canada, and especially the United States. Solange Khalil was born in Alexandria into a family of landowners originally from Minia. Her father, a cotton trader, endured serious economic consequences following the 1929 stock market crash. She spent time in Cairo with her grandmother, who lived to be over ninety, smoking like a chimney and never losing a tooth. Mother did not tell us in what year she was born. At one point, she and her three older sisters had to appear before a medical examiner, who would estimate their age and issue new birth certificates to replace lost ones. Ironically, after taking a good look at the four women, he determined that Mother, the youngest, was the oldest! Speaking of age, my maternal grandmother was married at thirteen and saw her husband for the first time on their wedding day. There was a fourteen-year difference between her and her oldest son, born in 1907, which was the same as the difference between him and his youngest brother. By calculating that the children were roughly two years apart, we figured that Mother, the sixth, was probably born around 1918.

She went to Girard, a renowned French Catholic school, never telling us for how long. She liked to speak of the fun she had with her brothers and sisters and their friends, at the frequent balls and dances of the famed Hotel San Stefano—the charming predecessor of the current unsightly mammoth. In the first half of the twentieth century, Alexandria was Egypt's most cosmopolitan city and one of the world's most attractive international hubs. However, after the

1952 Revolution—especially after the 1956 Suez Canal crisis and the war initiated by England, France, and Israel—mounting nationalism followed. Many among its cosmopolitan population left the country; Alexandria started to lose its charm and beauty and its very special quality of life. These distinctions, however, have not totally vanished, as they remain forever etched in the memories of those who, like myself, were privileged to have grown up in that era, or to have caught part of it. To the best of my knowledge, Alexandria is the only city in the world to have inspired the creation of an international organization that seeks to preserve its history and memory, the *Amicale Alexandrie Hier Aujourd'hui* (AAHA). Its members and friends meet regularly in different parts of the globe to maintain their links, to honor and celebrate their beloved city, and to keep its spirit alive.

As a child, I often accompanied my parents in the afternoon to the fashionable tea room, Baudrot. Afterward, Father would go to his clinic, while Mother and I would window-shop on the nearby elegant Sherif Street, before taking a *hantour* (horse-drawn carriage) to join him at the clinic. In his office, as we watched patients go in and out of the examination room, we became acquainted with them and witnessed the amiable and humorous way Father treated them. This was a one-doctor practice with two assistants, one male and one female, neither formally trained; the Faculty of Nursing at Alexandria University having been founded many years later. Appointments at my father's clinic were not necessary; patients were examined on a first-come first-served basis, unless they were family friends (or had been referred by friends) who had made prior arrangements. Money was no object, and patients unable to pay for the very modest office visit were not charged. Friends were never charged. Surgeries were performed at the end of the evening, and patients recovered for a couple of days in one of two rooms prepared to care for them. Life was simple, and so was medicine. Medical insurance and malpractice suits were nonexistent concepts for either doctors or patients.

This routine was well established, and as a child, I thought it would go on forever, but nothing ever does. The special places I recall are gone, as well as the humane medicine my father practiced. Many a night, a phone call from a desperate family would wake us all up; Father would get ready in a flash and hop into his car to go save the patient. There was no such thing as a free weekend, because even on Sunday, his only day off, he made house calls. Father's reputation as one of Alexandria's most popular, most cherished, and most renowned doctors lasted for many years beyond his passing in 1987, at age seventy-nine.

For several years, I walked to my nearby French school, the *Immaculée Conception*, a private institution run by Armenian Catholic nuns. Nothing major stands out in my mind during the routine of those peaceful years. The classes were small, and the students got along. We wore navy uniforms in the winter, off-white in the summer. The routine of summer vacations was also uneventful. We spent mornings at the beach cabin in Glymenopoulo, where we swam with friends, returned home for lunch, then went back to the beach in the afternoon. In later years, two or three evenings per week, we would walk with our neighbor friends to the nearby cinema San Stefano, an open-air theater, to see at least two of the three movies shown nightly. Sometimes we begged our parents to let us attend the third and last feature, but permission was rarely granted, as it would mean returning home after midnight. Curfews were a matter of principle, not caused by fear of crime or violence, which were never reasons for concern.

The Lycée Français, which became Lycée la Liberté following the 1956 war, is where I went to high school. Classes were larger, mixed gender, and multicultural. We were a naughty bunch who liked to play tricks on our instructors, especially the philosophy teacher, Monsieur Boussoulas. Our classroom was located on the ground floor; every so often, we paid a street-organ player to perform right by our window during that class. Monsieur Boussoulas got terribly irritated, as the music and our laughter disrupted his deeply entrenched train of thought. In the French Department of Alexandria University, a clique of seven girls, all graduates of French private schools, formed a lifelong relationship. Upon receiving BA degrees, our lives took us in different directions and different countries, but our friendship has remained as strong over the years as it was back then.

My dream for the future was to work in an international organization, where I would have the opportunity to satisfy my curiosity to travel and see the world. For a couple of years following graduation, I was employed in some interesting settings in Alexandria: the English Teaching Program of the American Cultural Center (a branch of the US Information Agency), which was burned by demonstrators at the dawn of the Six-Day War; a short-term project of the Food and Agriculture Organization (the predecessor of the World Food Program), and the regional office of the World Health Organization. Then, graduate studies took me to the University of Illinois, which had one of the largest and most reputable French programs in the United States at that time. However, the Midwest was no Hollywood, and the living conditions were not exactly what I had imagined. The environment was not particularly attractive, the weather was nasty compared with Egypt's mild Mediterranean climate, and confinement in a dorm room was a drastic change from the spaciousness of our multi-level villa in Zizinia. Life as a graduate student was a far cry from what I had experienced during my earlier years in multinational and multicultural circles, with privileged memberships at exclusive social clubs. In the late 1960s, however, the United States offered opportunities for a brighter future, in contrast with the oppressive Nasser regime that had deprived citizens of basic rights and freedoms, and left them with grim expectations and possibilities.

It was my hope that my PhD would reconnect me with the vibrant city life I so sorely missed. Unfortunately, that was not to be. Instead, in 1972, I headed for an even smaller town than Champaign-Urbana, in the ill-famed state of Alabama, where I did not wish to settle. However, a tenure-track position at Auburn University (AU) was not to be turned down at a time when university jobs were hard to find. Although an academic career was not my initial goal in life, I learned to adapt and make the best of it. Teaching and research became a fulfilling profession that I enjoyed for over forty years, and one that brought me unexpected recognition and rewards.

The cultural shock of going from the Midwest to the Deep South was greater than that of moving from Egypt to the United States. The first few years in the Heart of Dixie were undoubtedly the worst of my life. Personally, socially, and culturally, I did not belong. I felt removed from everything and everyone who mattered to me. The 1960s had come and gone, without changing much in a society entrenched in bygone traditions and a pre-Civil War mentality, whose conservative values were opposite my own liberal principles. My values were rooted in the French Enlightenment, which I had selected as a topic for my doctoral dissertation.

However, academic life provided advantages that compensated somewhat for the wanting quality of life in a small Southern town, with its absence of cultural activities, its limited vision and perspective, and its lack of interest in the rest of the world. Fortunately, I arrived at AU at a time when the institution was seeking to develop and grow. It was rewarding to participate in building the French program and expanding its scope by creating a variety of courses, organizing summer abroad programs and internships, and inviting distinguished speakers to inspire students and broaden their horizons. Many among them took advantage of the new opportunities and scholarships, and went on to achieve success in various professional fields. Some maintained their relationship with me beyond graduation; they became personal friends whom I invited to campus to share their experiences with their younger cohorts, and to serve as role models for them.

Summer vacations allowed me to get out of the "wasteland," travel, and recharge my batteries by returning to Egypt while our sons, Sam and Mark, were still young. In Alexandria, they made friends, with whom they learned to speak Arabic, and took Arabic lessons that enabled them to read street signs in order to go out by themselves, use public transportation, and find their way around town. At home, they mingled with my parents and their guests, became comfortable in the company of adults, participated in serious and not-so-serious conversations, and mastered the art of telling Egyptian jokes. They also accompanied me to France when I led student groups or worked on research projects, but their French was not as good as their Arabic, because we usually spent more time in Egypt.

Research provided opportunities for intellectual growth, and professional conferences were a welcome chance to meet and exchange ideas with friends and colleagues, while traveling to various parts of the country and the world. Thanks to generous funding from sources within and outside AU, I was able to share my work nationally and internationally, and above all, in the classroom with students. My own curiosity and upbringing in multicultural Alexandria colored my approach to teaching and research, as I sought to expand my academic interests beyond the doctoral program. Serendipitous events led me to focus on feminist scholarship, political women in France and Canada, and contemporary social and cultural issues in both countries. Through these new fields of research, I came into contact with a broad range of leaders in politics and diplomacy who inspired me, some eventually becoming close friends, thus adding personal fulfillment to professional achievements. While research and writing started out as an academic obligation, they soon turned into an inspiring activity and a real passion.

As our children grew older and were busy with lives of their own, as my parents and many in their generation passed on, as summer reunions with friends in Alexandria became less frequent, and as life in Egypt became more difficult and more complicated, the urge for regular visits to the homeland became less keen, although love of country remained unwavering. Meanwhile, I spent more time in Paris and Montreal during the summer and academic breaks—to collect research materials, update my knowledge, stay abreast of the latest developments, and meet with friends and colleagues, old and new. With time, it made sense to set roots in those cities, instead of being confined to hotel rooms or rentals. After I had established second residences in France and Quebec and was able to spend more time away from Alabama, life in the Deep South became more tolerable, even more satisfying.

Actually, the most exhilarating and exciting part of my personal and professional life occurred after retirement. Ironically, it was the result of the anger and frustration I felt while watching coverage of the ill-named Arab Spring, and the popular uprising in Egypt. Following Sadat's 1977 historic visit to Israel, Egypt was rarely present in the North American media. However, beginning in 2011, journalists and TV reporters were anchored in Tahrir Square, among crowds of demonstrators, providing information 24/7. As a scholar of women's studies, I was struck by the portrayal of Egyptian women. Ill-informed commentators described them in negative terms as illiterate and uneducated; victims of violence, rape, and police brutality; deprived of freedom; and controlled by men. The biased depiction and condescending remarks of so-called experts troubled and irritated me. I felt like the late Jack G. Shaheen, a brilliant Lebanese American author who published extensively on the portrayal of Arabs in American movies and TV programs. He wrote: "For years, I watched hordes of TV Arabs parade across the screen. It was a disturbing experience, similar to walking into those mirrored rooms at amusement parks, where all you see are distorted images of yourself" (*The TV Arab*, 1984, p. 4).

Looking around me, I saw a different group of Egyptian women, unlike those portrayed in the media. I saw brilliant and successful leaders in just about every professional field: academe, medicine, engineering, banking, finance, diplomacy, sports, international relations, and development, to mention a few. I wondered why the media disregarded them and concentrated exclusively on part of the Egyptian population that perpetuates arrogant attitudes, outdated stereotypes, and obsolete Orientalist clichés. I could not begin to understand their motives, whether intentional or unintentional, nor did I attempt to analyze them. I figured that delving into these issues was the business of social scientists and media experts.

For my part, I decided that instead of letting my resentment and bitterness prevail, I would turn the negative feelings into positive action. I could take a small step to counter the cynical reports and to remedy the grave omission by creating a richer, more accurate portrayal of the people and the country I know and love. I would highlight, in writing, the profiles of a sample of Egyptian pioneers and groundbreakers, who would narrate their own stories and explain how they had enhanced the quality of life in the societies in which they live and work. When I discussed the idea with some close friends, not only were their responses enthusiastic, they were overwhelming. It was also my purpose to let people know about the national and international recognition of these remarkable achievers, which is rarely reported beyond their immediate environments. Thus was conceived: *Daughters of the Nile: Egyptian Women Changing Their World* (Cambridge Scholars Publishing, 2016). Gradually, and with assistance from many friends, we identified a group of thirty-eight successful professionals, ranging in age from twenty-eight years old to ninety-two, from diverse family backgrounds, born and raised in big cities or small towns, who had grown up in Egypt or elsewhere, and were currently living and working in six countries on three continents. While nearly half now reside in Egypt, the others have made their careers mostly in Europe and North America.

Although the focus of the book was Egyptian women, Egyptian men also came out as winners, breaking the stereotype of the sexist chauvinist Middle Eastern man. Many authors gave credit to their supporting and loving fathers or husbands, for inspiring and encouraging them, and for standing by them on the way to achieve their dreams. In some cases, the exceptional attitudes of these Egyptian men wer far more enlightened and more progressive than those of most males in the East and the West.

None of the women engaged in the book project for personal or monetary gains. All royalties and profits from book sales were donated to two Cairo charities founded by book authors. One half went to an NGO founded by pediatrician Hanna Aboulghar, *"Banati,"* which cares for girls in street situations. The other half was gifted to an NGO founded by the late social scientist Marie Assaad, The Association for the Protection of the Environment, which seeks to improve the quality of life for the garbage collectors and sorters, known as *zabbalee*n. The authors donated their time and effort out of love for their country and their belief in the importance of the book's message. Their only satis-faction was to see their work in print. However, surprises followed, adding bliss and tremendous gratification to the impact the enterprise had on our lives.

As soon as the book was published, the authors were invited to launch the book in a number of venues around the world: in Ottawa, at the residence of the Ambassador of Egypt to Canada; in Paris, at the Egyptian Cultural Center; in Alexandria, at the Bibliotheca Alexandrina; in Cairo, at the residence of the US Deputy Country Manager; in New York, at the Permanent Mission of Egypt to the United Nations; in London, at the Embassy of Egypt and the Egyptian Cultural Center; at Auburn University; in Washington, D.C., at the annual meeting of the Fulbright Commission; in Switzerland, at the University of Geneva; in Los Angeles, at the residence of the Egyptian Consul General; at the University of California Santa Barbara; and in Morocco, at Al Akhawayn University in Ifrane, at Sidi Mohamed Ibn Abdallah University in Fez, and at the National Library in Rabat, hosted by the Embassy of Egypt.

Organizing, coordinating, and participating in these panels was extremely time consuming, with each event requiring the exchange of hundreds of emails and phone calls among the panelists and the hosting institutions, and the drafting of extensive documentation. In the end, however, it proved to be well worth the trouble. As the panelists traveled together, we became a special family that enjoyed spending time touring and exploring different cities, meeting interest-ing people, engaging in stimulating discussions with our audiences, and relishing the comments about the new images of Egyptian women and their successes. The bonds that formed between us are now deep and indefeasible, and our quality of life is immensely enriched. Even though many of us have spent years away from Egypt, we discovered that deep inside, beside our newly acquired second citizenships, we remain, above all, Egyptians at heart.

For my part, as a result of this experience, I am henceforth using my scholarly expertise to focus on the history of Egypt in the first half of the twentieth century, especially the women's movement—a period I call the "Egyptian Enlightenment." The icing on the cake was that during one of our presentations, we met Sandro Manzoni, a former Alexandrian, who created a charitable organization: *Association Solidarité Égypte*. He more than doubled the amount of royalties donated to *"Banati"* and The Association for the Protection of the Environment, and has continued to support them. This shows that a good deed never goes unrewarded: someone up there is looking after Egypt and its people!

———•———

SAMIA ISKANDER SPENCER had a brief career serving in various UN organizations in her native Alexandria and in New York City. She earned her PhD from the University of Illinois and spent most of her professional life as Professor of French at Auburn University in Alabama, where she was recognized with many honors. Her multidisciplinary publications have focused on the French Enlightenment, and women and politics in France and Canada. Recently, she has turned her attention to Egyptian feminism and the Egyptian Enlightenment (1850-1950).

HOW I CAME TO MANAGE BILLIONS
Sharif Abou-Sabh

I was born in Cairo, Egypt, on July 24, 1954, to Awatef Metwally and Abdul Khalek Abou-Sabh, their first born. However, my father insisted on registering my birth on July 23 because that guaranteed my birthday would be a day off for me, as that was the day we remember the Revolution of 1952, which is a national holiday.

My father was a colonel in the Egyptian Army and a free army officer. He was one of the officers who staged the coup d'état against King Farouk, and he fought with Nasser in the 1948 war at Flugga.

My mother was a homemaker par excellence, and the daughter of Abdel Hamid Metwally, a lawyer turned judge and the head of the Egyptian appellate court. Her mother was the daughter of Sheikh Taha Habib, who was Sheikh Al Azhar. The deputy prime minister during the Sadat regime, Anwar Habib, was also from the Habib family. Anwar Habib prosecuted Anwar Sadat when he was charged with the murder of Amin Osman during the Farouk regime, but rather than prosecuting him, he ended up defending him.

I never met my grandfather or grandmother on my father's side, as they both passed away before my birth. What I know about them is from stories that were told to me by my father, my uncle, and their contemporaries. They were vast landowners in the Garbieh governorate.

My sister Hayam was born in 1955, and my brother Ahmed in

1959. I was blessed with a warm and loving home and extended family environment throughout my childhood. I started kindergarten at the age of four at the English mission school in Heliopolis, where I stayed until 1962. The school was very rigorous on academics.

We lived a mile away from my school, and a mile away from the Heliopolis sporting club, to which my family belonged. I played water polo for fifteen years at this club. We won just about every league and tournament competition in Egypt, as well as at international events.

My grandfather on my mother's side was a stern and serious man.. My grandmother, Inayat Habib, however, was very warm and loving. They had seven children, and all of them came to our house every Friday for dinner, as well as on every holiday.

In 1961, my father was promoted to general in the Egyptian Army. He was sent as a diplomat to West Germany from 1962 to 1968. We all relocated to Germany with him, and I grew up with my sister and brother in the city of Cologne. We all went to a British school in a British army camp in Cologne. Every summer, we drove to Venice, Italy, and took a ship to Alexandria, by way of Greece, for a couple of days. A plethora of relatives would be waiting at the harbor to meet us. We spent the summer in Egypt and headed back to Germany to go to school in the winter.

Throughout my school years in Germany, we used the English mission school's syllabus and took the end-of-year exam in the Egyptian consulate in order to maintain our Egyptian school credentials. Our years in Germany were great because we learned another language and traveled to Holland, Belgium, Switzerland, Italy, France, Austria, and many other countries many times. This had a profound effect on me, as I learned what other cultures are about and that, at the end of the day, friendships are what matter, and that religions are about compassion.

We came back from Germany to Egypt in 1968 after the six-day war, when my father retired from the Egyptian army. He went through great anguish because he was only fifty-six years old—too young to retire.

My mother who was not only the best homemaker and chef, and most elegant person in the world, but she was also the financial planner of our family. She saved enough money while we were in Germany to build a villa in the Dokki neighborhood, right across the street from the Nadi Al Seed Hunting Club. My parents hired an architect to design the villa, under the direct supervision of my parents. They became the project managers and hired the contractor who built the villa. It was the most similar to a Frank Lloyd Wright design that you would ever encounter in Cairo.

I graduated from high school in 1972 and enrolled in Ain Shams University's Civil Engineering Department. During that time, I did nothing but study and play water polo every day, and what a joy that was. In 1976, I spent the summer in New York City as an intern at a structural engineering firm by the name of Le Messieurs Associates. I worked on several design projects, including the headquarters of CitiBank on Lexington Avenue and 54th Street, which was called CitiCorp Center, and which further defined the skyline of New York City.

After I graduated in 1977, I worked for the dean of the Engineering School, Dr. Al Hashmi, for a few months, designing shell structures over water treatment plants. My father had contacts in Kuwait and got me an assignment with a construction company as a site engineer on a fossil power plant construction. I hated Kuwait and its distorted culture and weather. I spent a year there, and then my father's cousin, Dr. Hussein Shahine, got me a job with a consulting engineering firm by the name of Parsons Brown, in Bristol, England. I designed a helicopter manufacturing plant, to be built in Helwan, Egypt. That was the beginning of my forty-five-year career, which I have enjoyed every day since.

I lived in Bristol for a year and a half, working on the helicopter manufacturing plant design and spending every weekend in London. I was then posted to Cairo, with the British engineering team, as a resident engineer during construction of the plant by two British contractors: Laing Construction and Cementation Construction. Laing hired Modern Contractors, which was owned by Abdel Hakim Abdel Nasser, who was Gamal Abdel Nasser's son.

In 1980, I applied to Columbia University in New York City for a master's of engineering degree and was accepted. I scored very high grades in the program: nine As and one C. That C was in the subject of finite element analysis, which was taught by a Japanese professor by the name of Shinuzuka, and I could not understand what he said. Luckily, my English mission school colleague Fikry Botros was doing his PhD at Columbia and helped me enough to pass the course.

When I graduated, I met two people who had great impact on my life at both a personal and a professional level: Dr. Mahmoud Agha and Hassan Mansour. Both were architects. Mahmoud was responsible for me staying in the United States, for me getting residency, and later, for me getting citizenship. Hassan Mansour adopted me as his younger brother. He was a pilot of small aircraft and flew us to different destinations almost every Saturday. What a lucky guy I was.

My first job was with a firm called Amman and Whitney, a long-span bridge design firm that was known all over the United States for designing and building the Verrazano Bridge, the George Washington Bridge, and hundreds more. The Verrazano Bridge was the longest span bridge in the world in 1981. My first project was designing the roof on the Transworld Airlines hangar at John F. Kennedy Airport in New York City.

In 1983, Dr. Hussein Shahine introduced me to a Saudi Arabian engineer who wanted to establish an office in New York City to design all the hospitals for which RBS&D Architects had contracts in Saudi Arabia. He wanted me to be his partner. This gave me the opportunity to work with Dr. Mahmoud Agha, who was the top architect at RBS&D and who later became a partner in the firm with Dr. Shahine. I ran the International Consultants Services Center (ICSC) for three years. We had over thirty-five engineers on our payroll and grew the business substantially.

In 1984, I met the love of my life: Linda Margret Casey. She was born in Dublin, Ireland, and grew up and was educated in England. She became my wife in 1986, and we are still going strong in our thirty-third year of marriage. We had two weddings: one in England and one in Agami, Alexandria. Also that year, I started a new career as a transit railroad project manager for the New York City Transit Authority (NYCTA), which has remained my specialty ever since. I learned the fundamentals of program management in the best sense ever.

So, what does a program manager do? A program manager actively manages the politics surrounding the program, because company politics are a natural part of any organization. Clients come with a variety of expectations, demands, personal goals, agendas, and priorities, all of which can conflict with one another. The program manager must rationalize and resolve these competing requirements by striking an appropriate balance between stakeholders' expectations and the realities of the program. In addition, the program manager must put into place a support team, together with the client, in these functional areas: program controls, project development, program support, design, and construction management. The program manager is also responsible for ensuring that the program is seamlessly integrated into the client's facility, and for making sure that all policies and procedures are observed to execute major multi-billion dollar infrastructure projects and programs. This includes (1) improving processes and promoting efficiencies; (2) planning, developing, and managing projects and their scope; (3) approach to and reporting of budget and fiduciary responsibilities; (4) approach to and reporting of schedules; and (5) training and mentoring.

Also in 1986, Linda and I bought an apartment on Central Park West in New York City, and a house in East Hampton on Long Island. We were the quintessential yuppy (young upcoming professionals) couple. Linda had one of the most successful catering businesses in Manhattan and I was running ICSC and then working at NYCTA. We had a blast traveling all over and enjoying Manhattan restaurants.

In 1988, we were blessed with the birth of our first son, Adam, and in 1991, we were blessed with the birth of our second son, Samy. Both have grown up to be fine men with incredible competitive spirits, both in sports (ice hockey) and life. Adam recently won an Emmy for his motion picture graphics, and Samy signed his first album record deal. Adam lives in New York, and Samy in Chicago.

In 1993, we bought a house in the town of Wilton, Connecticut, where our boys could attend good schools. I started the dreadful commute every day to New York City to support my family, and Linda stopped working so she could raise our two fine young gentlemen. It was the best decision we ever made, because it is reflected the values with which we had been raised. No regrets.

In 1999, I left NYCTA and joined the firm of O'Brien Kreitzberg as the project manager for the reconstruction of Penn Station, the second-largest station on the East Coast. It is a multi-modal station for several modes of train transportation and also the Staten Island ferry terminal. In late 2000, I won a program management contract to rebuild the Chicago Transit Authority (CTA), which was valued at $2.5 billion at that time. We moved to a suburb of Chicago called Naperville, where we lived for thirteen years. The boys got their schooling there—all the way to high school, and then university. Adam went to Loyola University and Samy to DePaul University. Adam did his master's at Parsons School of Design, and Samy did his at Columbia.

From 2000 to 2004, I was the vice president of my own company and program manager for my client, CTA. I was responsible for the planning and implementation of a $2.5 billion capital construction program, and for managing a staff of 120 professionals. I also developed and managed procedures and methods to plan, design, construct, monitor, evaluate, and document capital construction activity. I ensured that projects were implemented on a timely basis, consistent with established budgets and in conformance with CTA, state, and federal funding agency regulations and requirements. I also designed and implemented process efficiencies to streamline internal procedures and time ines related to construction procurement and project progress.

In 2004, I joined HNTB Corporation, a design firm with four thousand engineers, as a senior vice president. I became a partner in the firm two years later. As program manager for the Illinois State Toll Highway Authority, I was responsible for supporting the Tollway Engineering Department in the planning and implementation of the $6.3 billion Congestion Relief Plan. In 2009, I won a contract as program manager for the $3 billion CREATE program, a public-private partnership to invest in critically needed rail infrastructure improvements in the Chicago area, and to increase the efficiency of freight and passenger rail service throughout the region.

In 2017, we moved to California so I could be the program manager for the HNTB+PB joint venture for the Bay Area Rapid Transit (BART) Silicon Valley project to complete a sixteen-mile extension that consists of a five-mile fifty-five-foot diameter bored tunnel through downtown San Jose, with three underground stations, as well as a yard, shops, and an at-grade station in Santa Clara. BART's Diridon station will be the Grand Central Station of the West.

It has been quite a journey.

———•———

SHARIF ABOU-SABH is an experienced program and construction manager for complex, large-scale transit and transportation infrastructure projects, capital improvement programs, and commercial projects. In his 40 years of diverse engineering experience in the United States and abroad, he has managed a variety of technical aspects of construction and development projects. He serves HNTB as a senior project director, with responsibilities including the organization and direction of civil and structural engineering design and construction function, schedules, budgets, profit margins, and feasibility studies.

AN INCOMPLETE JOURNEY FROM THE MIDDLE EAST TO THE NEW WORLD

Mostafa El Khashab

A journey is never complete without a beginning and an end in its very traditional sense. A life journey, though, is more of an incomplete circle. One starts at a point and rotates around an axis, with stops along the way, and always has the next stops in mind. Anticipating those stops, and the process of reexamination of one's identity, are the hallmarks of the journey. The journey moves from one point in time to the next point, but within its confines lies the whole spectrum of human experience: love, hope, success, failure, disappointment, and at times, other feelings and perceptions that were never felt before.

Here, I will be hopeful and try my best not to deviate from the journey. People looking back at their lives never do so with two eyes but rather with one eye, while the other is testing the degree of truthfulness of the story. To me, examining my journey entails a multifaceted view of a life, seen from different angles. I believe our private personal lives do have a significant impact on our professional lives, and that both are intertwined more than we like to admit and accept. It is therefore quite apparent that what we think of our journey's goals is not necessarily dependent only on our vision of life but is often also shaped by those who have a great impact on our lives. Family members, friends, role models, and last but not least, idyllic figures shape our lives through the values and attachments they represent.

The most profound single force shaping my life journey has been my constant search for meaning—the meaning of work, the meaning of values, the meaning of religion, the meaning of family, and most significantly, the meaning of love and friendship. This quest, in my view, drives my thirst for the truth, for what is genuine in life, and for finding out what is worth fighting for in life.

One of the first lessons I learned when I came to the United States from Egypt was not to rush to judgment of events or people. It is in the very nature of things to take time to have an impact. At the age of twenty-four, one feels bigger than life and is in a rush to see results. It took me years to learn the lessons of perseverance and patience. And those are not the only two lessons I took years to appreciate. I don't believe personal experience can be imitated by others, or that mistakes can be avoided just by knowing how others have overcome their difficulties. I believe the best way to learn in life from others is by example. The lessons I have learned are wide ranging: some were purely professional, some related to character building, and others were related to attitude and thinking.

First Glimpse of the United States

I believe that the glamor and fascination of New York catches even Europeans by surprise. For those whose US experiences start with the Big Apple, something else goes through their minds. I would describe it as intimidating and challenging. This challenge was multifaceted. My most pressing questions were whether I could cope with life in New York and whether I could succeed amid the intense competition. I was concerned about how fast and how efficiently I could cope with the technological deficit I felt I had.

Failure was not on my menu of choices, but the challenge was immense, and I couldn't downplay or underestimate it. I had heard encouraging success stories of physicians coming from across the world, and in particular from the Middle East and Egypt. I also heard stories of people who could not cope with the cultural side of life or with medical progress on the professional side. The net effect of my first glimpse of the United States was a combination of intimidation, anxiousness, and most importantly, determination.

Cultural Impact

One of the first challenges that is vital to overcome is cultural in nature. Growing up in a middle-class family in Egypt was my cultural backbone. I consider myself lucky having been raised in my family; I will be forever grateful to my parents, who got me all the books I aspired to read. In the 1960s and early 1970s, my generation grew up in a multicultural society, which was a great influence on my vision of the world. We were educated in exemplary schools with high standards, and very early on, were taught to think and ask questions. We had great respect for our teachers, and the school system was pretty strict. In our teens, we knew what was allowed, as well as what was not permitted and would lead to disciplinary action.

I was privileged to have a good education that prepared me for college and medical school, and also introduced me to the humanities. The school system gave me an opportunity to learn the values of reading and the principles of culture. I also had a good introduction to history and the arts. The great writers from all different cultures were available to read. The world with theater, plays, literature, visiting scholars, and the arts represented some of the tributaries of cultural enrichment. I believe those formative years were extremely helpful to me, as I was about to leave Egypt to start medical specialty training and higher studies.

Cornerstones of Success During Medical Training

Lessons learned—at times, at a high cost—are never forgotten. As one lives through their life experiences, one may forget a lesson, but only after it has become an integral part of one's self. Some lessons are learned during everyday practice but are only recognized after untoward results follow our actions and our thinking.

One of the first lessons I learned early on, after three months of training as an intern, was about having a plan of care for a medical problem. I was asked by my attending physician about a newly admitted patient at 5:00pm, just before I was due to sign out to my colleagues. His question was about my suggested plan of care for that patient. In response, I analyzed my findings and the patient's status and explained the laboratory and radiological findings. I went on for ten minutes before my attending stopped me. He asked what his question to me had been. I told him his question was about the plan of care. He replied that I never mentioned the plan of care; I had just talked about my findings. He reminded me that instead of answering the question, I went in a different direction. He asked a specific question, and I did not answer the question. It was a lesson in my professional life that I always kept in mind.

Years later, when I became an attending neurosurgeon, I taught all my residents to listen to the questions asked and to answer precisely. Precision is the jewel in the crown of communication. It is the most effective way of communicating your understanding and ability.

Honesty and Integrity in My Working Environment and in Life

Character is a testament to the human spirit and personality. Six months into my training, our fourth-year resident was suddenly fired from his post, and after a very brief investigation. The magnitude of the shock in the training program was immense. In short, the fourth-year resident was called late in the night by a nurse to see a patient who showed some worsening symptoms after a brain surgery that had been performed earlier in the day. The resident gave a recommendation to the nurse but did not see the patient. The patient seemed worse at 5:00am the next day, and the nurse called the resident again. He said he would be seeing the patient on his rounds in thirty minutes. The nurse was worried and called the attending surgeon, who luckily was in the hospital and went immediately to see the patient and examine him. The attending was told by the nurses that the patient had taken a downhill course overnight, but when the resident was informed, he gave his recommendation over the phone.

The fourth-year resident arrived at the patient's bedside as the attending was talking to the nurse. The attending asked the resident about the unfolding of events overnight and why he had not been informed about the deterioration of the patient's condition. The resident said that he had seen the patient and was not worried. Earlier, the nurse had said the patient was not seen by the resident physically and he had given his recommendation over the phone. The attending asked the resident again, and the resident again answered that he saw the patient.

The patient had to undergo emergency surgery after the computer tomography scan revealed bleeding, which was the cause of the deterioration. The patient improved after the emergency surgery, but the issue was just starting to evolve for the resident. An investigation was launched, and within two days, extensive meetings took place between the faculty and the resident. The verdict was that the resident had lied about seeing the patient. The faculty concluded that many mistakes can be coached and forgiven but that lying destroys trust. Trust is the basis of the relationship between health-care providers. This breach of trust and lack of honesty were not something the program could forgive, and the decision was made to fire the resident. The program director and the whole faculty met with all the residents and gave an account of the reasons for the firing. We were told that if the resident had told the truth about not seeing the patient, matters would have taken a completely different course. The message to all of us was that honesty and integrity are nonnegotiable, and no breach of honesty would ever be tolerated. The lesson was clear, and the message was undisputable.

I believe that just as honesty and integrity are paramount in our personal relationships, they are equally so in our professional set of values. I can say after my years of training and practice that reputation in professional circles is of utmost importance and instrumental in establishing success and good standing. Over the years, I have seen very promising careers of medical professionals irreversibly tarnished, and at times destroyed, by breach of trust and confidence. Similarly, in my lifetime, I have seen some of the closest personal relationships severed and damaged by the betrayal of trust and by deceit. The pain and misery that result from breakups of relationships due to a breach of trust a very grave experience.

Dedication, Hard Work, and Precision of Goals

Integrity and a positive attitude constitute the most relevant basics for success in medicine. I can't stress enough the importance of clarity about goals, and the dedication to achieve those goals. I learned early on in my career that, in the presence of fierce and divisive competition, success requires very hard work and mental preparedness. To be competitive under those circumstances, I had to do my training under the harsh circumstances of working long hours daily and continuing the process of reading and participating in clinical and laboratory research after hours. Courses in time management and organizational skills were instrumental to me. They enabled me to make use of my time in the most efficient way. Oftentimes we think we can maintain our professional struggle while we are physically and emotionally exhausted. However, I saw fellow residents and colleagues who could not strike the correct balance between self-care and professional progress.

As I started to conduct clinical research on the topography of the brain, as well as speech dominance in different languages, I came to understand some of the factors vital to success in clinical research. Our scientific team consisted of eight young scientists who did special tests to examine the relationship between speech and visual images and the role of cerebral dominance in the determination of brain plasticity. We defined the areas of the brain responsible for carrying the functions of language, and their relationships to the rest of the brain. We were dedicated to figuring out the linguistic deficits arising from epilepsy and brain diseases. I published the results of three years of clinical research in my thesis, which was awarded magna cum laude. I presented the first steps to understanding the effect of brain injury on the speech functions of different age groups. I was fortunate to be able to cooperate with research groups in neuroscience centers in Europe and other countries to establish the foundations of research into language and dominance in the brain.

Cumulative Effect of Clinical Research on Medical Practice

The last ten years have seen increasing research into the use of genomic medical engineering to treat genetic disorders and to anticipate the appearance of disease later in life. The best-known areas of research have been in dementia and Parkinson's disease. In addition to this groundbreaking research, my group researched the genetic basis of childhood brain disorders. Research into hydrocephalus and spina bifida disorders in newborn infants, including preventive strategies, reached clinical trials and is expected to be influential in decreasing the incidence of these diseases, and more importantly, reducing the degree of disability resulting from the neurological impairment. My group wrote multiple scientific papers to expand on the role of treatment in decreasing disability and neurological impairment in children and adolescents suffering from these conditions.

Another area we worked on was increasing public awareness of preventive measures to avoid the development of severe disabilities from neurological disorders. As with chronic disorders, such as diabetes and hypertension, neurological impairment and strokes are preventable if we take into consideration the elimination of their risk factors. Working with community and educational efforts to increase public awareness was central to our group's work.

Lessons Learned from an Incomplete Journey

I call my journey incomplete because I am still building on my efforts daily and working full time to achieve some goals in my research. Considering that we learn all the time from our experiences and from our reflections on them, I was fortunate to have great teachers from whom I could seek help and advice, and later on, good colleagues who shared their thoughts with me.

These lessons are my conclusions from my incomplete journey and may not be the conclusions drawn by others. For what it is worth, I can enumerate them as follows:

1. A basic understanding of the history and geography of the United States is the cornerstone for understanding its culture and traditions. This knowledge allowed me to share the ideas, feelings, and understandings of the society at large and of the people I met. This had a great impact on my ability to anticipate events and responses as well as to have tolerance for and an understanding of the society at large.

2. Respect for other points of view and tolerance for differences in opinion are needed to cultivate a culture of mutual benefit and civility. Respect for decorum and the principles of communication are essential for one to be productive and to be successful.

3. Respect is not a given but an earned value. Showing respect to others and tolerance of their beliefs and culture are important.

4. The maintenance of good relationships with colleagues and the adoption of a principled view of work issues are mandatory. Not enough praise can be given to structured thinking and to a scientific approach to solving problems.

5. Keeping goals precise is important, as is working hard to achieving them. This is aided by a good education, building professional experience, and good mentorship.

6. Medical research derives its value from serving people and helping the sick and vulnerable; this is the basis of every valuable effort we can make. Working toward the common good of people is always rewarding. Service for others and dedication toward helping others give us value and appreciation.

7. I can't say enough about the support of family and the effect it has on our work and success. Happiness and emotional balance are of vital importance and have a direct impact on how we perceive life as a whole and how we perform on a daily basis.

8. Maintaining a regular and structured working schedule, alternating with some private and recreational time, is of fundamental importance to protect us from fatigue and burnout. It is not hard work

but rather irregularity and the lack of a system to live by that kills us.

9. Ultimately the value we attach to our principles and to our goals is what really counts. The most lasting values and goals are the ones that are directed at helping our society and giving back in gratitude. Fulfillment is what we all seek, and it can only be earned through good intentions, hard work, and complete dedication.

10. It is my conviction that, in the twenty-first century, with science and technology achieving unprecedented progress, the medical sciences will have new frontiers and challenges as well as unlimited potential and opportunities. It is the time for all of us, young and old, to work together to the benefit of noble and gracious causes.

———◆———

MOSTAFA EL KHASHAB is a neurological surgeon practicing in New Jersey and New York. He is committed to advancing the medical sciences and health-care sector in Egypt and giving back to his beloved home country. Over the years, he has maintained close connections there. He has lived in the US since 1982 and is married to Bakinam, a medical quality and safety expert. They have two children: Aly is in banking and Yasmin works in the medical field. He is passionate about modern art and history of the 20th century. He spends his time reading, painting, and traveling.

AN EGYPTIAN PIONEER IN AEROSPACE ENGINEERING

Awatef Hamed

"Scientists discover the world that exists; engineers create the world that never was."

—Theodore von Kármán (Hungarian-American mathematician, aerospace engineer and physicist)

Born in Mansourah, a mid-size town in the Nile Delta, I was the youngest of three daughters in my family. The oldest, Afaf, became a physician; the second, Azza, became a civil engineer. In his early career, my father was an engineer who worked on construction projects; later, he became a teacher, then an inspector in the public education system. Every time he accepted a promotion, the family had to move. When I started first grade at the age of five, I already knew how to add, subtract, read, and write. I loved school. Eventually, my parents became concerned about insufficient classroom stimuli, and I was allowed to take the test for admission to middle school. I successfully completed it and skipped sixth grade. Moving on, my interest in dancing, acting, and singing blossomed, while I continued to excel in math, trigonometry, and physics. In fact, I even received a certificate of excellence from the greater Alexandria District of Education for achieving a perfect math score in the comprehensive exam for admission to high school.

My father researched various high schools and learned that the Secondary School for Girls had the highest rate of acceptance among top-rated faculties. At age thirteen—two years younger than my peers—I enrolled in that school, where I knew none of my classmates. Three years later, I took the nationwide final high school exam, which was a memorable and unusual experience. That test was and still is the most important milestone for college-bound students; it is the only criterion to determine college options. That year, students had to take the exam a second time, after it was revealed that Israel had broadcast the questions as an act of sabotage. The information my father had received about the school turned out to be accurate. I graduated and was admitted to study engineering at Alexandria University; in addition, seven of my classmates were accepted in medicine, pharmacy, and engineering—an exceptionally high number for a girls' school at that time.

After completing my first year at Alexandria University, with a rating of excellent, I transferred to Cairo University, and my family also moved to the capital city. Our joy at finally living closer to our aunts, uncles, and the extended family, however, did not last long, as my mother was diagnosed with breast cancer. The year of my eighteenth birthday was one of the saddest in my life, as I lost my mother before I had a chance to know her better as an adult.

The College of Engineering at Cairo University had a program in the Aeronautical Engineering Department that started in the pre-junior year of the five-year major. I joined that program and graduated three years later, in a class of thirty-five students who had survived the rigorous course of study, out of the 133 who initially started the program. Degree in hand, I was immediately appointed to a position at the aircraft complex of the Egyptian General Aeronautical Organizations, in the Cairo suburb of Helwan.

When I started to consider graduate studies in the United States, the challenges I faced to obtain the required government approvals made it a nearly impossible endeavor. Soon after the 1967 war, Egyptian authorities stopped issuing exit visas to students who had been awarded personal scholarships based on their transcripts and qualifications. Nevertheless, I was able to overcome the difficulties, thanks to the advice and support of Professor Ibrahim El Demerdash, head of the Aeronautical Engineering Department, and dean of the Faculty of Engineering. He searched through piles of correspondence at his home and found an announcement about the Amelia Earhart Scholarship for women pursuing graduate studies in aerospace engineering. He provided a letter stating that, as the first woman to graduate from the Aeronautical Engineering Department, I was the only one in Egypt who qualified for the scholarship. I applied for an unpaid leave of absence and launched the process of getting the required approvals. It took more than nine months, with officials in each government office demanding the approval of all the others before giving his own. In short, all were reluctant to take responsibility for granting my request. A critical piece of advice came from Professor Osama El Kholy, whom I encountered while waiting for final approval of my exit visa by the Educational Mission Office. He advised me to go directly to the assistant to the director of that office and secure his signature before he left the country.

With all approved documents in hand, including one signed by President Nasser himself, I was off to start graduate studies at the University of Cincinnati (UC). My goal was to specialize in aero propulsion, a field in which I had become interested following one of my assignments that dealt with the performance of aircraft engines. Due to my lengthy delay in Cairo, I arrived in Ohio in late December, at the end of the fall quarter. It was a challenge to start in the middle of the academic year and catch up on course material that had been covered during the preceding quarter. This intense situation made me appreciate the very demanding nature of the aeronautical engineering program at Cairo University, where we had to enroll in up to thirteen courses each semester during our last three years.

At UC, I was passionate about my research and was encouraged by my advisor, Dr. Widen Tabakoff (1919–2015), to present my findings at professional conferences and have them published in specialized journals. Dr. Tabakoff was born in Bulgaria and received his PhD from the University of Berlin. He had been working for the Hoechst chemical company when he was approached by the US Army after World War II to join the team of Dr. Wernher Von Braun at the US Space Program, in Huntsville, Alabama. He arrived in the United States and received security clearance, but his wife was unhappy in that rural and provincial environment. While working on a project with the Army Research Lab in Cincinnati, Dr. Tabakoff visited UC, where he was offered a professorship in the Aerospace Engineering Department—the second oldest one in the United States. Established in 1929, it was headed by a navigation expert who was recruited from McCook Field in Dayton (currently Wright Patterson Air Force Base). From the start, the Wright brothers were involved in the development of the first cooperative engineering education program in the nation.

Upon joining the department, Dr. Tabakoff proceeded to modernize the program, introduced classes on space topics, initiated graduate studies, and established an advanced engineering program with General Electric (GE), through which more than a thousand GE engineers completed their graduate degrees while employed by one of the world's leading aircraft engine companies. In my course of studies, I had the opportunity to know many of these engineers as classmates. I also observed hundreds of students being guided, cared for, and financially supported, and their lives positively influenced by Dr. Tabakoff. His legacy has been honored by naming the UC Propulsion Lab after him. That was only fair, since that lab was established with the extensive research funds he brought to UC, and the air tanks were gifted by the federal government to support his research on wind tunnels. As my mentor, Dr. Tabakoff urged me to apply for a green card and was the reference in my application for US citizenship.

After completing my PhD, I was still very much interested in pursuing my research. Thus, when UC offered me an instructorship for one year, to be promoted to assistant professor the following year, I did not hesitate to accept. Although I did not look for other positions, I received several invitations to interview for research positions at a government research lab and Ivy League schools, including Arnold Research Laboratory and Massachusetts Institute of Technology. My name was most likely suggested by scientists who had attended my research presentations. At that point in my career, I became fully aware of the importance of having a mentor. Professor Tabakoff was instrumental in my appointment to a tenure-track position; I was the first woman to achieve tenure in the College of Engineering and remained the only one for twenty years. As my mentor, Dr. Tabakoff introduced me to the best scientists in the field and supported me as I conducted exciting, leading-edge research and compiled an extensive record of publications. These, in addition to my excellent teaching evaluations, resulted in my promotion to the rank of associate professor in three years, and full professor four years later.

Throughout my career, I had the opportunity to meet many outstanding engineers. Among others, they included Brian Rowe, the CEO of GE Aircraft Engines, and Hans von Ohein, the chief scientist at the Air Force Research Lab and the inventor of the gas turbine. Astronaut Neil Armstrong, the first man to walk on the moon, was my colleague when he joined the faculty of the Aerospace Engineering Department. Not only were these extremely competent engineers, but they also were outstanding leaders whose remarkable visions continue to have an impact on our lives to this day.

For many years, I focused my research on the propulsion field, with the goal of contributing to faster, safer, and more environmentally friendly aviation. My findings in this and other technical areas were rewarded by the National Aeronautics and Space Administration (NASA), the Pennsylvania State University Advanced Propulsion Lab, and the Aircraft Engine Committee of the American Society of Mechanical Engineers (ASME). I also received invitations to teach short professional courses in the United States and Europe, at Cranfield University in the United Kingdom, and the Von Karman Institute in Belgium. These courses were attended by engineers from leading gas turbine engine manufacturers, the government, and university research labs. In addition, I was asked to lead seminars at academic and research institutions across the United States, Europe, and Asia.

My commitment to research resulted in teaching innovations. For example, I initiated and taught a senior capstone engine design class with ten UC teams that won the national competitions of the American Institute of Aeronautics and Astronautics (AIAA) Airbreathing Propulsion Committee. My research also allowed me to enrich the quality of service I rendered to UC, to technical and professional organizations, and to government agencies. When I was invited to join the NASA Propulsion Technical Advisory Committee, I was surprised to be the only academic person; the remaining members of the committee represented industry and federal government labs. I served in that capacity for more than ten years—the lifespan of the committee. It is a great satisfaction to have advocated for continuing the support and funding of the Numerical Propulsion System Simulation (NPSS) software. Today, this is a powerful tool used across the aerospace industry and federal government labs to simulate complex propulsion systems and air cycles. My graduate students and I have been using NPSS in leading-edge research dealing with finding solutions to the challenging thermal management problems in future advanced aerospace systems.

My voluntary service to my discipline extends well beyond UC and NASA. It includes organizing international conferences and chairing and serving on several technical committees of the two leading professional societies in my field (i.e., the AIAA, where I chair the AIAA Airbreathing Propulsion Committee, and the ASME, where I chair the ASME Fluid Machinery Committee and the Gas Turbine Educational Committee). In addition to evaluating articles submitted for publication in leading technical journals and reviewing proposals for the National Science Foundation (NSF), the Army Research Office, and the Airforce Office of Scientific Research (AFOSR), I serve as editor of the *International Journal of Computational Fluid Dynamics* and of the *International Journal of Rotating Machinery* and as administrative secretary of the International Society of Airbreathing Engineers (ISABE). These opportunities allowed me to work with leading researchers from academic institutions as well as managers of industrial establishments and government labs.

In addition to my research, teaching, and service responsibilities, I have collaborated with students to create a student chapter of the Society of Women Engineers (SWE) and became its faculty advisor. This chapter is a focal point for the few female students in engineering to get together for friendly support and become involved in recruiting more women students for colleges of engineering. Upon joining Zonta International (a service society for professional women), I was invited to serve on the selection committee of the Amelia Earhart Fellows. In that capacity, it was a pleasure to meet and collaborate with fellow professors and women engineers from Germany, Australia, Canada, and NASA in the United States. More importantly, I was impressed with the caliber and drive of the applicants and their achievements, early on in their careers.

In 2001, when my colleagues selected me to chair the Aerospace Engineering Department—the first woman ever to chair an aerospace engineering department—I accepted the challenge at a time of budget cuts and a hiring freeze. In addition to securing external funds to support my own research, I wrote competitive grant proposals that won more than $32.5 million from the state of Ohio—$19 million for research infrastructure, and more than $13 million in endowments. With these resources, I was able to recruit outstanding faculty, build new research labs, upgrade existing ones, and support the establishment of the Center for Intelligent Propulsion. Its excellent facilities are accessible not only to students and faculty at UC but also to those at the University of Dayton and Ohio State University.

Being recognized as often as I have by peers and colleagues is a humbling experience. Among others, I was bestowed the following: in 2004, the YMCA Career Woman of Achievement, received at the Convention Center in the presence of local leaders and TV personalities; in 2008, the Aerospace Educator Leeland Atwood Award, sponsored by the American Society of Engineering Education (ASEE), the AIAA, and the Lockheed Martin Company; and in 2015, the UC Faculty Career Award, in recognition of my contributions to the three institutional missions of education, research, and service. Being elected fellow of both the AIAA and the ASME is an honor reserved to very few. My AIAA Fellow initiation ceremony in Washington DC was memorable. As keynote speaker, Pat Buchanan was very witty. Then, each of the seven fellows—every year one fellow is elected for each thousand members—was introduced and walked separately on the stage. Applause intensified and was definitely much louder when I arrived. Although I did not notice it at first, I was the only woman among the honorees. Later, the women in the audience told me how excited they were to see one of their gender among the fellows. After stepping down from the stage, I was approached by an embarrassed AIAA official, who asked me to give him my award certificate in order to correct the beautifully penned statement "for *his* contribution." It was later redone and sent to me by mail. When the incident was publicized on the UC campus, a female engineering student humorously wrote me: "Congratulations on becoming a fellow! I always thought you were a gal!"

Looking back, I realize that education and research have not only enhanced my career, more importantly, have enriched my personal life. In the process of organizing many seminars, presenting innumerable papers, and producing more than three hundred publications, I had the opportunity to meet amazing individuals and discover fascinating parts of the world. However, my greatest sense of accomplishment derives from having had the opportunity to lend a helping hand to many in my profession and my community when they needed me, and to assist others to reach their goals. A lifetime of hard work has taught me two important lessons: the first is the grievous reality when talent or potential for success is wasted for lack of means; the second is that the hand that enables or comforts is a source of boundless rewards. I have been most fortunate to achieve my goals and reach for the stars, thanks to the unconditional support of family, friends, and mentors who believed in me. Throughout my life and my career, I have made every effort to follow in their footsteps and give to others as much as I could. Although an intellectually challenging discipline, aerospace engineering is an important science that has a great impact on human connectivity. Lest we forget, it contributes to ensuring travel safely and human communication through satellites. Looking at the future, it is my sincere hope that more women will be involved in this fascinating field.

Previously published in 2016 in *Daughters of the Nile*, edited by Samia I Spenser.

———•———

AWATEF HAMED was the first woman to graduate from the Department of Aeronautical Engineering at Cairo University. She obtained her MSc and PhD from the University of Cincinnati, UC, and became the first woman to head an Aerospace Engineering Department at UC. Dr. Hamed is well recognized in her field of Aerospace Propulsion. During her career, she was awarded over 45 million dollars in competitive grants and contracts supporting her research and the establishment of two Propulsion Centers at UC. She has published over 300 refereed journal articles, and is an honored fellow of the American Institute of Aeronautics and Astronautics and the American Society of Mechanical Engineers.

MY JOURNEY IN BRIEF

Mohamed Elgamal

After graduating from Ain Shams University, I was very happy and excited to be appointed as a teacher (moeed) in the Faculty of Engineering. In July 1977, I went to start graduate studies in Sweden and stayed there for one year, during which I completed an MSc degree. Then I traveled to the United States to start my PhD, first at the University of Pennsylvania in September 1978, and then at Clarkson University in Potsdam, New York. One year later, I went to the University of Manitoba in Winnipeg, Canada, where I completed my PhD in electrical engineering.

My teaching assistant and research scholarships helped a lot; they paid for my student expenses ($11,000 a year), which was just enough for basic student life. My tuition and other school expenses were paid by the University. While studying in the University of Manitoba, I got a job as a research engineer in a government research laboratory. During this period, I lived in a house with a prominent Canadian family, with whom I had a great time and learned a lot. I appreciated their generosity and kindness. To this day, I have strong personal and family relationships with them.

During my studies at the University of Manitoba, I was active and very much involved in student life and in all aspects of life in the community at large. Of course, this was in addition to my academic work and research job. My interests also included the Egyptian community in Manitoba and nationally in Canada. On campus, I was selected to serve on some academic committees and was elected first as the social director and then as president of the Graduate Student Association (GSA). In 1982, while working as the GSA social director, I managed to introduce Egyptian foods, included falafel and kebob. A significant number of students and faculty members attended these social functions and very much liked the Egyptian culture in general and especially the tasty food. This continued for a long time, even after I earned my PhD and graduated.

In early 1982, after a successful launching of the Egyptian Student Association in Winnipeg, I contacted several active and prominent Egyptians in several Canadian provinces. We met in Toronto, and I was elected president of the Egyptian Canadian Association. A new TV program was launched with the help of the government and the Egyptian consulate in Ottawa and two prominent Egyptians in Montreal: George Saad and Mamdouh Ismail. His Excellency Ambassador Tahsin Bashir visited us several times, followed by Ambassador Mahmoud Qassim and others. Our goals included (1) introducing Egyptian culture to the Canadian communities; (2) helping Egyptian Canadians meet their needs in teaching Arabic to their first and second generations; and (3) explaining Egyptian causes to Canadian society.

In September 1982, while working as a research engineer at the Manitoba Research Council (MRC), I learned that the St. Boniface Research Foundation had decided to award its annual award to Egyptian First Lady Mrs. Jehan Sadat. We, as Egyptian Canadians, were particularly happy because this honor had only been given to world leaders such as Mother Teresa and Rosalyn Carter. This honor was so significant that I decided to invite Mrs. Sadat for a lunch, where we could show our respect and our joy for the honor she would receive. Preparations for the lunch started, and the Egyptian community in Winnipeg participated in the preparation. I coordinated our efforts with the Egyptian embassy and Ambassador Mahmoud Kasim gave us all the support we needed. Mrs. Sadat's office told us she was looking forward to the Egyptian lunch. I also coordinated with the Canadian Department of the Secretary of State, which supported the function and gave us financial support to partially cover the costs associated with it. I invited the Canadian minister of external affairs, who confirmed his attendance. Invitations were also issued to several provincial cabinet ministers and to the mayor of Winnipeg (Bill Norrie), and many others. All invitees confirmed their attendance. It appeared everything was in order, but it turned out it was not that easy!

While at work at MRC, I received a phone call from Mr. Campbell, who had the royal title QC. I knew of him, as he was a heavyweight and prominent personality, but I had never spoken to him. He sounded angry on the telephone as he said, "Mrs. Sadat is coming to us,St. Boniface Research Foundation, not to the Egyptian Canadian Society."

I replied, "Yes sir, but she is our first lady, and we want to show her our respect and support, especially in the wake of President Sadat's killing. We think the lunch is appropriate, especially since it does not conflict with your event. And Mrs. Sadat has already confirmed she will attend this lunch."

He tried hard to convince me to cancel our event and went on to threaten me: "You'd better withdraw the media advertisements and announcement you made and say you canceled the lunch." Then he hung up on me.

I tried to call him back, but he did not answer, so I called him again. When he answered, I said, "Mr. Campbell, you hold the title QC, and I respect you and your position, but I never expected you to hang up on me, sir. I want to work with you to find a solution."

He repeated his threats and told me, "None of the VIPs you invited will show up."

Two hours after that phone call, the MRC front office called and asked me to come to the front, where I found two police officers from the RCMP. They asked me to step out as they had some questions. They were polite and respectful. They asked about my plan to host Mrs. Sadat and what I was going to do. I answered truthfully and gave them the background and the plan. They looked at each other and then smiled and left me. I confirmed the plan with the media and the hotel and so on.

After work, I went home to find several FedEx envelopes from most of the invited VIPs, including the mayor of Winnipeg, the minister of education, and the minister of culture. I was disappointed and called them, one by one, to respectfully tell them the lunch was on and the election was coming soon, and we would campaign for those who stood by good causes and helped the community.

The lunch started, and I was pleasantly surprised to see the mayor and his wife attending. The minister of education, minister of health, and the Canadian deputy minister of external affairs were all in attendance. Mrs. Sadat was the keynote speaker and gave a very emotional speech that affected all the attendees. At the end of the event, the mayor took me aside and complimented our work and courage. He invited me to come to the city. We started a great relationship that is still going on to this day.

Subsequently, I was appointed chairman for community relations of the city of Winnipeg and served with the chief of police, Herb Steven, and Mayor Norrie, among other prominent personalities in Winnipeg. Maureen Hemphill, the minister of education, and Eugene Kostyra, the minister of finance, talked after the event about starting long-lasting relationships and friendships. The Canadian minister of the external affairs, Lloyd Axworthy, asked me to help in his campaign, which I did, and during this work, we started an interesting and good friendship. On the city level, I was involved with the community relations and race relations committees. Provincially, I joined the New Democratic Party (NDP) and became president of the Riding Association of St. Norbert and Richmond. Federally, I joined the Liberal Party and helped Lloyd Axworthy's campaign.

An interesting incident happened. A Native American chief from Northern Manitoba came to Winnipeg, and during his visit, he was drinking alcohol. He was walking on a Winnipeg street and got into a conflict and then a fight with a city police officer, who shot and killed him. This incident was brought to me as the chairman of the

City Race Relations Committee. I asked for a public hearing. Chief Stevens, who also was serving on this committee, said, "An internal police inquiry is enough." I insisted and called on the attorney general to do the public inquiry, which he did. The results were mixed, as the involved police officer sadly committed suicide. In fact, I felt somewhat guilty, but could do nothing except side with justice and defend the truth.

My life in Winnipeg was exciting and happy. Academically, I got my PhD in electrical engineering, and politically, I was elected president of the NDP for the St. Norbert and Richmond constituency. I was also elected as a member of the prestigious and influential budget, planning, and priorities (BP&P) committee in the Howard Polly government of Manitoba. I was also assistant to the energy secretary, Jerry Storie.

In December 1987, I accepted a position with the Aviation Department of Transport Canada. I was responsible for the national microwave landing system and guidance equipment. We were responsible for the design, testing, procurement, and installation and operation of this equipment on various runways in Canada.

One of my trips for aircraft testing was to Atlantic City, New Jersey. After doing the test, I had to drive back to Ottawa. On the way, I stopped in Allentown, Pennsylvania, to visit my hometown friend and relative Dr. Ismail Kashkoush, who was newly married. He invited me to a dinner with an Egyptian family in town and to meet someone "interesting," and I did! When I arrived at host's house, a beautiful young lady opened the door and welcomed us. I liked her a lot and I believe it was "love at first sight." We talked and our chemistry was good. I invited her and her uncle for brunch at a Greek restaurant the following day, and we continued our pleasant conversation. Subsequently, after phone calls and repeated visits, I proposed to her. We got married six months after our first meeting.

My wife came to live with me in Ottawa, where the weather was a big challenge for her. Practicing medicine in Canada also posed a challenge because she would have to go through a series of examinations and certifications. She had received her training and education in the United States and was certified and licensed as an internist in Pennsylvania and was ready to practice medicine there. When she got an offer to practice in North Carolina, we both decided it was best for the family to accept it. This decision was particularly difficult for us as my career in Canada was established and flourishing. However, sacrifices had to be made. It was very difficult for me and for my colleagues in the Aviation Group. I submitted my resignation with tearful eyes and a broken heart, after several years of service. I was confident I would resume my career in the United States, and in fact I did. Our family was a priority and of utmost importance to us.

We first resided in a rural area about one to two hours away from Raleigh or any other major city, and forty-five minutes west of Kinston. After settling in North Carolina, I met many good people, and within a month, became director of the Global TransPark Commission. This commission was set up for the economic development of a thirteen-county region in rural North Carolina. I had to report to Governor James Hunt and forty commissioners. We had to build infrastructure, such as an airport, road network, and harbor (a model can be applied to the Suez Canal region). I also taught electrical engineering at East Carolina University. During this period and in 1999, we were blessed with three children (triplets), in addition to Youssef, who was ten at the time. As of 2020, Hannah is a rising senior at the University of Toronto, and Omar at the University of Maryland. Sophie graduated from the University of Chicago in June 2020. Youssef is married and expecting a child as of August 2020.

The Eastern North Carolina region had a population of about 900,000 but was decreasing due to the fact that most successful high school graduates go to universities outside the region and never come back, due to lack of suitable jobs and because of the low quality of life. My job in the Global TransPark Commision was to reverse this trend and attract industries and companies to relocate in the region. This would result in jobs and enhance the quality of life. We made progress, and the work is still in progress. We started building transportation and technology infrastructure in the thirteen-county region and attracted some big companies, such as Air Cargo. We also introduced the internet to the region for the first time in 1996.

I was asked to provide connectivity and internet to schools, hospitals, health-care facilities, and some military bases in the region through a private business I started in 1997. I resigned from my position at Global TransPark to focus on the business I started. I subsequently started internet, engineering, and security companies. I created jobs for many youth and other opportunities for the people of Eastern North Carolina. I also provided video conferencing networks for farmers to market their crops and manage their farms. In fact, my company received a grant of more than $6 million from the US Department of Agriculture. I was also honored in 1998 with the governor's business award, and many other awards and honors. I became a well-known authority in the IT field and appeared frequently on the ABC, WRL, and other stations, as well as other forms of media, such as newspapers. When we first came to North Carolina, I was introduced at social gatherings as "the husband of the Dr. (my wife)." After I became more well-known, she was introduced as "the wife of Dr. Elgamal." Funny!

My companies continued to grow, and I hired more capable and prominent staff and advisors. Among them were the superintendent of Duplin County Schools, Mr. L. S. Guy, and a retired Air Force general. Without any serious marketing, and only based on the word-of-mouth, I worked with more than three hundred schools and many universities, health-care facilities, and businesses in twenty-five counties. I formed a board of directors the included billionaires and VIP personalities from within and outside the region. Steve Forbes of *Forbes* magazine visited us in 2001. I was the subject of a positive write up in this magazine.

In 2001, we built a fiber optics network that covered all of Eastern North Carolina and connected various businesses and institutions. This attracted Wall Street. I received offers to sell my company and I accepted. Subsequently, the company was resold to wealthy people in the region, who mismanaged it. I ended up advising them how to restructure it. Sadly, the company was divided into three parts: the fiber optics business was sold to Time Warner, and the internet and education networks went into bankruptcy. I then started a new company and was able to get back the schools and internet customers. I also focused on international markets. This business has been active since 2002.

Until 2011, I visited Egypt only to see my family and friends. I had neither political nor business interests in Egypt at that time. I felt business in Egypt was mainly reserved for those who had connections to the rulers and their people. This lack of trust was the main reason for my lack of interest in entering the Egyptian market. All that started to change on January 25, 2011. Seeing the youth, men, women, and people of all ages gathering in Tahrir Square changed everything I felt about Egypt. I had always had a deep love for my homeland of Egypt, but it peaked at that time.

Egyptian Americans in North Carolina gathered and tried to see what we could do to help and support the revolution. First, I called on all to send money to themselves or their relatives in Egypt to keep the Egyptian reserve of foreign currency going and to help the economy in general. Then we started to organize in the United States and Canada so we could provide needed support in an organized fashion. We were able to gather many Egyptians across all six continents and formed the International Association for Egyptian Abroad (IAEA). IAEA focused on (1) helping Egypt economically, culturally, and politically; and (2) helping Egyptians abroad by supporting their needs locally. We also participated in the revolution and stayed for a few days in Tahrir Square, where we met the youth leaders and members of the Supreme Military Council of the Egyptian Armed Forces. Our main goal was to find out how to support the country and its revolution. We also felt it was imperative to support the military as the main protector of the revolution and the country of Egypt.

In one of our many meetings, General Mohsen el-Fangary told us there was an urgent need to provide wheelchairs for people who were injured in the revolution. We immediately responded by providing more than just the required motorized wheelchairs. The cost of the chairs was paid by us and transportation from the United States to

Cairo was made free by EgyptAir. The wheelchairs were warehoused and distributed under the supervision of government and youth organizations.

My travel to Egypt increased because I wanted to ensure the success of the revolution. Our efforts to support the revolution and Egypt were intensified, not only in Egypt, but also in Washington and other capitals of the world. With colleagues and fellow Egyptian Americans, I made presentations to the US Congress during the period of 2011 to 2013 to ensure the continuation of US economic and military support to Egypt. I led campaigns in the US media, Arabic media, and Egyptian media to solidify support for Egypt and its leadership and also to unify Egyptians abroad and their efforts to help Egypt. We continued our campaign to increase the transfer of money to Egypt by Egyptian expatriates. The money transferred increased; it reached $6.8 billion in 2009, and according to the figures published by the Central Bank of Egypt, reached more than $22 billion in 2014.

In November 2011, I was invited to be a panelist at a conference in Washington D.C. entitled "Egypt, the Revolution." Many Egyptians came from Egypt, including Bothaina Kamel, Asmaa Mahfouz, and members of the April 6 Group. Near the end of the conference, I was surprised when these individuals suddenly called on us to demonstrate the following morning against our Egyptian military attachés office. I vehemently opposed such a call and helped to prevent it from happening. In hindsight, their expensive clothes and fancy shoes should have been a red flag to many of us!

We organized conferences and workshops in Cairo to continue our support and to show that all Egyptians were united, no matter where they were—inside or outside Egypt. In January 2012, we had a meeting in Cairo at the Four Seasons Hotel. It was attended by representatives of the Association of Egyptians Abroad and by prominent Egyptians, such as Abdel Aziz Hegazy, Ibrahim Badran, Ibrahim Mehleb, Amr Mousa, Fouad Abu Zaghlah, and Ahmed el-Burai (who was the minister responsible for the Association of Egyptians Abroad). We all wanted a new prosperous and democratic Egypt.

I personally communicated with the new government formed by Prime Minister Essam Sharaf and initially worked to provide technology for electronic voting. Although the technology did not materialize, our relationship continued and is continuing. I managed and coordinated his visit to North Carolina in 2013 to meet with Egyptians and government officials. He met with representatives of the US Department of State and US Treasury, and the treasurer and attorney general (who is now governor) of North Carolina. During these meetings, economic and financial offers were made to support Egypt.

Since the revolution, I have been a guest on many television channels in Egypt and abroad. In one instance, Al-Jazeera invited me to talk about the Egyptian economy, and Abdel Rahim Foukara, the anchor of the program (from Washington) said unfairly that the Egyptian economy had almost collapsed, and that the army controlled everything in the Egyptian economy. I told him and the audience that was not true. Yes, the strategic reserve had gone down significantly, but unlike the situation in Greece, it was still positive. Since then, I have not responded to Al-Jazeera's invitations to appear on their channel.

The Supreme Council of the Egyptian Armed Forces announced a new presidential election in 2013. There were thirteen presidential candidates. My fellow expatriates and I visited and had conversations with them to see whom we should support as the best candidate. We also had a conversation with Chancellor Abdel Aziz al-Jundi, who was minister of justice, and offered to enable Egyptians abroad to vote electronically. The idea was also discussed with Prime Minister Essam Sharaf. Voting for Egyptians abroad was granted for the first time, but it was done through a combination of electronic and mail voting. We also visited and discussed the future of Egypt with prominent Egyptians and former politicians and cabinet ministers.

My fellow expats and I were impressed with General Ahmed Shafiq's expertise and experience in administration and his clear vision of where to take the new Egypt. We were also impressed by Eng. Ibrahim Mahlab, who showed no interest in entering the presidential race. He ended up becoming the prime minister of Egypt in 2015, however. We decided to support Shafiq, although some wanted Amr Mousa; we examined the latter's experience carefully but thought Shafiq was the best fit at the time.

I personally campaigned for Shafiq and managed to get last-minute support for him from various stakeholders, including the Coptic leadership. He managed to win in the first round and had to face Morsi in the second round. For the second round, we had a choice between the Muslim Brotherhood and Shafiq, and the choice was clear to most Egyptians. We voted for Shafiq, and I played a role in his campaign. During this period, I was honored by his friendship, and we built a strong relationship that is continuing to this day. He is a man of honor and impeccable integrity. His love for Egypt is immeasurable, and I share this with him. Egypt is our love and hope!

The election resulted in a questionable victory for Morsi. Despite our deep disappointment with that highly questionable victory, we decided to support the new president only for the sake of Egypt. I even went to New York and met him to show our support to Egypt.

As the days went on, the new president made one mistake after another. At first, we tried to give him the benefit of the doubt, but it became obvious he had a plan to dismantle the Ministry of the Interior (police) and then the judicial system, with the goal of weakening the Armed Forces. In November 2013, he wrongly fired the Egyptian attorney general. We knew the attorney general and Department of Justice needed lots of reclamation, but we stood with Egypt. I was the first to write to President Morsi privately about how to solve this constitutional crisis and move forward. After many attempts, I had to go public and give two options: resign or call for an early election. He did neither.

I intensified my communications with youth groups, prominent Egyptians, and other political forces within and outside Egypt. We shared the belief that only one option remained to save Egypt: the Armed Forces must do the right thing and get rid of this bad system. Thankfully, they did so on June 30, 2014. Adley Mansour was installed as interim president, and a new cabinet was formed by el-Beblawy. I met el-Beblawy in his Dokky office on June 23, 2014, and he shared our vision that the Muslim Brotherhood government had to go. This period was a tough one for Egypt.

Morsi's supporters took to the streets and occupied public squares, and in effect, blocked the University of Cairo (Midan el-Nahda). Most notable was the occupation of Raba'a Square. Frankly, and for the sake of history, I must say here, as I said to Marshal al-Sisi (the minister of defense) in 2014, that the government had mishandled the situation because they were afraid of the world's public opinion. While we all respect the rights to peacefully demonstrate and voice our opinions, most democratic countries have rules on how to peacefully demonstrate, without occupying public buildings for months (as happened in Egypt). We should do whatever is in the interests of Egypt and its citizens and pay no attention to those who do not want Egypt to progress. I also voiced my concerns to various leaders and to the president of Cairo University, Dr. Gaber Nassar (who is a friend).

The prospects of a new presidential election were quite real, and no obvious candidate was on the ground. General Ahmed Shafiq was a potential candidate, but most people wanted the minister of defense el-Sisi. I had a phone conversation with Shafiq on this subject, and he agreed that el-Sisi was best suited for the presidency at that time. He said that if el-Sisi ran, then he would not run and would support el-Sisi. As president of the Association of Egyptians Abroad, I went with two other colleagues, Sabry Elbaga and Amir Barakat, to meet el-Sisi. In attendance were Generals Mohamed Al-Assar, Fouad Abdel-Halim, and briefly Abbas Kamel. We strongly encouraged el-Sisi to run and promised him our strong support. He ran for the presidency and won in mid-2014.

As an association, we supported el-Sisi around the globe, covering six continents. During the election, I represented him officially in New York and unofficially around the globe. It was a clear win, and we did what we could for the sake of Egypt!

After the presidential election came the parliamentary election, and we believed we had to take a role in it to ensure a good parliament that could work with the president and not against him. This was to ensure stability for Egypt, an essential requirement for progress and prosperity. We contacted all the major party leaders and concluded that each of them desired to be the "one" elected. I personally contacted these leaders and asked for unity but did not get the needed commitment. I tried repeatedly to explain that all the nonreligious parties had the same goal but were competing for the same votes, while the Alnoor Party, for instance, had its fair share of votes. Our association decided to "force" all the nonreligious parties to unite. We formed a list of candidates to run nationally and compete independent of the other parties. We formed the list, but none of us (the founders) were candidates. However, I had to suspend our list after we distributed it, because our candidates were included on other lists as well, such as for Hob Misr. The election was held, and a new parliament was installed. The legislative and judiciary branches were formed, and work begin in the best interests of the Egyptian people.

In September 2014, President el-Sisi attended the United Nations General Assembly in New York. We wanted to show the world this president had the support of the Egyptians. We organized and got many Egyptian Americans from all over the country to come to New York. It was a great show of support, as reported by all media outlets. A well-selected twenty-five Egyptian American businesspeople (including Dr. Mohammed Al-Arian) were invited to meet the president, and we met him. In that meeting, we again promised our continuing support for him and for Egypt. We told him we wanted to be a part of economic development and of building the new Egypt under his leadership. We also proposed certificates of deposits for Egyptians abroad and discussed how to implement this with Egyptian national banks, under the supervision of the Central Bank of Egypt. I think Egypt needs all of us, and as Egyptians abroad, we have the duty and the ability to give to and participate in economic development and to contribute in a more serious way and do our duty, as we should, toward Egypt. As a first step, we started with Cairo University (Drs. Gaber Nassar and Hala al-Said) to organize and unify the efforts to use

Egyptians' skills in various fields of knowledge and create a database. Then we matched the needs of Egypt with those skills and realized the benefits in the form not only of money transferred but also of the technology and knowledge transfer by the Egyptians abroad. This is still a work in progress.

We must work with the state to bring Egyptians abroad together and unite our energies in a proper institutional way, toward the clear objectives to serve Egypt's political, cultural, social and economic goals, on the one hand, and to serve Egyptians and their interests abroad, on the other hand. Unfortunately, the Ministry of Egyptians Abroad did not do its part, as we expected. We should continue what we started in 2015 at Cairo University with Dr. Jaber Nassar (former president of the Jama) and Dr. Hala al-Said, now the minister of planning and international cooperation.

M. ELGAMAL worked as a teaching assistant at Ain Shams University for two years before leaving Egypt in 1977, first to Sweden and then to USA. He worked for the federal and local governments in the US and Canada and taught at universities in Manitoba, Ottawa, and North Carolina. He is currently owner of a group of companies working in the high technology sectors in the USA, Canada and the Middle East. Elgamal has solid expertise in organization development and management in the areas of IT, security, aviation, transportation, education and economic development. A team builder and a goal and results oriented executive, he ensures that things get done in an effective, efficient, and economic manner.

BETWEEN EGYPT AND AMERICA
Mona Mobarak

My story is made of connected chains, sharing no clear beginning or end. Even though the end has not arrived yet, it has some sort of a beginning. How can I begin the story that led me to the United States, where I spent most of my life? I may start with a point that is close to the beginning, however. My mother was a housewife fully dedicated to raising us. We lived in a villa with six bedrooms, one of which belonged to me. It was my own little home. From the age of four, I attended the Sacré-Cœur (Sacred Heart) school. After graduating from high school, I went to college and majored in French literature. I did not complete my studies there. Instead, marriage opened a new chapter in my life.

My parents' family came from the village of al-Taʿbaniyya, the Ghonim clan. They were well-off to a certain extent. My father came to the world after a seventeen-year long childless marriage. After my father, my grandmother followed his delivery with two girls. When he was little, my father attended a Qurʾan school (kuttaab). One of his eyes caught a disease, so his mother moved with him to Cairo, where more than one doctor told her that he had lost sight in one of his eyes. He still was more fortunate than Taha Hussein, the Egyptian writer and thinker who lost his sight completely in childhood but nevertheless managed to earn a PhD from the Sorbonne University and become one of the most important intellectuals in Egypt in the last century. My grandmother gave in to the situation. She replaced the defective eye with a glass eyeball to minimize the harm caused to my father's looks.

After my grandmother moved to Cairo with my father, she made his education her central focus. She made sure he received a better education than what he would have gotten at the Qur'an school. With one eye, my father devoured all his textbooks and passed his classes with distinction. He went to law school and earned a degree. He moved through the judicial ranks until he reached the office of the prosecutor general. After the 1952 revolt, the Free Officers Administration tried to remove my father from his post. He refused to take another post. When they tried to transfer him, he resigned. After that, he continued to work as an attorney in the public sector in Cairo.

My father never paid much attention to religious rituals, even though he was a model of morality. His behavior and moral conduct influenced all of us. He wrote a personal exegesis of the Qur'an, based on his ethical and legal background. This enlightened exegesis, according to his older brother, was never published. Rather, it somehow disappeared from our home. We never knew what happened to it.

I was the only sister to five brothers. I was the last-born. My father never treated me differently than my siblings. One time, he took me to the bank to open a bank account for me. He distributed his estate equally between us during his lifetime. He wrote a letter to each of us every year detailing our assets. He always stressed that I should get an equal share from the inheritance and that we must divide things equally, six ways. I learned to treat my own children in the same way my father treated us.

All my brothers did well in school. They all started out working in my father's law firm; however, after a while, they took their individual paths. The oldest graduated from law school and became a judge. The second eldest finished medical school and became a physician and worked as an army doctor. The third became a judge in the Supreme Constitutional Court, while the fourth became a judge in the State Security Court. The fifth became a lawyer and worked in my father's law firm, which he later inherited.

Some of my brothers' stories are worth contemplating, as they give a good idea about our family. When my father knew my eldest brother was wanted by the authorities for being a communist, my father arranged security forces for him. My brother was not a communist, nor did he engage in any similar activity. Even though he was imprisoned, after his release, the case was dropped, and his name was cleared. He later became a lawyer, a writer, and a translator in the United Nations.

My second-eldest brother, Nabil, got to know a Jewish American lady. He met her on a bus ride between Cairo and Alexandria. The beautiful American lady sat next to him on the bus and they got to know one another. He volunteered to show her around Alexandria. She agreed. Then she went back with him to Cairo. At that time, our family was spending the summer vacation in Alexandria. Our house was nearly empty, except for a house servant. Nabil suggested that she stay over, and she accepted. She came back the following year to see Nabil. Their relationship deepened and they decided to marry without telling my family.

My father taught us to make decisions for ourselves and to take responsibility for our decisions, especially with regard to marital issues. The wedding of my two eldest brothers took place at the same time, in 1960, in a hall in the Shepheard Hotel, between six and eight o'clock, with a tea party.

Our family spent most summers in Alexandria, escaping the blazing heat of Cairo. We owned a beach hut in the beautiful area of Miami Beach. We spent most of our time in that hut, which had a small dressing room and a tiny kitchen. My father came from Cairo every weekend to spend time with us. He spent the mornings with his friends and later joined us for dinner.

One hot August day, while I was with my mother, drinking iced lemonade, chatting away and enjoying the beach scenery, an elegant young man in his early thirties stopped by. He said to my mother, "Hi, ma'am. Do you remember me? I'm Ahmad Mubarak. I used to study with Nabil in your house."

"Yes, of course!" my mother said. "How are you? What are you up to these days?"

Ahmad also wanted to get to know me. He asked, "Are you Mona?" I nodded. My mother invited him to join us for lemonade. He asked about Nabil. He hadn't seen Nabil for a long while and wanted to know where he had been and what he was doing. He asked for his number, saying he missed his friend.

My mother explained that Nabil was currently an army conscript.

Ahmad then drank his lemonade and left. He started stopping by after that, almost on a weekly basis. He would greet us as he passed by, chit-chat for a short while, sneakily look at me, and then leave. His interest in me was obvious. He is an admirable person and articulate, and he managed to make a good impression on me.

After our summer vacation ended, we went back to Cairo. My mother received a phone call from Ahmad's mother, asking if she could visit. My mother welcomed her, and she began to visit regularly. It became obvious I was the reason behind those frequent visits.

Then one day, Ahmad asked for my hand! I was seventeen years old. My mother replied that I was too young, but that she would nevertheless speak to my father about the matter. His reply was that we should look into the matter.

So, my mother asked Nabil about Ahmad, since they had been best friends and colleagues in medical school. His answer was that Ahmad came from a good family, even if they were not rich. Ahmad worked as a doctor in the public sector, had his own clinic, and secured a good income. He was an otolaryngologist. He had traveled to England to study in his specialty, which was deafness in children. He brought back a machine that could measure the level of deafness; it was the only such machine in Egypt at the time. Ahmad's salary from the public sector was thirty pounds. His income from his clinic was several times that.

Ahmad became known to my family. They saw no flaws in him. My mother was convinced he was a good fit.

After three months, Ahmad's mother called again, asking for a clear answer for her son.

My father's answer was crystal clear: "There nothing wrong what-soever with Ahmad, and if Ahmad is serious, I have no objections. However, he and Mona must get to know one another. They have to go out for a period of six months and decide for themselves."

That is exactly what happened and how we moved on to get married. The wedding took place in the same fashion as my brothers' weddings four years earlier, at the Shepheard Hotel. The belly dancer Soheir Zaki performed at our wedding. Afterwards, we moved into a spacious apartment in the Mohandsein neighborhood, with four bed-rooms and three balconies. In 1965, we had our first son, Muhammad, whom we nicknamed Hamada. Our second and last son, Ayman, was born in 1967. A very dignified nanny, Umm Abdou, helped me with the chores and taking care of the kids.

Moving to the United States

The year 1967 brought Egypt's resounding defeat. It was a miserable year for us and for other Egyptians. The regime was stripped in a disgraceful and painful way, and despair and gloom affected everyone in Egypt. Ahmad and his friends started thinking about migration. I had never entertained the idea of migration because it would mean leaving my mother behind. I didn't want to leave her, especially since she had begun to have symptoms of a weak heart. On top of it all, we had two children we needed to take care of. What awaited us in the United States? Our economic, social, and emotional life in Egypt was comfortable and easy. We would have to leave all that behind and knock on the doors of the unknown.

I ended up agreeing grudgingly. Ahmad resigned from his job in the public sector, and in mid-1968, my mother passed away. I was very close to her and was very sad about losing her.

The hardest thing for me was leaving my father alone after the death of my mother, his life-long companion. It was a period of severely conflicting emotions, pain, and uncertainty. One day, my father took me aside on our balcony and told me that the American consul, whom he knew personally, had told him we'd submitted our migration papers.

He stated that the decision was ours and we had to take responsibility for it. "You are my only daughter," he said. "You leaving me will be difficult, but now you belong to your husband and kids." He added, "I promise that if you decide to migrate, I will come to visit you once a year and buy you tickets to come to Egypt once a year as well."

Ahmad had the ability to either get rid of certain emotions or avoid showing them. Maybe the clearest emotion he showed as we prepared to migrate was his remorse at having to sell his 1965 Chevrolet. I think this was only a cover-up of other emotions he blocked out in order to avoid thinking about our uncertain future. Ahmad knew he was about to leave his mother behind. She was a second mother to me as well. I learned many things from her, and she always treated me as if I was her own daughter. Before we left, Ahmad encouraged her to write her autobiography, which she did. She wrote about marrying a doctor at the age of fourteen. Her husband was close to the ideology of the Muslim Brotherhood. Nevertheless, he was open-minded; he was an autonomous thinker, not a follower, and he separated himself from the Brotherhood after they resorted to violence and assassinations. Ahmad represented the third generation of doctors in his family.

The day of our departure came in July 1968. This was my first time out of Egypt. It was painful to leave all of Egypt, my father, siblings, and Ahmad's family. We first traveled to Beirut so Ahmad could pass his equivalency test. During the few days we spent in Beirut, we saw the main sights of this city, despite our anxiety and the endless unresolved questions in our minds.

When we reached the United States, Nabil, who had already migrated there, met us at the airport. He had completed his residency and started his work as a radiologist at Yale University. He and his wife, Judy, welcomed us as guests for three weeks in their apartment. Suddenly this tiny apartment was filled with four boys, playing together. One of Nabil and Judy's sons was born in Egypt and the second in the United States.

Four weeks from our arrival in the United States, we got the results of Ahmad's equivalency test. It was great news. Ahmad passed and was thus allowed to start working as a resident doctor. He submitted many applications and received a preliminary offer from Glen Cove Hospital, which was a modest hospital. It didn't match Ahmad's ambitions, but he accepted the offer nonetheless, until he could find a better situation. We both had to be interviewed before Ahmad could sign his contract. We passed the interview. The hospital chose a furnished three-bedroom apartment nearby to house us. The work was tiring for Ahmad. He left at seven in the morning and didn't return until seven at night. He ate dinner and then crashed, then repeated the same cycle the following day. In addition, he had two or three night shifts every month.

We bought a used car, a 1962 Mercury, for $200. I learned how to drive that winter. It wasn't easy, with all the roads covered with snow. Later, we bought a Dodge car, through installments. Slowly, we were pulled into the fast-paced rhythm of American life.

Without Umm Abdou, the dignified nanny we left behind in Egypt, I needed to perform chores I was not used to. In addition to buying groceries, I had to prepare meals and clean the house. The landlady was a kind Canadian. She helped by showing me where to buy groceries and showing me around town. She had a lot of time on her hands because her journalist husband worked long hours.

At the time, Hamada was four years old and Ayman was eighteen months. The landlady helped me register Hamada in a nursery. She also helped me become a volunteer in the nursery so I could see with my own eyes the quality of education, and to get to know the mothers of the children there. It was an extremely beneficial experience. In fact, Hamada and Ayman never had any problems adjusting to the educational system, because of their young age and their white skin color.

Numerous hilarious experiences happened to me at that stage. One time, I discovered that the can of tuna I thought I bought was in fact cat and dog food. Another time, I went to a butcher and ordered a big piece of meat, only to discover I didn't have enough cash on me. I called Ahmad and broke down in tears. He calmed me and instructed me on how to pay with a credit card. Such encounters ushered us into the American life, yet they stayed in our memory because of their strangeness to us then.

After finishing his residency, Ahmad was allowed to practice medicine. However, due to his lack of experience, his salary was modest. Most doctors had three to five years of specialized internships. Ahmad was not successful in finding an opportunity in his former specialization (otolaryngology). But we wanted to stay in New York State, near New York City. Therefore, he started to think about switching specializations. He ended up choosing psychiatry. He was delighted to be accepted at the New York Medical College for a training program that lasted four years.

We moved to an apartment designated for interns, which the Rockefeller Foundation gifted to the university. It was located near the college and had doctors from all over the world: French, German, Italians, Indians, Chinese, and Americans. The building was like the headquarters of the United Nations. I didn't feel like a stranger in this atmosphere. This was the United Sates: everyone was at once a stranger, and also ready to adjust, at least varying degrees. The apartment had two bedrooms, a living room, and a fully equipped kitchen. The cleaning team came daily to clean the apartment and change the bedsheets. This gave us more time to engage in different activities.

Ahmad's day started at 7:00am and he returned at 7:00pm. The kids left at 8:00am to take the school bus. They came back at 3:00pm. I took them to play in the park outside the building until dinner time. While their children were in school, most mothers attended to their weekly schedules. I joined them for their some of their activities, except for three days a week, when I volunteered at the kids' school. I also dedicated one day a week to studying English (my original education was in French). Another day was dedicated to buying groceries.

Some people attended classes in a nearby community college that had a two-year educational program. Afterward, one either worked, or went to a university for further studies. I enjoyed taking cooking classes. I also worked on developing my interests in photography, writing, and more. The kids acclimatized easily. They attended swimming and houseback riding summer camps. There were several avenues for entertainment on weekends. We also hosted many guests. However, I did not get to know other Egyptians; I only saw my brother, whenever his work shifts allowed.

In the summer of 1970, we visited Egypt. I was longing to spend time with my father, grandfather, uncles, and brothers. We stayed with my father in our old house. The cook, who was around when I grew up, would ask every day, "What would you like to eat tomorrow?" I was really missing Egyptian food. We spent every night with family and friends. In the mornings, we went to the Heliopolis Club and spent time with other kids from the family in the swimming pool. Hamada and Ayman were very happy during this visit.

On that trip, we also went on a beach vacation to Glim Beach, Alexandria. We had an enjoyable daily routine—spending the mornings in our beach chalet, swimming at Sidi Bishr Beach, and gathering in the chalet again afterward to drink tea and eat sweets made by our cook, Master Mursi. The nanny who raised me, Halima, came along. She helped with preparing dinner and putting the kids to sleep. After they went to sleep, Ahmad, his uncle (who was a lawyer residing in Alexandria), and I we went out to fish restaurants. These were the best nights during that summer. We spent the last week of this vacation with Ahmad's mother. She was an amazing cook. Anything Ahmad asked for, he got. She was happy to host us. We had dinner daily in her balcony, with Ahmad's brothers and friends.

The day we had to travel back to New York came quickly. I was sad. Saying goodbye again to my father was painful. He promised to visit us either in the coming summer or during Christmas. This became his regular routine for the rest of his life.

After finishing his internship at New York Medical College in 1970, Ahmad was hired at Cornell University in New York. He worked there until 1980. After that, he accepted a partnership with some of his colleagues. They opened a clinic in West Virginia. West Virginia represented a cultural shock for us since it was so different from New York, where we'd been living. The state was known as one of the Southern states with racial/ethnic bias against African Americans and Jews. We could not bear living there for more than six months and decided to move back to New York. Hamada and Ayman were able to complete the school year in West Virginia, despite their inability to get used to the conservative and racist atmosphere. I must stress that I found a severe gap in the quality of education between and within states in the United States. Apart from Hamada and Ayman's experience in West Virginia, their overall experience in public schools was positive and their education was of a high standard.

Ahmad went back to Cornell University and also joined two other psychiatric clinics on the side. We moved to Westchester, which is not far from New York City. We continued to live there for twenty years. During this period, Hamada and Ayman started to grow, mature, and live independently. Eventually, both went to Cornell.

Hamada interrupted his education at Cornell to move to San Francisco and take a handsomely paying job at Oracle for two years. He excelled with computers and found that a formal education no longer attracted him. A human being is worth what they are good at, regardless of whether they have a degree. After that, he decided to start his own company. He also worked with people from Stanford University on a research project for Toyota. During that period, he got to know a young woman named Kelly. She was a graphic designer working at her own company. They got married in a civil, nonreligious wedding. We were happy with the marriage. After honeymooning in the south of France, they organized a dinner party in a French restaurant for family and friends from both sides to meet one another. They decided not to accept any wedding gifts. After two years, they decided to move to France. Hamada found a job with an American company that had branches in Paris and Moscow. He traveled regularly between the two locations. Kelly started learning French and studying graphic design at the Sorbonne, to move ahead in her career. After two years, they moved back to San Francisco. Later, they moved to New York, where Hamada joined the management of Amazon, where he worked until recently. Kelly still owns her own graphic design business.

During a summer job at IBM, one of Ayman's managers advised him to study physics and mathematics. Nevertheless, he did not complete his studies in physics and mathematics because of concerns related to the job market. Ayman had an interest in music since childhood. After leaving Cornell, he joined with a few friends to form a band called Brown Fellinis. They toured throughout the United States for a year. It was a happy year for him, even though he did not earn enough. He then moved back to San Francisco to work for a biotechnology company, where his job was based on his experience with musical sounds. He met an engineer named Jenifer, and they decided to get married. Part of their honeymoon was on a cruise ship on the Nile. We also held a reception in Egypt for them to meet family and friends. One of the attendees asked me whether the wives of Ayman and Hamada converted to Islam. I said that was not a big deal for me or my kids—it is their life, and they can do with it whatever they wish.

After Hamada and Ayman became independent, I had more time on my hands. I started asking myself, "What can I do with this time?" I thought seriously about finding a stable job. By coincidence, I found an ad for a temporary job for Lloyd's of London, a large insurance company. One of the managers interviewed me and asked if I had any experience with computers. I told him I did. He then asked if I had previous work experience and I replied no, except for volunteer work at my kids' school and in some libraries and hospitals, as well as work on fundraising campaigns in Egypt for the Red Crescent.

The next morning, I received a phone call with another invitation to come to their office. They had decided to offer me the temporary position! They also offered me six months of computer training with someone from IBM. I learned a lot during that period. At the end of the six months, the company offered me a permanent position. However, that would require me to work in their office in Manhattan. I refused the offer because it meant I would have to take a train, which I was not used to.

When I mentioned this to my family, Hamada told me it was an opportunity not to be missed. "The company has trained you for six months," he said. "They took care of you. The issue with transportation is not the big deal you imagine it to be." He offered to take me on the train to Manhattan.

I went and saw the humongous Grand Central station for the first time. The company's headquarters were a few minutes on foot from the station. I called the company and accepted the offer. I continued to work for them for eight years. During the last year, I contracted Lyme disease, which is caused by a bacterium transferred to humans from a tick. When the disease is diagnosed early, it is usually easy to cure with antibiotics. This, however, was not my case. The disease spread and affected my nervous system. I needed hospitalization for a month and then medical treatment for a year. I ended up resigning from my job at Lloyd's. After recovering, I found work at Smith Barney, a company that invests people's money in funds that provide a variety of securities. The job required examining each case separately. Some of the clients were Egyptians, who took care of starting their funds from an early age. I remained there for seven years.

In the last twenty years, Ahmad suffered from a chronic disease that weakened his nervous system. It took five years to identify it as a rare disease called inclusion body myositis (IBM). Though it weakens the body, it does not affect the brain. Ahmad carried on with his life, nevertheless. However, his condition became more difficult toward the end, and his movement was minimal. According to his wishes, he remained at home, not in the hospital. I stayed by his side and attended to all his needs. A professional nurse also came and helped. During the last three months of his life, we had to move him into hospice care. Most days, I was with him around the clock. He told me he had been able to achieve all he wanted in his life and he was ready to die.

During that time, Hamada had been planning to travel on a safari in Africa. He wanted to cancel the trip to stay alongside his ailing father. Ahmad's response was that he himself had wanted to go on such a trip. He told Hamada to travel and send him pictures. He insisted this was what Hamada should do. And that is exactly what happened. Soon after the first batch of pictures arrived, Ahmad left us.

Now, I live in a small but beautiful apartment in White Plains. I enjoy numerous friendships with Americans and Egyptians. I'm always in touch with my children and grandchildren. I ask myself: "If I could go back in time, would I make any major changes in my life?" I don't think so. I was lucky and benefited from my circumstances.

———•———

MONA MOBARAK grew up in Cairo, Egypt and went to Sacred Heart School. While at college, she met and married Dr. Ahmed Mobarak in 1964. Four year later, they immigrated to the States, where she attended community college and studied hotel and restaurant management at Pace University Business School. After her two sons reached high school age, she worked at Lloyd's of London and later at Smith Barney. She has also spent time doing volunteer work. She currently lives in White Plains, New York. One of her sons works in New York and the other in California. She enjoys spending time with her two grandsons.

MY INTELLECTUAL, SOCIAL, PROFESSIONAL, AND CULTURAL JOURNEY IN THE UNITED STATES

Sherif Nasr

One can never overestimate the degree of acculturation one undergoes when one immigrates to the West. The saying "America is the great melting pot" should not simply be taken as referring to personal ethnic identity or character; America melts all traditional understandings, philosophies, epistemologies, and worldviews.

In looking back at the forty years I have lived in the United States, I am amazed how I came up with my very own organic synthesis of traditional religion and modern liberal values. I came up with a novel worldview I call "theomodernity," which is an amalgam of theology and modernity.

I grew up and went to medical school in Alexandria, Egypt. I'm an early-generation baby boomer who belongs to the upper middle-class. My dad was an academic physicist who studied in England for seven years. My mom was a housewife who only completed her primary education. I went to an English school for my primary education and then to a public school in an Arab country. My outlook on life was cautiously liberal. I was a traditional Muslim who lived a liberal upper middle-class life. I went to Friday prayers and then sat with friends to enjoy a glass of beer at Maamoora Palace. My liberal lifestyle was not just social; I believed in the full gamut of liberal views about social justice, free markets, and individual rights, and took a critical view of political despotism.

My focus was on my education and on my bridge game. I was addicted to playing bridge, eight days a week, for no less than six hours daily, throughout medical school. Therefore, religion never played a major role in my upbringing and youth. My dad read one chapter of the Qur'an daily during Ramadan. However, I criticized his liberal opinion that daughters and sons should receive an equal inheritance. In sum, I can be labeled socially conservative and religiously liberal.

When I came to the United States to start my residency right after I graduated from medical school, I was completely mesmerized by the new system and outlook on life. Initially, I was disappointed that New England was not as modern and urban as Dallas—a city I had become familiar with by avidly watching the soap opera from the 1970s that carried the same name. I didn't feel out of place in the United States, so much so that I was disappointed by the fact that Americans were not as smart or intellectual as I had imagined. I couldn't explain how simple, down-to-earth, unsophisticated people could create such a global superpower. It took me some time to reflect on and ponder over this discord. Finally, I came to the conclusion that the secret sauce lies in the system. The forefathers of this country brought enlightened insight to the creation of a dynamic system that is "idiot proof" and capable of continuous improvement and, most importantly, does not depend on the intellectual capacity of the masses.

I lived the typical modern liberal life. I attended Friday prayers but did not follow any of the Islamic edicts, other than fasting during Ramadan. However, when I decided to get married at the age of thirty-one, I looked for someone of my social and religious background who held the same conservative upper middle-class values. My wife is a Sunni Lebanese/Syrian woman. Like me, she didn't pray regularly but fasted during Ramadan. We started praying regularly as soon as we got married. We went for the hajj a few years later. We bought a house on a mortgage and lived the typical American life. On Christmas, we had a Christmas tree and invited my coworkers to parties and served them liquor, even though we never drank.

No longer intrigued by the liberal lifestyle, I gradually became more and more religiously conservative. I opted out of our mortgage and never dealt with interest payments in my private life or business. As I metamorphosed religiously, I gradually crystallized my religious worldview. I became intellectually content with the idea that any religion consists of a private set of beliefs, rituals, customs, and practices. In addition, the Abrahamic religion regulates the community of believers' social, economic, and civic/political lives. Once I came to this realization, the next natural step was to compare and contrast between this and secular worldviews.

Living in both worlds made me feel as though I was in no-man's-land. I had one foot firmly entrenched in the secular modern world and another equally entrenched in the religious world, but I was never totally content with either alone. I could see the grossly evident advantages of the modern system, but it was clearly evident that the humanistic dimension was missing in that world. Intellectually, I agreed with those academicians who critiqued modernity. They pointed out that it results in predictable cycles of wars, famines, financial recessions, and environmental pollution. More importantly, it leads to moral relativism and nihilism.

The theoretical underpinnings of modernity are problematic, to say the least, from a religious viewpoint. In one way, modernity can be understood as a philosophical viewpoint that starts with a scientific view, then adds a sociopolitical and economic view, and finally evolves into a comprehensive worldview. This worldview basically replaced God with man as the intellectual center of the universe. As a result, at best, modernity neutralizes religion and relegates it to the private sphere; at worst (e.g., in the case of the French Revolution), it is anti-religious. That is a historical fact. However, can we revisit this issue afresh in our times? What is the relationship between both worldviews? Do they represent parallel tracks, are they antagonistic, or do they represent two faces of the same coin? Can either represent a self-sufficient system that makes us capable of leading a wholesome life that takes care of our spiritual, physical and intellectual needs?

In the meantime, the Arab Spring made it clear to me that the utopian view of Islam clearly falls short of being a basis for achieving a viable modern civilization. We were so gullible to think Islam was a system you could take out of its box, and all you'd have to do is hit the *start* button, and voilà, the system would start working on its own, doing its magical work. Alas, our ahistorical view of religion is super simplistic and romantic. It lacks the modern values essential to build civilization, such as intellectual curiosity, valuing diversity of thought and ideas, empathy, democracy, scientism (e.g., Darwinian evolution).

Therefore, I took one step up in modifying my worldview from the concrete view of Islam as a complete social, economic, and political system into a view that considers Islam not as a system, but a set of values and principles from which we can derive a system. Most recently, I took an even wider bird's eye view in understanding that Islam is not even a set of values and principles (since these are global), but more fundamentally, a worldview (unity of God, or Tawheed) from which we can deduce a set of universal humanistic principles and values, from which we can in turn derive a system to guide our lives to achieve the following goals: (1) to live in peace with our physical and spiritual self, other human beings, animals, plants, and the inanimate environment (e.g., no pollution, depletion of resources, global warming, irradiation) and (2) to achieve our best potential as human beings.

Seen through this lens, there is now room to establish a dialogue between religion and modernity. Assuming such a relationship is not without its inconsistencies, how can we reconcile science and metaphysics, materialism and spirituality, the here and now with the hereafter? The relationship will never be harmonious; it will never reach an equilibrium, but it is more akin to a continuous back-and-forth tension in which each domain acts as a check on the other. In fact, Islam claims it embodies the secular domain within it. The story of the creation of man embodies this principle. God willed the creation of a being who has choice and is capable of balancing his spiritual and physical domains to achieve his full potential. He will only do so if, and only if, he successfully manages this tension between both domains.

So far, I have not encountered an example that disrupts this tension or disproves my hypothesis. The most classical example of such discordance is Darwinian evolution. The prevailing classical religious view is that the narrative of the creation of man should be taken literally. That places it on a collision course with scientific fact. On the contrary, I see no such inconsistency. Naturally, as a scientist, I fully believe in scientific evidence. Therefore, I'm not willing to engage in arguments about the worth of creationism and evolution. To me, Darwinism is a theory about how evolution occurred (by natural selection, as Darwin concluded) and not about whether evolution did or did not happen. Evolution itself is a fact and not a theory. Moreover, reading the Qur'an, I see verses that directly refer to the evolution of humans. Several hominids lived on earth, and then one species survived and flourished. Therefore, so far, I see no contradiction whatsoever between science and religion.

So, if this is true, then where did that division between science and religion, or modernity and revelation, come from? Even if you ask the common man, "Is there any conflict between religion and science?", their answer will be an emphatic *no*. Therefore, how can we explain such dissidence? I think the answer is psychological. We do not learn from people we do not hold in high esteem. The historical rubbing of shoulders between the East and West, between Islam and Christendom, created a psychological barrier that hinders healthy dialogue.

I see the risks and perils of adapting modernity as is. Yet I feel that if it is expressed within a framework of Tawheed, it will fulfill the two goals alluded to above. It is almost as if you have to swallow this bitter medicine in order to restore your health. Let's face it, the West has humiliated us militarily, scientifically, and culturally. Therefore, we are forced into a corner where we have only two choices: either be defensive or be imitative. How can we get out of this duality? Fortunately, for those of us living in the West, who has achieved some degree of professional and economic success, there is a third alternative. We are no longer haunted with the phantom of an inferiority complex. Free of any such prejudgments, we are grateful to the West and its civilization for everything it taught us. Yet we believe we can contribute to humanity's well-being and world civilization.

Therefore, I firmly believe secularism is actually part of religion. In traditional societies, everything is sacred: rulers, ancestors, useful objects, harmful objects, traditions, etc. Islam represented a departure and a major rift from this belief. It introduced secularism and separated it clearly from the divine. It is interesting that when we state our faith, we start by denying all deities before affirming our belief in the one and only God. This represents a radical departure from the religions of traditional societies and a venture into a modern worldview. Islam flies with two wings: revelation and acquired knowledge. Over time, at least three factors accounted for the gradual decline of the latter. These include the crises that happened to the Mutazilites, political despotism, and the creation of the clergy. These three forces—and probably others—contributed to mute and weaken the secular aspects of our religion. In the end, we are flying with only one wing—that of revelation. It is no wonder that, over time, our worldview will continuously get narrower as we are no longer able to critique our ideas and challenge our traditions.

I have no illusion that this worldview is a dialogue non-starter. To the traditional religious person, this seems, at best, an apologetic view on behalf of the West and, at worst, heresy. It will equally be rejected by secularists because the introduction of any religious or metaphysical reality is an anathema. Interestingly, we have a hadith (an oral tradition narrated by the Prophet, peace be upon him) that says Islam will start as a stranger and will become a stranger once again. I am not deluded by the fact that my understanding could be faulty. I am certain it is open to improvements and corrections, and possibly radically so. Therefore, I am humbled by the Qur'anic verses that point to those who believe they are doing good, while in fact they are doing the opposite. Therefore, I am hoping to create a platform where these ideas can be discussed, improved, and corrected.

So how has this worldview expressed itself in my day-to-day life? We placed our two daughters in parochial Islamic schools where my

wife, a PhD in molecular biology, was a teacher. One of daughters became a replica of my wife. She wears a hijab but holds liberal religious
and social views. Her center of gravity is her family, and her profession
only comes second. I don't think she is concerned about existential
questions. Life is just the way it is, and one has to go through it without too many questions, too many doubts, or too much trepidation.
My younger daughter is a social rebel. She made a full circle—starting
with a conservative religious view, moving to super liberal views, and
finally back to an improvised liberal religious and social stance. She
epitomizes the crises that face second-generation immigrants. Our
traditional religious views clearly fall short of providing second-generation immigrants with an acceptable worldview. We badly need to
generate one rooted in the modern societies we live in. We grew and
became comfortable in a world where we insulated ourselves from the
nagging inconsistencies between science and revelation. Traditional
religion, to us, is a ticket to enter paradise; it is not a tool to improve life,
let alone a universal worldview. This mindset may have worked for
our generation but will definitely not be sufficient or even acceptable
to the following generations. We keep deluding ourselves by repeating
that Islam is the fastest growing religion in the West and ignoring the
fact that religion is an extinct species in the West. We may be taking a
larger portion of a vanishing pie.

On the professional side, I joined a Fortune 500 corporation and
benefited greatly from learning how the corporate world has created
a system that can self-correct. However, I gradually realized that it
lacked a humanistic component. When I finally had to make a career
move, I saw an opportunity to put what I had learned into practice
and add to it a humanistic component informed by my religious
worldview. For example, I am blessed that I never had to raise capital
by borrowing money from banks on fixed interest. When I reached
out to angel investors (which all my friends truly are), I never used a
religious argument. Instead, I believed we should eliminate the mid-
dleman and his arbitrage. My accountant is bewildered about why I
have partners and investors when I can borrow money from banks at

a fraction of what I am paying them. More importantly, we treat others (e.g., patients, physicians, employees, vendors, insurance companies, government agencies) the way we would like to be treated. Therefore, selling the business is not one of our exit strategies, because we feel it will erode our social responsibility. The question whether such a socially responsible business can be scaled. The prevailing Western model is that when successful businesspeople, such as Bill Gates and Warren Buffet, become philanthropists and attempt to change the world for the better, they do so from outside their businesses. They set up separate foundations that focus on such missions. This is very commendable. However, is it possible to maintain and scale a business that is competitive and, at the same time, socially responsible?

Another dimension of my day-to-day life includes politics. At one time, I was engaged in national politics to reform our traditional societies and create a modern civic state. We learned a great lesson from the Arab Spring: changing the political figurehead is meaningless. Instead, we need to change the system to create a modern civic state that embodies the values and practices of enlightenment. Those who are critical of the status quo call for a change of the entire political regime. I now say this is still not enough. I offer as evidence the following metaphor. Let's hypothetically assume we will transfer the entire population of any traditional society—say, all one hundred million citizens of Egypt—and drop them in a modern state such as Germany, and do the reverse for Germans. So now the Egyptians are living in a modern state with all its resources, infrastructures, political institutions, rule of law, democracy, separation of powers, limited government, etc., while the Germans will be living in a deforested land with no such infrastructure, institutions, environmental resources, etc. Let's further assume we will examine both societies after two generations. Which one do you think will be a progressive society living in a modern civic state? No doubt it will be the Germans living in Egypt. This should not come as a surprise to anyone, because it is not the civic state that will rehabilitate its citizens but that the enlightened and empowered citizens will create such a modern civic state. They will not be able to do that without developing a worldview that will inform their ethics, values, and practices.

Therefore, my intellectual project is to create a worldview that takes care of the spirit and the mind/body. Theomodernity is such a project. The challenge is to how to extricate oneself from everyday life and focus on such a project. Naturally, debates and advocacy are not the way to go. We need to attract like-minded individuals who already believe in some elements of such a worldview. We are looking for the one percent of contrarians who are willing to question the status quo. Then again, only one percent of these curious individuals will have the interest and the wherewithal to stand against the crowds and swim against the current. Once a critical mass is reached, such a worldview will be expressed in different domains of knowledge (e.g., philosophy, social sciences, humanities, physical sciences). The end goal is to create a strain of religion that is as authentic as traditional, fundamentalist, spiritual, and/or political Islam. We will call this "contemporary Islam." Perhaps this would be one manifestation of the sun rising in the West, in the classical oral tradition in Islam.

I have no doubt that had I not moved to the West, I would not have developed such a dynamic, lively, and controversial worldview that is open to questioning and debate.

———◆———

SHERIF NASR was born in 1956 in Alexandria, Egypt. He graduated from Alexandria University Medical School. In 1981, immediately after graduation, he immigrated to the US. He is a pathologist working in the private sector and resides with his family in Northern New Jersey. Molded by his faith, culture and four decades of life in the West, his extra-curricular interest is to understand the relationship between modernity and religion. Although most dismiss as mutually exclusive, his project is to explore how they can interact in a complimentary fashion.

FROM CAIRO TO NEW YORK: THE CHALLENGES

Mona Mikhail

It is difficult for me to realize that it has been more than fifty years since I settled in the United States. In many ways, it could have been yesterday. A lifetime went by too fast.

I came the year my father passed away. A telegram with my acceptance—and a scholarship from the University of Michigan, Ann Arbor, to their PhD program in English Literature—arrived at the same time as dozens of others expressing condolences. I could easily have not seen it in the piles of telegrams.

At the time, I was an instructor at Cairo University, a position I had been appointed to after getting my bachelor's with honors. To continue my career, I needed a PhD. My elder brother, a physician, had been in the United States for graduate studies and specialization, and encouraged me to apply to the University of Michigan. He had returned to Egypt with his young family and was around when our father fell ill and passed away. It was very lucky for all of us that he was there during those hard times.

Very few Egyptian candidates were allowed to travel for graduate studies. My attempts became stymied at the university level. One day, I went to the office of an official who was clearly giving me a hard time. Just then, Professor Soheir al-Kalamawy entered the room and proceeded to tell the official to help, rather than create impediments for me.

I'm sure that resulted in my paperwork being expedited. Eventually, my papers, along with those of ten other candidates, were approved and signed by President Nasser. Such were the conditions in 1966.

I had a good life in Cairo, between teaching at Cairo University and a part-time job at an African embassy. I traveled to parts of Africa and attended some Pan-African conferences. Leaving all this behind was hard. And of course, it was hard to leave behind my grieving family and friends. Nevertheless, I was finally on my way.

We weren't permitted to leave with more than $11 stamped on our passports. Other arrangements were made with some family friends to supply me with extra dollars. I decided to make a stop in Paris, which was a dream come true for me.

I arrived in Ann Arbor on a cold September morning and settled into the Martha Cook Building, which was an all-women's dorm. My courses had already begun, so I had to immediately start work. One professor told me, "You are taking these courses at your own risk and peril." I took the challenge.

I had chosen a couple of advanced courses. I plunged headlong into them without knowing much about the graduate system in the United States. I quickly discovered how much more demanding it was than what I had experienced at Cairo University. Although we had excellent professors in Cairo, they hadn't trained us sufficiently to do graduate research. So, learning how to use the library and research tools in Ann Arbor was challenging. Also, Ann Arbor seemed small and isolated, compared with my vibrant Cairo. But it was also quaint in many ways, and somehow, I managed to take to it. My first semester ended successfully.

My first snow was memorable. My suite mate taught me how to make angels in the snow, which was a delight. However, I was not well-equipped for the cold and snow. I had brought more fancy clothes with me than I needed on a campus. In true Egyptian fashion, I had brought lovely outfits by some well-known seamstresses in Cairo, which were totally impractical for a student. So, I had to quickly equip myself with student clothes, especially a warm coat and boots for the proverbial snowy winters of Michigan. That summer, I took all my fancy clothes back to Cairo.

The Six-Day War in 1967, with its disastrous consequences for Egypt and the Middle East, was a hard time to be away from my family. My younger brother had enlisted in the army and was on the front fighting. During the years of the War of Attrition, we lived in great fear.

My political education went hand in hand with my graduate studies. Those were politically active years on campuses throughout the United States, and Ann Arbor was as active, or even more so, than Berkeley on the West Coast. As part of the antiwar movement, I participated in rallies against the Vietnam War. In November 1969, I joined friends going to Washington D.C. and we drove in packed cars from Ann Arbor all the way to the capital. Stopping on the way for food and gas, we met hundreds of students like ourselves. It was like going on a pilgrimage. When we arrived, we slept on the floors of student dorms at Georgetown University. The next morning, we marched in front of the White House and were immediately teargassed. That tear gas remained in our clothes for a few weeks. The officers watching over us were friendly; they would turn their lapels and reveal the antiwar pins they were wearing. It was their way of showing solidarity with us.

I also became acquainted with Arab student organizations on campus. The Arab students were very active. We had numerous meetings about Palestine, as well as clashes with pro-Israeli students. It was an opportunity to understand the Palestinian question in greater depth. Our activities encompassed cultural aspects as well: we organized dabke dances and musical evenings. It was a great opportunity to get to know students from throughout the Arab world.

After obtaining my MA in English Literature, I began to focus on comparative literature, and eventually made Arabic literature my specialty. This research led me to work on Naguib Mahfouz and Yusuf Idris. I investigated existentialist themes in their short fiction, which made my dissertation pioneering work in the field.

After I had defended my dissertation, it was time for big decisions about the future. Not long after my defense, I received an offer I couldn't refuse: the opportunity to teach at Princeton University. So, for the next two years, I moved East to that great institution. The library and general atmosphere of Princeton were instrumental in determining my academic career. I made good use of the library to work on my manuscript for publication. By the end of my second year, I received an offer to teach at New York University (NYU). It was not an easy decision. Many friends and colleagues advised me to remain at Princeton, where I'd also been asked to teach courses in the Department of French. But the lure of New York City was too hard to resist, and the Big Apple won out. I was lucky to have such opportunities early in my career.

I did keep in touch with Princeton since both universities shared a joint center. I benefitted from the Princeton library and the many lectures offered there by great professors. At the same time, I settled easily into the big city, especially since NYU offered great housing. I began discovering and enjoying the treasures of New York: the theater, opera, bookstores. I also gradually got to know about Arab organizations and events at the United Nations. I became an active member of the Islamic Cultural Society and was invited to give lectures. The Egyptian American Professional Society proved to be one of the long-lasting and important ways to meet a cross-section of Egyptians in the tri-state area. Throughout the years, I helped organize symposia and lecture series at NYU, through which I made long-lasting friendships. I enjoyed an invitation to the White House with a select number of academics. President Jimmy Carter invited a group of Middle East experts because he wanted to use us as an advisory group.

Two of Egypt's first ladies received honors at NYU for their contributions to their society. Jehan Sadat got an honorary degree for the work she did for Egyptian veterans of war and the joint efforts of the NYU Rusk Institute. I was involved in setting up this celebration. Suzanne Mubarak was honored for setting up libraries and museums for children.

The highlight of my career was the publication of seven books on the role of women in Arab society, the fiction of Naguib Mahfouz and Yusuf Idris, and Arabic literature in general. My book *Seen and Heard* won the Library Choice prize. My studies of the fiction of Mahfouz and Idris was translated into Arabic and published in Egypt.

In Egypt, I met several times with Naguib Mahfouz. One summer, when I was in the process of collecting information for my dissertation, I was told he was in Alexandria. So off I went, looking for him. I'd heard he usually went to a cafe in San Stefano, and I found him there, surrounded by a number of his friends. He graciously welcomed me and asked me to join them for coffee. On my way out of the coffee shop, I passed a lady seated with her daughter. She beckoned me and asked if I happened to be a journalist. I explained to her who I was. She then told me, with almost misty eyes, how lucky I was to meet Naguib Mahfouz. She said she came every summer and watched him from far. I immediately took her by the hand and introduced her to our writer. She was so happy to shake hands with him.

In the last five years, I have taken a leave of absence from NYU to teach at the American University in Cairo. It has been a great opportunity to give back to my home country the fruits of my experience in the United States. I enjoyed teaching Egyptian students as well as foreign students at the American University. It seems I have come full circle.

My sister, who decided to settle in Canada, had an equally challenging career. She decided to study library science and became a librarian in both grade school and high school. Her knowledge of French was also an asset. She received an MA in library science from McGill University. Years later, I read some very touching notes written by her students, who admired and loved her dearly. It was not possible for her to start all over with a new career in the United States, so we had to put up with living in two countries, though it would have been preferable to be together. We visited at least two to three times a year. Of course, we visited Egypt together in winters.

Today I enjoy the families of my nephews and nieces. I am proud to see them and their families have successful careers. One nephew teaches law at Georgetown University. One niece is a partner in a firm in Washington D.C., and another niece is working as a hospital administrator. Another nephew is a business entrepreneur. My youngest niece is teaching at Johns Hopkins University. Her brother has a position at Ford. The second generation and their successes are a testimony to what the United States is all about. Last year, their father brought them all on a visit to Egypt to introduce their spouses to their country of origin.

When I look back on my years at Cairo University, I realize how privileged we were as a generation. In addition to having excellent professors, such as Drs. Rashad Rushdie, Magdi Wahba, and Angele Boutros, we enjoyed a great social life. When I see pictures from that time, they which capture another era, compared with what is happening today on Egyptian campuses. As young women, we participated in sports and social activities. I was part of the swimming team and had no problem appearing in a swimsuit in mixed company at the engineering school pool. I won several championships at the university, as well as national prizes. Prior to that, I was a member of the swimming team and synchronized water ballet team at the Heliopolis Sporting Club, activities I enjoyed greatly.

At university, I took up horseback riding and rowing on the Nile, and even had dancing lessons. Mahmoud Reda gave us lessons, and we performed in the Grand University Hall of Cairo University. Today, this would sound like an unimaginable feat, considering the restrictive conditions women face.

———

MONA N. MIKHAIL is a Professor of Arabic Literature and Women Studies at New York University. She recently served as Professor at the Department of Arabic and Islamic Studies at the American University in Cairo. Mikhail is the author of seven books and over 40 articles. Her book *Seen and Heard* won the Choice Library Prize. She also wrote the screenplay for a documentary on the history of the theater in Egypt. Hailed as a great contribution to the Library of Arabic Literature, her pioneering work on Naguib Mahfouz and Yusuf Idris is well recognized.

ME AN ENGINEER? DEALING IN BANKING? I LOVE IT!

Samir Ansary

My father's family came from Tahta, Sohag, and my mother's family from Sinbelawain, Da'ahlia. On my father's side, I am a descendant of an Egyptian family that focused on education, going back to my great-great-grandfather Refaa Al-Tahtawi, the well-known Egyptian scholar (1801–1873). My father, Dr. Ali El-Ansary, graduated with a bachelor's degree in literature and started his career as a high school teacher in Zagazig, where I was born. He then moved to Cairo and furthered his education by obtaining a master's degree and a PhD in advertising from Cairo University. He became a cultural attaché at the Egyptian embassy in Baghdad and then in Somalia. He ended his government career as an assistant vice minister at the Ministry of Higher Education in 1967. He then became a professor of business administration and advertising at universities in Algeria, Benghazi, and Jeddah, until he retired in 1988. Throughout his life, he published and coedited several books.

My mother was born in Cairo, the youngest of nine children. Her mother was born in Albania and was a descendent of a prominent Albanian family named Freshrie. Her father was of second-genera-tion Albanian descent. Her father owned a large area of farmland in Sinbelawain. My parents were married in 1939. My mother stayed home to raise their four children. I was born first, in 1940. My brother

Samy came second, in 1944; my brother Refaat came third, in 1949; and my sister Rawyia followed in 1952.

Since childhood, I have wanted to be an engineer. I graduated from high school in 1957 and attended the College of Engineering at Baghdad University for two years, while my father was the cultural attaché there. Due to political disagreements between presidents Nasser and Abdel Karim Qasim, diplomatic relations between the two countries were severed, and we were expelled from Iraq and had to return to Cairo. The Egyptian bureaucracy forced me to enroll in the College of Science at Cairo University. I did not like it. Two years later, I transferred to the first class of the brand new High Industrial Institute of Petroleum and Minerals Engineering that opened in Suez. After the second academic year, our class was sent to West Germany for one-year of undergraduate training in our individual fields. This was my second exposure to international travel and my first independent living experience away from the family. During that time, I became fluent in German and was able to secure jobs the following two summers as an electric welder for VW car mufflers. I graduated in 1966 as a metallurgical engineer.

During President Nasser's era, engineers and doctors were drafted to serve in the Egyptian government for an indefinite period of time. I was assigned as a research engineer at the National Research Center in Dokki. My lab's research concentrated on minerals mined in Sinai. The fact that I was expected to become a government employee for the rest of my life didn't sit well with my upbringing, my entrepreneurial and adventurous character, and especially not with my desire for overseas travel. The idea of immigration started to crystalize in my mind and was shared by my best friend, Medhat Idris, who graduated as a veterinarian from Cairo University and was assigned to the Cairo Zoo. We both completed the immigration application for the United States, Canada, and Australia. Our applications to Canada and Australia were rejected due to the fulfillment of those countries' 1967 quota for Egypt. Luckily, we both were accepted by the United States, and specifically by the state of California. Our acceptance was based on the general US employment needs for our professions, as an engineer and a veterinarian. My situation was compounded by the 1967 War, during which Israel occupied the Sinai, causing my research materials to become unavailable and halting my research at the lab.

Resigning from the professional draft and completing my military service in order to obtain a passport were monumental tasks. My resignation took eight months to be approved by a sequential ladder of officials, eventually reaching the minister of industry and the prime minister. In 1968, I was drafted into the military engineer branch of the Army. Nine months later, I obtained a medical discharge due to flat feet. Finally, Medhat and I were ready to travel to the United States. Due to the currency control at the time, each person was only allowed to bring $200.

Medhat married his sweetheart, Siham, and they traveled to Holland for a week of honeymooning. We met in Amsterdam and then flew to New York on July 15, 1969 for three days of sightseeing, after which we planned to go on to our final destination, San Francisco. The next day, July 16, 1969, Apollo 11 was launched on the first lunar landing mission. We were glued to the TV to witness this historic event. On the second day, Medhat had a stomach ulcer that burst, causing internal bleeding and endangering his life. He was admitted to Bellevue Hospital and went through major surgery, which required blood transfusions, for which Siham and I donated our blood. The doctors instructed Medhat not to travel for a minimum of three months, so we had no choice but to stay in New York.

We had come to the United States without prearranged jobs and even without knowing anyone who could assist us in acclimating to the new environment. We stayed at an inexpensive Manhattan hotel, where many other Egyptians were staying. Our $200 did not go far, so Siham and I had to quickly find jobs. Employment agencies told us to forget about our college education and target employment as high school graduates. That was the right advice in order to be able to survive.

My first job interview was at Tiffany, the famous jewelry store on Fifth Avenue. The job was for a clerk in the accounting department and was listed as paying $90 per week. I passed the mathematics aptitude test with flying colors and was offered the job, with an immediate start at $110 per week. Siham went through a similar experience and was recruited in sales at a Lane Bryant department store, also on Fifth Avenue.

Now that two out of three of us were employed, we needed to find an apartment and furnish it. Our new Egyptian friends directed us to a building in the Bronx where several Egyptians were already living. I managed to rent the only available apartment, which was on the top floor—a fifth-floor walk-up, one-bedroom apartment for $65 a month. I also went to a furniture store and bought the necessary furniture on installment. When Medhat came out of the hospital, he and Siham occupied the bedroom, and I slept on a sleeper sofa in the living room. This arrangement lasted about one year, during which Medhat recuperated and was able to get a job as a cancer lab technician implementing research on mice. Siham became pregnant, and they moved to another apartment in the same building.

While working at Tiffany, I decided I needed a higher education for my engineering bachelor's degree to be recognized in this country. I met with the head of the Metallurgy Department at Columbia Engineering College, presented my undergraduate curriculum and scores, and explained my financial situation. After evaluating me, the department granted me a tuition scholarship for a master's degree. I attended evening classes for one year.

At Tiffany, I excelled in the accounting department and was sent to IBM School to learn programming for their tabulating machine (a first-generation computer). I became interested in computer technology and hence switched jobs to work the evening shift as an IBM 360 mainframe computer operator at Irving Trust Bank. My job application still said I was a high school graduate. I had to quit my Columbia University studies due to my evening shift work. After a few months at the bank, I confided to the head of the computer department about my real education and asked whether the bank had any computer programming/system analysis training. The bank did not have such a training program; however, he referred me to RCA Corporation, which had a computer system called Spectra 70 that was considered an alternative, or even a competitor, to the IBM 360 at the time.

I applied at RCA in 1971 and passed several tests and interviews and was hired for their four-month training program in Cherryhill, New Jersey. They recognized my undergraduate engineering degree and the one year at Columbia. I graduated as a system engineer and began work at the RCA computer department located in lower Manhattan. My first assignment was to design a computer system for the Staten Island Hospital. I enjoyed this work and was happy that my prior education was now being recognized, enabling a proper career and future employment.

During this time, Samy and his pregnant wife, Mona, obtained an immigration permit and joined me at my Bronx apartment. They occupied the one bedroom and I ended up, once again, on the living room sofa. Mona gave birth to their first daughter, Maha, in January 1971, and they moved to their own apartment on the same floor.

After one year with RCA, I decided to visit my family in Egypt and brag about the United States being the country of opportunity, if you worked hard at it. I took a ten-day vacation from RCA and went to Cairo. At that time, my parents had built a family home in Heliopolis, ultimately consisting of five floors. They gave me, my two brothers, and my sister each an apartment and maintained the roof apartment for themselves. My parents felt sorry for me living alone in New York as a bachelor, so they arranged for me to meet three or four potential brides, by inviting their friends with young daughters. I met all potential brides, as a courtesy to my parents, but explained it was unfair to ask me to make a hasty decision.

I returned to New York, only to find my pink slip from RCA, due to their sale of the computer division to Honeywell and the layoff of all junior system engineers. In November 1972, I registered with employment agencies to look for another suitable job. My father surprised me and my brother by arriving in New York to visit us, after a professional trip to the United Kingdom. For two days, I didn't have the heart to tell him I was unemployed, especially after I'd just returned from my bragging trip to Cairo. I initially told him I was taking time off from work, but on the third day, I had the courage to explain the situation.

That day, I decided to join him visiting his friends at the United Nations Egyptian mission. As we returned that afternoon, I noticed a crowd of people, fire engines, and ambulances at our building. As I looked up at my building, I found that my apartment ceiling was gone. It turned out that the gas company, Con Edison, had been working during the prior weeks to convert the building's heating system from coal to natural gas. Upon connecting the gas, an explosion occurred in my apartment due to gas being trapped behind my kitchen stove. Thank goodness there was no fire. The main damage was in my apartment, while other fifth-floor apartments only experienced broken window glass and some wall cracks. Samy and Mona were both at work, and Maha was being taken care of by a babysitter, who also lived on the same floor. Thank goodness no one was injured.

This incident was a major setback for all of us. We were not allowed back in the building for several days, during which my apartment was exposed to rain. Later I found that most of my furniture and clothes had been destroyed. The Salvation Army gave us some winter clothes, and the Red Cross provided two weeks of accommodations in a poor Bronx hotel for me and my father. Samy and his family were given four weeks. My father couldn't believe or comprehend what was happening; he felt sorry for us and started asking us to return to Egypt. It was extremely difficult to tell my father his presence was a burden and he needed to fly back to Cairo. We needed to deal with this setback on our own, without having to worry about exposing him to the experience. My father left with a broken heart, and extremely worried. He said he wouldn't be able to find the words to explain to my mother what had happened.

I needed to start a new chapter in my life that had a bit more stability. I moved to Bloomfield, New Jersey, rented an apartment in a two-family house, and later married my girlfriend. Luckily, I quickly landed a job with Price Waterhouse, a top CPA firm, as a programmer analyst in their computer division. I became responsible for developing the firm's partner's payroll system. To continue my career progress, after one year, I was hired by Chase Manhattan Bank as an assistant treasurer, first-level bank officer, and section manager at their system division. I managed a team of twelve professionals responsible for the enhancement and maintenance of the bank's commercial loan system. That system maintained a total loan portfolio of $30 billion. By 1976, I had been promoted to a second vice president, and my first wife and I had bought a house in Matawan, New Jersey.

The commercial loan system is the core business of any bank; therefore, while at Chase, I learned all about banking. I became interested in the banking side, and in 1974, I asked if I could take the bank's one-year credit development training program. My request was denied for two reasons: first, all my education and work experience was technical and I did not have any business administration background, and second, the program did not recruit employees with an officer title. The head of the program recommended I go to a graduate business school and study for a master's in business administration (MBA). The bank agreed to pay for my tuition, and I enrolled in New York University's Graduate Business School (now Stern Graduate Business School).

I started working full time and going to school three days per week in the evening. My daily commute to and from work was about an hour and a half each way. That was difficult. I returned to my home around 11:00pm, exhausted, had a bite to eat, and went to sleep. At the same time, my wife became a full-time student at the Brooklyn Law School and worked part time at her law firm to cover her tuition expenses. Our weekends were spent grocery shopping for the week and studying to catch up on our schoolwork. After completing the MBA courses of my finance major, I was allowed to enroll in the bank's credit program on a full-time basis and was granted an exception to retain my second vice president title. After finishing the credit training program, I joined the Middle East Institutional Banking Department of the international division. In 1975, I was granted US citizenship, and I completed my MBA degree in 1978. At the same time, my wife completed her law school and passed the New York bar exam to become a full-fledged lawyer at the same law firm. Now my wife and

EGYPTIAN AMERICAN JOURNEYS

I could say our career building blocks had been completed, and our individual career struggles were starting. We both worked hard to prove ourselves in our respective jobs, putting in long hours. Our long weekdays started at 6:00am and ended around 8:00pm.

In 1980, I was recruited by Philip Brothers, a major client of the bank's commodity division. The job was to develop a new Middle East market for their precious metals trading. At the time, the precious metal market was extremely volatile, and the prices of gold and silver were skyrocketing. I started a rigorous travel schedule, covering all Middle East countries. I succeeded in establishing trading relationships with banks and private trading companies. This business was very profitable for the company, and I was recognized and rewarded for my efforts. Also, in 1980, we bought a lovely larger home in Stamford, Connecticut, to be closer to our friends.

By 1984, my wife and I recognized that we had spent the past eleven years studying and building our careers at the expense of getting to know each other. This ended with an amicable divorce and equally splitting our assets. Such a dramatic event caused me sadness and a substantial financial setback. I continued my extensive business travel and managed a large and profitable client trading portfolio.

By 1987, my boss resigned from Philip Brothers and accepted the responsibility of establishing a brand-new company as president and CEO. This new company was called Elders Finance of North America, with headquarters in midtown Manhattan. The ultimate parent company was a multi-national Australian company. Elders Finance concentrated its activities on investment banking, commodities, and treasury products trading. I was initially recruited as vice president to duplicate the success I'd achieved at Philip Brothers attracting Middle Eastern trading partners. My job developed into managing the company's US banking relationship in addition to the Middle East business. Also, in 1987, I married my current wife, Debbie, and moved into my Stamford, Connecticut house. By 1990, the Australian parent company had decided to wind down the Elders Finance business, and I was asked to stay to the end to ensure the orderly payment of the company's bank lines.

At this point, a friend, who had established Intercap Investment Inc., asked me to join his company as one of the three executive vice presidents to help develop the Middle East business. The company offered merchant and investment banking services for its Middle Eastern clients, concentrating on investments in the United States. This was a short stint for me as Intercap was too small to attract larger transactions and participate in investments.

By then, I already commanded a respectable market reputation for extensive knowledge of the Middle East. During the late 1980s and early 1990s, most of the banks managed their Middle East business out of London. I figured that if I wanted to continue my career covering this region, I should consider job opportunities in London. Debbie was working at the Rockefeller Investment Company as an administrative assistant to the president. After sharing my thoughts with her and evaluating our situations, we agreed that relocation to London was an exciting prospect and she wouldn't have difficulty finding a similar job. I notified my Egyptian friends working in the London banking industry that I was available to relocate, and actually traveled to London three times for interviews with banking institutions. In the meantime, we sold our Connecticut house and rented another on a temporary basis. I finally accepted a senior director position with American Express (Amex) Bank's London branch to manage their Middle East private banking business. AMEX Bank secured my UK work permit and temporary living accommodations for me. I moved to London in January 1993. Debbie's boss accommodated her by offering her a job at their London office. Debbie singlehandedly did a great job of selling, disposing of, and donating all our Connecticut furniture and belongings. She finally joined me in London in August of the same year to start our new life.

At Amex, I found my job challenging. I was by myself, with minimal secretarial support. I was given a list of existing clients, with minimum documentation and old telephone numbers. During my first week on the job, a Lebanese client walked in and demanded to close his account of a couple million dollars. He explained that he hadn't been contacted for an extended time and that his account had been idle, without any investment opportunities. I explained that it was my first week on the job and asked him to give me a chance to prove my capability. He agreed and eventually became a very happy client for many years. In this job, I usually spent two to three weeks every month traveling throughout the Middle East, meeting existing clients and prospects and offering investment products. Over my twelve years of service at the bank, I built a team of four to support the growing client base, and their portfolio, which reached $360 million.

During our early years in London, we purchased an apartment in central London, within walking distance from my office. We also purchased a weekend home in Bognor Regis, in the southwest of England, on the British Channel.

At the end of one business trip, I stopped in Cairo on April 30, 1998, to start a ten-day vacation. Debbie flew in from London, and we planned to take my parents to Sharm El Sheikh for one week. However, my father felt weak and had low blood pressure the day before our scheduled travel. The doctor came to our home and gave him some medicine. His health did not improve the next day, so I canceled our Sharm El Sheikh hotel reservation. The doctor came again, but this time he suspected internal bleeding and recommended an ambulance take my father to hospital. Doctors worked on stabilizing his blood pressure and low body temperature and scheduled an MRI in the afternoon. Sadly, my father passed away during the MRI, as he had an abdominal aneurysm that had caused massive internal bleeding.

After the funeral, I decided to bring my mother with us to London. Her favorite sister was also visiting her son, Taher, in London. It was arranged that my mother and her sister would spend one week with us and one week with Taher. One day during the first week my mother was at Taher's, I suffered severe chest pains during the night. Unaware how serious my symptoms were, I called my office in the morning to explain I might be a bit late coming in. However, a colleague suspected a heart attack and called an ambulance. My wife rushed back from her office, and we went to the ER. It turned out I'd had a serious heart attack that caused a total blockage of a major artery (called a widow-maker). Because I didn't go to the hospital as soon as I felt chest pain, critical hours had passed, causing permanent damage to the heart muscle. That day—May 25, 1998—changed my life.

A few months later, I fell ill with pancreatitis. This is a serious and extremely painful condition. At the hospital, the doctors expressed doubts to my wife that I could survive the pain, given my heart condition. This was an unforgettable year of my life; however, I was blessed with a caring wife and a compassionate and supporting Amex bank management. During the next three years, I had two stents placed in other heart arteries, a pancreas stent, and surgery. At the same time, I resumed my regular workload. The job was interesting and challenging, and I enjoyed an excellent relationship with my clients, the majority of whom were top-tier wealthy businessmen.

In 2001, my doctors recommended I slow down and drastically reduce my travel schedule. Such business trips were very stressful because I had to see many clients and prospects every day, as well as cover five to seven countries each trip. I took my doctors' recommendation seriously and made an arrangement with Amex management to move my office to my home in Cairo. I would continue to manage my team in London and would cover the Egyptian clients, and my assistant would cover the remaining countries. This was a perfect arrangement, and I was happy the bank was accommodating to my needs.

I moved to Cairo in July 2001 and set up an office at my home that was fully equipped with internet, fax, and a computer connected to the bank's server. I was able to see all my clients' accounts and function as if I were sitting at my London desk. Debbie resigned from her job, and we accepted an offer to sell our London apartment. I went back to London in early September to help Debbie make the move to Cairo. I was at my London office when the September 11 tragedy happened. I witnessed the event on TV. That was an unforgettable, sad day. Amex's Manhattan tower was damaged during the collapse of the World Trade Center, and all the staff were relocated to a backup site in Jersey City. An executive order directed at senior management prohibited us from taking international flights. Debbie and I were finally able to return to Cairo several weeks later.

As a result of my illness and the doctors' warnings, I decided to secure a residence in my wife's name. We, therefore, bought an apartment in Ossining, New York, which is where her mother and two of her three brothers live. In Cairo, we lived in our apartment in the family building and looked after my mother, who lived in the floor above us. Debbie went to the British counsel to learn the Arabic Egyptian dialect. She was able to adapt quickly to our way of life. She loved our history, culture, music, and food. She enjoyed taking Egyptian cooking lessons from the family's best chef—that being my mother. Samy had resigned from his job as a pilot with USAIR airlines and returned to Egypt. He bought a piece of land in Nuwaybah, Sinai, and built a twenty-five-room resort called Mermaid. He loved his resort and commuted every two weeks between Cairo and Nuwaybah. We also loved his resort and visited him frequently. In Cairo, he stayed at his apartment in the family building. His older daughter Maha lived with him in Cairo and attended American University. His younger daughter, Nadia, married an Egyptian American man named Hany, who was the son of one of Samy's friends, and they stayed in New Jersey. She had graduated from Rutgers University and was studying for her PhD at Columbia University.

My brother Refaat pursued a diplomatic career after college and was employed by the Ministry of Foreign Affairs, where he progressed through the ranks. His assignments included London, Tel Aviv, Vienna, and Budapest. As an ambassador, he served in three African countries and Albania. He usually spent a year or two in Cairo at the Ministry of Foreign Affairs' headquarters between assignments. When in Cairo, he would stay at his apartment in the family building.

In October 2003, Samy was at his Nuwaybah resort happily entertaining his guests. For the first time ever, he decided to snorkel with the guests. Upon his return, he decided to take a shower and planned to join the guests for lunch. Sadly, he passed away while in the shower at age fifty-nine. He had always been healthy and had never complained of any illness, except occasional migraines. I had the shock of my life when I received the news. Refaat and I drove to Nuwaybah and brought Samy's body back to Cairo. My most difficult task was to tell my mother the news. Upon comprehending it, she suffered a three-day coma and was not able to attend Samy's funeral.

This event had a major effect on my perception of life and death. I decided to take an early retirement, and Amex Bank sympathized with my situation and granted me the retirement effective February 29, 2004. It took me over one year to settle Samy's estate and distribute his assets. At the same time, some of my clients asked if I could continue to advise them on their investment portfolios. I declined to take any official role but continued my social contact with some Egyptian clients.

Having retired, Debbie and I wanted to be close to our respective families and also have time for ourselves. To achieve this, we spent winters in Egypt, spring and fall in New York, and summers in Bognor Regis. My mother was aging and having heart problems. Refaat was assigned as an ambassador in Tirana, Albania, where he was able to locate members of the Freshrie family. Mother enjoyed spending extended periods visiting Refaat and was introduced to her Albanian family. Debbie and I visited them in Albania. At the same time, Debbie's father's health was deteriorating, and she wanted to spend time with him. While in England, we also took trips to various European countries with my cousin Taher and his Dutch wife.

In 2008, a Swiss bank approached me to assist in their private banking efforts in Egypt. I accepted and successfully contributed to their market expansion over the next ten years. In May 2010, my mother passed away at her home in Cairo at the age of ninety-two. We all were with her during her last few months. Debbie's father's health was getting worse and she wanted to spend more time helping her mother take care of him, so we sold our Bognor Regis home and decided to spend most of our time in New York, returning to Cairo during the winter for only a few weeks. In 2012, Debbie's father passed away.

In 2015, we decided to buy a second home in Sarasota, Florida, where many of our friends had become residents. We became what

Floridians call snowbirds, because we escape the cold and snow in New York by spending the winters in sunny Florida. Since my retirement from Amex, I have continued to enjoy being engaged with jobs and volunteer assignments as well as managing our personal assets and investment portfolio. At the same time, I resumed my sailing hobby, joining two clubs in New York, where we sail on the Hudson River and train beginners, and one club in Florida, where we race remote-controlled one-meter sailboats three days a week on a large lake. I also go to the fitness center and play pickleball twice a week.

I volunteered as the treasurer of a charitable organization, Life Project for Africa, based in Ossining, New York, where we live. The organization was created to save lives and give hope to the poor in Tanzania. We raised funds to build and operate a hospital in a rural area that provides mothers with a safe environment to deliver healthy babies, and that treats the poor and sick children. Debbie volunteers as a board member of Life Project for Africa, as well as for church activities and for a food pantry that feeds the poor and homeless.

In my fifty-one years living in the United States, I have met and overcome challenges in my career and personal life. I quickly adapted to the culture shock after I arrived, and I made several career and personal changes. All in all, one can say my life was full of struggles, adventures, events, challenges, experiences, luck, successes, travels, health setbacks, sadness, and happiness. As I approach eighty, I consider myself lucky to be alive, with a loving and caring wife—enjoying the many friendships we have cultivated over the years and maintaining an active, balanced, and healthy life.

———◆———

SAMIR ANSARY spent his entire career in investment banking. His story charts a path of a young Egyptian man's journey in pursuit of the American Dream—from arriving in the United States with $200 in his pocket to becoming a successful banker with one of the largest firms in the world.

MY LIFE IN TWO CITIES

Sylvia Iskander

How do I write about the most emotional, life-changing experience in my life—leaving my homeland for a new one? These are some of the thoughts that went through my mind when I was asked to share my experience immigrating to the United States. I mulled over what approach I should take: a personal and emotional narrative, or purely biographical? I guess the two can't be separated, so it will be a mix of them. In essence, Egypt is my first home and where I grew up, the youngest of four. America is my adopted home, where I raised my own family. They complement each other, and I love and need both.

I was born in 1948 in a Cairo neighborhood called Zamalek, which is surrounded on all sides by the Nile River. It has several sporting clubs and many gardens. It was a quiet neighborhood, with many attractive villas. Today, most have been converted to embassies or schools.

My family was considered upper middle-class. My parents and three older siblings were closely knit. Nadia is the oldest, followed by Sonia, and then my brother, Wagih. Nadia was the chief political analyst for the American embassy in Cairo and head of the research library. Since she retired, they renamed it after her to honor her expertise and service. Sonia fell in love with a US Marine and moved to the United States after they married. She became a social worker and dedicated herself to helping people until she retired. Wagih immigrated to Canada and opened his own medical practice as a pediatric neonatologist.

In the early twentieth century, my father, Kamel Abdel Shaheed, was a young man studying law at Cairo University. Egypt was going through tumultuous times due to the British colonial occupation. He became politically involved in the resistance movement. As a result, he and his brother Munir, who was studying medicine, were arrested, along with twenty-eight other activists. Most of the activists were students at Cairo University or Al-Azhar University. Egyptians were unified against the British occupiers. But six British judges conducted the trial and charged the defendants with conspiracy and incitement to murder. Of course, the judgments were cruel, and both my father and uncle were imprisoned, along with many other defendants.

In 1919, a revolution against British occupation broke out in Egypt. It was led by a young man named Saad Zaghlul. When the British were defeated in 1924, he came to power and freed all the activists, including my father and his brother. He is considered the father of Egyptian independence.

My father spent his career as a judge, eventually becoming the chief justice of Egypt's court of appeals. He was a passionate nationalist who loved Egypt, even when his cotton gin in Beba, in the governate of Beni Suef, was nationalized in 1961, during Gamal Abdel Nasser's presidency. After my father retired, he took care of the land we owned in Beba full time. It was important to him because he was born and grew up there. He spent a lot of time traveling back and forth between Beba and Cairo to inspect the land and make sure everything ran smoothly.

My mother and I would join him for a few weeks during summer vacations. I loved going there and staying in the house my grandfather Girgis Abdel Shaheed had built. It was big, with many beautiful rooms. An Italian artist had painted the walls and ceilings. The bathing room was built in marble and had a basin you could fill with hot water, and then you could scoop up the water with a container to pour over you. It had a domed ceiling with several stained-glass openings, allowing light in. To me, this was exciting, as it took me back in time and I felt connected to my grandparents, whom I'd never met. My favorite room was a big terrace enclosed on three sides by stained-glass windows. I have fond memories of playing with cousins who lived close by. We also had a *hantour*—a horse-drawn carriage driven by a man named Sayed. Sometimes he would let me drive, which was a real treat. These are wonderful memories, but many years later, after my siblings and I had left Egypt, the house stood empty and we decided to sell it.

My mother, Adele Ishak, was a vibrant woman. She attended a French school called the Bon Pasteur. She began studying art when she was a young girl, and it became her lifelong passion. She attended the Academy of Art in Cairo and became an accomplished painter, focusing on portraits. She was prolific and painted portraits of the extended family. She had a clever way of getting her grandchildren to sit still so she could paint them: she was an excellent raconteur and told them wonderful stories from *The Arabian Nights*, also known as *One Thousand and One Nights*. The children were mesmerized and would sit motionless. I have an audiotape that I cherish of her recounting some of these stories. She was also active in volunteer work with other women; they sewed clothes for underprivileged people and raised funds to help them. They visited these families frequently and helped them according to their needs.

I attended a coed school, called the Gezira Preparatory School, in Zamalek. Years before, Edward Said, the public intellectual who became a professor of literature at Columbia University and a founder of the academic field of postcolonial studies, was also a student there. When I first attended this school, it was run by the British, and our headmistress's name was Mrs. Wilson. After the 1967 war, all the British citizens left, and the school was run by an Egyptian head mistress, Mrs. Mahmoud, and Egyptian teachers.

I later attended high school at Port Said School, previously known as the Manor House. This school was for girls. We had an excellent headmistress, Miss Salama. Both schools were excellent, and I still stay in contact with my school friends and see them every year when

I visit Egypt. We always compare our fate in life, between those who stayed and others who left for America, Canada, Europe, or other Arab countries. Interesting scenarios emerge, suggesting how my life would have been different if I hadn't made the choices I made.

After graduating from high school, I pursued my passion for science and mathematics by applying to Cairo Engineering School, which is the top university in Egypt and the Middle East and admits only students with high grades. I was very happy when I was admitted. Women made up about 30 percent of the student body. After five years, I graduated with a major in civil engineering, specifically in highway design.

During my years attending university, Egypt was going through a very hard time in the wake of the 1967 Six-Day War. I graduated four years after the war, and the idea of leaving Egypt during what it was going through was not an easy decision. My friends and I were nationalistic and wanted to contribute to our country. However, there seemed to be a surplus of engineers, which made my decision to leave somewhat less difficult.

I met my future husband, Sameh Iskander, at Cairo Engineering School. I was attending my first year and he was in his last year. He was the brother of my friend Mary Iskander, who was attending Cairo Architecture School. We fell in love and got engaged in 1969. He had applied for immigration to the United States, and soon after we got engaged, he left for the United States. I stayed behind so I could finish university. We kept in touch by letters and occasional phone calls. After I graduated, two years later, he returned, and we got married in September 1971.

The idea of my immigrating to the United States tormented my mother. I was the youngest and closest to her. However, at no time did she try to dissuade me from leaving Egypt. If she had done that, it would have been very difficult for me to make a decision. My father was wise and gentle and was also reserved. But he always encouraged me to pursue my own dreams and choose my own future. He was sad to see me go but was still happy for me. It was bittersweet for me, as I was leaving my mother and father and my sister Nadia and my friends. But I was excited for a new adventure. I'd been to Europe as a young girl, but never to the United States. I was ready to start a new life.

Sameh and I lived in New York City. Communication with my family in Egypt was not easy then: there was no FaceTime, email, or Viber. We stayed in touch by letters sent through the post office, which took a long time to arrive. We rarely spoke by phone since they couldn't make long distance calls from home and had to wait in line at a central station.

New York, I quickly discovered, was an exciting place. In a way, it reminded me of Cairo, with its vigor and energy—both big metropolises. It is the world's epicenter of culture, finance, the arts, and entertainment. We discovered experimental, avant-garde theater and film, without the religious or cultural constraints that existed in Egypt. Our five years of engineering study had not offered any courses in the humanities, so we immersed ourselves in the cultural life of the city. We frequented museums and galleries that contained a wealth of collections representing historical art movements and signed up for art courses on such subjects as pop art and minimalism. We also took advantage of the rich musical scene in the city: concerts, operas, new experimental music, theater, as well as cinema—none of it subject to censorship. I fell in love with New York City, and after traveling to other parts of the United States, it would have been difficult for me to live in any other city. It is a melting pot of myriad ethnicities.

Within a short time, I landed a job as an engineer, designing roads and highways. I was lucky because engineers don't always find jobs to match their major. One of the projects I worked on was designing a portion of the Taconic Parkway, a major highway system in New York State. The environment played a big role in the design; our design took into consideration saving any streams, trees, and other natural features in the area. Another project was designing a highway in Nigeria. Part of the work dealt with checking plans for public works in different areas of the city and making sure the sewer and water grid systems were adequate and efficient. I was surprised to find out that most of the women engineers I worked with were not American. They came from places such as Hungary, Poland, and Czechoslovakia. In Egypt, gender did not play a role in our academic choices.

For our vacations, Sameh and I traveled extensively to visit and view the art, architecture, archeology, and natural beauty of different countries. We trekked along the Great Wall of China, took safaris in Kenya, skied the Alps of Switzerland, and discovered the ancient wonders of Sudan and Yemen. In my free time during the rest of the year, I pursued my burgeoning passion for art by taking classes at New York University, including courses in the history of classical music, history of opera, ancient Egyptian history, interior design, and literature. I also studied drawing and painting at the Academy of Art in Manhattan. At the Brooklyn Museum, I took a course on stained glass.

Eventually, I majored in pottery making, which I studied for six years. Working with clay, and the idea of creating art from a lump of clay, appealed to me. I set up my own studio, which had a pottery wheel and a kiln; I mixed my own glazes and fired my wares in my studio. I veered toward sculptural ceramics, using the female body as my prototype and as a representation of Mother Earth, who is life giving and whom we should respect and preserve for future generations. These stoneware sculptures evoked the subtle yet powerful presence of the Egyptian landscape, linked with the equally important sensuality of the human figure. The colors I used were deep burnt sienna of the cliffs in the western desert, playing with the lighter ochers of the desert floor, all surrounding the delicate nuances of green crop fields and complemented by cracks, fissures, and incisions that reinforced the sensual shapes of the human figure. The deep cobalt and ultramarine blues I used evoked the Nile River. I was also strongly influenced by ancient Egyptian and Coptic art. I had several solo exhibitions of my ceramic sculptures in the galleries of Chelsea (the district in Manhattan now considered the art center of New York), Westchester, Long Island, and Connecticut. My work was also exhibited in Paris for several years.

As Egyptian immigrants, we wanted to meet and socialize with other Egyptians who had come to New York. We joined a secular organization called Egyptian American Professional Society (EAPS).

We made many new friends at the monthly meetings, which included talks and presentations by different speakers. Afterwards, we socialized over dinner. Children were welcome, and we had different programs for them in an adjoining room. We also brought our two daughters along with us. We discovered that many of the members had artistic talents, so we organized art shows once a year. I curated these shows with Giselle Haki, who was also a member of EAPS.

Our eldest daughter is Mona; she is a TV producer, with a master's from Columbia University. She worked for PBS as a correspondent and is now an independent journalist working for outlets such as MSNBC. She has produced political and social programs about domestic and international issues. Her work has taken her to the small South Pacific island of Kiribati to report on climate change, to Egypt, where she reported on the revolution, and to Jordan and the West Bank, where she covered the plight of the Palestinians. Mona is married to Jawad Metni, and they have two beautiful girls, Amina and Mira.

Joyce is our younger daughter and has a master's in elementary education from Columbia University. She traveled to Chile, where she taught English for one year. She also spent two years in Egypt teaching at an elementary school. In her spare time, she volunteered to teach English to refugees in Cairo. Currently, she is working with my husband in real estate development. Joyce is artistic like me and her grandmother and has taken courses in painting at the Student Art League in Manhattan. She also works with stained glass. Joyce is married to Mike LaHaie, and they have two handsome boys, Francis and Nile.

In 1981, Sameh established a real estate development firm in New York City, after working as a civil engineer for several years. Later, he decided to pursue a childhood dream to be an Egyptologist. He obtained a PhD in Egyptology from New York University. After getting his degree, he launched a new archeological project in Abydos, 500 kilometers south of Cairo, with one of his colleagues. The mission of the project was to document, restore, and preserve the three thousand year old temple of Ramesses II in Abydos, also known as Ramesses the Great, who ruled Egypt for sixty-seven years (1279–1212 BC).

I was involved with the project from its inception, in 2008. This expedition is still ongoing; now we are digging outside the temple. My engineering experience and art background has come in handy in two ways. I surveyed the architectural layout of the temple, with its intricate details. I also worked with other Egyptologists to document the fascinating inscriptions on the walls. I could almost sense the hand of the artist drawing those lines. The temple contains beautiful painted images carved in raised and sunk reliefs, many of which can still be seen in parts of the temple. In other parts, architectural components and images have been damaged or destroyed, and plans are underway for conservation. Interestingly, the temple is known for the depiction of the best-documented battle in ancient history, the battle of Kadesh between the Egyptians and the Hittites, the two superpowers of ancient times, which ended in a historical peace treaty. A copy of this treaty is displayed at the entrance of the General Assembly of the United Nations, to show that enemies can live in peace after military hostilities. A book, *The Temple of Ramesses II in Abydos*, was published and has become a reference for universities and libraries.

After thirty years of living in Queens and then Brooklyn, we settled in Pelham Manor, Westchester. It is a good place to raise children and we love the proximity to Manhattan. We are only thirty minutes from midtown, where we can still take advantage of its cultural activities. Pelham is a small community with many amenities. We have an art center that is very active and offers many classes in art, photography, graphics, painting, ceramics, etc. There are also many art exhibitions, presentations, and performances throughout the year.

In May 2016, I and my friend, and fellow Pelham resident, Candy Taubner, working in conjunction with Alwan for the Arts (an organization that caters to Middle Eastern arts, music, culture, and film, and that is run by Ahmed Issawi) brought an exhibition called "Creative Dissident: Arts of the Arab Spring Uprisings" to Pelham. This traveling exhibition was organized by the Arab American National Museum (AANM) and the University of Michigan Ann Arbor in 2013. It was designed to immerse visitors in the creative vitality of the continually evolving uprising movement commonly referred to as the Arab Spring. The exhibition merged freedom of speech with artistic expression that captured the anger, frustration, and hope and employed different media, including street art, photography, and video. With over thirty works, it took the viewer on a social, economic, and highly political journey of recent Middle Eastern history. The Pelham Art Center was the final stop on the three-year tour of this exhibit. I was glad to introduce my community to the events taking place in the Middle East. The exhibition was an eye opener for many people and had good attendance and a lot of interest.

I think I have the best of both worlds: I love where I live now, and I also look forward to going back to Egypt every year and seeing family and friends. I also see many changes in Egypt that make it feel a world apart from the country I knew growing up. New slang words pop up each year, demonstrating that language is always evolving. New art galleries are opening in certain parts of Cairo, and new TV channels, movies, and theater cover interesting subjects. The city is growing at an unprecedented pace: new neighborhoods have sprung up around Cairo that I am not familiar with, such as Katameya and El Sheikh Zayed. There are new highways linking these new areas to American-style malls.

There seems to be a general conservative, religious tendency in Egypt now, much more than when I left in 1971. I see the same thing happening in the United States. That is everyone's right, as long as there is freedom of religion for all, and no one infringes on the rights of other denominations—whether Shia, Christian, or other—to pray in their own places of worship. Fanaticism should not have any place in the world.

New York and Cairo together are my beloved homes. American and Egyptian are my identities.

—•—

SYLVIA ISKANDER grew up in Egypt and graduated in 1971 from Cairo Engineering University as a civil engineer. That same year she married Sameh Iskander, also an engineer, and immigrated to New York. She worked for several engineering companies. In addition, she pursued her passion for art by taking up painting and sculptural ceramics, which led to exhibiting at galleries in New York and Paris. She worked with Sameh, who is also an Egyptologist, on documenting the Temple of Rameses II for eight years. In 2019 and 2020 they unearthed the palace of Rameses II and the store rooms located south of the temple. Today, they are continuing with their work and hope to restore and conserve the temple and palace. Sylvia and Sameh visit Egypt every year and enjoy sharing their time between New York and Egypt. They have two daughters and four grand kids.

FROM EGYPT'S FARMLAND TO NAGASAKI AND EVERYWHERE IN BETWEEN

Tarek Nazir Saadawi

Al-Pots and the Village of Monshaat Demo

I was born in Cairo in 1951. My father was Head of the History Department at Ain Shams University in Cairo. My mother was an English professor at Helwan University, Cairo. They raised my three brothers and me on the fundamental belief that education and innovation are the basis of growth and progress on a personal and societal level, and that these same qualities are needed for nations to advance. Our house was constantly alive with debates on public, social, and cultural topics from the 1940s onwards. My father was an active member of The Young Egypt Party (Hizb Misr al-Fataah), a nationalist socialist party formed in 1930s. At the time, university and civic life was bustling and strong in Egypt—with all sorts of events, activities, debates, and demonstrations which my father participated in, calling for Egyptian independence from British rule and political reform away from a monarchy. This eventually culminated in the Egyptian Revolution of 1952, in which my uncle, Mostafa Mourad, was the youngest officer in the Free Officers, a group of Egyptian nationalist officers that instigated the revolution. Following the revolution, there was constant change and dynamism. My uncle later joined the opposition forces in 1956. My father would take his students, and often one of his four sons, on educational, historical, and cultural trips to various places across

Egypt: the Red Sea, Sinai, and Western Oases, among others. While we grew up in Cairo, he would often take us to visit our family's origins in the village of Monshaat Demo in Fayoum governorate, just southwest of Cairo. These visits were some of our most beautiful moments of our childhood. We enjoyed being in the midst of the lush farms, open fields, and splendid nature. We also went to the valley of Al-Pots, which is a large water canal located between two hills in Fayoum. As kids, Al-Pots was our gathering point, where we played and enjoyed the greenery majestically surrounding us. These childhood trips stayed with my brothers and me, and when we had our own children, we also passed this onto them. While my children were born and raised in the US, every year in the 1990s-early 2000s, my wife and I spent our summers in Egypt. Between taking them around Egypt to also witness the country's vast history, culture, and nature, our children always insisted on visiting the village in Monshaat Demo—climbing the same mango trees, and walking the same dirt paths that my brothers and I did some 30+ years beforehand.

In our last visit in December 2017, however, we were saddened to witness the extreme deterioration of the Egyptian countryside. Green farms, fields, and different plantations were all erased at the hands of the mighty invasion of cement structures and buildings, as populations in the villages grew from 2,000 to over 20,000 per village. Garbage overflowed the streets; litter could be found everywhere, replacing the shrubbery and dirt. The beautiful water canals like Al-Pots, that used to be clear and teeming with ducks, were now filled with trash and even animal corpses! For decades now, the countryside was neglected. No oversight has been exercised. The role of the state has been completely absent. The countryside is the nucleus of the Egyptian society and its food basket. Most of the historical and current competent talents and leaders of Egyptian society—in the arts, film, politics, education, etc.—came from rural backgrounds. Neglecting the countryside to this extent is a tragedy. Unless we give sufficient attention to the Egyptian countryside, our current situation will not be fixed.

My mother, Fatima, the daughter of the noble engineer Mourad

Refaat, was a student at the Faculty of Arts, Cairo University in the late 1930s. She was one of seven female graduates of her class. My parents were friends and colleagues with the different Egyptian Ministers of Education from that era, including the iconic intellectual Dr. Taha Hussein (1940s) and Army Major Kamal El-Din Hussein (1950s). During this era, education and literacy were high in Egypt, and English was a core subject in both public and private schools. In fact, fellow Egyptian American friends of mine, including Dr. Hani Al-Sadr and Dr. Mustafa Al-Khashab, would reminisce about our childhood days in Cairo, where we attended Asmaa Fahmy Elementary School near Cairo University Bridge. Ms. Raheel, our English teacher, at the time, was firm on making sure we learned English correctly from a young age. Similarly, middle school and high school also had core English courses. We credited our public school system with our ability to be completely bilingual and fluent in English from a young age. In 1978, however, when my mother came to visit me in America, she seemed sad and rather down. She told me the new president of Helwan University removed English as a core subject and made it just an elective. This seemed to begin the degradation of education in Egypt. During my forty years in New York, I met with scores of Egyptians, journalists, members of official Egyptian delegations, or members of diplomatic missions. Increasingly, since the 1990s, I found that many of them have no command of the English language and are sent on these foreign posts without any ability to properly converse, let alone learn and innovate! This phenomenon prompted a journalist to write an article in the Arabic Al-Shorouk newspaper on July 6, 2018 titled "Journalists who do not know English." The degradation of Egypt was not just physical in its green lands, like that of the village of Menshaat Demo, but also in the degradation of the minds and education of the Egyptian people.

The Strawberry Fields and the Black Forest

In the summer of 1955, my parents traveled to England as part of a scientific and educational exchange between United Kingdom and

Egypt. They decided to take my brothers and me along. We traveled by boat to Piraeus, Greece, then to Genoa, Italy, then to Marseille, France. Afterward, we took the train to Paris. We stayed there for a few days to visit the tourist attractions of Paris. We then traveled by train to Calais, where we took a ferry across the English Channel to Dover, England. From there, we took another train to London. From a young age, my parents instilled in us the importance of travel, learning from other cultures, and interacting with people who think and speak differently.

In addition to my academic achievements, I had other interests and hobbies as well. For example, during my first year at Cairo University, I was a member of the rowing team. One of the most beautiful moments in my life at the time was training on the Nile River at dawn. I continue to be baffled at Egypt's lack of interest and investment in sports, and specifically water sports, in the same manner as I have seen in the Charles River in Boston and the Hudson River in New York, among others. In the summer of 1969, following my first year in university, a friend and I decided to spend the summer working as strawberry pickers in a farm to the North of London. There, we met dozens of students and young people from Italy, Spain, Morocco, and around the world. During this summer, we were glued in front of the television to witness the historic moment when the first man set foot on the moon. It has been incredible to witness the advancement of space travel and exploration since then. Now, according to NASA, humans are expected to reach Mars by 2030. Similar advances are also witnessed in the private sector, as in the case of the efforts led by Elon Musk, the innovator and owner of SpaceX, and the electric vehicles and clean energy company, Tesla. There is no doubt that human aspiration and scientific progress is unlimited. As the World Economic Forum made clear, the world is now undergoing its Fourth Industrial Revolution. One of the features of this revolution is the "internet for things," where devices communicate with each other via the internet—everything from home appliances, factory machines, robots, sensors, self-driving cars, etc. For example, the existing escalators in malls can now be linked to contact the computer server of the manufacturer, which contains intelligent software. The software can monitor the escalator's performance and maintain it automatically. We are now in the era of machines communicating with one another through the internet.

The following summer, in 1970, I traveled to Germany for an engineering apprenticeship in a factory. There, I befriended an Australian young man, also conducting his apprenticeship, and every weekend we traveled around Germany and Europe. We visited the Black Forest, a dense forest and spectacular nature bounded by the Rhine River and valley to the west and south. We also visited the beautiful city of Colmar in northeastern France and the Austrian city of Salzburg.

While in Munich, I met an American family, where the father worked for NASA. It was during this trip, and countless conversations with the family and many others, that I decided I wanted to obtain a PhD from the United States. Upon returning to Cairo, I graduated top of my class with honor and distinction and was offered a teaching assistant position in the Department of Electrical Engineering at Cairo University in 1973. I completed my master's degree in electrical engineering in 1975. I went on to publish three research papers from my master's thesis in a British journal. This would be the first of countless research papers that I would publish in my career.

At the time, there were two ways for Egyptian students to join a PhD program abroad. The first approach is through a government-sponsored scholarship. In the 1930s, Egypt established the General Administration of the Missions, with the mission that state-sponsored scholarships will help Egyptians learn the latest scientific advancements and research and bring it back to Egypt and apply it in the country. Similar state-sponsored programs were developed around the Arab World and in places such as China. In Egypt's case, the program was not administered correctly and, after eighty years of existence as a program, Egypt has yet to make any leap towards scientific independence or progress. Meanwhile, as a professor at The City University of New York since the 1980s, I have had the pleasure to work with dozens of Chinese researchers who joined the PhD program under a similar state-sponsored research program. I even recall that they would often wear a uniform emblazoned with "the People's Republic of China" with the symbol of Chinese leader Mao Zedong. However, China's program lasted for just a decade, sending thousands of Chinese across to US universities, bringing back that knowledge to China, and building momentum and a new stage of progress, self-reliance, and scientific independence.

The second approach was to apply on your own and find other means to raise funds, such as obtaining a scholarship. This is the approach I went with. I applied and wrote to dozens of universities and eventually chose the University of Maryland, which offered me a full-ride scholarship to obtain a PhD in electrical engineering and provided a monthly stipend in exchange for me teaching in the lab. My fellow Egyptian colleagues, including Dr. Hashem Sherif, Dr. Mohamed El-Sayed, and Dr. Magda Nassar, also went with the same approach.

Washington, D.C.

My life in America started in 1977 at the University of Maryland, 10 miles from Washington, D.C. I obtained my PhD three years later, in 1980. My dissertation focused on the fundamentals of information and communication networks. At that time, the concept of the internet was not understood as it is understood nowadays. But at the time, my research group and I believed in the power of telecommunication networks, and felt it was the way to unlock some of the greatest inventions of the twentieth century. My PhD research has been published in scientific journals and conferences, and continues to be referenced in academic papers, even today, 40 years after publication. ResearchGate is a website where you can access research papers on a wide variety of scientific subjects and information on the researchers. This website is free and open to all. I myself have over 300 published papers that can also be accessed on ResearchGate. Science and knowledge, like air and water, are available with equal access to everyone, without distinguishing whether the people acquiring it are from advanced or developing countries or whether they are rich or poor.

At the University of Maryland, I also partook in a number of extracurricular activities. I played bridge (a cards game) with my Chinese friend, Sean. I went horseback riding and played karate with my Iranian friend, Farid and my American friend, Ted Kramer. I also participated in a debate hosted by the Rotary Club, where I debated an Israeli student during the time of the historic Camp David Accords (1978). During the holidays, I traveled with a number of other foreign students to discover America. One of the most memorable and enjoyable experiences for me was visiting the Library of Congress. The Library is home to more than 160 million books, manuscripts, letters, etc. The Dome of the Main Room depicts human civilization and progress through history. It starts with the Pharaonic civilization, all the way to the birth of America. Somewhere in the middle is the representation and progress of the Islamic civilization. I wonder when the Arabs will appear again in this depiction of progress and innovation.

New York and the Catskill Mountains

In September 1980 I moved to New York City, where I started a job as an assistant professor at City University of New York (CUNY), City College, in the Electrical Engineering Department. After a few years, I was tenured, and until today, I am a professor and Director of the Center for Information Networks at the same university. New York is a bustling city, with endless activities. During summer times, I would take my family to Central Park, where we would bike all day and attend concerts, theaters, and shows. I remember my late father-in-law, Dr. Mahmoud Elmarsafy, telling us about his biking trip in Europe. He spent one month biking through European countries. This was after he had finished his PhD from Imperial College in London in early 1950. We would walk along the Hudson River, play tennis, and check out different restaurants and museums. The number of museums in the city is astonishing, and many offer discounted or free entry for families. During the winter, we took up skiing, something that I had never experienced growing up in a desert country. It quickly became a favorite activity, and we would take weekend trips to the Catskill Mountains, a few hours' drive north of the city.

In 1985, I got to know my wife, Boussaina Elmarsafy, through my cousin, Sahar Mourad. At the time, my wife worked for the Fulbright Foreign Student Program in Egypt, which facilitated cultural exchanges between Egypt and America and is funded by the US government. In America, my wife worked as an accountant in a company. However, after giving birth to our third child, she decided to become a housewife, devoting herself to raising our kids and maintaining a proper household. This has undoubtedly helped in forming their strong personalities and a sense of community. She insisted on getting them involved in different after-school activities, and making sure they have active, well-rounded lives not just centered on academics. Ranya, my eldest daughter, graduated from Barnard College, Columbia University, with a degree in Political Science and Middle Eastern Studies and then obtained her master's in Public Administration (MPA) from the London School of Economics (LSE). She is currently Executive Director of Pearl Initiative in Dubai, working to improve corporate accountability and transparency in the Arabian Gulf region. My second daughter, Marwa, obtained her master's in Psychology at Fordham University, and went on to become a child therapist for kids with special needs. She launched her own startup, Indira Jewelry, reviving and promoting silversmith and silver making, another traditional art in Egypt. My youngest son, Nader, graduated from Marist College with a Business degree, and went on to work for large American corporations and high-tech startups. He is also an avid basketball and soccer enthusiast, playing competitively on the US national junior level and through university.

In addition to my work at the university, I started an engineering consultancy with my colleague, veteran professor Don Schilling. Afterwards, I set up a private company and acquired engineering contracts from the US government and other entities. In 2000, my company won a contract with the United States Agency for International Development (USAID) to provide consultancy services to the Egyptian Ministry of Communications and Information Technology (MCIT) between 2000 and 2006. We conducted a comprehensive study of telecommunication networks in Egypt and issued a strategic plan to develop Egypt's telecommunications infrastructure, including how to technically update the Egyptian network, and how the public and the private sectors can cooperate in a balanced way to build a modern network. My colleagues, Dr. Mohamed Elsayed, Dr. Ali Elrefai, Dr. Amr Badawi, among others, contributed to this study. In mid-2005, we designed the protocol for the tender process to obtain the third license for wireless communications networks in Egypt. The Emirates Telecommunications Group Company PJSC, "Etisalat," won the contract and paid the Egyptian government the value of the license, which was 16 billion Egyptian pounds (3 billion dollars at that time). This was one of our company's most important achievements for the Egyptian government.

This period witnessed the introduction of Egypt into the era of modern information technology. It is at this time that MCIT was established and became the main engine for technological advancement in Egypt. Its mission was the digital transformation for various government sectors. This technological progress continued in Egypt from 2000 until 2009, as the growth rate decreased and then later flattened after the Egyptian revolution of 2011.

Along with a group of experts, I decided to establish the first International Conference and Symposium on Computers and Communications specific to the Mediterranean region. The first conference was held in Cairo, in the Mena House Hotel, in 1995. The founders of this conference were Egyptian Americans. This included, Dr. Mustafa Hashem Sharif (AT&T), Dr. Ahmed Tantawi (IBM), Dr. Adel S. Elmaghraby (University of Louisville), Dr. Hussein Abdel-Wahab (Old Domenin University), Dr. Reda Ammar (University of Connecticut), myself, and others. 2020 will mark the 24th year of this annual conference. While Egypt's participation in this conference is acceptable—in fact the founders were all of Egyptian origin—sadly over the decades, their presence has been eclipsed by other Mediterranean countries and there has not been enough effective participation of Egyptians.

In 2010, I participated with the nonprofit group, called the Alliance of Egyptian Americans that promoted culture, diversity, and civic engagement among Egypt and the US. The Alliance included my friends, engineer Mahmoud Al-Shazly, Dr. Fikry Andrawes, and others. The Alliance organized conferences, in which they invited prominent Egyptian intellectuals and thinkers to discuss the future of Egypt. The purpose was to highlight all the different point of views—everything from progressive leftists to Islamists to traditionalist holders. Two conferences were held in 2010: the first at my university, the City University of New York, in June 2010, and the second was held in Washington D.C. in September. There was quite a bit of momentum and interest, with each conference attracting around 200 participants.

In December 2010, the Alliance organized a visit for Egyptian Americans to go to Egypt, with the aim of discussing various political trends in Egypt. We also planned to provide a call for a collaborative solution, encouraging all the different political parties to come together. We used our network and sent requests to meet with the Egyptian President, the prime minister, the heads of political parties, various influential associations, and public figures. The delegation was led by Mr. Mahmoud Al-Shazly and ten members from Connecticut, New York, New Jersey, Kentucky, Virginia, Maryland and Washington, D.C. On that trip in Egypt, you could feel that something was different in the air. There was a lot of movement, a lot of clandestine meetings, and a lot of anger and frustration with the lack of general consensus and deterioration of Egyptian society and way of life.

One month after our trip, the people in Egypt rose up, on January 25th, 2011. For 18 days, all Egyptians came together under the unified slogan: "Bread, freedom, and social justice." Remotely, we, fellow Egyptian Americans, stood in solidarity with the people's call for these basic principles. In early February 2011, the office of Senator Bob Menendez, the top Democrat on the Senate Committee of Foreign Relations, contacted me and asked for a meeting to discuss the situation in Egypt. We met on February 9th, two days before President Mubarak would eventually step down. I attended the meeting along with a few prominent Egyptian Americans, including Mahmoud Elshazly, the head of the Alliance of Egyptian Americans, Dr. Mostafa El-Khashab, and Dr. Mona Tantawy. I presented to the Senator an overview of the revolution. I demonstrated to him that all Egyptians, of all religions, of all socioeconomic backgrounds, from all parts of the country (cities, rural areas, desert), joined forces in Tahrir Square, in a scene that brings to mind the Revolution of 1919 in Egypt.

As the after-effects of the revolution played out in Egypt, with power struggles, and a counter-revolution, we as Egyptian Americans felt our role was to focus on how to revive Egypt's economy. In November 2017, we organized an economic conference at Cairo University, on the celebration of the anniversary of the passing of Talaat Harb, founder of the modern Egyptian economy. Mr. Mahmoud Al-Shazly, Dr. Hala El Saeed, who later became Minister of Planning, Monitoring and Administrative Reform, Dr. Gouda Abdel Khalek, former Minister of Supply, and myself organized the conference with the hopes of spurring new economic planning and strategy for Egypt, which suffered greatly following the 2011 revolution. While the protests had stopped, the fight for true justice and economic and innovative reform was still elusive.

We continue to host similar economic and historical conferences to showcase the long, arduous road to progress ignited by revolutions, but only when combined with collaboration, innovation, and systemic approach to change. One such conference which I organized is a historic look at Egypt's 1919 Revolution, which took place in 2019 in New York City. Egypt has had a long history of different forces, different rulers, and different uprisings. Modern-day Egypt can draw on key lessons from our long history to help shape a better future.

The City of Nagasaki

Currently I work as the Director of Center for Information Networking & Telecommunication (CINT) at the City College of New York. In collaboration with the Japanese university, Kyutech, we won a three-year grant (2018-2021) from the National Science Foundation (NSF). The research team consists of ten professors: four from the City College and six from Kyutech, Japan. We study and design the new generation of the internet and its security from cyberattacks. Currently, the network-ing and telecommunication lab at the City College is being connected with its counterpart in Kyutech through Internet2 (a network exclusive to universities and research centers). This network will enable con-ducting joint experiments between the two universities. I have been impressed by the dedication, respect, and innovation of our Japanese colleagues. They are extremely humble, hardworking, punctual, and highly respective of all systems and governments. Their advancements are impressive. For example, the director of the laboratory showed me how they had designed a robot to assist nurses in hospitals, and it was already being widely used. This was in 2019.

While most of our collaboration is done remotely, we have arranged several trips to Japan. During one of the trips, we visited Fukuoka in the south of Japan, where we learned about Shintoism, the main reli-gion in Japan that truly seeps into their culture and work ethic.

One day, two of my colleagues and I took the express train to Nagasaki, a coastal city in southwestern Japan. Then we took the tram directly to the Nagasaki Atomic Bomb Museum, a museum dedicated to presenting the destruction of the city by detonation of an atomic bomb by the US. It shows the effect of the temperature reached three thousand degrees Celsius, as a part of the detonation. Nearly 80,000 people were burned to death immediately and the entire city was destroyed. I was impressed by how a country, that had witnessed such devastation just 75 years ago, was able to rebuild itself and become a pioneer and center of innovation.

The world has now become a small village. Information and science have become accessible to all. There is a fierce competition between nations for progress and advancement. It is time for Egypt to rise up and join this train of progress. There is no doubt that Egyptian Americans can contribute effectively and strategically to such a pur-suit. There are at least a million Egyptians in North America alone, pioneers and leaders in various fields and industries. There are esti-mates that there are about 100,000 Egyptian researchers in universities and research laboratories in private companies abroad. All of them are ready to collaborate with Egypt. In return, Egypt muſt open its arms to cooperate with them and work with them ſtrategically. In my 40+ years abroad, while I have found individuals and small timeframes where Egypt fully cooperates with its talent abroad, it is sadly not long-laſting or inſtitutional. Egypt requires political clout and collaboration and cooperation with Egyptians abroad, as well as its neighbors, in order to truly advance and grow. As we say in a common Egyptian proverb—it takes two hands to clap.

———•———

TAREK SAADAWI is an Egyptian American professor of electrical engineering. He currently resides with his family in New Jersey, USA. He has had an inherent love for travel, different cultures, and hiſtory and intersection of technology in globalization. Raised in Cairo, Tarek's life experiences have been shaped by the farmlands of his anceſtors in Egypt, his early travels to the UK with his professor parents in the 1950s, and his adult journey through ſtrawberry fields and factory training across Europe. His life in America, which began in 1977 with his PhD program, has been filled with excitement, adventure, and the intersection of work and cultures across countries in Europe, Asia, and the greater Middle Eaſt.

WORK IN PROGRESS

Dina Samir

I never knew my eyes could hurt so much from crying. For the twenty-four hours following the day I left Egypt, I couldn't handle looking at any light, even if it was not bright. It felt as if someone was poking my eyes with a stick. July 27, 2011 was indeed one of the saddest days of my life.

I was excited to move to the United States, accompanying my husband, Bahaa, on his journey to become a professor through the PhD program at the prestigious University of Texas at Austin. Despite my deep love for change and my excitement about new beginnings, a new land, new friendships, and new smells, the day I had to say goodbye to my family, I felt nothing but pain. It was the type of pain you can't take a painkiller for. It was the type of pain you have to experience every detail of in order to get through it.

On the airplane—after a long, sad night that felt longer than a year—for the first time, I wasn't able to enjoy my favorite part about flying: watching the 3D clouds. Every time I tried to look out the window, my eyes hurt. I kept thinking of my family—how my sister hugged me and couldn't let go, how I saw my mother crying like a baby for the first time in my life, how my brother looked heartbroken and silent. Every time I thought of them, I cried. And every time I cried, my eyes hurt more.

On our stopover at JFK International Airport, where we had a connecting flight to Austin, my heart started racing as I approached the visa officer. My husband had obtained a green card through the lottery years earlier, but I was traveling on a tourist visa. I kept praying as I waited in line that the officer would give me a six-month stay in the United States, the maximum any tourist can get. When I finally reached the officer and saw the stamp on my passport for a six-month stay, I felt we had overcome the first hurdle of our journey. At least I could stay with my husband for six months, and hopefully the green card he had applied for a year before would be issued by the end of that period. On such a mysterious journey, hope is not optional.

When we finally reached Austin, the summer heat greeted us as soon as we stepped out of the airport. We didn't know anybody in Austin. When my husband considered getting his PhD in the United States, he had applied to several universities. The University of Texas at Austin was the one that accepted him. So, we did not really choose Austin; it was chosen for us.

The early days and weeks in Austin were a mix of excitement and nostalgia. I was excited every time I walked down a new street, saw a new place, or met new people. However, my family was always at the back of my mind. The pain of being away from them was woven into my new life in Austin.

Our activities during the first weeks revolved around settling down. We focused on getting the most urgent things. First, cell phones. Second, an apartment. "I'm going to faint," I told my husband after we had walked for an hour in the heat and humidity to get to the mall to buy cell phones. Since I have a history of low blood pressure and had fainted in public before, I knew I had to listen to my body's signals telling me I was close to fainting. So, I rushed into a bar we had just walked by and asked for water.

Our search for an apartment was relatively easy. We were lucky to find a realtor who drove us around in his car to different apartment complexes, and we were able to find one that was not expensive. It was small and far from Bahaa's university, but it was exciting to have our own place in Austin.

After we settled into our apartment, I started to enjoy my new life. I appreciated the wide, uninterrupted horizons, the smell of freshly cut grass, and the sense of freedom I felt whenever I went out. I could walk around without feeling conscious of being a woman, without worrying about how my movements would be interpreted by men on the streets.

My husband was already starting to feel very busy and over-whelmed with his classes and work at the university as a teaching assistant. Everything was new and challenging for him. I, on the other hand, was not busy for the first time in my adult life. Before moving to the United States, I led a very busy life in Cairo. I was working full time at the American University in Cairo and I was also doing a master's degree in journalism and mass communications. Additionally, I had a fairly active social life. Busyness in life was the norm; it was the only thing I knew as an adult. In Austin, I found myself sitting in our small bedroom alone, not sure what to do. Since I was not allowed to work yet because I didn't have a green card, I found myself wondering how to spend each day, each week, each of the six months. It didn't take me long to realize that boredom was more challenging than the busyness I used to complain about in Egypt.

While I was in the midst of my daily fight to pass time, a volunteer opportunity presented itself through my husband's university. I was asked to help students learning Arabic as part of the Middle Eastern program. I was excited to find anything that would get me out of the apartment and let me engage with my new world. As a language part-ner, I met with three students once a week for an hour to simply talk in Arabic. Unlike tutors, a language partner's role is to talk with students the way friends engage in conversation.

"How was your week?" was a simple question I started my ses-sions with.

As soon as I started doing these sessions, I realized they were God's gift to me. Not only was I able to do something meaningful with my life, but I had an opportunity to do what I enjoyed most in life: connect with other people. My sessions also allowed me to understand more about American culture and college life and helped me meet beautiful young people, some of whom are still my friends.

Dickie Fisher was one of my favorite students and is now one of my good friends. Born to an American father and a Spanish mother, Dickie's warm personality, big heart, and interest in social justice issues caught my attention. Arielle Levine is another student I connected with and continue to be friends with, despite our vivid differences. Arielle's free-spirited personality and unique of way of looking at things challenged me to think differently. People, like me, who grew in up collectivist cultures, are inclined toward thinking and acting in ways that agree with the societal norms and what is socially accepted. Everything about Arielle challenged my inclination to conform.

I was grateful to get the opportunity to mentor students and to deepen my friendships with Dickie and Ariele. However, these sessions were not enough to keep me busy because they took up only three hours of my week. I found myself nostalgic for a busy schedule and deadlines. Yes, deadlines. As much as we complain about pressing deadlines, when I didn't have any sort of urgency, I found myself at a loss for meaning. Work had always been a source of fulfillment and joy in my life. Without it, I wasn't sure how I could find fulfillment for myself.

The other major thing my life revolved around was my husband. While I was struggling with boredom, he was struggling with busyness and stress more than he ever had. My days all looked alike. I woke up in the morning, made my husband his coffee, then packed his breakfast and lunch. I kissed him goodbye. After he left, I started cooking dinner for both of us. Despite how much I loved to support my husband—in fact, this was the reason I left my family and stable career in Egypt and decided to come to the United States—it felt out of balance to have my life now revolve around him. Sooner or later, I believe any unbalanced situation will bring unpleasant consequences. Bahaa was beyond busy, and I was beyond bored. Whose marriage wouldn't be challenged by that?

The one person who supported me through all of this was my friend Ekram. Although Ekram and I had only been friends for about three years, she was the closest to my heart during that time. I felt I could tell her anything without feeling judged. During our Skype calls, I could be myself. I could cry if I needed to. I was able to express how unhappy I was. I could share things I couldn't share with my mother and siblings, despite how close they are to me. I didn't want them to worry about me. It was enough that I had left them with a void and a burden when I left Egypt.

Ekram helped me connect with an editor in *Al Ahram Online*, an English-based newspaper in Cairo. I started pitching story ideas and working with *Al Ahram Online* as a freelance writer covering Texas news.

I was able to extend my tourist visa, but after ten months had passed—slowly for me and quickly for my husband—we faced the moment we hoped we wouldn't have to face. I could not extend my visa again. My husband had applied for my green card, and we were hoping to hear from the US Citizenship and Immigration Services on that long-waited card; however, the process was taking even longer than how my days felt.

"You have two options: either overstay your visa and stay illegally in the United States or move back to Egypt until you get your green card," my immigration attorney said.

My tears were falling down my cheeks by the time he finished that sentence. Those two options were equally difficult. After many discussions, tears and more tears, we decided I would go back to Egypt to wait for my green card. Despite how harsh it would be to be separated from my husband—and to feel millions of miles away from him—a solution that entailed breaking the law was not an option for us.

So, a year after I said goodbye to my family in Cairo, I found myself saying goodbye to my husband in Austin. I again cried my eyes out. I packed my summer clothes and traveled to Egypt with a one-way ticket in summer 2012.

When I arrived in Cairo, I stayed at my mother's house. I was happy to be reunited with her and my siblings—Sally, who lives with my mom, and Ramy, who is married and lives with his wife very close to my mom's house in new Cairo. Yet, after ten days of indulging in family reunions, relaxing, and catching up with friends, it was the time to start a new chapter. I didn't know how long it would take for the green card to be finalized, so I took my luggage and moved into the apartment in Heliopolis where Bahaa and I had lived before moving to the United States.

Soon enough, I found myself asking the same question I asked in 2011, when I moved to Austin: what do I do with my life now? While I couldn't commit to a long-term job because my plan was to go back to Austin as soon as I got my green card, I could pursue job opportunities that were interesting to me and had no strings attached.

Thankfully, I had already worked with *Al Ahram Online* as a freelance writer covering Austin-related news. In Cairo, I started working with them as a freelance journalist covering Egypt's news. I was able to pitch a few ideas here and there that kept me busy and made me feel fulfilled and happy whenever I saw my published articles. Since the newspaper had full-time journalists covering news in Cairo, I was assigned fewer stories over time. Soon I was fighting boredom again, this time in Cairo. The fight was easier, however, because in Cairo I had my family and friends.

I did not stress too much about not working and enjoyed the new social opportunities that life offered in Egypt. I started to meet new people, go to new places, and rediscover Cairo. It felt as if I got to have a fresh start with Egypt. I was able to catch a train to Alexandria to spend time with two dear friends, Arielle and Dickie. Yes, the same Arielle and Dickie I met in Austin through our Arabic language sessions. Life is not short on surprises. It happened that, in the same year I went back to Egypt, both Dickie and Arielle traveled to Egypt for one year as part of their Arabic language program at UT Austin. I stayed at Arielle's apartment in Alexandria, which she shared with her roommate, another American student from the Arabic program.

Alexandria is the city in Egypt closest to my heart. Because my mom is from Alexandria, I grew up spending summers there at my grandparents' house. Despite countless trips to Alexandria as a child and adult, my trip in 2013 was one of my favorites. I got to see Alexandria with fresh eyes and experience it through the eyes of my American friends—not only as foreigners, but also as college students ten years younger than me.

Six months after I arrived back in Cairo, I had received no word about my green card. Since my freelance writing with *Al Ahram Online* had phased out, I started to look for other short-term job opportunities. I was fortunate to be hired as a communications manager at HarassMap, a volunteer-based initiative that works to create a society that does not tolerate sexual harassment. My experience there was a breath of fresh air, despite how tiring it was. It was my first time working full time in Cairo on a social cause—a cause close to my heart. Like so many women in Egypt, I grew up with an increasing anger from the daily sexual harassment I experienced every time I walked in Cairo streets. I was happy to get the opportunity to channel the anger I'd been sheltering for years toward a positive action.

After working for HarassMap for three months, I finally heard some news about my green card. I was scheduled for a green card interview. My husband was visiting Cairo during this time so he could spend the summer with me. We were both beyond happy to hear the news. In the following months, we finished the required paperwork for my green card, I got the needed vaccination, and the two of us spent some quality time together.

Finally, the long-awaited day arrived. I went to the American Embassy in Cairo for my green card interview, the last step on this journey I had started three years before.

"What is the date of your marriage?" the embassy officer asked.

"August 4," I answered.

He frowned and replied with another question: "What happened on July 27, then?"

"I don't remember," I said, starting to feel very nervous and perplexed.

"How come you don't remember?" he asked.

Only after I had left the interview, did it hit me that July 27 was our official marriage date, when we signed the marriage contract. August 4 was the date of our church wedding ceremony, which had become our wedding anniversary. To my surprise, the officer proceeded with the process and no delays happened due to this incident.

A few weeks later, I found myself packing again and getting ready to go back to Austin, after spending one year in Cairo waiting for my green card. This time, I have to admit, saying goodbye was easier. True, it would be hard to be away from my family and friends again, yet I was ready to leave Egypt. Although life had surprised me by making the year fulfilling, eventful, and full of new experiences, I longed to unite with my husband. I also missed my quiet life in Austin, my sense of freedom there, the smell of fresh grass, our small apartment, and my bike rides. I was excited to start a new chapter in Austin as an American resident entitled to work and have a life of my own.

Certain situations, times, and days remain like mental pictures in our memory. I cherish the memory of my husband holding red flowers in the Austin airport as he waited for me after we had been separated for one year because of my green card. I cried in his arms. There had been days when we both feared this moment would never come. There was a rainbow in our hearts that day.

The first thing I was excited to do after returning to Austin was search for a job. Before moving to the United States, I had a relatively well-established career in Egypt in the field of communications, but now I knew I had to start from scratch again. "You have to make compromises," any old immigrant would tell a new immigrant when it came to starting a new career in the United States.

My husband sent me a notice about a part-time job he came across, receptionist at an English-language center that provided intensive English classes to foreign students in the United States. Because the center had a high percentage of students from Saudi Arabia who came through fully funded government scholarships, they were looking for a candidate who spoke Arabic to help facilitate conversations with students with limited English. The position was part-time, only four hours a day, so I thought, "Why not try it until I find a full-time job?" At least it would be a source of income. Even though this job was irrelevant to my career background and ambitions, when I was offered it, my attitude was nothing but positive. My approach has been to always pursue every opportunity as if it were the last one.

Not long after I started the job, I was able to make a contribution and received many compliments from students and staff. The students with limited English skills were relieved that I was there to help them get accurate information and to translate their issues and concerns for the center's management. Some students were just happy to find someone who could converse with them about any topic in their native language. I enjoyed connecting and talking with students. As a people-oriented person, being around students most of the time was a source of joy to me.

When the management realized my contribution to the students' experience, they offered me a full-time job, which they created for me. I would spend four hours working as a receptionist, covering the lobby, and the other four hours as an assistant to one of the directors, helping him with administrative work. Again, I was excited about the full-time position, despite how irrelevant it was to my career path and aspirations. All that I could think about at that time was that I had a full-time job in the United States and a stable source of income.

The full-time job came at the right time, because two months after I accepted it, I learned that I was pregnant. I could not have been happier. Although I spent the first three months of my pregnancy feeling nauseated and throwing up, I was grounded by a sense of happiness and hope that surpassed any physical pain. I felt as if a happy song was always playing at the background of my life.

That happy song paused when the director made a change to one of the work arrangements we had agreed to when I accepted the full-time position. Since I am a rebel by nature, I requested to meet with the director in the presence of my direct manager to express my refusal to accept the situation. My argument included an expression widely used in American culture: "This is not what I signed up for." I expected the director to negotiate the agreement and try to reach a middle ground that would be fair to both of us. To my surprise, his answer was, "Well, Dina, if you don't like the change, you can return to being part-time." His answer felt like a slap in the face. What made it more difficult was the fact that I could not refuse it. I accepted the new terms without protest because I could not afford to lose my full-time job, given that my husband was a student, and I was pregnant.

My daily work experience took a different turn after this incident. While I was happy to continue to help students and connect with them, every time I saw the director, my anger was triggered. Nevertheless, the happy song playing in the background continued overpower any challenges I had at work. The hope I was carrying and that was growing within me gave me a strength I had never experienced before. I learned that the power of motherhood starts before you actually see your baby.

When I was five months pregnant, that song suddenly ended with the loss of our unborn baby. The details of that loss were lengthy and painful. The one only glimmer of light during that period was my family's support, especially my mom's. On the same day that the news about my loss reached her, she booked the earliest flight to Austin to be with me.

While this was one of the most difficult seasons of my life, it was also the time I connected with my mother and felt her love more than ever before. As a child and teenager, I had issues with her that resulted in a deep wound in my heart that I carried over the years. As an adult, I learned to forgive her as I understood she was doing her best in the difficult circumstances she was going through, especially having been widowed at the age of forty-four. Our relationship was healed, and the wound I had harbored for years finally saw the light of healing.

After the loss of my baby, I channeled my energy and grief into searching for a new job. There was no more reason to continue my current job. Fortunately, work was never busy, so I was able to find time every day to search for a job. I searched desperately every single day. Months passed, but my relentless efforts didn't produce any results.

Only after seven months of tireless searching did doors finally start to open. In one week, I found myself doing interviews for three jobs. First, I received a call that I was accepted by the Communications Department of the Department of Health and Human Services, the equivalent of the Ministry of Health in Egypt. The other door that opened was from a local magazine called *Austin Chronicle* that I had knocked on out of desperation, hoping to even join as an intern. When the editor saw the articles I had published with *Al Ahram Online*, she told me I was ahead of the game and could join as a freelance journalist. All of a sudden, I found myself with both a full-time job and a freelance writing job.

I enjoyed my job with the Department of Health and Human Services. My manager there was one of the best managers I have had in my life. The downside of my job was the amount of bureaucracy I encountered. Like in any governmental organization, I witnessed how bureaucracy was killing the birth of new ideas and delaying projects I was responsible for. I found myself sitting in a gray cubicle, with few tasks and eight hours to kill every day. Despite my efforts to find and create work, there was not really room for that to happen. My saving grace during that time was my freelance work with *Austin Chronicle*, which connected me with my passion for writing and gave me the opportunity to do something fulfilling.

Freelance writing also allowed me to meet great human beings who had dedicated their lives to support certain causes, and who spent most of their days advocating for the rights of others. The joy I experienced every time I saw my article published overrode the boredom I experienced every day in the gray cubicle of my state job.

I never thought my heart could race as fast as it did when I heard my husband's name called during his graduation ceremony. When the presenter said, "Bahaa Gameel," and I saw Bahaa walk on stage to receive his PhD degree certificate, I stood up from my seat, screaming and clapping. I could feel my legs shaking. It was the highest moment of our journey in Austin. That day, we saw another rainbow shining for what we had fought for over five long years. We walked around the campus afterwards, holding hands as lovers and winners.

In August 2018, we packed up all of our stuff in Austin, including our furniture, put it into big a truck, and drove thousands of miles to our new destination, Saint Petersburg, Florida. Bahaa was lucky to be accepted as a professor at the University of South Florida in Saint Petersburg. We were both excited to leave Austin. As much as we loved the city and the great people we had met there, our time in Austin had been difficult. We were excited to have a fresh start in a new place. With its warm weather and beautiful beaches, Saint Petersburg felt like the perfect place for a new start.

We enjoyed our first days discovering new places in Saint Petersburg while still trying to recover from our three-day drive from Texas to Florida. Right after we settled in, Bahaa started to get busy with his new job as a professor. I also started to get busy applying for jobs. I came across a job announcement online that was in communications and hit the apply button since it was simple, and no application was needed. After I hit the apply button, I learned that the company ran juvenile justice facilities and was one of the biggest private providers in Florida. I wasn't sure how I felt about private companies running juvenile justice facilities for the Department of Juvenile Justice, even though it is an accepted business model in the United States.

To my surprise, the day after I applied, I received a call for an interview. I was not keen on this job and had mixed feelings, but I thought I would use the opportunity to learn more and to brush up my interviewing skills. Having nothing to lose, I decided also to interview the company leaders who interviewed me. "How do you see your role in bringing reforms to the juvenile justice system in Florida?" I asked the chief operating officer during my interview. The next day, I received a call from the human resources department telling me I had been accepted.

Despite my doubts about the company, I was happy to have found a job in Florida so quickly, without the struggles I went through in Austin. A few months into the job, I started to realize it was better than I had expected. I got to learn new skills and step out of my comfort zone. For the first time at a job in the United States, I felt challenged. It was a good feeling.

Six months later, however, the company was bought by an invest-ment firm, which gradually laid off the company's leadership team. The environment became turbulent, and the company's declining prof-its added to the stressful environment. So, I started job hunting again.

I came across a good position as communications manager at a Fortune 500 healthcare company. Without having to think about it, I applied. "What can I lose?" I thought. The same week I applied, I received a call from human resources requesting an interview with the direct supervisor of this position and her manager, the vice president of communications. As I always did, I prepared for the opportunity as if it were the last one.

A few days later after my interview, I received a call from human resources telling me that I had moved to the second level of interview-ing. They scheduled me for three back-to-back interviews with three executives in the organization.

"Give me an example of a project you led that did not succeed," the top executive asked me.

I thought about it, but nothing came to my mind. "I'm thinking," I told him, trying to buy more time. Then I replied jokingly, "Every project I lead succeeds." I said it with a facial expression that conveyed cockiness and sarcasm. *Did I just say a silly joke in my interview with a top executive?* I thought to myself. "Sorry, I know I'm not supposed to joke in interviews," I quickly told him.

He smiled and said it was fine, and we resumed the interview. One week later, human resources called to offer me the job. To my surprise, they offered a higher salary than I had requested. It is amazing how sometimes we have to knock on so many doors for one to open, while other times, doors open without any effort.

The first six months of my new job were overwhelming, with so much to learn about a new industry and the corporate culture in the United States. I reminded myself how bored I'd felt in all my previous jobs since I'd moved to the United States. It didn't take me long to re-alize I had landed the best job opportunity of my career. Besides work-ing in a booming industry in Florida, the company offered a dynamic work environment that encouraged creativity and allowed me to grow and learn. The best part about my job, however, was my supervisor. I had never had a supervisor who was as kind as Susan Dunlap. Susan also believed in me as no other manager had. She was able to focus on my strengths and was impressed by how accomplished I was as an immigrant. She quickly noticed that I have a talent for being on camera. Eight months after I was hired, Susan pitched a new idea to me. She asked me if I would be willing to host a news show that would broadcast to the company's employees across the country. As someone who studied TV broadcasting and wanted to be a TV presenter, I was beyond happy to start this new project.

On March 11, 2019, the first episode of the news show was broadcast to the company. I received emails from various coworkers across the organization that I had not met—including a top executive—complimenting the show. I felt like a champion that day, not because I did something successful that was recognized by many, but because I was able to look back at where I started in the United States and how I had been able to build my communications career here against all odds. While I don't know what the future holds for my career and life in the United States, I know I have what it takes to succeed, which in itself is a win. I also realize that my career journey, similar to most journeys of our life, is a work in progress. I might not be where I aspire to be, but I am where I need to be today. I have faith in the journey. It will take me to where I need to be.

———•———

DINA SAMIR SHEHATA lives with her small family in Tampa, Florida. She started her career in Corporate Communications in Egypt and has worked in the same field in the US. She also worked as a freelance journalist and TV presenter. Shehata likes to write about marginalized communities and the "invisible" people in our world. She likes to call herself a "student of pain." She is passionate about learning how pain transforms who we are as human beings.

SEEING THE WORLD WHILE WORKING

Fayek Andrawes

I was born into a typical, interconnected, middle-class Egyptian family and lived the first nine years of my life in Aswan, Egypt. The roots of our large family run deep in Egypt and spread across Esna, Edfu, Naqadah, and Aswan. Our home in Aswan always welcomed relatives and guests who were visiting or staying, temporarily or permanently.

Our family had, and continues to have, strong ties to Sudan. My father, who was born in Edfu, went to Sudan at a young age to work in the Sudanese postal service, but became immersed in politics and joined the White Brigade Association, whose main goal was to expel the British and unite the Nile Valley. Due to his political involvement, he was arrested, jailed for nearly two months, and expelled from Sudan, along with a wave of deportation of Egyptians active in the resistance to British colonialism. This was a concerted effort to keep England involved in Sudan, without Egyptian interference.

My father returned home in search of work, found a position in the Egyptian postal service, and settled in Aswan for a long time. In addition to his government position, he worked with an Italian company that secured the contract for the second capacity increase of the Aswan dam in 1925. This company used a granite mine registered in the name of my father, whose work on this venture represented significant additional income for him, but the project's activity diminished by the 1940s.

In 1949, my father quit his job with the postal service and began working in a completely different field. Through Abdul Rahman Hamada Pasha, a member of the company's board of directors, he found work at the Egyptian Spinning and Weaving Company (a cotton textile producer) in El-Mahalla El-Kubra. My father worked in administration, overseeing some of the company's facilities, the most important of which were modern restaurants that provided full meals for thousands of workers and employees. In 1952, he began to work for company in Kafr El-Dawar, and our family moved to Alexandria. My father continued this work until 1968 and then transitioned to free contracting activities between Suez, Esna, and Aswan.

The year we moved to Alexandria, 1952, was the year both Egypt and our family witnessed major events. The Free Officers Revolution, which represented radical changes in Egypt, ended Muhammad Ali's dynasty rule of Egypt and transformed Egypt into a republican system. Egypt transformed into an optimistic country. The aristocratic mass-land holders began to weaken, some even collapsed, and the poor and middle-class experienced improved living conditions and prosperity. My father was a Wafdist (national political party) and, like many Egyptians at the time, lived through and supported the revolution of Saad Zaghloul. He had doubts about the rule of the officers who successfully staged the July 1952 revolution, despite some of their important achievements.

Alexandria was a beautiful, clean city, with a pioneering culture characterized by diverse ethnic and foreign people living harmoniously in one society. The Egyptian education system was good, and good foreign schools were available, though they were expensive, so not many could afford them. My two younger brothers and I attended public schools, and my younger sister enrolled in the French school École Girard in Alexandria at an early age. She transferred to a public school so she could attend an Egyptian university, but she got married and immigrated to America instead.

Every summer, our house in Alexandria resembled a beehive, as it was always swarming with guests, some visiting and others who would come to stay. Our moves from Aswan to El-Mahalla El-Kubra, and then to Alexandria, were major cultural shifts for each of us, especially my two brothers and sister. Our parents wanted us to receive a strong education, so my father brought us books he borrowed from his company's library. The schools we attended in Alexandria were as good as the schools in more developed countries, and our schools encouraged us to join clubs and take part in various activities. My father collected antiques, including furniture, paintings, and oriental rugs, and he encouraged us to adopt a stamp collecting hobby. We joined our school's philatelic societies and later the Egyptian Philatelic Association, in which many hobbyists, doctors, engineers, and professors participated—both Egyptians and foreigners. Some collected an impressive amount and quality of Egyptian and foreign stamps in excellent conditions. Some even became experts in certain stamp issues. The president of the association at the time was Ahmed Mazloum Pasha, who also served as the chief justice of the Supreme Court.

Interest in politics became part of our culture and was difficult to avoid. The Free Officers Revolution ended the British influence in Egypt, with the nationalization of the Suez Canal. This led to a war between Egypt and the aggressor alliance of the United Kingdom, France, and Israel. During that crisis, I volunteered for military training, which was not serious or rigorous. That catastrophic war ended when President Eisenhower mandated the withdrawal of the aggressors, and with the rise of Gamal Abdel Nasser, who became a populist leader whose influence extended outside of Egypt. Other world events that affected Egypt, both directly and indirectly, were the Cuban Revolution and the Vietnam War. The nonaligned movement between countries began, which included Tito in Yugoslavia, Nehru in India, Sukarno in Indonesia, and Abdel Nasser in Egypt. Egypt ended the Western monopoly over the country and turned to the Eastern camp for armament and construction of the Aswan High Dam after the West withdrew its financing of the vital project. Defeat followed in

1967, shedding light on flaws in the Egyptian regime. Depression soon followed.

After the war of 1956, many foreigners began to leave Egypt. During that period, we moved to an old but well-designed house. The house occupied a corner city plot, with six rooms and two halls, two balconies, a salon room, a semi-formal lunchroom, four other bedrooms, two bathrooms, and a spacious kitchen. The bedrooms had wooden floors, and the salon rooms had white-and-black marble floors. The building consisted of three apartments, owned by a friendly elderly Jewish woman named Sarina, who was controlled and manipulated by a junior military officer.

After high school, I enrolled at Alexandria University, which was made easier by my family living in Alexandria. I tried to be a good student but did not excel in my studies. Alexandria University offered a great educational program with a limited number of students. The professors hailed from famous Eastern and Western European and American universities. The syllabus and course load were not easy and were similar to those of the European educational systems I later experienced in the United States. The academic way of thinking stayed with me. The truth is I was lucky with my family and teachers in high school and later on in college.

Alexandria was one of the most beautiful cities on the coast of the Mediterranean Sea, full of cultural and social activities. We had great times with many friends and enjoyed taking part in political discussions, especially in university.

After retiring from the textile company, my father started a contracting business, which took him to Aswan for the summer and fall of 1963. As I neared the end of my studies at the Department of Science at Alexandria University, I worked with my father on several projects. The projects included saving several of the Pharaonic temples that were under threat of being flooded and drowning under the rising Nile water after the Aswan High Dam was completed. The company's contracts included cutting and transporting the ancient Temple of Wadi es-Sebua, a project that lasted until 1965. This temple dates back to the

Ramesses II Era of the nineteenth dynasty and is the second largest temple in Nubia, after the temple of Abu Simbel. I also worked on the Temple of Amada, which dates back to the time of Thutmose III in the eighteenth dynasty and is estimated to weigh six hundred tons. This temple was transported as a single block on a specially built railroad. My work during that period brought me closer to the great history of Egypt—all Egyptians belong to that heritage, which the world is proud of. Regretfully, however, I was not able to see these temples in their new location before I left Egypt.

I was fortunate to find work right after college, which was not an easy feat at the time, especially since I did not graduate with high grades. I did not expect to find a job other than maybe teaching in a public school. However, a family relative happened to be working for United Geographica Geophysical, an American seismic company in Alexandria, and he got me a job. The company was a contractor for Phillips 66, which had a concession area in the western desert, under the supervision of the Egyptian Petroleum Corporation.

My position was as a trainee and considered temporary, but I took my job seriously. I sought to learn as much as I could and sometimes worked ten to twelve hours a day. My salary was twice what the government paid its employees, and I never asked for a raise, but I think the company appreciated my hard work, because they gave me annual bonuses. I was happy with my job, which ended up lasting three years. I learned a lot about geophysics and was able to work and socialize with the diverse group of expatriates in the company. I was also able to live amid my family. That ended with the great exodus from Egypt.

After the war of 1967 and the general state of depression in the world, one of my Egyptian friends and colleagues began talking about immigrating to the United States or Australia. He suggested I also apply to the American Embassy. I agreed without giving the matter much thought. I was not aware how long embassies took to process applications before they accepted or refused them. I was eager to immigrate because my job was short term and unstable, similar to those at all foreign oil companies in Egypt at the time. I was liable to lose my job any moment. I was surprised to receive approval two years after I applied to the American consulate. Following the approval, I had to go through a medical examination and a personal interview with the consul general, both of which went smoothly.

I had to obtain the approval of the Egyptian authorities to get a passport, which required a lot of official papers. Despite the fact that I was working at a foreign company, I faced some difficulties obtaining these papers, but I got them nonetheless. I got the rest of my required papers in order, completed the procedures with the American consulate, and obtained my required visa to leave Egypt and my immigrant visa to the United States. The most difficult thing for me was to say goodbye to my family and friends. I'll never forget the sight of my father in the last moments before my departure from the Cairo International Airport. He looked as though he felt he was never going to see me again. In fact, he passed away less than three years later, before I was able to see him again. I returned to Egypt for the first time after his death. Although we were constantly in touch, and although my parents were reassured of my future in America, we missed each other very much.

I was allowed to leave Egypt with 137 US dollars marked on my Egyptian passport. I was ready to work immediately upon my arrival in the United States, and my goal was to find work in the oil sector in California or Texas. My airline ticket's final destination was California, but I stopped in Michigan for a short visit with my uncle, who was a mechanical engineer and who had immigrated from the Belgian Congo years earlier. He tried to persuade me to stay in Michigan. My uncle owned his house and had a stable livelihood; though I was somewhat familiar with how things worked in the States, I didn't know my uncle very well. He had left Egypt in the 1940s for the Congo after he failed to persuade officials in Egypt to start an agricultural project in the Sinai Peninsula.

It so happened that my uncle came across an engineering company very active in finding and using underground water. Eager to have a member of the family close by, he urged me to apply for a job at that company. "What do you have to lose?" he asked. And so I did.

The company was small, and I met with the director of geology, who managed the company technically and was also a professor teaching hydrology geology at the University of Michigan. I was offered a position with a satisfactory salary. I reluctantly accepted because my heart was still set on working in the oil exploration sector. I took my job seriously and spent long hours at the company and at the university library, reading and gathering data on the groundwater and geology of the region. It was all very new to me. I spent four months there, learning a lot, and presented my research findings directly to the company's clients. That was in the summer months. By the time autumn and winter came, I was ready to move to California or Texas and escape the extreme cold. I submitted my resignation to the director, who told me they would send me a return plane ticket from wherever I landed and that I was welcome to return any time.

I went to California and lived in the YMCA in Los Angeles. I obtained the addresses of all the oil companies with regional offices from the yellow pages (remember, dear reader, I'm speaking of a time before the internet). The only offer I received was from a geophysical company that wanted to send me to Alaska. I quickly turned it down due to Alaska's climate, and decided to go to Houston, Texas. I bought a train ticket (which was $20 cheaper than a plane ticket) and arrived in Houston two days later, having seen a lot of the States. There, I looked for companies in the yellow pages again, but this time I received more than one offer in a matter of a week. I accepted a tempting offer with a substantial salary from Mobil, one of the largest oil industry companies.

At Mobil, I worked hard and for long hours because I loved my job. The company sent me to a university to pursue advanced technical and language courses. I started working in the Department of Domestic and International Geophysical Petroleum Exploration and subsequently moved to the General Exploration Department as a senior explorationist. The projects were located in the Gulf of Mexico, the Gulf of Alaska, Nigeria, Libya, Indonesia, and Egypt. In Egypt, Mobil had two concessions: one in the Gulf of Suez, where our work led to the discovery of the first oil well in the Ashrafi Field, and another in the

Mediterranean that led to the discovery of the Temsah Field (translated to Crocodile Field in English). I chose its name and supervised the work leading to the drilling of the initial successful well. I was on the drilling location during the first test of the well. Mobil was unsuccessful in procuring the gas from that site as it was not considered commercially viable at the time; however, it was later successfully produced, thanks to advanced technology, and was transmitted through a pipeline to feed Egypt's needs.

I made some Egyptian friends in Dallas, Texas, and was happy when we met to eat *ful medames* (fava bean stew), which I missed a lot. I have retained many of those friendships and memories, even as life led each of us down different paths and to different locations.

In 1973, I married a wonderful woman who came from Mexico to study the respiratory system at a college in Dallas. She was living in the same building, so over a year, we got to know each other, and then got married according to the Coptic traditions. Before our wedding, my mother visited me because she was not comfortable with me marrying a non-Egyptian. She soon accepted my choice. My wife, Rebecca, was a traditional woman and helped me by bringing stability into my life. My work was stable and provided a solid income, experience, and a future. We had two children. The oldest is Janette, who is fluent in Spanish and English, and who gained a basic knowledge of Arabic and French after spending a short time in Egypt and Tunisia. Janette has worked in marketing, branding, and communications for startups and arts organizations. She won an Emmy Award for a commercial she produced and currently works in San Francisco as the vice president of marketing for a tech company in the real estate sector. Janette has one child, Rafael. Our youngest, Alexander, lives near us in Austin, Texas, and has two children of his own: Sophia and Amelie. Alexander founded and is the CEO of Pervino, Inc., a wine conglomerate. He became a distinguished expert in wine and wrote *Investing in Fine Wine* (2017). Alexander created and is the CEO of another company, Green Ocean Sciences, Inc., which specializes in purifying natural plants for medical use.

My career at Mobil advanced my technical acumen to the point that I attracted the attention of my colleagues and leaders in my field. Some of my colleagues started a company that would employ modern technology to detect gas and offered me an attractive monthly salary and a share in the firm. But such an adventure was not part of my plans. I was happy with my work, and going into business for myself and creating an independent company was something I never seriously thought of doing. I rejected such offers, and I realize now how limited my thinking was. As the old Egyptian saying goes, "If a government job bypasses you, roll in its soil." I'm glad my son thinks differently and that he took the risk of starting two companies.

I received a job offer from the United States Geological Survey that I also rejected, but that was because I knew I would grow faster in a private company than in a government job bound by routine work. But in early 1980, I accepted a position at the Marathon Petroleum Corporation as Southeast Asia's chief geophysicist at the company's Singapore headquarters. In 1981, I was transferred to work at the company's London headquarters as explorations manager for the European continent and Middle East. During my work at Marathon through 1983, I attended many classes and lectures, perhaps the most important of which was a three-month university-level, full-time executive management course. When I was transferred to Tunisia, where we lived for six years, I was appointed exploration director. The family had a wonderful time in Tunisia, and our children often speak of our happiness there and of their unforgettable experiences.

After that, the company decided to transfer me to Egypt. I faced problems there that caused me a great deal of pain, but I will not touch on them. Needless to say, I was unable to work in my country. I was supposed to be the manager of the company in Egypt, but I only remained six months. Upon my request, I was transferred to my company's Houston headquarters as area manager, managing exploration operations in Africa and the Middle East. At that time, my work took me to Syria for six months.

While working at Marathon, my responsibilities expanded to cover new ventures and business development for Europe, Africa, the Middle East, and the countries that were separated from the Soviet Union. In 1998, my position was eliminated, and I was let go after eighteen years. I worked as a consultant for some time after that, primarily for small companies working in oil exploration. By then, I had worked in many countries, including Benin in West Africa. I stopped consulting to work for Petroleum Geo-Services (PGS) as director of new ventures and marketing and was responsible for business in Europe, Africa, the Middle East, and former USSR countries, including those in Central Asia. PGS was a geophysical company that enabled me to work in London once again for two and a half years and then in Dubai for about three years.

As I approached retirement age, I began to wonder what I could do to occupy my time. I'm not the kind of person who can spend all day watching television. I decided to buy a medium-sized hotel to manage and reside in. It had twenty-five suites, meeting rooms, and two restaurants. My younger brother helped me, as he had extensive experience managing large hotels. The hotel kept my wife and me busy for four years, but then old age caught up to us, especially after a heart attack that led to bypass surgery. I finally decided to sell the hotel and retire in Austin, Texas.

I traveled to more than seventy-five countries during my career. My daughter and son saw many countries around the world and attended schools in England, Tunisia, and Egypt, which increased their exposure to other cultures before they attended the University of Texas. While living in Tunisia, we leased a creatively designed house that was part of the palace of the bay (king) of Tunisia, decorated with Tunisian mosaic. It overlooked the Gulf of Tunis, in a small town called Sidi Bou Said, where the homes and buildings were all white and blue. Sidi Bou Said remains the most beautiful place I have ever lived in. It attracts many international artists, especially from European countries. I was fond of antiques and local arts and crafts and acquired many along my travels. Our home became full of these antiques and memories.

I acquired many antiques during my travels, but I did not have room in my home for all of them, so I gifted some to a Texas university.

Life's journeys contain different curves and surprises. Now I have time to enjoy my children and grandchildren and the things I missed during their formative years, as my many travels took me away from them. During my long-life journey, Egypt has never left my mind. I went back there on a short visit with my brothers after the massive January 25th revolution. How I wish Egypt would return to what it was when I left in 1969! I often wonder what happened to Egypt and to the Egyptian people.

———•———

FAYEK ANDRAWES graduated from Alexandria University with a degree in geology. Upon graduation, he worked as geophysicist for an American company based in Egypt. Three years later, he immigrated to the United States. After briefly working in Michigan in the area of ground water production and disposal, he took a job with Mobil doing oil field exploration. For the rest of his career, he stayed in the same field, albeit working for different companies. His work took him to sites all over the world. Now retired, he lives in Texas with his wife. He has a son, a daughter, and three grandchildren that bring joy to his life.

FROM EGYPT TO ENGLAND TO AMERICA

Giselle Hakki

When I look back at my early years in the 1930s and 1940s, I think of silence. Although we were a large family with four children and we lived in a suburb of Cairo, it is the quiet that I mostly remember.

The suburb was called Ein Shams. It was close to Matareya. We lived on Gharb el-Shereet Street, but there was no house number. On one side, there was the railway and on the other side, there was a rural road that led to a village called Ezbet el-Ewtad. People went to and fro on that road. We had a kind of jasmine hedge that was quite dense around our garden, but we children could peer through the hedge and see the world go by. Sometimes funeral processions passed, with paid mourners who shrieked now and then. We weren't alarmed by these sounds because they were commonplace. Now and then peddlers would go by; especially intriguing was the Roba Bechia (street Arabic for Robba Vecchia, which is Italian) man. When he came around, a maid we had would give him bottles, and he would give her something in return. I once got some glass bracelets through this exchange. I had no jewelry because my mother didn't like jewelry, and we girls didn't even have our ears pierced. So, I was pleased with my gift!

The gate on the side of the railway was never opened, except when my father ran for parliament and lost. At the time of the election, the garden was filled with people being served coffee. Cars drove by, with people chanting, "Al doctor ma al Doŝtour," which rhymed and meant, "The doctor is on the side of the Conŝtitution." My father loŝt that election to a very rich man from the Shawarby family, but later (from 1943 to 1946) he became a senator.

On the other side of the garden was the back entrance, flanked by two large eucalyptus trees. That was the kitchen side. My brothers and I loved to shine sunlight through a magnifying glass onto the eucalyptus leaves, causing them to burn slightly and emit a medicinal smell a bit like Vicks. The leaves and branches of these trees would crackle and whisper at night as we lay in bed, making it a little eerie. We could also hear the regular creaking of the waterwheel, as the ox belonging to someone who had an orchard across the road went round and round all night to turn the wheel. I felt terrible for the suffering of the blindfolded ox. Across the road, there was a mulberry tree at the side of the road. Village children sold the mulberries to passersby.

At the back of the house, there was a vegetable garden and a walkway with pine trees on either side. And there was also vegetable garden, where we grew vegetables and herbs, such as arugula, toma-toes, purslane, and mint. I loved to eat the purslane ŝtraight from the earth. There also was a loofah tree—a miracle tree that grew loofahs you could use! On top all that, there was a lemon tree. Our garden in the back also had a tall hedge, but you could see the road if you peered through it.

When one went out of the kitchen side entrance and turned right, and then left, one went onto Wilson Street.

Wilson Street was a European enclave. A Danish eye doctor, who treated the peasants for very little, or even for free, lived there, as did Sir Robert Allason Furness, who was in the Egyptian Civil service, and his wife, Lady Furness, and their daughter, Lucy. We were on visiting terms with them. My father knew Dr. Wilson, after whom the ŝtreet was named. There was a drinking fountain for animals in Dr. Wilson's garden wall.

We passed through Wilson Street when we were little because our governess took us in a three-seater carriage every afternoon to visit an ancient Egyptian obelisk. We generally sang French songs with her, especially "Au Claire de la Lune/Mon ami Pierrot." The governess's name was Madame Clotide Forenbacher, but we called her Nanitza. She was the most wonderful addition to our family. She was a Yugoslav, who had lost her Austrian officer husband and come to Egypt as a companion to a German countess named Sizzo-Norris, but stayed on as governess to the Abozbaa family when the countess returned to Europe.

Nanitza brought her daughter, Jennie, to the Middle East and placed her in a convent boarding school. When the Abozbaa children, Nihad and Samiha, no longer needed her, she came to us, replacing an Italian nanny named Peppina, who had been working for my parents but who wanted to leave when my father refused to shoot all the owls. She regarded owls as a bad omen and wanted us to get rid of them.

Nanitza told me that when she took up her position in our home, she was told that my older brother, Adel, would be looked after by his wet nurse and that she would have to look after my younger brother, Samir. So, she asked, "What about the one on the sofa?" They told her Guzetta (that was my nickname) was the middle child. However, she ended up being in charge of all of us, including our younger sister, Leila, who was born a few years later.

Nanitza was the most wonderful, moral, decent, and kind person anyone would love to have in their family. She remained with us until the end, and when I had my daughter, Yasmina, in 1959, in Zamalek, Egypt, she came to stay with us for a while. When we were children, she did everything for us all day long. At night, we donned woolen sack-like coverings she'd made for us, which she called "peau d'ours" (bearskin). She made us sit in a circle, and after we had eaten some homemade yogurt, she read to us from Victor Hugo's *Les Misérables* and other edifying books.

She was a Catholic, but she respected other people's religions. She felt at home with Muslims, like us. Her daughter, Jennie, eventually became a governess to the Astras, a Jewish family who owned a well-known company that made Astra cheese, and she felt perfectly comfortable living in their environment. I often accompanied Nanitza when she went to the Catholic Church in Matareya. My parents didn't object, because we were all comfortable in our own religions and we knew that our three religions were somehow linked. The church in Matareya was famous as the resting place for Mary and baby Jesus.

My two brothers went to the English School in Heliopolis, where Jews and Muslims left the room when it was time for scripture class for Christians, but my sister and I went to the English Mission School, where I attended scripture classes and we sang hymns. No one minded. I used to wait for the English Mission School bus in Matareya with my dear friend Lawrence Moftah. We each brought a multi-layered lunch container to school. I still see Lawrence when she comes to the United States to see her children. I was transferred to the English school when I was twelve so that I could be with my brothers in one school. My sister went to the same school, but she was in the junior school because she was a lot younger.

In those days, Egypt was secular and liberal and religious in the best way. My mother was educated at home after a certain age; her governess and tutors were European. My aunts and my mother-in-law, however, went to Sacré-Cœur Catholic schools. Muslim parents liked the strictness of nuns. Our aunts told us that when they were at school as boarders, they wore a gown for modesty when they showered!

But of course, that was a liberal and rational time. Extremism was not known and would have been frowned upon. Nowadays, God's name is brought into every conversation. That would have been considered poor taste in our day. You did not drag religion into every conversation. We were good Muslims, by which I mean that we tried to be decent and moral.

My maternal grandmother, Gameela, had the misfortune of losing her son Saad when he was a student in Belgium. He and his brother Mohamed had been to French schools run by the *Frères*. My mother taught my grandmother to read the Qur'an, which helped to console her. Also, in my grandmother Gameela's house in Zeitoun, which was about twenty minutes away by car, a sheikha used to come and stay in what they called the sheikha's room and read the Qur'an to my grandmother.

My grandmother's mother was Circassian and could not speak Arabic properly. She had been awarded by the khedive to my grandmother Gameela's grandfather, whose name was el-Gretly for his services in the army. She was a white slave and had been abducted by the Ottomans when the family got her, but she was given her freedom and married off to their son, Mahmoud Bey Zaki el-Gretly. I have a copy of the document, which states that she was freed by the Gretly family. The Gretly family had originally been Greek and were from Crete.

My mother had lived in a grand house with a salamlek (guest house) and stables. The house was probably designed by my grandmother's cousin, Mustapha Pasha Fahmy. He was the Royal architect and he also was the architect who built Cairo University.

My father was born on November 13, 1886, in Alexandria. Dr. Abdel-Aziz Ahmed did not come from a rich family; in fact, when he was a student, he was rather poor. He waited until he was forty-five and well-established in his career before he got married to my mother. His family name was originally al-Seran; they traced their family to shipbuilders and sea captains in the time of Muhammad Aly the Great. His grandfather was a prominent religious personage who rode with the khedive in his carriage when the khedive came to Alexandria. His own father was a religious scholar, who had instilled a love of learning in his children. My father told us that one floor in their childhood home was filled with books.

There was some belief that my father's family, the al-Seran family, had originally come to Egypt from Tunisia and intermarried with Egyptians. However, according to a cousin, there was also a Turkish connection. An area in Turkey is called Seran; the inhabitants of that area were Greeks who had converted to Islam. The al-Seran family is mentioned in an old Arabic dictionary called *Qamus al-Arus* as being religious scholars in Alexandria. The name Seran was dropped by my father and his siblings because, when the word Seran is pronounced in Arabic, it means "rabid!"

My father's father was appointed to the religious High Court, and they moved to Cairo from Alexandria. He died soon afterward, and they had to go back to Alexandria. The eldest brother had to go to work to support the rest of the family; he even postponed getting married until his brothers and sister all grew up.

My father went to school where English was taught by English teachers, and he said they were excellent. Although my father knew the Qur'an very well because he had to memorize it, he also excelled in English. He later went to Fouad I University. He had very little money, so he walked to save bus fares, and he told us he often just had a glass of milk for supper. However, he worked very hard and did well in engineering, so in a few years, the English professors sent him to Birmingham University in England to get a graduate degree. He was told to get the degree in physics. My father said the British professors knew he wanted a graduate degree in electrical engineering, but they didn't want him to do that. But he was lucky, because his professor at Birmingham, Professor Kapp, allowed him to also get a BSc degree in electrical engineering in 1914 and an MSc degree in the same subject in 1914. Professor Kapp encouraged my father and convinced the British authorities to allow him to get a PhD in electrical engineering in 1922. He was awarded a DSc degree in electrical engineering in 1923.

He formed a lifelong friendship with Professor Kapp, and when we went to England many years later, he introduced us to Professor Kapp's son. He also formed a close friendship with an Egyptian medical student who became a doctor and remained in Birmingham for the rest of his life. Dr. Sidky and my father were like brothers and many years later, when my father went through troubled times and ill health, Dr. Sidky was there for him.

My father was probably one of the first Egyptians to get a DSc degree. When he went back to Egypt with the DSc, he was appointed professor of electrical engineering at the age of thirty-nine. He later became the first Egyptian-born dean of the Engineering School at Cairo University. I have several photos of him as dean sitting, in the center of the front row, with his British professors on either side—some of them wearing a *tarboush* (fez)—and with the engineering student class behind them.

By then, I guess he could afford to get married. The marriage was arranged through a Turkish woman marriage broker, Amina el-Torkeya. First, she arranged for him to propose to Aisha, who was the daughter of Aly Pasha Hussein. Aisha turned him down, saying he was too old for her. So, Aisha married a diplomat, Abdel Rahman Pasha Hakki, who is the father of my own husband, Dr. Ahmed Hakki. My father was then taken by Amina el-Torkeya to propose to my mother, Ikbal Abou Seif Rady. My mother was glad to get away from her father, who was generally too controlling, and she agreed to marry my father.

Her father, Ibrahim Abu Seif Rady, was a landowner who had a lot of land in Aboxa, in Fayoum. His father had owned land in el-Menya and Bani Souef, and had a home in el-Helmeyah el-Adima. His grandfather was the head of an Arab tribe, called Banu Fazzara, that originally came from Northern Hejaz. His mother, who was my mother's paternal grandmother, was an Albanian.

We, however, loved our grandfather Ibrahim Abu Seif Rady. He was a hands-on farmer, and when we visited him in Aboxa, he got up very early and stood on his balcony and shouted to people, telling them what to do. We were fascinated and we loved the smell of the orange groves. He also built a cheese factory on his land. He was a fun-loving person in his own life, and he and his friend Zaki Bey Wissa often gave parties together. Sometimes Out el-Koloub would attend.

My mother was twenty-two when my parents got married on March 13, 1931. In spite of their age difference, our parents were very happy together. When my father bought the house in Ein Shams, it was a modest house surrounded by an orchard. His mother and two nieces lived with him. His mother, Zeinab, who was pure Egyptian, was disabled due to arthritis and lay in a hammock in the garden during the day.

Before my father got married, he added another floor to the house and turned the orchard into a garden. Over the years, it became a beautiful garden. Both my parents loved the garden. My father designed small irrigation canals with little bridges and had an engine to water the garden. He brought seeds from England and built a large greenhouse to propagate plants. He built metal trellises for bougainvillea and sweet peas, and a kiosk for us to sit in. He also built a small area that was a sort of maze with tree trunk seats.

The lawn area where we sometimes sat with guests was surrounded by flowerbeds with delphinium, poppies, lilies, wisteria, asters, nasturtiums, and more. My mother could often be seen working alongside the gardener, measuring flowerbeds. There was also a small cactus area nearby. It was wonderful to sit and have tea on the lawn and smell the flowers.

We also had two large fir trees, which is not so common in Egypt. One day, we found flags stuck on the top of the trees! My two brothers had secretly climbed and put up the flags.

Once, when I was about eleven, a prince named Omar Tousson, resplendent in a white suit, came to look at the garden. Someone had told him about it. He wanted to buy the house because he loved the garden, and he made a fair offer. My mother was inclined to accept because she thought she could then move to Heliopolis and be near her sisters. In the end, my parents decided not to sell the house.

Although my mother had never completed her education, she spoke and read Arabic and French. She took advantage of the fact that my father's house was full of books to enrich herself. She was interested in the French intellectual movements and read a lot of avant-garde French novelists and philosophers. She regularly purchased books and often donated books to the library at the Heliopolis Sporting Club and the Gezira Sporting Club.

Our house was filled with books. My father was an avid reader and could freely quote Shakespearean verse and much poetry. He read widely in literature, history, philosophy, and science. He loved Bertrand Russell and the Greek philosophers. Our entrance room had a lot of copies of Greek sculpture and famous paintings. In his study, he had a photo of Gandhi, whom he admired. When I woke up very early and crept downstairs, I would find my father sitting surrounded with papers and writing. He always got up at dawn and worked.

At the end of the garden, next to the gardener's room, was a room filled with books. We freely helped ourselves and we all loved nothing better than to curl up with a book. We also listened to music. My father had a collection of classical music and opera. Now and then, my parents took us to the opera house to see operas or Shakespearean plays or *La Comedie Française* performing Racine and Moliere. My mother liked to play Cole Porter tunes on the piano and also strummed Arabic tunes by ear.

I took piano lessons with Mademoiselle Aziza Ghareeb, who lived nearby. Her father was very old and was known in the neighborhood for the long walks he took. I was not good at the piano and I specially hated Czerny exercises. But my sister, Leila, played the flute well. She was also a gifted athlete and broke a national record in running.

Everything seemed idyllic in Ein Shams; however, that was only one side of life with our parents, as my father had a difficult career, and that spilled over into all of our lives. When he was a young engineer, he stood in the way of a government minister who wanted to personally benefit from a project. My father lost his job and was accused of using a boat on the Nile in Upper Egypt for his own benefit. When he lost his job, we were short of money. My mother didn't want to ask for help from her father. Some people at that time stopped talking to my father. He became very depressed. Finally, the case came to trial, and the judge threw it out, saying my father was the most innocent man to set foot in his court. It is interesting that, at that time in history, although the minister suing my father was a very powerful man, justice prevailed! Congratulatory telegrams poured in when the newspapers published that he had won. And his friends rushed back to him.

Then my father was appointed Chairman of the Hydroelectric Power Commission and set about working on the electrification of the old Aswan Dam. Again, interested parties tried to get contracts for themselves and their business partners, and even to bribe him. It was a difficult time. *When Capitalists Collide: Business Conflict and the End of Empire in Egypt*, by Robert Vitalis, a book that was published in 1995, describes how my father was harassed by some people who wanted only personal gain.

However, when the electrification project was completed, an opening ceremony was held at Aswan. I have a newspaper photo of King Farouk talking to my father, overlooking the Aswan Dam. The prime minister at the time, Nokrashy Pasha, is also in the photo. The king made my father a Pasha at the time, but sometime later, the title was withdrawn. No matter, the papers and people continued to call my father Pasha. None of us were sorry that Farouk was drummed out of Egypt on his yacht. He was too much of a playboy to be missed.

Then came the era of Nasser. Initially, people were willing to give him a chance. When land reform laws were passed, my mother's father, Abou Seif, who was still alive, lost a lot of land. It was confiscated and then distributed to the peasants. Grandpa moved out of the Zatoun house and rented it to a technical school. Then Nasser passed a law that renters could become owners, so the school became the owners of the Zatoun house, and it too was lost to the family.

My father was quite old and suffered from polycythemia vera (and later leukemia), but he was still working as Chairman of the Hydroelectric Commission when Nasser's most important project, the Aswan High Dam, was conceived. Nasser was very anxious to have this project carried out. When my father examined the High Dam project, he had reservations because he felt the loss of silt would be a huge disadvantage. He had other objections as well.

When my father expressed his objections in writing, the minister ordered him to get rid of them.

My father requested an open discussion with Dr. Hurst, the British engineer involved with the High Dam project. Dr. Hurst was scientific consultant to the Ministry of Public Works in Egypt. My father knew him well. But Dr. Hurst and the Ministry refused to have an open discussion.

My father resigned. Some newspapers wrote that he was fired, but he was not fired. He wrote a paper laying out his objections. Then he went to London to present his paper to the Institution of Civil Engineers, where Dr. Hurst and other engineers involved in the High

Dam Project were members. The paper, entitled "Recent Developments in Nile Control," was published in *Proceedings of the Institution of Civil Engineers* (17[2]:137–80) in October 1960.

My father was himself a member of both the Institution of Civil Engineers and the Institution of Electrical Engineers. When he was about to return to Egypt, after reading his paper, he received a warning that if he returned to Egypt, he would be sent to jail. I was in England at the time, and for a whole year he could not return Egypt. People tried to help, especially the journalists Ali Amin and Mustapha Amin. My father's oldest friend, the physician Dr. Sidky in Birmingham, was there for him and helped.

During his absence from Egypt, my father was awarded the state medal by the professional body of Egyptian engineers. They expressed their appreciation for the work he had produced during his career. It was a very important award. The medal came with a little money, but the medal and the money were confiscated by the Egyptian government. At the time, my parents were in desperate need of any money.

Years later, after my father's death, my Aunt Zenab's husband, who was a prominent lawyer and a very good person, was able to get us the money that came with the award. Still later, a relative of my husband got the government of Sadat to release the medal.

My parents were very idealistic and very fair. They made no distinction between girls and boys. All four of us took the entrance exams to Cambridge University in England. We were all accepted, and we all graduated from there. It was a great sacrifice on my parents' behalf because it was expensive for us all to go. Also, they did not have us near them when they needed us.

They had very high principles and never compromised. We hope we lived up to their expectations. When my brother, Dr. Samir Ahmed, got a job with NASA at Princeton, my mother made it clear that he should never agree to work in the nuclear armament field, and he never did. My sister, Dr. Leila Ahmed, is a distinguished scholar. She is a professor of Divinity at Harvard University. She has written and published many books, including an autobiography.

My two brothers, Dr. Adel Ahmed and Dr. Samir Ahmed, had very distinguished careers as electrical engineers. Adel is in the New Jersey Inventors Hall of Fame for his work on the ground fault interrupter; he had numerous inventions in electronics. Samir is a Herbert Kayser professor of electrical engineering at City College, where he was also chair of the department for many years. He has spearheaded original research in laser atmospheric sensing and satellite monitoring of oceanic water quality.

I am the only one who did not get a PhD. After my graduation from Cambridge, I got a job as language instructor in the English Department at Cairo University. Dr. Magdy Wahba and Dina bint Abdul-Hamid (former queen of Jordan) were teaching there at the time. I enjoyed it. After marrying my first husband and having my daughter, Yasmina, we went to England, and I started to work toward a graduate degree. But due to various reasons, including my divorce, I did not complete the work.

I met Dr. Ahmed Hakki, who was a friend of my brothers from their Cambridge days, and we got married. We emigrated to the United States, and I had a second child, whom we named Adam. We started our life in Hyde Park, New York.

My husband had a wonderful career in psychiatry and was a great example of dedication and decency. He worked at the Albert Einstein College of Medicine and in the Bronx. He became the clinical head of the Kirby State Hospital on Wards Island and was also the chief of an outpatient clinic at Our Lady of Mercy in the Bronx. He had no difficulty adjusting to life in the United States. As a diplomat's son, he had lived in different countries. He cared lovingly about his patients and got up at 2:00 in the morning when he was on the crisis team. I never ever heard him complain!

His father and mother were also tolerant and ambitious self-sacrificing parents. His father, Abdel Rahman Hakki Pasha, who was a career diplomat and ambassador to Rome and London, had extremely high moral standards, as did his mother, Aisha Hussein. She was the daughter of Aly Hussein Pasha, who was a lawyer and minister of

Wakf, and, like my mother's father, came from Bani Souef. Aly Hussein Pasha's wife descended from a Cretan royal concubine, donated by the khedive to her ancestor, el-Nagdali. Aisha was also a relative of the poet Ahmed Chawki and she had three brothers: Dr. Ahmed Hussein Pasha, who was Minister of Social Affairs and later Egyptian Ambassador to Washington during the 1956 Suez crisis; Dr. Abdel Aziz Hussein, who was Minister for Sudanese Affairs and Fisheries; and Mohamed Aly Hussein, an engineer who was married to Mona Abboud, Abboud Pasha's daughter. Aisha and her brothers, like my parents, did not pray on a regular basis, but Abdel Rahman Hakki Pasha did. We did not care about appearances. They were all good people. And that's what counts.

I am also very proud and grateful for my two children and my granddaughter, Sophia. My only regret in life is that I wish I had spent more time painting, writing, and fighting for those who do not get a fair chance in life. I hope Egypt industrializes and puts its large, capable population to work soon. They need a chance!

When we came to the United States, we realized our own success is greater when we allow others to also fulfill their potential.

———•———

GISELLE HAKKII's life journey took her from Egypt to England and later to the United States. In 1953, she and her younger brother Samir became undergraduates at Cambridge University. At the same time, her older brother Adel was about to graduate from Cambridge. Six years later their younger sister also went to Cambridge and earned her PhD there. Upon graduation, Giselle returned to Cairo and taught at Cairo University in the English department and at the American University of Cairo (AUC). After her marriage to Dr. Ahmed Hakki, a psychiatrist, they immigrated to the United States and have lived ever since. They have two children: a daughter who lives in England and a son who lives in New York. She is an avid painter and her oil paintings have won prizes at art exhibitions.

A COMMON LIFE WITH UNCOMMON BLESSINGS

Norm Toma

As I think about what I could write related to my experiences as some-one born in the United States of parents who emigrated from Egypt, a lot goes through my mind. There is so much I could write. I choose to write about what comes to mind first. The first feeling I have is of luck. I was raised by great parents, who came here when they were in their twenties. My parents learned to assimilate quickly because in the late 1960s, there wasn't much of a choice.

My father arrived in New York City, like almost every other im-migrant at the time. He came to the United States based on a full-page ad in the national Egyptian newspaper *Al Ahram* encouraging people with science, engineering, special trades, or medical degrees to come here almost immediately. What different times those were. He came with a few hundred dollars, made a life for himself, decided to return to Egypt for a short time to marry my mother, and built a life for his family. It took guts for my father to take that risk. It took extreme will to leave everything he knew and start almost from scratch. He did it knowing he could be successful. A few months after seeing that ad, my father moved to Louisiana to pursue his dream of getting a PhD. He aspired to be a college professor and he also made that dream a reality.

The love story of my parents, and my father's hard work to estab-lish himself, are two stories I won't cover here, except to say my parents came with little money, not knowing anyone, and still managed to assimilate. They came to a community where segregation was prevalent, not only for Blacks and Whites, but for foreigners. Even facing strong bias in the South, they helped the people around them learn to be more accepting. Due to my parents' personalities, it was hard not to like them, even after meeting them only once or twice. Some old friends speak about the time my parents got them out of a highly tense segregated situation. Other friends told me, "Your parents used to get along with all the White Southern folks." Once my parents went to a dinner party and brought a friend of theirs who was Egyptian but who looked Black. Everyone was in shock, but my parents acted as if there was no issue. Because of the way they handled themselves, everybody else was put at ease. My parents pulled this kind of love and respect for all people from their Egyptian culture and they spread it to everyone they met. Thinking back on this helps me realize the luck I had to have such parents.

When you get into your late teens, you start to feel your roots. When you get a bit older, you start to see how lucky you were if your parents blended the good from both cultures. My parents gave us the perspectives of both cultures. From the time they came to the United States, until they passed into the hands of the Lord, they were open-minded and accepting. They taught us the value of hard work, they taught us to respect everyone, and they showed us how to succeed if we wanted to succeed at something. All this came from taking the positive aspects of Egyptian culture and bringing those into what was going on around them in the United States.

My parents loved Egypt. They raised my brother and me to speak the language and learn the culture. At the same time, they made sure we knew the faults of Egyptian culture, so we didn't bring that into our lives, especially here in the United States. When we were young, we didn't realize how blending cultures could work, but now that my brother and I are a bit older, we see the value of a lot of things they taught us. We grew up with typical Egyptian food, typical traditions, and most of all, with a very tight immediate and extended family.

You could say we were rooted as a family. In addition, our Christian Orthodox religion was very central to our lives.

While these fundamentals of an Egyptian household might be typical for any immigrant family, our parents also made sure my brother and I were totally American from the point of view of attitude, language, assimilation at school, making friends, and so on. They had the foresight to realize we could not be sheltered by the Egyptian culture. They wanted us to be fully immersed in American culture, but not to the point where we forgot our heritage.

My dad and I often had talks about life and life lessons. It was his way of teaching me how to live. He was a great teacher. After all, he was a professor. My mom was also a teacher. Due to their strengths as teachers, they taught in ways they knew we could learn. That said, during our talks, my dad and I had lessons to learn from each other. When I heard his thick Egyptian accent, I would sometimes say, "Ramses, thirty years in this country and you still can't pronounce.... correctly?"

My dad always focused on the positive. Once he said, "You know, in this country, you can make anything happen. You can live on $10 a day or $10,000 a day. You should always use your head. My PhD advisor said, 'You're a foreigner and a minority. Use that to your advantage. Apply to teach where you will be the exception, not just where you are another foreign professor.'" To me, that says a lot about my father's experiences and the kind of man he was. He became that man in part because he was an Egyptian American.

I took my parents' advice and what I learned from their experiences and translated that into the person I am today. I don't look at anyone differently. I try to have a positive outlook on everything. I believe there are many opportunities available to those who want to work hard. I still use their advice to guide my path in life.

At different times, my parents thought about going back to Egypt. I imagine that all immigrant families who don't need to stay here think about such an option. At the end of the day, it was God's plan for them to stay in the United States. They always told us the United States was "the best country in the world." Although the United States has plenty of deficiencies, we do live in a place with great opportunities. We live in a country where immigrants like my parents can come with limited money, get graduate degrees, work in professional jobs, raise a family, and build some modest wealth. Although this can also happen in other countries, the opportunities can be more limited in those places. My parents truly lived the American dream.

As the son of successful immigrants, seeing them live the American dream made me want to be successful. I wanted to succeed, not just to make my parents proud, not just to be successful, but also to see if I could accomplish my goals. I had and still have a strong desire to help my community and my country. One of the career aspirations I had that was similar to my father's was serving in the military. His service in the Egyptian Army was not voluntary, due to a draft. Mine was voluntary. I wanted to serve my country. I felt obligated to give a small piece back to the country that gave us such a large gift. I felt blessed and still feel blessed to have cultural Egyptian roots while being American.

Another reason I am who I am today is my mother. She played an equal role to that of my father in so many lives, not just mine. She and my father served everyone in their community: their neighbors, their fellow church parishioners, and most significantly, their students and their students' families. My mom was the model of a mother, a teacher, and a friend to all. She and my dad were true servants. In fact, I think my father, as strong as he was, looked to my mom as a guide for serving people. She worked part-time and gave up a lot of her career aspirations, and even some of her life, so she could help others. I learned these qualities from her.

I believe my mother developed a lot of these characteristics based on her personality. It had little to do with being Egyptian or Egyptian American. I believe if she grew up in any nationality, these qualities would have been part of her personality. At the same time, I believe her culture growing up in Egypt and then going through the experience of immigrating also contributed to the way my mother was.

After my father passed away, my mom and I became even closer. I saw a closer relationship grow between my mom and brother as well. After all, sons have a special bond with their mom, no matter how close they are with their father. My brother and I both believe that had our parents been from another country and not come to the United States, we would be totally different people today. Some things might have turned out the same, but many of the good qualities we received from their teachings were due to them being great Egyptian Americans.

When we have family gatherings, we reminisce about old times and those who are no longer with us. Our family always has a sense of humor. Part of what we joke about is the big gatherings, people arriving late, the chaotic nature of being together, and other Egyptian qualities. You might ask, "What are other Egyptian qualities?" To be immersed in a large family, with all the food and loud voices that go along with it, may seem normal to anyone who is Italian, Mexican, Indian, or another ethnicity. To truly experience the qualities of any ethnicity, you have to go to one of their gatherings.

I did not aspire to become a teacher like my parents. Although I always saw the value in being able to teach anyone anything, I desired to enter the business world. I was able to graduate from a good school, The Citadel, The Military College of South Carolina, with dual majors and a double minor. That helped set the stage for my career, not only because of my military experience but also due to the discipline I received by getting a degree there. Some of my experiences in business also helped mold me. I have been fortunate to work in positions where I've been able to run and manage large-scale teams and large business projects. I worked for a few companies and then returned to client services, where I got my start after college.

We all come from somewhere but being American and having an Egyptian background is unique in a very positive way. When I talk to people now who may not know me, I often see a look in their eyes that tells me they're wondering about my origins, about my heritage. Even if you speak without an accent, people wonder about you based on the way you look. It used to bother me a bit, but now it doesn't. I think some people are surprised to learn that someone can hold onto their culture and speak their parents' native language and still be "totally American." It may amaze them, but I think that's just due to their own background.

For about thirty years, I did not visit Egypt. A few years ago, we decided to go back to attend my cousin's wedding. That trip helped me realize many things. I saw that it took more guts than I thought for my parents to leave their familiar country and go to a totally different place. The trip also made me realize how similar my family there is to my family in the United States. If you put a bunch of Egyptians from Egypt in a room, I feel I would be able to pick out my relatives even if I haven't seen them in decades. From that point of view, it's not about what background you have or where you are from, but more about who you are. This is an idea I learned from my parents, which I think comes from an old-school Egyptian mentality. My parents grew up in a time in Egypt where it didn't matter who you were or what you were. The son of a Christian teacher could have a friend whose dad was a well-off Muslim business owner. When I went to Egypt last time, I saw that in some places. In others, I saw people divided by class and religion.

Seeing those divisions made me realize my blessings again. Growing up in a classless environment depends on the family's values. In my family, I could be friends with the child of a billionaire, and I could be friends with the child of someone who barely had a few dollars. Looking at the basis of old Egyptian culture, you see that's what they used to believe. A Muslim child who was poor could be in a classroom next to a Christian who was well-off. I see this value in older Egyptians quite a bit, and now it's becoming more widely acceptable.

My closest dealings with Egyptians and with people who were born and raised here, but who came from Egyptian roots, are through my church or are involved in the work my church does. When they ask what I think about how to raise their kids, I give them a breakdown of how I was raised. I say this not because my parents were the best parents or because I was raised in a better manner than anyone else, but because the way I was raised allowed me to freely decide what I would take away from American culture and from Egyptian culture. I was raised with freedom of expression, love for all, understanding, and seeing the good and bad in cultural norms. I feel that if more people were to take this approach in life, people in the world would be able to understand each other better.

As I reflect on what may be next in life, I wonder if I will be able to continue to blend the cultures I was raised with. If I have kids one day, will I be able to raise them with the same flexibility? If I don't have kids of my own, will I be able to demonstrate this ability to promote both cultures in my dealings with others? I hope so. Time will tell.

—◆—

NORM TOMA had an unlikely journey in life, partially due to the grace from his Egyptian parents who emigrated from Egypt to the US in the late 1960s. As some of the earliest Egyptian immigrants, Norm's parents assimilated well. When Norm and his brother were born, their parents raised them with the good things from the American environment without losing their attachment to Egypt and Egyptian culture. This upbringing helped Norm develop into the person he is today—both as a person and within his career and business ambitions. Norm is a Veteran of the US Army National Guard, a Certified Management Accountant, and enjoys a successful career in finance and accounting.

EXCERPTS FROM MY LIFE IN EGYPT AND THE STATES
Rawya El Wassimy-Agha

My name is Rawya Morad Helmy Mansour El Wassimy. I was born on June 15 in Zagazig. the capital city of the Sharkeya governorate in Egypt. I have always been proud to mention my birthplace when asked, because it is who I am, and it is where my roots are. I was born at home, in a neighborhood called Mensheyat Abaza, named after my mother's family.

My mother was Fatma Mokhtar Abaza, from the prominent Abaza family in Sharkeya. The family's origin goes back to the Abkhazia region, located in the northwest part of the former Soviet Union. The Abaza name was attributed to a revered and beautiful Abkhazian woman who, in the eighteenth century, married the head of the Al Ayed, an influential family in Sharkeya. This wife bore him many children and was the favorite of several wives, so he referred to her children as "the Abaza children." Many of us take pride in this fact, which speaks to the strength and uniqueness of this woman, considering that Egypt is a patriarchal society, and as such, children normally take the name of the father.

My mother always referred to her family, with great pride, as "the family of Pashas," since, at one point, there were seven Pashas serving at the same time in the Egyptian parliament in the mid-twentieth century. The Abaza family was sometimes referred to as "Egypt's oldest parliamentary dynasty" and it contained members who were prominent figures in the history of the country. Ismail Pasha Abaza, my mother's grandfather, for example, was famous in history for refusing to extend the British mandate on the Suez Canal, turning down their offer of one hundred gold English pounds.

My mother was French educated, and studied at the Notre Dame Des Apotres, a Catholic school run by nuns. My mother's brother, Aly Abaza, was a judge at the highest court in Egypt, Mahkamet Al Iste'naf, equivalent to the US Supreme Court.

My father was Morad Helmy Mansour El Wassimy, from the El Menoufeya governorate. The El Wassimy family was among the prominent families who owned lands in the governorate. My father was an architect and had six sisters and two brothers. I am blessed with three sisters. The eldest is Gazbeya. I was born after her, and my mother was thrilled to have a sister for her, because my mother did not have sisters of her own. Tahani followed me, and finally, the youngest of us is Azima.

As youngsters in Zagazig, my sister Gazbeya and I went to the same school our mother had gone to. On our morning rides to school, we had our own private horse-drawn carriage, with Osta Aly as the driver. We made one stop at Nonna's house (my mother's aunt) to pick up her daughter, Fatma Abaza. Fatma is the cousin I was closest to and who we considered to be like our fifth sister. Nonna was more like an older sister to my mom than an aunt, and she was a second mother to us as well. She lived about ten minutes away and was the disciplinarian of the family—we somehow feared and loved her at the same time

On our numerous visits to Nonna's house, Gazbeya, Fatma, Hatem (Fatma's brother), and I played in the field that surrounded the house. We often spread an old sheet, gathered some fresh onions, arugula, and tomatoes, and had a fun picnic. While we ate, we listened to Hatem recount cowboy movies he watched on his visits to Cairo.

Nonna had a small French poodle, Lucky, who visited us quite often. Somehow, Lucky's visits always coincided with the day of our piano lessons, so whenever Gazbeya played, Lucky would hide behind the piano and howl in protest. We always joked that Lucky didn't appreciate my sister's music.

When I was ten, my father accepted a job offer in Cairo, so our family had to relocate. We lived in Zamalek, in apartment number 4, building number 36, on El Mansour Mohamed Street. This apartment continues to play an important role for our family, including for our children and grandchildren. My daughter Jehan wrote an emotional paper in high school describing how apartment 4 is a metaphor for all the goodness and the love in our family, headed by my mother, and the attachment she felt toward Egypt, which my mother embodied. Apartment 4 is where my sisters and I all got engaged. It is also where we had our *Katb Ketab* ceremonies, as did our daughters. Apartment 4 was where my mother waited for my children and me, with open arms, to welcome us back to our roots; it is where our home base was during our summer visits to Egypt, and where we celebrated countless birthdays and happy occasions. It is where our cousins and aunts and neighbors came during the 1967 war, because it is a first-floor apartment, which was safer in case of bombings. Apartment 4 is also where my mother chose to pass away. This apartment houses many of our family's memories and secrets, and it is where my sister Azima still resides, and where our family continues to meet.

When we moved to Zamalek, the four of us went to Lycée Français, an all-girls school a few blocks away from where we lived. Zamalek was a safe neighborhood then, so many of our friends who went to the lycée walked to school with us without a chaperone. Our class had fifteen students, and French was the main language of instruction, with a few subjects taught in Arabic. Three of my teachers made an impact on my life: Ostaz Metawea, the Arabic teacher, who was such a caring person; Miss Aida, who made history and geography fun subjects to learn; and Madame Zoe, the math teacher, who was a terror, and whom I have to thank for feeling overwhelmed to this day when I deal with numbers!

After middle school at Lycée Français in Zamalek, I went to high school at Lycée Français du Caire, which was in downtown Cairo. In my senior year, I ranked thirteenth nationwide in the final exam. This ranking might sound impressive, but I was disappointed because only the top ten students got to shake the hand of President Gamal Abdel Nasser, including my sister, Gazbeya, who ranked seventh. When I learned of my grades, I locked myself in the bathroom and cried for hours. My cousin Hatem was visiting and he talked to me through the locked door. He thought I had failed high school because I was so upset. When I told him why I was crying, he sarcastically said I should consider repeating the year so I could get a perfect score. He made me laugh, so I unlocked the door.

My father's work frequently took him to different cities in Egypt. When he was home, he played games with the four of us, helped with our homework, and organized short trips for us all to be together. He would laugh as he got down on his hands and knees and let my two young sisters ride on his back. Unfortunately, his life was cut short when he was fifty-one by a brain aneurysm while he was traveling alone on a business trip. My mother was only forty-five and suddenly had four girls to raise on her own: Gazbeya was twenty, I was eighteen, Tahani thirteen, and Azima was eleven.

My father's sudden death was my first experience of losing someone close. After he passed, everything seemed different—people, places, and streets. It was a surreal feeling, as if I were in a continuous nightmare.

My mother was determined to have all of us complete our school and college education and encouraged us all to have careers. I went on to study in the Faculty of Economics and Political Science at Cairo University. Dr. Boutros Boutros-Ghali was our professor of international organizations and had a profound impact on my intellect. Dr. Ghali eventually became the United Nations Secretary-General from 1992 to 1996. The war with Israel took place while I was at the University, in 1967. That year was also a personal milestone in my life because it was when I met my friend, life partner, children's father, and beloved husband, Mahmoud. Mahmoud's father and my uncle went to law school together, and they thought to arrange a get-together at a country club in Cairo, Al Ahly Club, so Mahmoud and I could meet.

We often went to that club to meet friends and spend time with my uncle and cousins, so it seemed to be an afternoon like any other. My sister and I walked to the pool area, where we usually sat. There was my uncle, his wife, and Mokhtar, my cousin, sitting with my uncle's law school friend and his son. I immediately sensed this was an ambush and I was being set up. The meeting did not go well at all because Mahmoud was quiet throughout. When I returned home, my mother and uncle asked what I thought of him. I replied with a firm *no!* I was furious that I had been kept in the dark and not told I was going to meet a potential suitor. I also did not understand how they expected me to have an opinion about him when he didn't utter a word.

After much negotiation, I requested to go out with Mahmoud alone to judge for myself whether or not we were a good fit. My mother and uncle were infuriated by my request because it was totally unacceptable at the time for a girl from our family to go out alone with a boy. Doing so, in their eyes, put our family's stature and reputation at risk. They came back with a counteroffer: I could go out with Mahmoud, but my sister and her fiancé, Mokhtar, must chaperone us. I thought it was reasonable and I agreed to their offer.

The four of us decided to go to Tamarina, a pleasant outdoor restaurant on the Pyramids' road, for dinner and dancing. Mahmoud picked us up in his white Fiat, and from the moment I stepped into the car until we finished dinner, he didn't stop talking. He talked about his work, his family, his friends, and the mutual friends he and Mokhtar had. At one point, my sister and her fiancé claimed they had to find a phone to make an important call (there were no cell phones then), so they left us alone to give us some uninterrupted time to get to know each other. I started to pay attention to Mahmoud and discovered he was interesting and not shy, as I thought him to be (anyone who knows Mahmoud is clearly aware he is far from shy). I also realized he had a great sense of humor and was very honest; he wasn't embarrassed to tell me about the girlfriends he had during his college years in Germany. That impressed me, and I saw him as savvy and outspoken. After we finished dinner, on our way out of the restaurant, he looked at me and asked if we could all go out again next week. I said yes. Later, he told me he was ecstatic when I agreed to see him again, meaning there was a good chance for us to be together. After many dates with chaperones, Mahmoud grew on me and I ended up falling in love with him. We were engaged for two years and got married on July 6, 1969.

In December of the same year, Mahmoud decided to continue his graduate studies in the United States, regardless of the dismal relations between Egypt and the United States. He turned down a full scholarship to study in East Germany and went through a difficult process in order to travel to an unfavorable country. I was still in my senior year of college, so we decided that I'd stay behind until I finished my degree. Mahmoud was accepted into the PhD program at the University of Pennsylvania (UPenn) and left for the United States in January 1970. I moved back with my mother and concentrated on my studies. Every week, I received a long letter from Mahmoud, describing how lonely he was and how much he longed for me to join him as soon as I finished my studies.

By June 1970, I had completed my BA in political science, with a major in international relations, and planned to join Mahmoud in Philadelphia. I was apprehensive and anxious because I had never traveled alone, and I had never been on an airplane before. I would now have to do both on an eleven-hour trip! I was very sheltered, very young, and extremely close to my mother, sisters, and extended family. Our family held the belief at that time that when one immigrates to another country, it was either because of financial need or because of a lack of family. It was very hard to understand why I was leaving when these two criteria didn't apply in my case.

My mother was furious at Mahmoud and couldn't understand why he would take her daughter away and uproot her from her family. That said, she was a wise woman, so she didn't stop me from joining my husband, especially because she knew how much he loved me. Yet, for decades, she wouldn't accept the fact that one of her daughters lived far away, and as a result, she never visited us in the States. I was torn because I felt extremely guilty for leaving her behind, but at the same time, I wanted to join my husband. To this day, I get a knot in my stomach whenever I step into an airport, because I relive the separation anxiety of that first trip. The guilt was finally lifted off my chest after thirty years, when my mother accepted that I had a happy life here, that I still remained connected to Egypt and to the family, and that I was raising my children with this strong connection.

I landed in New York City on the evening of July 20, 1970, and I felt as if I were on a different planet! I was so happy to see Mahmoud waiting for me at the airport, but everything else was unimaginably foreign to me. We spent a few days in New York City, where I met Hassan Mansour, Mahmoud's close friend, and his wife, as well as few other Egyptians. We were invited to Hassan's apartment, and I sat there shell-shocked, watching everyone being loud, drinking, and dancing. It was an overwhelming feeling that I will never forget, and I promised myself never to feel that way ever again.

We spent the first five and half years in Philadelphia, which is my second favorite city, after the Big Apple. Mahmoud had a full-time job in an architecture firm and studied for his PhD in the evenings. We made friends with Philip, a Lebanese Christian graduate student, and with Martin, also a graduate student, who was an American Jew. Along with Mahmoud, an Egyptian Muslim, they formed a unique trio, especially since this was after the 1967 war and relations between the United States and the Arab countries were at a low point.

After a few weeks, I started to look for a job and was hired in the Physics Department at UPenn. I was working with graduate students, recording their data into the computer, which at the time consisted of punching cards. I was always homesick, and the only thing that consoled me was writing the weekly letters to my mother and sisters. I wrote about every detail of my life in Philly: how I ate lunch every day with Mahmoud from a food truck at the campus that specialized in hoagies and Philly cheese steak; how Mahmoud and I had picnics in the park, along the Skullkill River; how Mahmoud was hired at Kling, one of the city's famous architecture firms; and how we became good friends with several Egyptian families. I wrote about how every weekend we got together with friends at a nearby lake to barbeque and exchange news about the mother country. During the month of Ramadan and other holidays, our community always got together to celebrate with food, prayers, and music. These gatherings were the closest thing to a family far away from home.

The year 1973 marked the Yom Kippur war between Egypt and Israel. The Egyptian army crossed the Barleeve Israeli defense line in the Sinai and proved that Israel was not invincible, as it always claimed to be. Egyptians reclaimed their pride, which was lost in the 1967 war. Those of us who were away from Egypt felt a great sense of dignity and self-respect.

In 1974, I applied for and got a scholarship at Villanova University for a master's degree in international relations, with a concentration in Middle Eastern studies. The highlights of my program were working with my advisor, Dr. Fred Khoury, doing research for his book *The Arab Israeli Dilemma* and teaching his class on international organizations while he traveled.

At the time, Mahmoud was writing his PhD dissertation. One night during its final stage, he woke up with pressure on his chest and pain in his left shoulder. I knew immediately that something was wrong with his heart. He had a mild heart attack and had to be checked into a hospital. Mahmoud was so distraught and concerned about finishing and submitting his PhD on time, so he asked if he could have few days to present it before checking into the hospital. The doctor replied that of course he could choose to wait, but that he would be choosing death. The doctor asked me to drive Mahmoud to the hospital, and his exact words were "Drive carefully; you have a ticking bomb sitting next to you." I was very anxious because I had just obtained my driver's license two days before. Thankfully, the school gave Mahmoud an extension, and after a few weeks, he was discharged from the hospital and finished his dissertation.

For the longest time, I blamed Mahmoud for separating me from my family. At the same time, I was in denial that I would stay permanently in the United States. Actually, Mahmoud was also convinced that after we finished our graduate studies, we would return to Egypt.

All this changed when we moved to New York City in 1976, when Mahmoud got a job offer there. I started working as a tour guide at the United Nations, giving tours in English, Arabic, and French. Mahmoud was working in an architectural firm, heading the Middle East division, where he eventually became a partner. We also became naturalized US citizens. Although life was good and we both enjoyed the city, I was still planning to go back to the mother country.

One warm summer evening, as Mahmoud and I were having dinner at Mitchell's Place restaurant, located on the rooftop of the Beekman Towers, he surprised me by saying he was seriously considering living permanently in the United States. He said he knew how close I was to my family; he wanted both of us to make this decision together. I immediately started to cry. I was speechless. After a long discussion and loads of Kleenex tissues, we reached an agreement that we would make the United States our adoptive country and embrace being Egyptian Americans on one condition: that we kept our ties with Egypt and devoted a few months every year to visit. Since then, we have kept our close connection to our families and to our culture and raised our children to do so as well.

In 1978, we were blessed with our daughter Jehan, who filled our life with love and energy. As new parents, we had never handled a baby before, so we had to improvise. The first time we changed her diaper, we put it on backwards. Luckily, we were still at the hospital, so the nurses showed us the right way. I sometimes called Dr. Brown, Jehan's pediatrician, five to eight times a day to ask him about everything concerning her care. He was such a supportive man and nicknamed her Queen of the Nile. I also had a great support from my youngest sister, Azima, who came from Cairo and stayed with us for a couple of months. I decided to leave work and stay at home to give Jehan my full attention, knowing I would not have family support around. I wanted her to learn about our traditions and our culture. I talked to Jehan in Arabic, teaching her about our family in Egypt and sharing lots of stories from my childhood. We had an important rule: while we were at home, we only spoke Arabic, which we called our secret language. She was excited to show off her secret language in front of her friends when they came for playdates.

After a few years, Mahmoud and I wanted a second child and tried, but I had two miscarriages. After the second one, I was hospitalized for twenty-one days because of complications. Mahmoud thought I was dying, so he asked my sister Tahani to come and help take care of Jehan. She was an important factor in my recovery, as was our network of friends. Tina and Jean took care of Jehan and Mahmoud while I was in the hospital, and our friends, the Loveras, drove from Philadelphia to New York to check on me.

In December 1986, my miracle child Mostafa was born. We used the same rules for language practice we'd used with Jehan, but Mostafa totally refused to speak in Arabic, although he understood every word. At five years old, he suddenly started to reply in Arabic and became very proud of his heritage. I am blessed to have these two amazing human beings in my life who are different in character, yet are magnificently similar in being smart, empathetic, compassionate, and kind. Every year, we went to Egypt for the summer months, which was a crucial time for our children to learn more about our roots and our religion.

Since we had decided the United States would be our second home and we would raise our children here, we worked diligently to combine the best attributes of the two cultures into our lives. We succeeded in bringing up two well-adjusted adults who are proud of being Egyptian Americans, respect differences, embrace family traditions, and understand their rights as well as their duties. Jehan and Mostafa went to the United Nations International School (UNIS) in Manhattan, where I taught kindergarten for nineteen years. At UNIS, and whenever I had the opportunity elsewhere, I always tried to serve as a bridge between the Arab world and the West, and between the Muslim faith and other faiths.

Every year during the month of Ramadan, I organized an assembly for the kindergarten classes. The main purpose was to share the festivities of the holiday and explain why Muslims fast. We had music and food from the Muslim students' countries; each child wore their national outfit and shared two to three reasons they liked about Ramadan and how they celebrated it in their home countries. When my turn came, I explained that fasting meant to stop eating and drinking, from sunrise to sunset, which helped Muslims understand what being hungry felt like, so they, in turn, would share what they had with the needy. I also stressed that, throughout the month of Ramadan, fasting meant we not only stopped eating and drinking, but also refrained from hurting, offending, and upsetting people around us. These assemblies helped the Muslim children feel included in the kaleidoscope of holidays celebrated at the school, such as Christmas, Hanukkah, Kwanza, and Diwali. In addition, the assemblies helped teach non-Muslim students about Islam and helped them recognize similarities between the various holidays, such as the importance of family and the idea of giving back.

One day—on a regular day at school—I passed Jeremy, one of my previous students, in the hallway. He was in fifth grade then. He stopped me and proudly told me he was fasting. I was confused, knowing he was Jewish. His mom was with him and explained that he remembered the Ramadan assemblies of his kindergarten year and was curious to know how Muslims felt when they fasted. She was very supportive of this and appreciated that her son had reached out to understand and learn about another culture.

In 1993, when the bombing of the World Trade Center took place and the wave of Islamophobia began, I felt an obligation to defend my religion. I constantly answered questions from friends and colleagues about Islam and I participated in panel discussions in several forums, where I explained the basic tenants of the religion. One of them was at Tina's son's Sunday school. She invited me to answer the boys' questions about what they had heard in the media related to the bombing. The class had around twelve boys, ranging in age from ten to sixteen. I asked a simple question: "What comes to your mind when I say the word *Arab*?"

Their answers included violent, desert, killing, dirty, bare feet, tents, aggressive, towels on their heads, camels, and hate.

I was very quiet. Then I turned around and wrote on the board "Assalamo alaykom" and I greeted them in Arabic.

The whole class went silent.

I said, "I'm an Arab, a Muslim, an Egyptian, and an American."

They were shocked, and some commented that I looked and dressed like them. We then had a constructive conversation about learning not to judge a race by the mistakes of few, to welcome differences, and to understand other ways of life.

September 11, 2001 introduced a new order in the world that changed the basic trust and understanding between countries, as well as between people of different faiths. Fear, mistrust, bigotry, hatred, and aversion to differences became the new normal. Arab and Muslim communities in the United States faced a great amount of backlash. My daughter still remembers that I gathered a suitcase with our passports, official papers, and some clothes, for fear of deportation. Even UNIS was not immune to the climate of fear and bigotry. A day after the World Trade Center crumbled, the school resumed classes, and I was thunderstruck by a verbal attack from a UNIS parent, Mrs. Victor, who accused me—just because I was a Muslim—of cheering for the attack. She even threatened my son, who was a peer of her son in high school. I was in disbelief and saddened by this incident, especially given all the efforts I had made to encourage mutual understanding. That said, I didn't let this experience discourage me from participating in events and discussions that encouraged dialogue.

These are just a few instances in which I saw changes take place. Some will see them as insignificant, but I believe this is how each individual can work toward ending bigotry and fear of others. I am still following my mission and I am confident each stride done with conviction can build a strong bridge between the various cultures of the world.

My mother's passing in 2004 made a significant impact on my identity. I was thankful to be in Egypt at the time, as I don't know how I would have handled this great loss if I had been in the United States. I mourned her for the longest time. She was a major figure in my life, and she instilled in me substantial values, which I continuously practice and which I passed on to my children. She was also my strongest connection to Egypt, and our apartment in Zamalek personified her. It took years until I was able to spend the night there again without mourning my mother. She will always live in my heart, and I will be indebted to her as long as I live.

Another defining moment for my identity was when I read Jehan's master's thesis. Fittingly, she focused on the issue of identity politics. She explained how identity is fluid, according to events and time and places. When I read that, a light bulb lit up in my brain. I had seen identity as something static that needs to be preserved, but after reading her thesis, I saw how my identity had changed throughout my life—first being totally an extension of my mother as a youngster; then being an extension of my sisters and family; then when I came to the States, evolving and becoming layered, as I was an Egyptian, a wife, and a mother, and eventually being a proud Egyptian American Muslim.

Most recently, a pivotal moment for my identity was the Egyptian revolution of January 25, 2011. The people had three basic demands: bread, freedom, and social justice. Tahrir Square, or El Midan, was the focal point where people demonstrated and camped out for eighteen days, until President Hosni Mubarak stepped down. During those days, I went down to El Midan several times with Jehan and Mahmoud's nieces. My participation in the demonstrations and visits to El Midan were euphoric. All kinds of Egyptians stood side by side, regardless of what normally would be considered societal dividers, such as religion, gender, or class. Everyone was communicating in a cordial and civil manner—Christians protected Muslims as they prayed, women wearing a hijab or niqab stood next to ones with t-shirts and jeans, and sons and daughters of the elite held banners next to individuals with less privilege. People were walking around offering water and snacks. Surprisingly to us, there was no sexual harassment (unfortunately, Egypt normally struggles with a high rate of sexual harassment), even when it was so crowded that men and women were squished next to each other.

I call those elated, but short-lived, moments utopia. What I saw in El Midan was the potential of what Egypt could become if given the chance. The revolution awakened the citizenry to their commitment to community. It gave us a slight but heartfelt hope that we finally owned our country and we'd better take care of it. After the demonstrators were promised their demands would be met and after El Midan was vacated, people took it upon themselves to clean the streets of our newly owned country. Jehan, Mahmoud's nieces, and I went down with our mops and brushes to clean the streets of our neighborhood.

Unfortunately, different political actors started advocating for their agendas and usurped the revolution from the idealistic, leaderless youth who started it, and that led to a tumultuous few years. To this day, the basic demands have not been met, and many are convinced the revolution was a conspiracy to throw our country into chaos. Because of this, the revolution was and continues to be a polarizing topic for many in Egypt, including my family. Many in Egypt still take it personally if you disagree with them, especially when it comes to politics. My position to back the revolution angered several close members of my family and friends, and it definitely strained our relationships. It pains me that I was accused of many things, such as lacking love for, and loyalty to my family and not being Egyptian enough to understand what was really happening because I lived abroad. The hostility toward me shook me to the core because I was accused of betraying the two things closest to my heart: family and country. Since then, my family and I have made an effort to heal by putting our family first. I don't believe we will ever see eye to eye on the subject, so we decided not to discuss politics and I decided to forgive all the aggression I experienced, even though it still hurts when I think about it. Life is too short to hold grudges, and family is the most important thing to me.

I believe that events in our lives are planned even before we are born; I like to think there is always a time and a reason for them to happen. After Jehan decided to go back to Egypt and chose to work and live there on her own, a significant event happened in her life: she met Ahmed Akel through mutual friends. They fell in love and got married, and their daughter, Sherifa, was born in 2015. When I met Ahmed for the first time, I felt as if I had known him before. He has a kindhearted face, which makes it easy to trust him. Ahmed and I were present with Jehan all throughout her labor of almost twenty-six hours, which ended in a C-section. We bonded over this time spent together, and I witnessed firsthand how kind and supportive he was to my daughter. He is also a great father to Sherifa, who has a special bond with him, but also who has him wrapped around her pinky, as most daughters do with their fathers. To have a granddaughter is such an incredible feeling; just being with Sherifa and listening to her stories makes me feel alive and on top of the world.

Mostafa met Wiebke Reile (V) at a mutual friend's party after they both graduated from college. The first time when Mahmoud and I met V, we knew right away that the two of them were very much in love and committed to each other. I developed a close relationship with V over the years, and the better we get to know each other, the closer we get. I see her as a wonderful member of our family who is keen on achieving her goals, is supportive of Mostafa, and genuinely would like to learn more about our culture.

Now that we are in our golden years, Mahmoud and I are healthy and enjoying each other's company in New York City. We are each other's family and support system, as this city made us resilient. With good luck, we will continue our annual trips to Egypt to see our families and our granddaughter; will cross out a few more things on our bucket list; and will try to travel as much as our health permits.

RAWYA AGHA EL WASSIMY lives in New York City with her husband Mahmoud. She is French educated at the Lucee' du Caire in Egypt. She has a Bachelor of Science degree in political science from the School of Economics and Political Science at Cairo University and a Master's degree in international relations and Middle Eastern studies from Villanova University in Philadelphia. Rawya worked for 19 years at the United Nations International School in NYC. Her daughter Jehan lives and works in Cairo and her son Mostafa lives and works in NYC.

TWO DEVIATIONS CONVERGED TO CORRECT MY PATH

Reda Athanasios

I was born in 1954 in the warmth of Shoubra, fourth of five children to Boctor Athanasios and Magdoline Faltis. I have three older sisters and one younger brother. My father was a director at the Minister of Treasury (مدير عام), and my mother was a housewife who volunteered in several charities. My mother's family was an old Coptic Orthodox family from Manabad (منقباد), in Upper Egypt. My father hailed from an Asiout family. In the middle of the nineteenth century, my paternal grandfather was the first Egyptian to become a Protestant and help establish the Protestant presence, first in Asiout and later in Cairo. Shoubra, then, was a cosmopolitan part of Cairo, adjacent to downtown, with a considerable presence of Egypt's ethnic and religious minorities. There, we grew up saturated in the coexistence of and mutual acceptance between Muslims and all different Christian denominations. We genuinely embraced each other's differences and learned to find common ground. We celebrated all our holidays together. We celebrated Coptic Easter and Occidental Easter, Christmas and the Coptic Christmas, the Byram and Eid El-Adha, and Ramadan almost equally. We ate *aashoura* (عاشورا), a traditional dessert dish, with the Shia (الشيعة), a minority Muslim sect, and ataief in Ramadan. We ate sweetmeats (حلاوة المولد) in both Moulid Elnabi and Moulid Mary Guiguis, just the same.

My father solemnly believed the Muslim Brotherhood would one day rise and take control of Egypt. He thought they would gain power by turning against Egypt's Christian minority. He felt that when this happened, Shoubra would be the safest place for a Christian family. Yet, we also always kept our outside gate locked and our German Shepherd running freely between the gate and the inner door. Growing up in Shoubra influenced my character in many ways, as I learned tolerance, acceptance, and adaption to others' cultures and customs. It also made me comfortable with different classes of people and those with different educational backgrounds or foreign nationalities.

My great fraternal grandfather, Athanasius El Assuiti, was the founder of the Episcopal Church in Egypt. We belonged to the Episcopalian denomination, which was a minor group of the Protestant churches. The Protestants, in turn, represented a small part of the Christian minorities of Egypt. I made no choice of my own to be in this minority of the minority position. Still, I must have subconsciously liked my minority status, as I chose to be a Zamalkawi fan, which is a minority among sports fans in Egypt. My minority position established a deep feeling in me that I always need to work harder and be smarter if I want to have equal opportunities, which in turn taught me the importance of competition, commitment, and passion in all my endeavors.

Religion and the church were a large part of our family life. We read the Bible and prayed together every night before bed. My mother fasted a lot. She fasted with a strict vegan diet before that became a thing. She had us children convinced that it was proper to fast but to keep drinking our milk daily. Our home church, All Saints Cathedral on Cairo's Nile Kournich, was an integrated part of our weekly lives. All Saints Cathedral had an Egyptian congregation and an international (predominantly British) congregation that worshiped in shifts.

Education in Egypt

I attended the prestigious Tawfikia High School and was a very active social and sports leader. The Tawfikia had its hands in Egypt's intellectual communities and its leadership was in control throughout the last two centuries. In Tawfikia, I learned fair competition, comradeship, and assertiveness. I was captain of the school's volleyball national champion team and participated in the volleyball team that prepared for the 1976 Olympics in Montreal. An automobile accident ended my Olympic volleyball ambitions. It also deterred me from graduating with my peers and had me spend an extra year in high school. That redundancy caused me to use the additional year in productive services to my church's mission, Center in Boulac, where I ran the young youth program and organized events for all its fundraising needs.

I finished high school with grades that would have allowed me to go to one of the medical schools in Egypt away from Cairo. Still, since I enjoyed leadership and managing projects most, I chose to study business administration instead. My parents were progressive enough to believe that what you do is not as important as how well you do it. I enrolled in the Institute of International Trade's (IIT) Business Administration Department in the beautiful spot of Zamalek Island of Cairo. The IIT was an independent accredited Institute founded by Nasser to attract international students of Arab and African origins. It later became a college.

As I started college, All Saints Cathedral had to be relocated because redesigning Greater Cairo demanded the building of a long bridge and freeway in its original place on the Kournich. The congregation had a very negative view of the project. I saw it as a necessary evil that was forced upon us, regardless of any merits or disadvantages. The new location was in Zamalek, where I attended college. As the church's leadership had confidence in my organizational skills, I was assigned the responsibility of moving all the cathedral compound's contents to the new building. It was a massive project, with international coordination, as we retained British and Italian subcontractors for moving the delicate organs and stained glass windows. The project required precise planning and a disciplined commitment of time and effort. During this project, I came in contact, and at times, worked closely with the English congregation leadership of All Saints Cathedral. I also came to consider the Cathedral's provost, Rev. Brian De Seram, as a mentor. I started attending the international congregation's services to learn more from my new mentor. This interaction broadened my horizon and opened my eyes to many different cultures and ways of life. I was very proud that I had been trusted with such great responsibility.

Career in Egypt

The success of the All Saints Cathedral move established me as a go-to person for all other active new projects around the parish that needed energy and organization. During my senior college year, a few members of the cathedral's international community approached me with opportunities to join their open-door policy (سياسة الإنفتاح), newly established firms in Egypt. I chose a post as the administrator of the British International School, Cairo (BISC) because I admired its founder, Leslie Casbon, OBE, whom I knew from our joint church activities. I started with BISC before I graduated and was immediately immersed in its development and phenomenal rise to becoming the elites' preferred kindergarten school through grade 12 in Egypt. I was the highest-ranking Egyptian national at the school, which was mostly staffed by British education professionals. I earned quite an autonomous responsibility as I managed all the noneducational professionals in the school. The school was fundamentally a start-up company, and I learned and became experienced in all aspects of growing a business, which aided me throughout my career. My life was busy, productive, and worthy. I was both appreciated and highly motivated. My biggest motivation was that if I failed, a Brit would take my job and manage my team. I did not want that.

In general, the 1970s, with its new open-door policy and President Sadat's desire to become an Islamic leader of an Islamic nation, created many misfortunes for Egypt. The biggest of these was the rise of Islamist influence across society—from the addition of article 2 to the Egyptian Constitution, to the early release of Muslim fanatics from their jail sentences. The fluid movement of young Egyptian laborers between mono-religious Arabic states meant Egypt had a real security threat. That threat was perceived most seriously by Egypt Christians. These critical new dynamics were felt in everyday life in Egypt. Big-bearded but small-minded men in white short galabias started appearing, preaching, and recruiting jihadists in the streets. Christians felt more insecure than they had at any time since the 1919 Revolution, which had managed to unite Egypt and alleviate all these sectorial threats. This new threat, coupled with the availability of some desirable immigration options, shook the sense of belonging Egyptian Christians had held throughout history. For many, it was time to jump ship. With all their international contacts and relations, my family and all my closest childhood friends were ripe targets for the appeals of immigration and the better career opportunities it allegedly promised. Most loyalists were starting to flee the sinking ship. I was the lone holdout, who was never attracted to the idea. Maybe it was because I had a stronger sense of patriotism or perhaps because I was doing so well and had no worries or responsibilities. In any case, I parted ways with the rest of my family and my best friends and remained in Cairo.

First Deviation

By the late 1970s, my parents and all my siblings and their families were either already living in California's Bay Area or waiting for the right time to move there. All my closest friends were living on the East Coast. I was still adamant about remaining in Cairo.

I traveled to England in 1979 to conduct BISC business. While I was in London, my father had to undergo surgery in San Francisco, and I wanted to be near him for the duration. With BISC's approval, I traveled to San Francisco. BISC continued to keep me on their payroll. Reunited with my whole family for the first time in well over a decade, and in closer proximity to all my best friends, the temptation of living in California became real. Yet I remained steadfastly bent on going back and resuming my rewarding and fulfilling life.

As my father recovered well, a systematic campaign to have me stay in the United States ensued. I wanted my life in Egypt, and everyone else wanted me in California, along with my parents. My older sisters were rightfully persistent, but my parents were very understanding and accepting. The threat in Egypt that would soon after cumulate in Sadat's assassination was growing, and so the pressure was justified. Also, as the oldest son, I had responsibilities toward my aging parents. Finally, we found a compromise that almost satisfied all. I should stay for a short while to convert my visitor status into permanent resident status. That way I would have a legitimate contingency plan to living in Egypt, which appeared at the time rocky at best. This process was only supposed to take a few weeks, and BISC was on board with the plan to extend my paid leave. Generously enough, they suggested that, with a green card, I would become eligible to be compensated as an expat and earn multiple times the already-good salary I enjoyed.

So, I applied to the US Immigration Services to convert my visa into a permanent one, and I began to enjoy my visit to California while I waited. Unfortunately, some immigration clerks filed for an incorrect procedure, which prolonged the waiting period for months and ultimately required me to reinitiate the whole process again from scratch. I seriously considered leaving the United States and forgetting the entire thing. Still, Immigration Services told me in no uncertain terms that departing before the matter was settled would potentially result in blacklisting me from ever reentering the United States. Taking that risk was not an option, considering that my aging parents and the rest of my family were all now US citizens or permanent residents. So, I decided to wait it out. BISC was very accommodating and patient. Immigration Services, realizing my awful situation, granted me a permit to work while my permanent status was pending. This clerical slip cost me eleven months, which was two more than BISC could remain patient, but by then, I was too involved in California and family life to mind.

Career in the United States

My first and very lasting impression of the United States in 1981 was how pervasive and powerful computers had become, and how personal computers were becoming ubiquitous in everyone's everyday life. My anger at the US government because of my visa problems turned quickly into a desire to excel and to compete to prove my viability in the United States. I made an obvious and easy choice: I got into the computer industry in its most competitive marketplace, Silicon Valley. I enhanced my skills by taking a very compressed computer course, which allowed me to apply for computer-related jobs.

While visiting with a friend's family in Minnesota, I applied, took tests, and interviewed for the infamous IBM. I was assured a post but decided against it for personal reasons. I ended up with a position in a boutique computer services company based in San Francisco, in the buzzing financial district. Its data center was in Santa Clara, the beating heart of the then-young Silicon Valley. After a year on the job, I grasped what business in corporate America is about and understood the type of commitment and dedication it took to succeed.

There was one piece of advice I failed to understand. My first boss, Mr. C, whom I consider one of the smartest people I ever met, used to tell me, "Always remember who is number one." Initially, I assumed he meant the customer is number one, but after a few months, I learned that he meant to advise me to always look after myself before anything else; I'm number one. I learned a lot from Mr. C, but failed to quickly learn that one ugly principle—or rather, I refused to accept it.

Working for a mid-size but well-run company was a great way to learn and grow. The company was a vibrant and conducive place for me to excel and climb up the corporate ladder. After seven years of committed, hard, and smart work, I was made a vice president, responsible for the division with the most significant revenue and expense budget. I was always proud of what we did. Since nothing good lasts forever, however, the company was a target for a large conglomerate in Dallas on an acquisition spree. My job was to secure the acquisition. That I did, reluctantly.

After the acquisition, I was the most senior person left from the old guard, with a big responsibility to protect our large employee pool and our satisfied client base, while we all struggled with the cultural changes and making adjustments. I had a simple philosophy: each corporation had three major stakeholders (shareholders, employees, and clients) and as a corporate executive, my method was to focus on the employees and to empower them, prepare them well, motivate them, and justly compensate them. They, in turn, would work hard and take care of the clients, who, in turn, would expand and reward us with more of their business. That way, we assured the shareholders' happiness, while keeping them at bay. That was also the cultural approach I always strived to instill in my team. In contrast with that, the new company's motto was one word: "Hustle." Their focus was on profit, to satisfy the greed of their shareholders at any cost and by any means. Their shareholders come first, last, and everywhere in between. I thought this was a short-sighted and short-lived objective. They overpaid us to ensure our loyalty and tried coaching us to do business through friends, while I was much happier making friends through business, as we satisfied their needs. These Machiavellian ways did not sit well with me.

Gradually, the new culture took root, and the larger company started to expect our business practices to bend and twist to accommodate theirs. I was no longer proud of what we did. I saw the slippery slope and feared I might fall into the allure of the new ways, as many of my colleagues did. I dreaded my monthly reporting trips to the Dallas headquarters because the trips were nothing but attempts to fatten us up and to lure us in with the potential shiny new but false, materialistic gains. I had to get out of this rabbit hole. I stayed long enough to ensure that some of our team employees negotiated fair, binding contracts for primary clients, and then left to join our old company's owner in a new start-up venture. I was proud I could walk away from what I perceived to be a false corporate temptation and leave behind its spoils.

In the new venture, we worked tirelessly to employ recently released internet tools to innovate and establish a new higher education learning model, now referred to as "online education." Our model used access to the internet to deliver education to those who needed I,t rather than only to those who desired to have it. It was conveniently delivered at a distance, to where they worked or lived. It leveled the playing field for all because it made higher education available economically to less-privileged individuals and to latecomers who wished to switch careers or adjust to new global dynamics. Today, the model we devised is educating tens of millions of individuals through thousands of higher education institutions around the globe—people who otherwise could not receive a higher education. I consider this our team's business legacy and a fair contribution to humanity's collective knowledge. It's my pride and joy.

Capitalism reared its uglier side. During the dot-com era, our company became a favorite for venture capitalists, then investment bankers who were looking for pie-in-the-sky opportunities. Our major shareholder, who was older than me, thought this was his last opportunity for a significant upside return, so he decided to roll the dice and maximize his chances for a phenomenal exit via a primary public offering. I was satisfied with our substantial financial success and rock-solid, steady, traditional growth. So, we agreed to disagree, and I left with my gains to pursue the American dream. I also decided that if I wished to continue to apply my moral values to business, I needed to be the controlling shareholder. Therefore, I financed a new venture all on my own. Once again, steady hard work, along with the credibility of my established name in the online education industry, and an extended business network, paid dividends. My self-financed venture, which was designed to help higher education institutes provide virtual campuses to online students, managed to thrive and produce stable profits in its second year—a small miracle for a self-financed technology start-up. Fewer than 4 percent of such companies achieve that success. Fewer than 8 percent ever produce a profit.

By then, I had married Soha, an industrial engineer with a PhD in ergonomics, and we had two daughters. Churches in the United States were either social organizations or shallow evangelical ventures. The Egyptian Coptic Orthodox churches that grew everywhere around us thrived, but most became dens for closed inner culture. A generation or two earlier, as they struggled to get out of Egypt, church members always cited their fierce intolerance for the religious (Islamist) influence that was creeping into the rule of the state, as justification for giving up our homeland. This view stems from Jesus's teachings about the separation between the state and our faith. Now, we live in a country where the separation of church and state is guaranteed by the Constitution, yet almost all church members are feverishly dedicated to having the religious (Christian) influence creep into state rule in the United States. The fact that many relatives and friends, whom I fully respect and love, advocated for this hypocritical paradox never ceases to amaze me. After my very religious upbringing, I found that my intellectual growth and life experiences lead me toward a much more secular life. I went to church less frequently and did so more as a tradition, rather than because I had faith in organized religion. The church and its dogmatic beliefs are not a major source of reference or reverence for me anymore.

Having a family—and for the first time in my life, feeling vulnerable—I realized I could only be as strong as my weakest child. But life was good, and my daughters were thriving. We gave them easily pronounceable Egyptian names that could be culturally identifiable to most people in the United States. We went to great lengths to ensure they grew up in a multicultural environment and were independent thinkers. They both went to church with friends and ended up with deep Christian values, but eventually stopped going to church. Now, nothing makes me happier than to see their strong cultural identities and their strong sense of belonging to Egypt. My oldest daughter, Hana, graduated with a degree in political science from the University of California, and my younger daughter, Neda, is taking a similar route.

At that time, we lived in a large house in a charming, quiet suburb about twenty miles east of San Francisco. I played squash competitively; Soha cooked and threw large parties, mostly for fundraising and other Egyptian community purposes. For the first time in my life, I felt I should make some money to secure my daughters' future. Life was excellent.

Second Deviation

Unfortunately, my overprotection and desire to control the venture was a double-edged sword. Having no depth or backing left us vulnerable and, somehow, overexposed to business risks and costly challenges. My business thrived for twelve years, and then problems crept in. We started to have unexpected capacity problems. No matter how much we increased capacity, we were jammed again and again. Finally, we discovered that our largest client was allowing excessive unauthorized users into our cloud systems, thus stealing our services. They denied our suspicions for months. When we eventually managed to document and prove their contractual violations beyond a doubt, they fessed up to it. They accepted the responsibility verbally and in writing and promised to compensate us. As we continued to provide our services to them in good faith, while waiting for compensation for their illegal access, they were just buying time to get their annual bonuses and to find an alternative to our services. When the time came to pay the piper, they started strong-arming us and left us with no option other than to pursue them legally. Because they were big and mighty (and the most significant religious sect in the world), they acted self-righteously, as if they were entitled to cheat. They became adamant, bent only on protecting their already-tarnished image because of other public scandals. They spent over $12 for each dollar owed to us so they could avoid looking guilty publicly. They made threats and told us they would spend all it took to bury our company. With literally bottomless pockets, they spent sixteen months using every legal maneuver they could muster to force a longer and longer undue process upon us to ensure we were always stretched thin and financially extended. And they succeeded. While the judge agreed with our evidence and grievances, and reflected that materially in a summary ruling that completely supported our violations claims, they refused to settle and insisted on a jury trial. My attorneys and expert legal witnesses seemed very sure of a victory and ample compensation at the end.

At the civil trial, my opponent's counselors switched their strategy to one that was theatrical and took advantage of the newly prevalent xenophobic culture. They secured a jury of individuals who would be easy targets for manipulation and religious bias and played to their emotions and prejudices. The jury decided that the self-claimed benevolent adversary should not have to pay this Arabic millionaire for stolen services. "Reda Athanasios" became one of the first victims of Islamophobia in California. Never underestimate the naivete and ignorance of most Americans. The judge, having been exposed to the detailed, indisputable facts and to my adversary's admittance of guilt, wished to grant us a new trial. I wanted nothing to do with that, as no amount of money was enough to make up for the agony of another civil prosecution and the company of attorneys for many months to come.

I was left shocked, disenchanted, and betrayed, to put it mildly. Until then, I had felt 100 percent Egyptian and 100 percent American and was vehemently grateful that the United States had allowed and accepted my dual loyalty. After that case, I was not so sure anymore. I perceived this severe loss as a very major failure in my business career but accepted it as a cost of being in business. However, continuing to carry on with the business, as a small fish in this poisoned nationalistic and xenophobic climate, became distasteful to me. I continued to self-finance and support the business until my last contractual obligation concluded and then I wound it down.

Path Correction

A few years before my business's demise, I was fortunate enough to be introduced to Egypt's most exceptional and noblest charity. I felt they granted me a gift by allowing me to participate and help. I always thought that the best way for us, as Egyptians Americans, to help our motherland was to use US philanthropic generosity to aid non-governmental organizations in Egypt. The Egyptian government can never do enough, and the Egyptian private sector is too greedy, self-centered, and random to provide long-term solutions to Egypt's most desolate. I took full advantage of this opportunity by founding a US 501(c)(3) foundation dedicated to supporting the charity in Egypt.

When my company was promising and very profitable, I made

promises of future support to the charity. When I saw most of the financial fruits of my decades of hard work so easily and quickly evaporate, I felt no reason to renege on my promise. Whether it was my disillusionment with corporate America or a response to old feelings of guilt for leaving my home country, the final solution for me was the decision to put all my efforts, knowledge, and experience into helping the charity in Egypt. So rather than continuing to pursue money making, I'm now running the 501(c)(3) foundation I launched in the United States. Now, all I am invested in is supporting my less-fortunate brethren in my beloved Egypt, our motherland. The foundation is growing and thriving, my path is corrected, and life is good again.

Conclusion

I'm always puzzled by the assumption our young folks in Egypt make, that immigrating will provide them with better lives. I beg to disagree. Your commitment, hard work, and some luck are what determine such an outcome. As I reflect on my inadvertent decision to immigrate and on my life in Egypt versus my life in California, I wonder what would have become of me had I stayed in Egypt. I can see with some clarity that there is no distinct advantage either way. Each country has advantages and disadvantages, and one can never predict with any precision which will suit a person better. We should all have the discipline to weigh our circumstances, opportunities, relationships, trials, tribulations, disposition, and priorities, and then decide which suits us best. We just have to commit to the goals we choose and work wholeheartedly, purposefully, and with a passion for achieving set goals. "To each his own" is the only advice I can dispense.

———◆———

REDA ATHANASIOS is the co-founder and executive director of the Magdi Yacoub Global Heart Foundation. As an investor and entrepreneur, he serves as advisor to several Silicon Valley technology companies. He is an enthusiastic squash player and an avid reader. He is married to Dr. Soha Athanasios, with whom he has two grown daughters, Hana and Neda. They live in the

East San Francisco Bay Area among relatives of their extended family who have also settled there.

FROM EGYPT TO AMERICA
AND BACK TO EGYPT

Nahla Bakry

I was born in the city of Cairo in 1968 during the attrition war with Israel. This was a few years before the great victory of October 1973. I was five years old, and my little mind didn't grasp the complicated cause of the war. I came to understand much later how Egypt had deteriorated because of an enemy implanted along its borders. Despite the war, we had fun playing and goofing around as children. When we heard the air raid sirens, we hid and switched off the lights. Later, we heard another siren clearing any danger. We then went back to playing. Our family had many chats about our memories of the previous wars of 1948, 1956, and the defeat of 1967.

My family's background is traced to the ancient city of Damietta, a city situated on the Nile banks, where the Damietta branch connects to the Mediterranean. My grandparents moved from Damietta to Port Said, where my father was born. Later, they moved to Cairo, where my mother was born.

After Port Said reopened, we went for our first visit. The roads had been destroyed by bombs, and our car kept bumping because of the potholes and rubble. We finally reached Port Said, an unforgettable scene of destroyed houses and the suspended half-standing staircases. We went to Port Said every weekend and spent our summers there. My father took us on nostalgic tours, telling stories about his past. I hoped the city would revive its glamour; instead, the old houses began to disappear, and one by one, were replaced by modern ones. The last standing antique wooden ferry, which crossed the Suez Canal to Port Fouad, was replaced by an ugly metal one.

Piano Tunes

I learned the piano at six. It became my best friend, always by my side, day and night. I dreamed of becoming a famous pianist. I attended piano lessons passionately, always striving to impress my teacher, the great pianist Rachel Salib. She believed in me and consistently told me I had a bright future. I spent countless hours practicing, expressing all my emotions and dreams of my future.

My Father: Glamour Architect

My father was an architect. I grew up in his glamorous office, spent my childhood surrounded by art, classical music, drawing, and playing the piano. Architects debated the downfall of architecture in Egypt, and how to stop the demolition of the remaining historic buildings. I noticed the deterioration myself: the erosion of farmlands, the demolition of historical houses, the dismantling of the Abou El Ela Bridge, and the emergence of rural blocks replacing the palm fields. Ugliness had dominated all parts of Egypt, I wondered how Egyptians could accept this. How could the farmers sell their lands to be turned into random red cement blocks? What about our ancestors' vow to preserve the land and the purity of the Nile? I realized that our identity was stolen. The socialites have become weak and unable to resist the extreme capitalism and the petrodollar's reign. Its influence brought upon new rules by means of intimidation and manipulation of our slang, dress code, and names, all changed. They felt helpless and alienated.

My Mother: Super Woman

My mother worked in the airline and tourism sector, working morning and evening shifts. She was always elegant, an excellent cook, and fluent in several languages. She could sew, knit, and crochet. Despite her workload, she participated in community volunteer work; she and the women in the family helped impoverished women through NGOs. She also took a nursing course and volunteered in hospitals after the war. It was natural that I dreamed of becoming like my mother: a working woman, and at the same time, an amazing housewife—not forgetting her patriotic duty, helping NGOs, and volunteering to support her country. She was truly a role model.

Identity in Danger

A fierce fundamentalist campaign called "Islam is the Answer" started at the beginning of the 1980s, forcing women to cover their hair, stay home, and drop out of school. They instructed men to grow beards and wear short galabeyas as a symbol of allegiance. The rationale was to return to the Arab-Islamic identity European colonialism and its agents had stripped us of. The common dress of female peasants changed from the authentic, colorful Egyptian galabeya and traditional bandana, which showed their beautiful braids, to an ugly black burka that lacked taste and authenticity. The upper Egyptian traditional men's galabeya was replaced with the white one worn on the Arabian Peninsula. Women's clothing became monstrous looking, lacking individuality. The veil became our main concern—as if we'd fulfilled all our dreams and the only thing keeping us from becoming a superpower was our dress style!

What about our Egyptian identity? It was subject to a plan, with fatwas declaring ancient Egyptians to be infidels and their statues prohibited. The authorities banned people from visiting Egyptian antiquities. Everything related to Egypt, the cradle of world civilizations and the mother of Arab civilization, became taboo. They forgot that Egypt was the mother of Arab civilization, since Prophet Abraham's wife, Hajar, was Egyptian. The radicals didn't read history but instead followed the orders of their imams and foreign-funded agents, who were on a mission to deface our identity.

Identity Preservation

My father devised an educational plan to counter the effect of this campaign. He ordered my sister and me not to follow anyone blindly. He emphasized that reading and research were the means of personal knowledge and growth. Whenever I went to him with a question, he would give me a book to read. It became my habit to read a book every month, then discuss it with him. I noticed that my peers fell into the trap of indoctrination: fearing and following the extremists, which resulted in a sense of alienation. I was scared of getting into a relationship with a person who might transform my life into absolute darkness.

My father was keen to anchor our Egyptian identity. He took us, every weekend, to the pyramids, the ancient necropolis Saqqara, and Khan al-Khalili bazaar. He also took us to mosques, churches, and ancient monasteries. He wanted us to be acquainted with the great history of Egypt and its various arts and culture. We waited anxiously for the weekend so we could have a picnic in the desert or on a farm, eating sugarcane, corn, kebabs, or Egyptian pies (*fiteer*). We learned about authentic Egyptian attire, regional cuisines, and the authentic traditions that distinguished us. We rode horses, camels, and donkeys around the pyramids, after which we had lunch in one of the authentic Egyptian restaurants in Mariotteya, while watching folkloric performances. We visited the National Circus weekly to watch the famous al-Helw family show with lions and tigers. We went regularly to the Balloon Theater to watch the Reda Folkloric Dance Troupe. I grew to love the beautiful and diverse folklore of Egypt from Nubia, Upper Egypt, to the northern delta.

Education

I clashed with the Egyptian education system several times. During elementary school, in the Saint Joseph Schools in Zamalek, the religion teacher accused me of cheating. She proceeded to hit me with a sharp ruler and broke my finger. My father was furious and rushed to the school principal and demanded my sister and I never again be made to attend the religion class with that savage teacher. She was appointed by the Ministry of Education to teach religion, but instead she made us fear God and religion.

For middle school, I went to Gezira Languages School. This was in the 1980s, during the uprising of the fundamentalist movement, a period marked by the spread of the veil and calls for segregation between boys and girls. As a result, the Arabic teacher separated girls from boys during class, explaining that he was applying Islamic order (*iltizam*). It was one of the new foreign words that had started to infiltrate our lives. During the middle school exam, the monitor forced me to share my exam papers with my peers. This angered me, as I was a hard-working student. I got the same grades as careless students, which led me to leave the school and transfer to a foreign education system that was equal and fair.

My father suggested I join a student exchange program and go to the United States, but I refused. I didn't want to leave Egypt. I attended Cairo University in the Department of Engineering, where the fundamentalists were very active. They offered Islamic dress and books and helped students follow the path of Shariah. I transferred to the Commerce Department, where the same scene repeated itself. Bearded students broke into classes and yelled out verses from the Qur'an, calling on their colleagues to join them in jihad and pursuit for guidance. This was supposed to inspire awe, but instead it was a farce.

I switched to distance learning in order to avoid these painful scenes. I resorted to seclusion and found refuge in the world of art and music. I worked for my father in his office, while completing my music and art education. I thought fundamentalism was a temporary fad, but it infiltrated all aspects of life in Egypt.

World Journeys

We traveled abroad every summer. My mother's work in the aviation and tourism sector enabled us to visit many places around the world. My first trip was when I was seven. I compared the countries we visited to Egypt. At the time, Cairo's airport was better than the Greek, Turkish, and Bulgarian airports. Germany and Austria, however, surpassed Egypt. I longed for our trip back to Egypt, when I wrote diaries, collected pictures, and compared different civilizations and peoples. This caused me to acquire a wider perspective; I started to see the world as a small village.

In the mid-1980s, the gap between Egypt and the West widened tremendously. While other countries worked hard to develop, we were drowning in a sea of fatwas, rural settlements, street children, and systematic demolition of historical buildings. With the future looking foggy, I started to think about leaving. I asked my father why he didn't leave Egypt, despite having many opportunities to do so. He explained that he couldn't detach, but that the opportunity for me was there, should I wish to take it.

Marriage

My fiancé chose to complete his postgraduate studies in the United States. He had to resign from his job. We weren't sure whether that was a safe step, or an improperly calculated jump into a world of uncertainties, in a country far away from Egypt and our families. We got married, and I caught up with him in Texas to start a long path of expat life.

After I left Egypt, I cried every day for four years. I was severely depressed and gained forty kilograms. While my husband worked hard on his studies, loneliness killed me. This pushed me to join a program for weight loss, where I lost all the weight I had put on. They then recruited me, which started my path in nutrition.

We lived in College Station, a small college town in Texas, centered around the university, with a population of around eighty thousand at the time. We started off modestly, surviving on a small salary. Our income wasn't sufficient, so I worked in a restaurant to make ends meet. I then began to give piano lessons at home. I started to adapt and observe life in the United States and the community of students around us. It wasn't what you see in Hollywood movies: there was prejudice toward students from the Middle and Far East, and favoritism toward rich White students.

American Dream or Nightmare?

Everyone talks about the United States as the land of opportunity. What is the American dream anyway? I only see a nightmare. The United States is nothing but a huge labor camp, like a kibbutz, where you work and pay taxes from the second you set foot in it. You can only vote when you get citizenship. Millions of people seek US citizenship to land the majestic American dream.

One thing I like about the United States is that the US Constitution ensures justice and equality. It allows everyone to feel they will get justice, no matter how long the process takes. There was a continuous debate in the Egyptian community in the United States about whether immigration was a good decision, or if it was better to return home. The majority favored immigration: they portrayed Egypt as the sinking Titanic, with the smart people jumping ship before it was too late. Only a minority supported moving back. I got tired of this senseless debate; it became obvious to me that no one's opinions would change. Whoever wishes to stay can stay, and whoever wants to leave, go ahead! I, for one, decided I would leave.

The Outcasts

The university had student clubs: we had the Egyptian club, the Lebanese club, the Palestinian club, etc. However, the Muslim Brotherhood fundamentalists controlled all of these clubs. This caused a group of Muslim and Christian students from different Arab countries to come together and form a club for the outcasts, which was named the Arab Club. We decided to represent our cultures through this club; every year, the university organized an international week. Every country represented itself with a small booth that showcased its local food, artifacts, clothing, and traditional dances. I collected some Egyptian artifacts for our booth, and papyrus paper to write the names of the visitors in hieroglyphics.

The day of the festival, I found that all the booths for the Arab countries were represented by bearded men, with no women in sight. Their booths lacked culture and identity—except for the flag of each country, copies of the Qur'an, and Qur'anic recitation playing. I couldn't stay in our Arab Club booth while the Egyptian flag was hijacked by those fanatics. So, I went to the Egyptian booth and placed our artifacts and papyrus on the table. One of the men told me I wasn't allowed in their booth, explaining that they had decided who would represent Egypt, during their mosque meeting.

I stopped him in his tracks and said, "I have an Egyptian passport, just like you! I represent my country in the same way you do. You have no authority to decide who is suitable to represent Egypt and who is not!"

He was astonished that I didn't care about their opinions.

I started welcoming visitors to the booth, giving every visitor a small piece of papyrus with their name in hieroglyphics. I also agreed to give presentations about Egypt in several schools, which I later did.

That was my first encounter with the Muslim Brotherhood outside Egypt. Is there nowhere to hide? I left my country because of them, just to find them in Texas, recruiting new members, especially foreign students and citizens who aspired to preserve their culture and religion.

Motherhood

My first son was born in 1994 in College Station. I began to mingle with other families and visited various educational and entertainment places for kids: museums, parks, playgrounds, and nurseries. I could leave him in childcare for a few hours to go shopping or exercise. In Egypt, the battle to move a baby's pram around the Cairo streets was next to impossible. I felt bad for Egyptian mothers, who lived without public spaces designated for kids. Egyptian mothers devised a solution: either hire a nanny, if it is affordable, or bring the kids along anywhere and everywhere, whether it is suitable or not. As a result, no place was suitable for anything. When I went to a cinema, restaurant, or museum, kids cried loudly, while mothers went about their business. I was shocked to see kids being pulled by their nannies, while the mothers weren't attentive. Every time I went back to Texas, I thanked God I didn't live in Egypt and my child didn't live such a lifestyle. The decision to go back to Egypt became harder after the birth of my eldest son. I felt stuck between two worlds.

Work or Fate

We moved from our student quarters to our first owned house. After failing to find work in Egypt, my husband was offered an appealing job in College Station, with the prospect of getting US residency and then citizenship. Russia and Korea attracted their citizens to return after graduating from US universities, while Arab countries let their citizens float, without offering them any incentive to come back. In the United States, it was customary to value distinguished students and offer them good jobs. We were left with a difficult choice between going back to Egypt without a job or staying in the United States. I felt the threads of the American dream weaving themselves around my neck slowly but surely.

Our next step was to change from student visas to working visas, which meant we had to travel out of the United States and then back. Our lawyer prepared documents that proved employment, in order to receive the stamp needed. After checking the easiest and safest way to do this, we decided to go through Mexico.

We began our trip early in the morning. We took a plane from College Station to the border town of El Paso, in southern Texas. We then took a bus across the border to Ciudad Juárez, Mexico. At the border checkpoint, they asked us for a Mexican visa, which we didn't have, so they asked us to step out of the bus. The lawyer assured us that the visa was not necessary. As soon as we handed the inspector my baby's US passport, he pointed to my son and said, "I will allow you to pass because of your American son!"

This was the beginning of an unforgettable trip. We arrived at the gates of the American Embassy in Juárez at 5am. We weren't prepared for the cold weather there, since the weather was always hot in Texas. We stood in line until the embassy opened at 8am. We almost froze, so we used newspapers to shield us and the baby, taking turns standing in line to protect our son from the cold. At 7am, a security officer from the embassy appeared and started organizing the disorderly queue. He had a stick with which he hit those who were not in order. I couldn't believe my eyes! Was this how Americans behaved outside of America? I felt the immigration rope tightening around my neck. There was nothing to do since we were at the mercy of the job, which would secure a dignified life for us and our son.

After finishing the procedure, we took a taxi to the airport across the Mexican border. Hundreds of cars were stuck in a queue, waiting to cross; it looked impossible for us to make it on time for the plane in El Paso. We stepped out of the taxi and ran across the border, with the baby in the pram. It looked like a scene from a movie.

By crossing the border, our legal status in the United States changed. We had taken our first steps toward gaining residency and then citizenship. I wasn't sure whether I was happy or sad. But now the rope was officially tied around my neck, with the blessing of my country, Egypt. Unlike the United States, my country did not see any value in us.

Between East and West

We visited Egypt once a year during Christmas. It was a long and costly journey. We saved money all year long in order to spend this vacation with our beloved families. We normally traveled via the Netherlands, waiting in transit for as long as twelve hours and renting a hotel room at the airport.

One year, they divided the airport, and we found ourselves stuck in the section without a hotel. Egyptian passports were on the unwelcome list. We tried to plead with the security officers, and they only agreed to let us cross to the other section when we showed them our son's US passport. Just like that, our status changed. I wondered, if we were the same people, with the same citizenship, why the sudden segregation? I was amazed by the change in attitude when I pointed out that my son held a US passport. All doors would be opened with a smile.

Egyptians Abroad

Our life in Texas was quiet. We had a family away from home, with our Egyptian friends, cooking our favorite foods, our kids playing together, playing our favorite games; it was a happy atmosphere.

I taught piano to our friends' children. Our kids bonded and made lasting friendships. I used to leave my son in my friends' care when I had to. Sometimes I needed to lie in bed for weeks, unable to move, and my friends were with me every step of the way. We spent nine years in this small town in the heart of Texas, home of the deeply rooted traditions of Southern culture and the Bible belt. When we moved to our new house, some neighbors came to welcome us to the neighborhood. When they heard our foreign names, one of them dropped the homemade cake that was supposed to welcome us and ran away. I compared the warmth I received from my Egyptian friends with the treatment I got from our American neighbors. When my toddler ran away one day, I screamed for help, only to get the cold shoulder. I felt like a stranger among them.

I never imagined that the Ku Klux Klan still existed. I had seen them in American documentaries, wearing white gowns, roaming the streets on horses, carrying torches, and burning homes and churches of African Americans. I was shocked to see them rallying in our city, which was the home of a university, but seemed fine with their racist ideology. It was sad to see how popular their ideas were among the people of our city. I also discovered that some shops in town supported them by displaying their initials, KKK.

Residence

After my second son's birth, in 1999, I finally got my green card, two years later than I should have gotten it. I turned to the member of Congress in my district for help, after my lawyer failed me. He found out that my files were lost, that was the reason for the delay. I was amazed by how easy it was to meet my Congressman and by his welcoming attitude. I was stressed because we were being transferred from Texas, without having obtained residency. I compared the government services in the United States with those in Egypt and the daunting obstacles one had to go through to meet a state official or a member of parliament in Egypt.

Temporary Repatriation

We moved to Cairo in 1999. I had to prepare my five-year-old for the transition, so I drew the plane that would take us to Egypt, the pyramids, and our family. We started the steps needed for the move: closing bank accounts, transferring medical files, looking for schools, selling our cars, the house, and our furniture, and shipping the rest. We had to sell the swing my son played with daily. While they were dismantling it, he stood watching with great sadness and tears in his eyes. How could he understand that we had to follow wherever our job took us? I observed the psychological impact on our kids every time we transferred from one country to another, leaving behind family, friends, and memories—each time building and destroying.

I enrolled our son in the Cairo American College so he could continue with the American educational system. In the class, when the children were asked to introduce themselves, my son wrote, "I am half Egyptian, half American, and teensy-weensy French!" His answer baffled me. Obviously, he was confused about his identity. I couldn't blame him; he had just moved from one country to another. I started teaching him everything a child his age should learn about his genetics, identity, family, history, and country. I explained that he was a hundred percent Egyptian, that he was born in the United States because we happened to be there, and that we were not French, we just spoke the language. I wanted him to be anchored and to be proud of his identity.

We stayed in Egypt for three years. We decided to buy a farm, where my kids could plant trees, keep pets, and organize birthday celebrations. We made beautiful memories: I taught them all about Egyptian culture, customs, and traditions. I showed them the traditional ovens, peasant life, and cows and buffalo returning from the farmlands at sunset. That scene captured my little son's attention—watching until the very laſt cow went out of sight. We celebrated Egyptian holidays on the farm with our family. I organized competitions for the kids and gave them prizes. I tried very hard to give them a taſte of the Egyptian dream so they wouldn't be fooled by the American one.

Difficult Choices

After 9/11, our lawyer advised us to return to the United States to complete our citizenship papers. At the time, the company where my husband worked gave us a choice between India and Dubai. But the lawyer insiſted we return, so we asked to be transferred back to the United States. We moved to the beautiful city of Denver, Colorado in 2002. I had to prepare the kids for moving yet again, and for leaving their friends and family. I told them about our new house and the mountains there covered with snow, where they could play and learn to ski.

Denver was a totally different experience from Texas. There was no prejudice as there had been in Texas. When we moved into our new home, the neighborhood's kids dropped by. Each of them handed us a piece of paper with their name, address, and phone number. They greeted us and welcomed our children. Intimate friendships between our children sparked from that firſt moment. I was very happy to see my kids adapt and blend in. I wished to ſtay in that house for a long time. I ſtarted giving piano lessons and went back to diet coaching. We all ſtarted adapting to our new lives.

Six months after moving to Denver, my son fell ill suddenly. He was admitted to the nearest hospital. For a week, his condition deteriorated, until most of his body systems had collapsed. They finally asked us to leave so he could die elsewhere. It was a horrible night, as his condition deteriorated rapidly, and his body swelled like a balloon. The doctor cried telling us he was going to die if we couldn't save him, and we should transfer him immediately to the children's hospital.

An ambulance took us to the hospital, where a doctor checked him, told us his chances were slim, and said he would go through a critical twenty-four hours. They might have to intervene surgically. I cried and started praying to God to save him or bestow his mercy on him to end his torment. I placed my son in God's hands. I was completely in despair regarding the possibility of his survival. I started to weave a mental image of our return to Egypt, with my family receiving my child's coffin. It was pure horror.

After that horrid night, we received some good news. My son was presented to a group of specialists in endemic diseases. They were able to identify the problem as Kawasaki disease. My son was isolated and treated for another week in intensive care, and then released. His treatment continued for a whole year. He dealt with strange symptoms and depression, until he was completely cured. The doctor considered it a very special case and a miracle.

This painful experience had an impact on my already fragile back. It began to deteriorate to the extent that I needed a wheelchair. A serious operation on my spine was necessary. We had to move again after we obtained American citizenship. We were transferred to Paris, France. I was given the choice between having the operation in the United States or France. Because I was very angry with the American healthcare system that had led to this condition, I decided to have my operation in France. We sold our cars, home, and furniture, closed our bank accounts, transferred schools, and did all the other procedures required for the move. We all felt sad to leave our beautiful home, friendships, and memories behind; we didn't have much choice but to move with the job.

Paris: The Recovery

The trip to Paris in 2006 was physically painful. I suffered from pain in my back and legs until we finally reached our new home. A new life awaited us in a new world, and a new language that I barely spoke. Five days after our arrival, my legs gave out on me; hence, an emergency surgery was scheduled. The French surgeon advised me to sue the American doctors for neglecting my case, but I wasn't ready to do that. A few days after the operation, I started a year-long rehabilitation journey in order to be able to walk, stand, and sit again. I took long walks in the Marly Forest, near our house, to exercise my back muscles. When I visited my surgeon a year after the operation, he was amazed by the results.

Life in France was totally different from the United States in terms of culture and services. Bureaucracy ruled in banks, schools, and government papers. But the surrounding art and beauty overshadowed all. I enjoyed living in a country that held s its heritage sacred. I participated in cultural groups for museums visits. I learned a great deal about the history of France and its development from a monarchy into a democratic civil republic.

Our new friends were very supportive after my surgery—cooking and helping me in various ways until I regained my strength. I went back to giving piano lessons; I could always rely on the piano, my companion throughout the journey.

During our two years in Paris, I lost my father and my aunt. We were then supposed to transfer back to Texas. But my recovery was in such a critical stage that I couldn't afford anymore hard labor in the United State; thus, we decided my husband would leave the company and we would return to Egypt. I wanted to anchor my children in their home country. I knew they would go back to the United States for college. I told them I would return to my country, and in the future, they should choose the place they wanted to live in, regardless of my decision.

Homecoming

We returned to Egypt in 2008. It was the first time my father and aunt were not waiting for us at the airport. Every immigrant experiences this type of bitterness. Our boys returned to their American school, where they made lasting friendships. They were happy to find friends from the same culture—the third culture that stands between the East and West. The boys adapted to life in Egypt. We spent summers by the north coast, with its beautiful seaside and sun. They also went on vacations with their friends to Sharm El Sheikh and El Gouna. I wanted them to get to know their country, so we traveled to Alexandria, Port

Said, and Aswan on educational trips, visiting historical sites and traditional markets. I wanted them to be connected to this great civilization, so that even when they left, they wouldn't forget who they were, what they owned, and owed.

I asked my children about their feelings regarding our relocation and finally returning to Egypt. They said they were happy to be pulled out of the comfort of the United States. They lived a beautiful dream in the United States, but they were blessed to see the world and rediscover Egypt, while making lasting friendships. They questioned my parenting skills until they saw their Egyptian friends' mothers saying, "We learned you're just Egyptian and not crazy!"

Country in Turmoil

The January 25 revolution took place after years of turmoil. I participated in community work, as I'd always dreamed of. I chose to help public university students develop their skills for the job market. The revolution created a high interest in wide-spread behavior change. A new stage of enlightenment and rejection for the extremists began. Finally, my childhood dream began to materialize. I had lived many years deprived of my family and had lost dear family members; finally, I returned to help my country, to anchor my kids, and to give them a taste of Egypt.

My Children's Independence

My eldest son was accepted into the engineering department in a university in Indiana. We all traveled to help him prepare for his new life. He would be totally alone, and we would not be able to help him from thousands of miles away. On the day we bid him farewell, he got out of the car and walked away without turning to us. His head fell down in grief, and my tears did not dry for weeks. Nor did my fear dwindle. He now works in Chicago. My second son followed him five years later. He is studying engineering in New York. The same scene was repeated, but he had his older brother in the United States for support. This move was much easier than that of my eldest, who was left completely alone. I remained in Egypt, seeing my sons twice a year on holidays.

It has been years since I moved back to Egypt. Many changes have taken place: the rehabilitation of my exhausted body, my return to the arts, finally specializing in nutritional sciences and earning a postgraduate degree from the United States. I opened a weight management center for weight loss and lifestyle change.

I am Egyptian

I fulfilled my mission as a mother. My children have established roots in Egypt. I don't regret the journey, however hard it was. It enriched my children's knowledge and developed their personalities. They became citizens of the world, able to adjust and live with any people or in culture. I was happy to return to my homeland and participate in the cultural revolution that leads toward enlightenment.

I don't like going too frequently to the States; it reminds me of the pain and suffering of the indigenous people who were massacred for the sake of America, and the Africans who were enslaved, tortured, and brutally murdered to make America a superpower. The "American Dream" was built on the bodies of innocent souls. I prefer to stay in Egypt, even with the ignorance, poverty, and disease. Egypt needs every citizen's help to fulfill its dream. Egypt is my home and destiny.

———————

NAHLA BAKRY was born in Egypt in1968. She moved to the United States in 1990, but decided to return back to her home country in 2008. She is a nutritionist by profession and an artist at heart. She works on behavioral change in all aspects of life. Nahla was successful in changing her outlook on life, thereby changing her destiny. Nahla has two sons, one working in Chicago and the other studying in NewYork

FROM A NILE DELTA VILLAGE TO THE LONG ISLAND SOUND

Mahmoud A. Elshazly

I hail from a village called Kafr Elhawashem, four kilometers south of the town of Kafr Elzayat, in the middle of the Nile Delta, on the Rosetta branch, where the Elshazly family represents more than 50 percent of inhabitants. When I was barely ten years old, two events happened that I still vividly recall as if they happened yesterday. The Elshazly family celebrated, within a short interval, the return of two members, after long years of estrangement. The village had only one telephone, which was at the Umda's residence, and was operated by a government employee, to send and receive official messages between the police station in Kafr Elzayat and the Umda, and vice versa. As such, all communication between the two men and the village was cut off, and their respective absences were accentuated by the lack of communication.

The first to return was Ahmed Elshazly, after his release from the Tora maximum security prison. A fight had broken out fifteen years before, involving his brother and a member of the Zanaty family. Ahmed Elshazly, who was the head of the small security detail in the village at the time and didn't witness the fight, heard a rumor that his brother had been killed. He pursued Zanaty around the village streets. He caught up with Zanaty, who was protesting that the rumor was false. Nevertheless, he shot him dead with his government-issued shotgun. The rumor turned out to be false, and the only victim in this tragic incident was poor Zanaty. Ahmed Elshazly paid for his haste by spending fifteen years of hard labor at Tora prison.

The second event was the return of Elsayed Elshazly, with his family, from Switzerland. He had gone there on a scholarship from King Fouad University's (now Cairo University) engineering school in the late 1930s and received his PhD in the early 1940s, becoming the first member of our village to attain such high honors. He had to wait for the cessation of the war before crossing the Mediterranean, until it was safe from German U-boats and he could return. The contrast between the two returning men could hardly have been greater. Nevertheless, the Elshazly family's celebrations for the two were the same.

My father graduated from Teachers' College in the mid-1920s and was appointed as a teacher in the Ministry of Education. The schools where he taught were determined according to a list made by the ministry before the start of the academic year. I pursued my primary and middle schooling wherever my father was posted. After my sophomore year at the secondary school in Kafr Elzayat, I needed to relocate and live with my Uncle Mostafa in Alexandria and enroll in Ras Eltin secondary school, where I received *thaqafa* (fourth year) and *tawgihya* (fifth year) in preparation for attending the School of Engineering at King Farouk (now Alexandria) University.

There were, of course, no social media such as Facebook and Twitter in the early 1950s. We didn't even have television yet. However, this didn't mean our life was devoid of rich, cultural activities and entertainment. We never missed an important soccer match over the radio. We drew a rectangle over a piece of paper, divided it into eight squares, and gave each square a number from one to eight. Then we followed the ball, according to what the announcer said, moving from one player to another between the squares until it hit the goal.

Hollywood movies were shown immediately upon release in several luxury theaters: Metro, Amir, Royal. But prices for even the cheapest seats were beyond the modest pocket money most of us had. The Cinema Plaza came to the rescue! Located on Fouad Street, within walking distance of those expensive theaters, Cinema Plaza showed two full-length feature films a couple of months after their release. And the tickets of two and half piaster were affordable. Our attendance at Cinema Plaza became a weekly routine, just as at any important lecture. We became as familiar with Hollywood stars—such as Burt Lancaster, Kirk Douglas, Yul Brynner, Rita Hayworth, Sophia Loren, and Esther Williams—as we were with Um Kalthum and Abdel Wahab.

Primarily due to this thorough exposure to American culture and way of life, I developed an overriding desire to visit the United States. The lack of US colonial experience—similar to, say, Central America or the Philippines—made a positive impression. The idea of permanently immigrating, however, never crossed my mind. The ideal scenario was to go to the US for graduate studies to obtain a master's or PhD degree.

After graduating with a BS degree in mechanical engineering in June 1956, I was drafted to work at the newly built, publicly owned, petroleum refinery in Suez. The system of drafting newly graduated engineers to do specific jobs in the industry was instituted by Nasser's government, as its relentless drive for industrialization was underway. Motivated by the general manager, Salah Nesim, a young colonel (who died a few months later in a car accident on the Cairo/Suez Road), we were conscious of the competition from an older and larger refinery owned by the British/Dutch company Shell.

Going home to Alexandria one weekend, I found a letter from Ahmed Tawfik Elbakri, general manager of Misr Spinning and Weaving Company, in Mehalla, Elkobra, inviting me to visit the mill for an interview, with the possibility of being offered a position that included a two-year scholarship to the United States to earn a master's degree in weaving technology. I was beyond myself with joy.

Starting to work in Mehalla, I realized that this invitation had included several top graduates: from Alexandria, Ahmed Abo Elwafa and Abdel Monem Khowisa, and from Cairo, Ahmed Elbaz, Ahmed Yassin, and Hussein Anbar. We spent several months training and waiting for our respective applications to be processed by the various universities. Finally, we were assigned to start in the fall. Ahmed Elbaz, Ahmed Yassin, and I went to Raleigh, North Carolina, and Hussain Anbar went to Lowell, Massachusetts. Abo Elwafa and Khoweisa went to Leeds, in the United Kingdom.

Our air trip from Cairo to Raleigh took a full thirty-six hours. We needed to stop half a dozen times for refueling, maintenance, and crew changes, before finally arriving at Idlewild (now JFK) airport. A domestic flight took us to Raleigh/Durham airport. Landing in that very modest airport, there was only one waiting limousine. It took the few passengers, including us, to town, where we chose a motel near the state college campus.

After a few hours of rest, we ventured outside to explore the surroundings. We walked in the direction of downtown, where we thought the shops, movie theaters, and restaurants should be—only to discover that we were the only pedestrians in sight and there was no trace of public transportation. Without a car, it was as if we were under curfew. Mehalla's sister company in Kafr Eldawar had sent a few of its engineers for graduate studies in Raleigh a couple of years earlier. One of them, Fathy Ahmed Aly (who later became its chairman), had just finished his studies and was preparing to return home. He had a few items to sell, among which was a 1950 model Studebaker auto. Price? $150. Since my first month's stipend was still mostly available, I gave Fathy the money in exchange for the keys. Fathy volunteered to spend a couple of hours teaching me how to drive. So, the three pedestrians from Mehalla had their own car, even if the driver was just learning the ropes.

We each moved to a semi-permanent residence. I had a furnished room with a retired couple. At this stage, food was my primary concern. Most of my meals upon arrival in Raleigh depended on the college cafeteria, with its totally unfamiliar cuisine. As a result, I lost several pounds of my already slim weight. In late November, I was invited to Thanksgiving dinner by my landlords. I had heard that families usually celebrate the occasion with turkey dinners. So, my hunger fed on that dream, until we sat at the dinner table and I discovered my hostess had substituted smoked ham for the turkey. She obviously didn't know that I did not eat pork. So, my long-anticipated Thanksgiving dinner was limited to one corn on the cob and some turnip greens.

I then moved to an independent apartment, along with one colleague, and started experimenting with cooking. I had missed fried rice since my arrival, as it was the main staple of any meal for me in Egypt. After many attempts, during which the bottom burned while the top stayed raw, I eventually became an expert cook—especially of Egyptian-style fried rice.

The background of the newly recruited engineers was in mechanical and electrical engineering. Textile technology was not yet a discipline of instruction in Egyptian universities. Therefore, our program in North Carolina was designed for us to spend the first year studying along with the beginners (freshmen) at the textile school, then spent the second year preparing for a master's degree. I couldn't bear the boredom for even one semester. I decided to switch and get my master's in mechanical engineering, majoring in air conditioning. A professor of mechanical engineering I met in Raleigh, Dr. Black, who had spent one year visiting the University of Alexandria, gave me a letter of recommendation to his professor (Dr. Konzo) at the University of Illinois, where he had received his PhD. This proved pivotal in my being accepted, starting in September 1958.

At the end of the school year, in June 1958, I said goodbye to Raleigh, put my few belongings in the trunk of my Studebaker, and with one of my Arab student friends, headed for Chicago. We spent a few weeks there. On a sunny day, we went to the beach, where hundreds of sunbathers enjoyed the beautiful shore. I laid down my towel on the sand, and remembering the hours I'd spent in the warm waters of the Mediterranean, dashed into the crystal clear water of Lake Michigan—only to have the heart-stopping shock of ice cold water. I quickly turned around and rushed back to shore. I learned my lesson and never ventured to swim in Lake Michigan again. After spending August on a small family-owned dairy farm near the border with Wisconsin, I drove south to the town of Urbana to start my studies.

The Egyptian cultural attaché's office in Washington used to send me a monthly check to a post office box in Raleigh. I didn't dare to give them a change of address, because my curriculum change from weaving to mechanical engineering was not authorized. Instead, I gave the box key to Ahmed Elbaz, who retrieved the monthly check and mailed it to me in Urbana.

I found about a dozen Egyptian students studying at the University of Illinois; all except one, were graduate students. Among them was a group, headed by Atef Ebaid (the future prime minister and architect of privatization of the Egyptian economy), working on their PhD degrees in business. After two semesters and a summer, on September 13, 1959, I sent a report back to Mehalla composed of one sentence: "I received today my master's degree in air conditioning."

Despite an initial uproar, I was welcomed back, as management had already realized the importance of sophisticated control of the environment—in particular, by maintaining a steady high level of relative humidity—in weaving sheds, on productivity and product quality. The honeymoon lasted only a few months for me, because the rigid compensation structure meant no relief from a salary of only about 25 LE per month. In early May 1960, I accepted a job with the Arab Contractors (Ossman Ahmed Ossman), who had just been awarded a contract to build the Aswan High Dam. They gave me a decent salary. I was among the early arrivals at the site, but within a few months, the handful of engineers had swelled into scores. The unmarried lived onsite, and work proceeded 24/7 in order to complete the diversion of the water flow before the arrival of 1964 flood. Otherwise, the construction schedule would have been delayed by a full year.

At the beginning of 1963, I accepted one of the scholarships offered to Helwan University by the West German government to be guest lecturer in mechanical engineering for two years. Helwan University had planned its engineering school using the model of—and with technical and financial assistance from—the German engineering schools. While teaching and living in Saarbrueken, near the West German/French border, I met and married my wife, Marliese. At that point, I had reached the limit of my deferral from possible military service and had to submit to the Egyptian armed service headquarters in Shatby, Alexandria. My pregnant wife took a job in Heidelberg, and I returned to Alexandria. After taking the physical and other required exams, I was told I remained subject to the draft, if needed, for one year. Fortunately, I wasn't needed!

Mehalla was in the midst of a major expansion, eventually more than doubling its spinning and weaving production capacity. They were eager to welcome me back to head the air conditioning engineering department. I was joined by my wife and our infant son, Ossama, who was born in Heidelberg on New Year's Eve 1964.

Toward the end of 1966, construction on the new facilities was nearing completion. Prospects for professional advancement in the newly nationalized company were geared to seniority rather than merit. Life in Mehalla started to look less promising. At the same time, the attraction of the American experience was becoming irresistible. We applied, along with other colleagues, for immigration to the US consulate. To our great pleasant surprise, we received a letter of acceptance within a couple of weeks, in February 1967. Being the only applicants from Mehalla to achieve that result, we learned later, was due to the small number of German applicants, compared with Egyptian applicants.

We spent the following year applying for and getting all the needed approvals from the various ministries and departments that were required for an exit visa. By January 1968, we had received that exit visa, and we flew out of Cairo on February 1. After spending the night in Geneva, the next morning, we split the US $240 between Marliese and me 40/200. She, along with Ossama, now three years old, flew to Frankfurt, and I flew to New York.

From JFK Airport, I went to the 36th Street YMCA, with which I was already familiar. There, I met another Egyptian engineer, Husni, who graduated seven years earlier from Cairo University, in aeronautics engineering. He had arrived a couple of months earlier and planned to fly to Los Angeles, the center of demand for jobs in his field. I had the same intention to start our life in Los Angeles. I'd applied to UCLA to study for my PhD in jet propulsion and had been accepted to begin in September 1968. I convinced Husni to drive with me instead of flying. We drove a Chevy Impala, which we were delivering to its owner, a marine at Camp Pendleton, south of Los Angeles.

Ten days into the trip, we arrived one afternoon in Las Vegas. Husni, who had not been to the United States before, but was nevertheless familiar with casinos, wanted to see one from the inside. I parked the car in front of one major casino and stayed at the steering wheel while Husni went inside for a quick look. After waiting for a long time for him to return, I locked the car and went in to look for him. To my big surprise, I found him sitting at a blackjack table, with a wide grin on his face. He had just doubled his original (small) fortune. It was not possible to peel him off the table!

I had about $100 on me, and soon he had about $1000. So, I sat down next to him, thinking that if I lost my $100, we'd still have enough between us to manage. Being a novice at gambling, it took me only minutes to lose my $100. I spent the next couple of hours walking around, enjoying the various entertainment activities. When I returned to Husni, I found him sweating, his luck gone south, trying to recoup his losses. At that point, he had only a one dollar chip left. I grabbed that chip and told him we needed that one dollar for gas to reach Los Angeles.

And that was exactly what happened. We left the Las Vegas casino around midnight, got one dollar's worth of regular gas, and headed to Los Angeles. On the road, we slept in the car—the first time we had done that on the trip—for a couple of hours. We arrived in Los Angeles in the early morning, without even a dime (the price of a cup of coffee at that time). We drove around and stopped in front of a pawn shop and sat in the car waiting for it to open. I took off my watch and offered it to the shop owner. He examined the watch with a magnifying glass for long minutes before pronouncing his verdict: $10, plus $1 in interest, payable per month for three months. If the $10 had not been paid back after three months, the watch would be forfeited. I pocketed the $10, a small fortune, and said goodbye temporarily to my watch, and we headed to the nearest diner. I ordered a big breakfast, and most importantly, plenty of coffee. Husni refused to touch the food because it was haram, paid for with pawn money. After breakfast, we delivered the car to its owner and recovered our $40 deposit. We were ready to start our respective job searches.

The mammoth Apollo project to land a man on the moon was nearing completion. NASA and its collaborating contractors were starting to wind down and were laying off thousands of their aerospace engineers. Efforts were underway to retrain those engineers to acquire other skills. It was the worst time to be looking for a job in that specialty. Husni spent a few months looking and eventually decided to go back to Egypt. I, however, immediately forgot about resuming my studies and started looking for any engineering job.

Husni had, in the meantime, introduced me to a classmate of his from Cairo University, Kamal Asfour, who had come to Los Angeles seven years earlier, right after he graduated. Kamal, who, like Husni, had graduated among the top of their class, had come at the right time. He had already reached a good position with the prestigious consulting firm TRW. Being a religious Copt, he had started, with other likeminded Egyptian expats, to form a Coptic Church. They had formed a board of directors, for which Kamal was the treasurer. The board decided to bring in a pastor from Egypt to lead their fledgling congregation. As the pastor settled into performing his holy duties, he felt it was his prerogative to handle the finances himself, without any cumbersome treasurer. The board, with Kamal out in front, insisted on transparency and good accounting practices. The conflict ended with the holy man excommunicating Kamal. I had never seen a man suffering under such agony, as if he had just gotten a death sentence for a crime he didn't commit, or the decree excommunicating him had come down directly from the heavens, signed by God Himself.

Shortly after our arrival, with the help of a management recruitment firm, I was able to secure a job in Culver City, a suburb of Los Angeles. Having lived in the United States ten years earlier, I was able to adapt quickly. I opened a bank account, financed the purchase of a new Ford Mustang, and got a credit card to purchase airline tickets to bring my wife and son from Frankfurt to Los Angeles.

A colleague at work introduced me to a professor at Santa Monica City College, who had accepted a two-year teaching assignment in Liberia and wanted to rent his house, completely furnished. We rented the top floor, while his mother, Frau Buchholz, lived in a downstairs apartment. The small house sat on top of a hill in Pacific Palisades, north of Santa Monica, and had a glass wall overlooking the Pacific Ocean, through which we could see from Los Angeles International Airport in the south all the way to Santa Catalina Island. Its garden sloped down to Sunset Boulevard. Frau Buchholz had emigrated as an adult from Germany and still spoke German as her primary language, which made her the perfect companion for Marliese, who at that time spoke nothing but German, in addition to the Arabic she learned in Mehalla. We seemed to be fast realizing the American dream. Except that my job in a small manufacturing company did not promise much of a future.

A phone call from the management recruiter I'd dealt with in the past told me that a major company had seen my curriculum vita and was inviting me for an interview with one of its consultants in San Francisco. At dinner after the interview, at Fisherman's Wharf, the consultant arranged for me to fly to Detroit for further interviews at the Park Davis headquarters. There, they made me an offer I couldn't refuse. I was to join their extensive engineering department.

We put our suitcases and sparse belongings in the trunk of our convertible Mustang and headed east along Route I-80. For several days, we enjoyed the unparalleled natural beauty of the Sierra Nevada Mountains, the Grand Canyon, and the Great Plains, with their thousands of flat agricultural acres, before finally arriving in Detroit. The Park Davis offices were located on Joseph Campeau Avenue, along the river. To house hunt for a residence within driving distance, we started by driving twenty miles in every direction. Marliese could not contain her tears. The contrast could not have been starker between Santa Monica and the bleak Detroit winter.

During my first meeting with my future boss, Lou Landau, he said, "Mahmoud, I am Jewish. How do you feel about working for me?" He knew, of course, that I was an Egyptian Muslim. It was 1969, and the American media were digging into the still-raw wounds of the 1967 defeat. I explained my thoughts to Lou honestly and clearly. In my view, there is a great deal of difference between Judaism as a religion and Zionism as a political colonial ideology. In business, as well as in my personal and social interactions, there is not an iota of difference for me between a Muslim, Christian, and Jew. However, I oppose Zionism as I oppose all forms of colonialism—especially settler colonial regimes, of which Zionism represented the ugliest mode. Lou understood my position, and we started our relationship on the right foot. He later promoted me and recommended me for significant responsibilities. I proceeded to perform my job designing production facilities to produce antibiotics and other drugs, for which my background in air conditioning was a key factor in preventing the cross-contamination of products.

A year later, the nation's awareness of air and water pollution came into increasingly sharper focus. Park Davis thought to establish a special department to deal with this issue within its manufacturing facilities, and I was selected to establish and run that function. While meeting with Bob Miller, vice president, in charge of engineering to present my plans, he pointed to a sleek sailboat crossing the Detroit River that we could see from his picture window. He said, "I bet the owner of that yacht isn't an employee, regardless of rank. He must be one who owns his business." That remark is etched in my memory.

Within months of establishing and starting to implement a comprehensive company-wide pollution control program, Park Davis was acquired by Warner Lambert (now a part of Pfizer). Warner Lambert, in turn, was contemplating establishing a department to handle this vital function. I was chosen to handle the job as corporate manager of environmental control.

We moved from Detroit to Morris Plains, New Jersey, where the Warner Lambert headquarters were located. Before we left Detroit, our daughter Salwa was born at a hospital in Royal Oaks, one of Detroit's suburbs. My tenure with Warner Lambert was quite satisfying professionally. I established and ran the pollution control program for its hundred-plus plants worldwide. In the process, I acquired the knowledge and expertise to be able to contribute four chapters to an important book on the subject: *Handbook of Pollution Control Management*, edited by Herbert F. Lund, and published by Prentice Hall.

The 1973 war and its aftermath of quadrupling oil prices created enormous fortunes for the oil-exporting countries of the Middle East. Those countries were spending lavishly on refurbishing and expanding their infrastructures and attracting producers and contractors for those projects. Gould, Inc., out of Chicago, was the third largest producer of electric power generation and distribution equipment after General Electric and Westinghouse. Gould offered me a job establishing and running their regional office as the managing director of the Middle East and Africa. Although some in management wanted to locate the office in Dubai, I prevailed, and the office was located in Alexandria.

I hired a deputy director, Gamal Elzarka, a former colleague of mine in Mehalla. Then came Safaa Abo Taleb, office manager. Safaa was born and educated in San Jose, California, where her father, Naim (who later became governor of Alexandria) was studying for his PhD, before returning to teach at Alexandria University's engineering school. As such, Safaa was truly bilingual in Arabic and English. Then I hired a driver/expediter, Abdel Aziz Maharem. Abdel Aziz's responsibilities were as important as those of any of us with respect to the proper functioning of our regional office. The only mode of communication between our regional office in Alexandria and corporate headquarters in Chicago was the telex. There were two public telex offices in Alexandria. Abdel Aziz used one or the other daily to send and receive messages from the main office.

Our family enjoyed living in Alexandria during this period immensely. Marliese was able to drive all over in a less-congested Alexandria, and we enjoyed the salary of an American corporate manager. One of my small pleasures, whenever I made the periodic rounds of Gulf capitals to visit Gould's agents and distributors, was to leave Tehran to the last stop. Flying back to Cairo, I would bring with me a quarter kilo of black caviar from the duty-free shop, packed in dry ice.

The relentless capitalist drive toward consolidation finally reached Gould. But it was too big to be acquired by one company, no matter how colossal. So, a consortium of three multinationals divided Gould's businesses between them. Siemens of Germany acquired the low-voltage plants, Braun Bovary of Switzerland got the high-voltage plants, and the Japanese Matsuchita got the electronics. Gamal Elzerka remained with Siemens and relocated to Kuwait, where their regional office was. He remained with Siemens until he retired and returned home to Alexandria.

I decided to leave and try my hand at starting my own business, remembering Bob Miller's famous remark as we watched the yacht sailing across the Detroit River. My first attempt was a joint venture with a Saudi businessman in the construction business, Sheikh Ali Abo Khamseen. We started a ready-mix concrete business in his native town of Alkhober, a few miles north of Dhahran. We imported the equipment from Britain and Germany and started operating, with great potential. It took several months to get the necessary residence permits for the family. We rented a comfortable furnished villa, brought in Abdel Aziz, the driver, from Alexandria, and enrolled the children in the American school in Dhahran. Marliese couldn't drive as she had been able to in Alexandria. It became obvious very quickly that no amount of money could compensate for the quality of life we had enjoyed in Santa Monica or Alexandria.

The same week the children's school year ended, we were on a plane heading for New York. On the way, we planned to stop for a couple of days' transit in Amsterdam. At passport control, we faced a problem. Salwa and I carried our US passports. Marliese had kept her German passport. Ossama was still travelling with his Egyptian passport, issued while he was in Mehalla and renewed from Alexandria. After a long deliberation, the agents decided to let the two Americans and the German out, but not the twelve-year-old Egyptian. It took a couple of hours of explanation and appeals to higher authorities to finally let the entire family leave the airport.

We eventually settled in Connecticut, where we remain to this day, having lived for the past forty-plus years in Greenwich, New Canaan, and Stamford. Marliese, recognizing the great need for quality childcare, and capitalizing on her background in pediatric nursing in Germany, decided to try her hand in that field, together with Nick Snow, whom we had gotten to know socially as a parent of one of Salwa's middle school classmates. We together purchased a villa on one acre in Stamford to house the business, The Baby Cottage, Inc. Nick had worked earlier as a partner with the accounting firm Arthur Anderson. His accounting and financial expertise proved to be the right complement, ensuring the success of the business, which has been one of the most reputable and recognized names in the industry for more than thirty years.

I opened an office in Greenwich to import cotton textiles from Mehalla and Kafr Eldawar and export construction materials for Egyptian and Saudi infrastructure projects. Eventually, the activity was narrowed down to exporting American lumber to Egypt. Then I opened an office in Cairo (Alfustat Import/Export) to stock and distribute that lumber in the Egyptian market. During the past twenty-plus years, Alfustat has become a significant player in the Egyptian hardwood trade.

On the cultural and social side, we were fortunate to be equally active. While in Detroit, I had joined the Association of Arab-American University Graduates (AAUG). Through that group, I was fortunate to get to know some distinguished personalities. Among them was Ibrahim Abu Lughod, AAUG's second and most influential president, who was at the time teaching at Northwestern University. He later went back to Ramallah, in the occupied West Bank, to participate in establishing and teaching at Bir Zeit University. I also got to know Drs. Edward Said, M. Cherif Bassiouni, and Saad Eldin Ibrahim. I presented a paper during AAUG's second annual convention in Chicago about the Luxemburg Treaty (Luxemburg Abkomen), which obligated West

Germany to pay billions of Deutsche marks to the newly established state of Israel as reparation to Jews for the Nazi atrocities. The paper was published in the proceedings of the conference.

Then I participated in the founding of the Association of Egyptian American Scholars and served as secretary on its first board of directors. Dr. Mohamed Elwakil, then professor of nuclear engineering at the University of Wisconsin at Madison, was president, and Dr. M. Cherif Bassiouni was vice president. In the summer of 1974, we held a conference in Cairo under the title "Egypt in the Year 2000." At the conclusion of the conference, President Anwar El-Sadat received the attendees at the presidential retreat of Elkanater Elkhayria. I delivered the association's presentation, as both Elwakil and Bassiouni had left Cairo the day before.

Finally, in 2005, I participated in founding the Alliance of Egyptian Americans, along with Dr. Kamal Elsawi, Mr. Mohsen Khalid, Dr. Safei Eldin Hamed, Dr. Samia Harris, Ms. Amy Ekdawi, and many others. The Alliance was incorporated as a cultural and educational 501(c)(3) corporation in Florida, with Dr. Safei Eldin Hamid as its first president. In 2009, I succeeded Dr. Hamed as president. Members of the Alliance, as most Egyptian Americans, were keenly aware of the increasingly urgent resistance to President Husni Mubarak's attempts to hold onto power, either through seeking reelection for a sixth term or by grooming his son Gamal to succeed him. That resistance manifested itself through a movement called *Kefaya*, or Enough.

In May 2010, the Alliance held a major conference in cooperation with the Graduate Center of City University of New York. Many distinguished and leading figures from Kefaya in Egypt were invited to participate. Among them were Dr. Hassan Nafaa, Dr. Yehia Elgamal (who later served as deputy prime minster), Dr. Gouda Abdel Khalek (who was a visiting professor at Rutgers University at the time), Counselor Mahmoud Elkhodairi (retired deputy chief justice), Dr. Ossama Elghazali Harb, and others. That conference was the culmination of hard work and months-long preparations. Assisting me in organizing that conference were Dr. Sherif Nasr, Dr. Fikry Andrawes, and Mr. Ahmed Issawi. Ahmed Issawi had, several years before, established the Arab cultural organization Alwan. Alwan, to Ahmed Issawi's credit, remains to this day the principle Arab cultural venue in New York City. The conference commanded the attention of major Egyptian media outlets—although more critical than complimentary, as its theme debated the future of democracy in Egypt. This conference was followed by a similar one in September in Washington, D.C., and a visit by several members of the Alliance to Cairo in December. Prominent among them were Kamal Elsawi, Mohsen Khalid, and Tarek Saadawi. We gave a series of interviews to print and TV media. All these activities served as preparation for the soon-to-follow Arab Spring in Tahrir Square, on January 25, 2011.

Most recently, my friend Dr. Tarek Saadawi, professor of engineering at CUNY, succeeded me as president of the Alliance. We organized an economic conference in November 2018, in collaboration with Cairo University and Bank Misr, to coincide with Talaat Harb's birthday. For the keynote speaker, we invited Dr. Eric Davis of Rutgers University. Dr. Davis had lived in Egypt and written the most authoritative English study of Bank Misr and Talaat Harb: *Challenging Colonialism, Bank Misr and Egyptian Industrialization*.

In the spring of 2019, the Alliance, in collaboration with CUNY, organized a conference in New York to celebrate the centennial of the Egyptian 1919 Revolution. Dr. Mohamed Abolghar came especially from Cairo to deliver the keynote address. The conference culminated in the creation of a permanent seminar within the curriculum of Middle Eastern studies, chaired by Dr. Beth Baron at CUNY Graduate Center, under the name "Egypt Salon." The first lecture was delivered in the fall of 2019, also by Dr. Abolghar and was on the modern history of Egyptian Jews.

It is now more than half a century since our family came to live in the United States. Looking back to evaluate, I ask: Did we make the right decision to immigrate? How do we view the changes in the quality of life in the United States over that period? The answer to the first question is easy; it is definitely in the affirmative. The meritocratic system in society, coupled with the quasi-Darwinian nature of contemporary capitalism, allowed our family, with its above average advantages in education and skills, to prosper—while never losing our ties to the mother country, Egypt. All family members, including my German-born wife, our two children, and our two grandchildren, enjoy dual citizenship: US and Egyptian. Additionally, opening a business office and maintaining a residence in Cairo, starting some twenty years ago, allowed us to spend an extended period of time in Egypt and visit relatives in Germany several times a year.

Evaluating human progress over that period and its contribution to the quality of life, however, we come up with a mixed bag. In the fields of the physical sciences, unimaginable progress has been made. We landed a man on the moon and robots on Mars. We now fly nonstop in ten hours from New York to Cairo. We've gone from communicating via telex to 5G now. For the 100 million Egyptians, there are now about 110 million mobile phones in use. But in the fields of the humanities, we are still largely prisoners of the sad inheritance of colonialism and slavery. Such a state of affairs is putting the brakes on the potential available for humanity to fully benefit from our scientific progress. Social scientists have even been mobilized to justify and legitimize colonial wars and conquest, as was eloquently articulated in Edward Said's classic, *Orientalism*.

Challenges and opportunities are endless. We are full of both hope and anxiety as we hand over the torch to the next generation, who are already showing ample signs of rejecting the status quo and effecting changes to the better.

———

MAHMOUD A. ELSHAZLY received his BS and MS degrees in Mechanical Engineering from the University of Alexandria, Egypt and the University of Illinois at Urbana. After working on the construction of the Aswan High Dam then at Misr, Mehalla El-Kobra, he immigrated to the United States with his German-born wife Marliese and their son Ossama. Their daughter Salwa was born in Michigan. Elshazly first worked in pollution control management for the pharmaceutical industry, then business development in the Middle East for the American electric power generation and distribution Industry. He later established his own Import/Export business, which is still active today, with offices in Cairo, Egypt and Stamford, Connecticut. Elshazly and his family enjoy sailing aboard their boat *Nefertari* on the Chesapeake with friends in the summer.

SABA, GAMEELA, AND ME

Nimet Habachy

My father's mother was illiterate. Her second son, my father, won a scholarship to the Sorbonne's Law School and, upon return to Egypt, became a professor of law at Cairo University and one of Egypt's youngest judges, and eventually a cabinet minister in the government of King Farouk. After Nasser's 1952 Revolution, my father left Egypt and settled in the United States, where he began a second career, arguing a landmark case for the Arabian American Oil Company and becoming a professor of international law at Columbia University.

It was in this latter period, when I was 15 years old, that my father, Saba Habachy, agreed that, if my grades were good enough, and if I got through Thomas Carlyle's *The French Revolution: A History*, he would take me to Paris. I was already a committed Francophile, loving the sound of the language, especially the poetry of Baudelaire, the history of the Bourbons, the gossip I could understand in *Paris Match*, the paintings of Sisley and Pissarro, the songs of Piaf and Jacqueline Francois, and the music of Debussy, whose *Clair de Lune* I mangled mercilessly as I tried to master it for a school recital. I aced the year academically and struggled through Carlyle, with the dizzyingly complicated philosophies of Danton and Robespierre, wept over the fate of Marie Antoinette and her children, and flew to Paris one wonderful June day.

True to his word, my father took it upon himself to take me through Paris' wealth of museums, starting of course, with the Louvre—that is to say, *his* Louvre. Given that his taste was extremely good, I did get a fabulous grounding in what mattered. The Venus of Samothrace did get more attention from him than I felt she deserved, but I was willing to wait for my first viewings of Watteau and Fragonard, who were high on my bucket list. My father did an impromptu lecture on ancient Greece and democracy and I listened enthralled, along with an audience of total strangers, which he had attracted. This happened a lot. My father could discourse on virtually any subject. Throughout his life, he read voraciously in Arabic, English, French, and German. A fluency in languages was to be a great asset all his life. To hone his skills, he would often read the same book in two languages simultaneously. I prize my father's copies of the Bible, in several languages.

My father marched me all over Paris. One afternoon, we seemed to be lingering in an undistinguished little square in the Montparnasse district. I was impatient, anxious to get to the Conciergerie, which boasted a particularly grizzly artifact—the blade of a guillotine. My father said amiably "You see this square?"

Somewhat impatiently, I said "Yes." All there was was a bench, a bit of a lawn, and a streetlight. My father then told me that this was where, as a young law student, he had studied, under the streetlight until it went out. At that point, he would go to his student digs and burn what little kerosene he could afford. We did not get to the Conciergerie that evening. Instead, we talked of what it was like to grow up poor in Egypt. My father was the cleverer of two brothers, but what money there was went to his older brother. My grandfather had been a gambler and my grandmother would sometimes dispatch Saba to fetch his father from the gambling tables.

But, my father had caught the eye of the elderly matriarch in the family, Tante Galila who was his first cousin. Tante Galila was the daughter of Boutros Ghali, Egypt's Prime Minister from 1908 till 1910. Their mothers were sisters. One sister had married well, and one had not. The latter was my grandmother.

When I was a child, I always wondered if Tante Galila had ever been young. I remember her as being gray. She had gray hair, wore gray, and had one rheumy gray eye and one very alert brown one. How the eye had been lost I never knew. But the other eye missed nothing and had a twinkle in it. Needing a reader and seeing the promise in her young cousin, Tante Galila invited my father to come regularly to read to her from the poems, plays, and novels of Alfred de Vigny. And then they turned to Vigny's translations of Shakespeare. My father not only learned French, but also acquired a permanent champion in Tante Galila. She gave him a stipend to help see him through his Paris student days when he won a scholarship to the Sorbonne. When she was in Paris, she would take her young cousin out for a good meal at the Rotisserie Perigourdine.

And now, some fifty years later, my father and I left Montparnasse and headed for the same Pergourdine, to rendezvous with my mother, who'd been shopping. I was enjoying watching them deal with disparate aspects of Parisian life. Here we were, in an elegant restaurant, and quite soon my father was faced with his nemesis, the enthusiastic Sommelier, hell bent on selling his best and preferably most expensive bottle of wine. My father apologetically told the man that we didn't drink alcohol. The man looked genuinely wounded, and then horrified, and then he became downright angry. My father's prowess in the Egyptian courts had earned him the title of the "Tiger," (*nimr*) but he was totally cowed by a Parisian Sommelier. My mother laughingly took on the offended Sommelier and deftly and elegantly defused the situation.

Not only was my father's Paris immensely enjoyable, but my mother's was rich and exciting in a different way—hers was the Paris of the opera, the theaters and the nightclubs. Paris was offering a number of variety shows that summer at the Mogador and the Olympia. Maurice Chevalier, in his straw boater hat, sang about every little breeze whispering the name of Louise. It was corny but charming and the ladies in the audience were lapping it up. And there was operetta at the Opera Comique. It was a rich summer of theatricals for a teenager and her musically oriented mother.

My mother, Gameela Gindy Younan el Mallakh, was a pianist who had, despite coming from a conservative Coptic family, managed to get herself to Germany to continue her musical studies. What made her departure for Europe alone at the age of 17 possible, was that her eccentric uncle Ramses, who was studying chemistry and lived in Berlin, could be her chaperone. No one seemed too troubled by the fact that my mother would be living far away from Berlin in the town of Baden-Baden on the Rhine. My mother found lodging with a widow by the name of Frau Kuppler, who ran a tight ship that taught my mother Germanic principles, like punctuality, that stayed with her the rest of her life, to the irritation of her children. My mother and Uncle Ramses got together in Berlin upon occasion for important things, like attending Wagner's Ring of the Niebelung. Uncle Ramses would have to be woken up periodically, as he managed to sleep through even Wagner's brass-heavy orchestration.

My mother loved those two short years in Baden-Baden, which, though a small town, was quite sophisticated, having once replaced Paris as Europe's cultural center, while that city was under siege in 1870 during the Franco-Prussian War. My mother went about with Cora, her friend from the boarding house. She and Cora would greet young men wearing caps representing their universities. One or two had a slash across their cheek, acquired honorably in a duel fought for some ludicrous reason. One shy young man presented himself to my mother, who apparently found the approach not undesirable.

As they strolled on a winter evening, the young women nursed hot sweet potatoes warming cold hands. One night, out of the blue, someone hurled a shower of coins at Cora. My mother was shocked; Cora was not. Cora hurried them away towards their rooming house and patiently explained to my horrified mother that the insult implied that Cora was a prostitute because she was a Jew. The next morning my mother woke up to the news that Cora was gone—Frau Kuppler had asked her to leave.

My mother returned to Egypt in the early thirties. She received a letter from Cora asking if she could come to Egypt if she could get out of Europe. My mother wrote back that she would be very welcome and waited and waited for a reply that never came.

My mother had no choice but to leave Germany. The family fortune that had allowed her the luxury of a European musical education had run out because of her grandfather's bad business dealings, and because the Wall Street crash dealt a severe blow to Egypt's cotton industry. The Gindys not only owned land, but they were in the business of shipping cotton to Alexandria for export abroad.

My grandmother showed up to take her daughter home. My Granny was a product of the PMI, the Protestant Missionary Institute in Assiout and was staunch in her Protestantism, but respectful of her husband's devotion to the Coptic Church. Before bundling my mother off to Cairo, my grandmother attended a traditional German event that meant a great deal to her—the Passion Play at Oberammergau. The inhabitants of Oberammergau had vowed in 1634 that if they were spared from the Bubonic Plague, they would re-enact Christ's Passion every ten years. They were spared and had kept their word, performing the Passionsspiel to the delight of the faithful and the tourists. With great solemnity and religious fervor my grandmother and her daughter joined the Lutheran faithful in this rite over several days. One evening, returning to their lodgings after the performance that had included the Crucifixion, they walked past a beer hall, and there was Jesus Christ, swilling what was probably a well-earned beer with Joseph of Arimathea. My grandmother, to hear my mother tell it, never quite got over it.

My father saw my mother at a club where he was playing tennis and where she was with friends at a table overlooking the tennis courts. A European might have sent over a bottle of champagne. My father sent over an order of tea. Thus began a courtship. My father seemed to be a man with few prospects. But he was promising. He had distinguished himself already as a very young lawyer, helping in the defense of Egypt's nationalists, trying to free their country of the British yoke. But the nationalist hero, Saad Zaghloul, and his cohorts, wound up exiled to the Seychelles islands despite my father's best efforts. My father had apparently impressed General Edmund Allenby, who was made High Commissioner for Egypt and Sudan just after World War I. Allenby suggested that perhaps Saba Habachy should be included among those exiled to the Seychelles. Clearly, he was a dangerous new addition to Egypt's political scene.

When they married just before the war, my parents lived modestly. My father had recently been sacked by his Prime Minister. He was a member of the Saadist party and had disagreed with members of the opposing Wafdists. Running afoul of the prevailing political winds was characteristic of my father. He was known to resign with some frequency. King Farouk was heard saying that when Saba Habachy resigns, there is usually something going on that reeks of corruption.

By the time I was born, my parents had moved to Kubba Gardens, where they shared a villa with my maternal grandmother. My Granny ruled the roost in her quiet way, and made sure that I was well on my way to knowing many Bible stories, which she recounted in English and in Arabic. I grew especially close to her, as she and I were frequently the only members of the family in Egypt over the summer. At this time in the Habachy family's life, my father was being frequently called abroad on business. He took his wife and my older sister and brother with him. ESSO, BP, Shell et al had discovered a most valuable legal mind that could navigate between the Napoleonic Code Civil and Sharia law—in three languages. My father was one of the draftsmen of the oil concession agreement between the Arabian American Oil Company and the Government of Saudi Arabia.

I was delighted to be holed up with my Granny in Alexandria's Beau Rivage hotel, right on the sea in the district of Laurent. We lived in a bungalow that was like an individual tiny house with its own porch and stairway. Every day, I went to the beach with my Egyptian nanny, who fought valiantly to see to it that I didn't get too dark in the mercilessly strong sun. It was a losing battle; no amount of ugly sun hats could keep the Egyptian sun off of a true daughter of Egypt. My mother was fair, had brown hair, and came across as Middle European or Slavic. I came away from those summers looking as though I'd changed races. Despite my mother's distress, I played on happily in the sand with my floppy hat and built sandcastles. My little friends were Brits, Poles, and French. I was in the minority on my beach and I never really understood why there were only Egyptians on the next-door beach, and why they were swimming in their clothes, with no silly hats and no constricting bathing suits. I thought they were having a lot more fun than I was. The foreigners and a few Egyptians built intricate castles with sluices that let in the Mediterranean at our command, until a big wave swept everything away.

My parents stayed abroad for 2 to 3 months. There was lots of time for Granny to inculcate her brand of fundamentalism in her grand-child. I liked the idea of this kindly father figure who "suffered little children to come unto him." Granny's stories were buttressed up by the presence of an American missionary whom Granny insisted looked just like Jesus Christ. He had a brown beard and was fair and therefore beautiful and looked just like the Christ figure in my Bible lessons for children, which came out of a book by the English writer, Enid Blyton. Jesus Christ and his family frequently came by to visit this staunch member of the Presbyterian Church.

We picked up our Cairo lives at the end of summer. My siblings went back to school and my father spent his days at the *barlaman* (parliament). I watched the parade of people that came to visit. During my childhood, I was aware people respected my father but really didn't know why. My father was Minister of Commerce, Industry, and Supply in King Farouk's government, hell bent on industrializing Egypt with the help of the Europeans, but then getting rid of them. He was instrumental in starting several Egyptian industries. He had earned his place in the public eye during the war when, in his capacity as Minister of Supply, he had chosen to supply the British in the desert. In choosing to side with the allies, he went against his king, who was pro-Axis. Farouk had been promised by the Germans that if they won the war, he would cease to be the vassal of the British that he was now.

It could be argued that my father's decision to supply the British at El Alamein helped hasten the end of the war—it certainly was the end for Rommel's Afrika Corps. But now he was in the uncomfortable position of knowing he was on Rommel's hit list, and the German forces were only a hundred and fifty kilometers from Cairo. Bombs could already be heard in Alexandria. My parents had the local shelter in their Cairo home. My father used to tell the story of a *fellah* who arrived asking to be let into the shelter with the family *gamousa* (water buffalo). He argued, quite rightly, that without the gamousa, his family would lose its livelihood.

Rommel entered neither Cairo nor Alexandria and after the war, the British saw fit to honor my father with a knighthood.

Life in post war Cairo was lively. My mother hosted gatherings for her famous and much sought-after husband. But she still found time to play piano for me while I sang from the Golden American Song book. My nose reached the keyboard on the upright piano and I could point to the song I wanted by the picture that accompanied it. We spent many a happy afternoon that way. These are among my happiest memories of her.

My Egyptian childhood ended after several foreign bastions in Cairo were burned over several days in January 1952. I remember seeing a very red sky from the roof of our home. In the aftermath of this insurrection, the British were finally ejected from Egypt and a new anti-capitalist army regime swept in on a wave of nationalism and pan-Arabism. My father was going to be identified as having been pro-British during the war and being part of the old regime.

My family left quietly for America with two weeks' worth of clothing, ostensibly to attend Columbia University Commencement exercises where my father would receive an honorary doctorate. We did not return for 18 years. The family started a new life in a much less gentle environment, where it took some time to learn how to belong. I remember my father gathering us together and making it quite clear that life would be harder here, since we'd left and lost everything in Egypt. But he said he could do one thing for us, perhaps the most important thing of all. He could give us a good education. And that he did. The three of us have gone on to make good lives in what was then a generous and welcoming America. My sister had a distinguished career as a United Nations Civil Servant, my brother is a respected Corporate Lawyer with a Middle East firm, and I'm a radio broadcaster with National Public Radio and a lecturer on classical music.

I was lucky that my father considered Paris part of my education that wonderful summer. I was there with two of the most fascinating people I will ever have had the pleasure of knowing in my lifetime. My parents were good teachers. I like to think I was a good student.

———◆———

NIMET HABACHY celebrated a 40th anniversary working in radio and continues to host night broadcasts on classic music on WQXR, part of National Public Radio (NPR). She also continues her work with the Association for the Protection of the Environment, the organization that works with the *Zabbaleen*, the garbage collectors of Cairo. APE works primarily to improve the lives of the women in the community who instead of just sorting the detritus of Cairo, learn about hygiene, gain literacy, and acquire other life skills, earning them a place in a patriarchal society. She looks forward to seeing a dream come true—a new school in the *Zabbaleen* area that will be devoted to educating the next generation.

THE MANY JOURNEYS BETWEEN EGYPT AND AMERICA

Fikry F. Andrawes

Deciding what to include or omit in this short autobiography was challenging. I decided to share some of the memories that mean the most to me.

I was born in Aswan, Egypt, in 1941, and spent my early years there. The family later moved to El-Mahala El-Kobra and then to Alexandria, where I attended school and university. I immigrated to the United States in 1970 and have lived here for fifty years, visiting Egypt annually. But my early memories of Egypt are still vivid and dear to my heart.

Our house in Aswan was full of life. In addition to my parents and siblings, grandfather, and an aunt and uncle who lived with us, the house nearly always contained relatives and guests, who stayed with us while traveling back and forth between Sudan and Cairo or beyond. One of the highlights of those early years in Aswan was the Coptic community's annual pilgrimage to visit the ruins of Anba Hidra's ancient monastery, across the Nile in the western desert. The monastery dates back to the seventh century. I and the other kids enjoyed eating delicious food from different families, and most importantly, playing in the infinite desert sand surrounding the site.

Another trip was a beautiful voyage from Aswan to Wadi Halfa, on the northern border of Sudan. One of our uncles was an engineer assigned to inspect the banks of the Nile. The government provided him with a *dahabia* boat that had several cabins, so he took me, my brother, and two aunts along with him. It was a trip back in time that lasted for two weeks.

Before the High Dam was built, the Nile flowed peacefully through Nubia, with no interruption. We visited some of the ancient Egyptian temples, including the famous Abu Simbel temple, in its original site. This was before the entire temple was cut into blocks and reassembled on higher ground so it wouldn't drown in the new Lake Nasser that would form when the dam project had been completed. During this trip, we met up with another uncle, who was a medical doctor inspecting the banks of the Nile for mosquitos that could carry malaria. The government had also provided him with a dahabiya, equipped with a small laboratory, so we were able to visit between the two boats. Along the way, we also were invited to attend a Nubian wedding. We saw crocodiles and dined on delicious meals of freshly caught fish.

After my family moved to El-Mahala El-Kobra in 1950, I didn't visit Aswan again until 1980, when I came back with my American wife, Alison. In thirty years, the small, beautiful town had changed significantly. It had become unrecognizable to me. I knew that the house I grew up in was on the corniche, overlooking the river and separated from it by the main street in town. This street was decorated with a line of Albizia lebbeck (شجر اللبخ) trees, often called *Dekn El-Pasha*, meaning the Pasha's chin, because their flowers have delicate yellow whiskers. Now, the trees and the quiet old town were gone, and the changes filled me with sadness.

One evening, we went out to have dinner in a restaurant on the Nile's bank. The restaurant was very new, and the owner, in his long white galabiya, was watching a sign painter write the name of the place in English. There was a mistake in the spelling, which my wife noticed and corrected for them. After we enjoyed our fish *tagan* dinner, I asked the owner where the post office building was. The man looked at me and asked, "Which post office?"

I replied, "The old post office in town."

His second question was "Why you want to know?" I said, "Because our old house was very near the post office." His third question followed: "What is your father's name?" "Fouad Andrawes," I told him.

The man looked at me and said, "Come, my son, I will show you your house."

It turned out to be very close to the restaurant. We crossed the street along the corniche, with its line of new tall buildings, and then entered a narrow inner street that ran parallel to it. Our guide pointed and said, "This is your house." Pointing to an old gray building he said, "This is the old post office."

We thanked him, and he left. The house, with its two balconies, and the nearby post office building had not changed, but they were no longer on the Nile's bank. A new block of tall buildings had been built between my old street and the Nile. My old riverside home was now on a small alley, a block from the water. Building the High Dam had revolutionized Aswan and destroyed its original character. Each of my visits since has revealed more changes. Now Aswan is a big city. It has changed just as much as I have.

The 1980 trip was Alison's first visit to Egypt, so I wanted to show her the major sites of Cairo. Of course, we went to the Giza pyramids. It turned out she was the third generation of her family to stand in the famous tourist spot. Her grandparents had visited Egypt in 1926, two years after Carter discovered the tomb of King Tut. We have an old family photograph of her grandparents sitting on camels, with the Great Pyramid in the background. Her father, then a six-year-old boy, is seated on the saddle in front of his mother. The same tourist photos are still taken in the same place today.

During this trip, a friend of ours arranged for us to go with some other friends to the New Valley in the Western Desert. We spent a few days at our friends' date palm farm, escaping the very busy, overpopulated, and noisy Cairo. We enjoyed the good company of our friends.

In 1950, my father changed jobs and moved the family to El-Mahala El-Kobra, a center for the textile industry in the middle of the Egyptian

Delta. In 1952, we moved again, this time to Alexandria, where my siblings and I attended high school and college. During my years in Alexandria, Egypt was undergoing political, social, and economic upheavals brought about by the military revolution of 1952. The British colonization of Egypt that had lasted for eighty years finally ended. King Farouk was deposed, ending the old Mohamed Ali dynasty, founded in 1805. Egypt became a republic, headed first by General Nagib and then by Gamal Abdel Nasser. The regime nationalized businesses, encouraged industrialization, and initiated projects to serve the poor and the middle class. It also turned the country into a police state in which the government controlled the media and limited the freedom of the press. Living through these dramatic events as a teenager gave me a lasting interest in politics and history.

After graduating from Alexandria University in 1963, I got a job with the Agricultural Research Department and was posted to Assiut in the south of Egypt. But my interest in politics continued. Like most Egyptians, I sympathized with the suffering of the Palestinian people, as a result of the creation of the State of Israel. In my lifetime, Egypt had gone to war with Israel in 1948 when it was founded, in 1956 after the nationalization of the Suez Canal, and now again in 1967. This latest conflict was shockingly brief. The combined forces of Egypt, Jordan, and Syria were defeated in a matter of days, during which time Israel seized the rest of Palestine, including Jerusalem.

The war of 1967 exposed serious faults within the Nasser regime. Many Egyptians were shocked at the outcome and felt betrayed. They felt their government had mismanaged the war and lied to the people about how it was progressing. I was one of those who were sadly disillusioned. Like many other educated Egyptians at the time, including my siblings, I decided to leave Egypt and immigrate to the United States. This outflow became the first mass wave of emigration from Egypt in modern times.

But before I could leave Egypt, I had to get approvals from many officials, including the Minister of Agriculture, even though my job was of little significance. Under the centralized bureaucracy of Nasser's government, lower-level administrators had lost their authority to make decisions, so they kept forwarding my request upward until it reached the minister's office. This took time, but was ultimately successful. Egypt would allow me to leave, but would the United States allow me in?

I prepared all the application documents the American Embassy required for immigration. Then I had to be interviewed by the American general consul. During this interview, the consul asked me questions about my plans. I answered them and mentioned to her that I expected to have some difficulties, but that I also expected I would be able to do well. I had a brother who was a geologist working for Mobil Oil Company, and also an uncle who was an engineer and had immigrated from the Belgian Congo and was doing very well in the United States. The consul looked at me and said, "All Egyptians say something like that, but they fail in the States." She finally gave me her approval to immigrate, but I didn't like her discouraging and prejudiced comment. It stayed in my mind. Years later, after I had gotten my master's and PhD degrees and was working at NASA, I wished I could remember the name of the American general consul who had interviewed me in 1969. I would have liked to send her a letter describing my success, reminding her of her denigrating remarks and pointing out that her own ancestors at one point had been immigrants themselves.

I arrived in the States in 1970. Even before leaving Egypt, I realized I would have to make a serious adjustment to a new life in a new country. My first big challenge was the language barrier. My education in Egypt had included eight years of English, but the quality of my language education hadn't been very good, and it had ended ten years earlier. When I arrived in the States, I confronted the additional problem of understanding American regional accents.

My first place of residence was Dallas, Texas, where I stayed with my brother, who was already established there. I got odd jobs working in restaurants for a while, until I landed a job working on the assembly line of an ice cream factory. I started school to study English and also attended a course in chemistry at the University of Texas.

Within a year, I met another Egyptian immigrant, Ahmed Galal, who came from Houston to Dallas for a weekend visit. Ahmed mentioned that he worked in a new plastics factory, called Valeron Strength Film. He told me the company was hiring laboratory technicians. My brother bought me a new Ford Maverick car, and off I went to Houston. I got the job Ahmed mentioned and was able to stay as a guest in his apartment until I got my first paycheck. I then moved to a nice apartment by myself, but I'll always be grateful to my brother and Ahmed for their help and generosity.

The job in the plastics company was simple and didn't require any intelligence or much effort on my part. While chatting with an American engineer at the factory, I received a useful piece of advice. He told me that, in the United States, you can choose what kind of work you want to do and where you want to do it, and then you just have to go out and get it. To me as a foreigner, the language barrier and its subtleties were additional barriers, but what that engineer said was correct at that time. There were many opportunities. I decided I had to take action if I wanted to get ahead.

To improve my vocabulary, I bought a notebook and alphabetized it with plastic side tabs. Then, with the help of the English-Arabic dictionary I'd brought with me from Egypt, I began to write down words from television and newspapers that I didn't know. This was my personal dictionary for a while. Gradually, I acquired others. Now, in my study, I have five dictionaries, one of which is all in Arabic and which I still find difficult to use. Both the Arabic and English languages are still a challenge for me.

I applied to attend graduate school at the University of Houston (U of H). After I completed the forms, the head of the International Students Office told me, "Your degree from Egypt doesn't mean much to us. We regret to tell you that your application to graduate school has been denied. You will never get a degree from here." So, I asked to attend classes as a post-baccalaureate student, not a degree candidate. This was accepted, but the official repeated that I would not get a degree from U of H.

During this time, I continued working at the plastics factory. Employees worked rotating shifts around the clock, 24/7. The most-hated shift was the graveyard shift, which started at midnight and ended at eight in the morning. I arranged with my coworkers to take this night shift so I could go to school during the day. Naturally, they welcomed this. In addition, though work in this shift was necessary for the continuous production of the lab, it was very slow and allowed me time to read and study freely. I was the only person in the lab most of the time.

At U of H, I took two courses in English as a second language and one in chemistry. The next semester, I enrolled in a graduate-level chemistry course and received a good grade. After passing these courses, I applied again as a graduate-degree candidate and this time I was accepted. I started the program for a master's degree in chemistry. I also got a teaching assistant position, which allowed me to support myself. I quit my job at the factory, sold my car, bought a bicycle, and moved into the dormitory. It was hard to go back to school full time, but it was also challenging and fun.

Before I finished my master's in science degree, my advisor decided to relocate to Germany. I had to choose another professor to oversee my research. Albert Zlatkis welcomed me. He currently had an Egyptian graduate student, Fred Shunbo, who was about to finish his PhD, and I learned that Zlatkis's very first graduate student had also been an Egyptian. They must have left a good impression on Zlatkis, for he never discriminated against his Arab students. We discussed Middle Eastern politics and the Arab-Israeli conflict in particular. In one of our political discussions, he quoted Nasser as saying he would "throw Israel in the sea."

I challenged that, knowing that Nasser had never said it. Someone else used this phrase, and it was misattributed to Nasser in Zionist propaganda. I turned around and mentioned to him that Golda Meir, the prime minister of Israel, said, "Who are the Palestinians? They never existed."

He said, "Oh no, Golda couldn't have said that."

I remembered that she had said it in an interview published in London's *Sunday Times*. So, I got a copy of the newspaper from the library and showed it to him.

My relationship with Zlatkis remained good after that. Many years later, I organized a retirement party for him in honor of a conference he had organized annually.

I finished my master's degree in 1975. When I had trouble finding a job, Zlatkis offered me a scholarship and assigned me a research project to work on. I went to Egypt to visit family for a short vacation and then came back to the university and worked hard on the research assigned to me. After about a year, I showed the preliminary results to Zlatkis. He looked at them with amazement and then he looked at me and said, "With this work, you've earned your PhD. Now just finish the academic requirements and keep working on the project."

That I did with pleasure and enjoyment. But I have to admit, I was very lucky. By the time I'd finished my PhD in 1977, I'd already started a job at NASA analyzing lunar samples obtained from the moon by the astronauts.

During my time at U of H, I was fortunate to meet a beautiful young woman, Alison, who was taking chemistry classes. She already had a BA in art history from Wellesley College and had finished her coursework for an MA in religious studies at Rice University. Studying psychology of religion got her interested in how the mind works. She decided to go to medical school to learn about the brain and become a psychiatrist. To do that, she needed to take pre-med sciences. U of H offered the best schedule, so she enrolled there as a non-degree candidate, and that is how we came to cross paths in the chemistry department. We got to know each other, and lived together for a year, unsure whether we would find a job and a medical school in the same city. Luckily, Alison was accepted to the University of Texas Medical Branch at Galveston, which was about a thirty-minute drive from my job at NASA in Clearlake.

We got married in August 1977, one day after I defended my PhD dissertation. Within two weeks, we had moved from Houston to Galveston, and Alison had started medical school. It was a busy time.

My job at NASA was interesting and very challenging. NASA had purchased an analytical machine to do a very specific analysis on some extraterrestrial materials, including samples from the moon. But they had been unable to use the machine, due to misunderstanding some aspects of the theory behind how it worked. I developed a better theory that allowed us to use the instrument. I also designed and built an elaborate closed system to allow us to analyze tiny amounts of gas in lunar rocks, without letting the Earth's air contaminate the sample. This was quite challenging, but the difficulties were finally overcome. The system I designed had wide applications and allowed me to collaborate on various projects with other researchers in the United States and abroad. I published many scientific papers and was asked to review scientific articles being submitted for publication in peer-reviewed journals.

As a result of my work at NASA, a new commercial instrument was introduced to the market by a private company. The manufacturer gave my laboratory one of these instruments for free, knowing they would benefit from the free advertising they received whenever I published results of work using that instrument.

I stayed at NASA for five years. But the geochemistry work at NASA didn't interest me all that much, so I applied for jobs in academia and in the industry. At the same time, Alison was finishing her medical degree and interviewing around the country for residency training programs in psychiatry. I was offered a job working at the central research laboratory of American Cyanamid Company in Stamford, Connecticut. Alison was delighted at the prospect of moving back to Connecticut, where she had grown up and where her parents still lived. She took an internship at New York Medical College, followed by a residency and fellowship training at Cornell Medical College in Westchester, New York—all within easy commuting distance from Stamford, where we bought a house. I was able to walk or bike to work.

Living near New York City allowed us to enjoy some of the rich cultural activities the city offered, including museums, shows, and special events. We sometimes spent the weekend in the city and enjoyed shopping at the Arab food stores and eating at our favorite Yemeni restaurant on Atlantic Avenue in Brooklyn. At this point, our life was stable, but we both worked hard. I continued my work in the research lab, published scientific papers, and participated in local and international conferences. It was gratifying to receive awards and recognition for my work.

After moving to Connecticut, we met a community of Egyptian Americans in the greater New York area. This was something I had missed in Texas. Two Egyptian American psychiatrists introduced us to the Egyptian American Professionals Society (EAPS), where we became regular members. This organization met monthly for dinner and a lecture, initially in individual homes, but later in a rented space, where up to eighty people would gather for a potluck buffet. I served as president of EAPS for some years and added to these activities an annual conference, which was usually held at New York University or Columbia University. Speakers came from the United States, Egypt, and Europe. In addition, the organization sponsored an annual gala, attended by three hundred to four hundred persons.

Once my career was well established, I started to go to Egypt annually, and became a contributor to the monthly magazines *El-Helal* and *Weghat Nazar*. I started to write books in Arabic and English on topics related to Egypt.

In the late 1990s, as I was approaching retirement, Alison started thinking about building a small hut in the woods of northwestern Connecticut as a weekend camping retreat. We both loved nature and hiking. We found a beautiful piece of woodland with a clear stream running through it. After exploring many possibilities, the idea of building a hut there mushroomed into building a house where we could live full time when we retired. Alison had seen her parents build their family's home in the Connecticut woods when she was young, so the concept wasn't foreign to her. But this whole idea was totally foreign to me. It was a great learning experience for both of us.

We wanted the house to be energy efficient, so we chose a sheltered south-facing site on the side of a small mountain, with a view of the valley below. Here it would be sheltered from cold north winds in winter and receive cool breezes in summer. It took a year to build an access road up the mountain, including building a bridge over the stream. We also had to bring in electricity, dig a well, and install a septic system. Heavy-duty excavators built the road and cleared the house site. It took three hundred pounds of explosives to blast the foundation hole. All this was new and fun for me to see. The project entailed cutting a large number of trees. Many of the felled trees were cut to log size and set aside for later use. After the house was built, they were split into smaller pieces, stacked, and allowed to dry. The dry wood was then used to help heat the house in the winter. During this process, I learned how to cut trees and split and stack wood so it would dry properly. We burned two twenty-five pound loads of wood a day, in a stone furnace specially designed to conserve heat inside the house. But I'm getting ahead of myself.

It took two more years to build the house. We worked with a talented local architect to design and draw plans that incorporated features and ideas Alison had collected over the years. She had taken design courses in architecture at Massachusetts Institute of Technology when she was an undergraduate at Wellesley. Building this house was the fulfillment of a life dream for her. By now, she had retired from private practice and teaching and could be at the building site every day to keep an eye on the project and address problems that arose. We were also fortunate to have the architect, contractor, and crew we had. They all took great pride in their work. Several became personal friends.

The house featured Japanese elements inspired by the work of Frank Lloyd Wright. Natural materials were used whenever possible. High ceilings, stone and wood floors, and large glass windows featured in the design. The overhanging roof was designed so the sun would enter and heat the house from sunrise to sunset in winter but would shade the interior in summer. The interior was decorated with things we had collected over the years from Egypt and the States.

When the house was completed, it was a piece of heaven. It overlooked thousands of acres of wooded hills, with almost no buildings in sight. Nature surrounded us on all sides. We saw black bears, foxes, coyotes, and exotic birds. Bobcats walked across the deck. Wild turkeys roosted in the trees. Sometimes nature got a little too close. Skunks and mice had to be ushered out when they tried to move in, and a hungry porcupine had to be trapped and relocated after he developed a taste for chewing the cedar trim. Once we saw a fisher, a small, weasel-like animal that is shy and rarely seen.

We tried to landscape along the road and around the house, without intruding too much on Mother Nature. I worked outdoors for four to six hours a day in the growing season. In the winter, we shoveled and plowed snow—lots of it. It was good exercise.

Then, the year after we moved in, during a routine physical examination, I was diagnosed with an incurable form of non-Hodgkin's lymphoma, a type of blood cancer. Luckily, it was a slow-growing kind. Second opinions from Yale and Sloan-Kettering recommended chemotherapy, but a local oncologist (and lymphoma specialist) offered the option to watch and wait in order to see how fast the tumor actually grew. We chose the latter. Within a year, the tumor had started to enlarge and cause side effects, so in 2002, I had my first course of chemotherapy, which was well tolerated and brought about a complete remission. Lymphoma is not considered curable; it recurs every few years, but so far, I have responded well to treatment.

The cancer diagnosis got me and Alison interested in researching ways to improve our health and my cancer-treatment outcomes through food and lifestyle changes. This interest resulted in a book written in Arabic, *Your Food is Your Medicine*. Abdelgelil Mustafa, a professor of medicine at Cairo University, wrote an introduction to the book and took five hundred copies to distribute to doctors' unions in Egypt. The information in this book was taken from research done in the United States and Europe. The scientific findings were published in English, but I wanted to make the information easily available to an Arabic-reading public. Someone must be reading it, because the Egyptian publisher has already issued a third printing.

We spent many wonderful years at the house in Connecticut. Each season had its special beauty. In spring, the forest was full of flowering trees and bird songs. Summer was a season for gardening. In autumn, the woods blazed with brilliant color. In winter, the air was clean and crisp. After a fresh fall of snow, a glittering white carpet covered everything in sight. But as the years went by and we got older, the winters were less enchanting. We started to visit Alison's sister in Hawaii during the holiday season. We enjoyed Hawaii so much that each year we wanted to stay longer. We began renting an apartment for a month, then two months. Finally, we decided to buy a condo surrounded by tropical gardens in a small town on the windward side of Oahu. For several years, we split our time between Hawaii and Connecticut, six months in each place, before returning to the East Coast in summer to put the house on the market. Eventually, the perfect buyer came along, and we said a reluctant goodbye to our beloved house in the Connecticut woods.

Living in Hawaii is like living in paradise. We eat our meals outdoors on a balcony overlooking a landscaped pond populated by rare birds from the abutting nature preserve. Now, at eighty years old, I feel I'm starting another phase of my life. I enjoy walking on the beach, exercising, reading, and writing. And most importantly, I make my annual pilgrimage to Egypt to see friends and family and just walk in the streets. Getting Arabic books is an important benefit of visiting Egypt. Through the years, I have accumulated a good library, which is invaluable for my research and writing. So far, I've had ten books published, all on topics related to Egypt.

When the revolution of January 25 started, I wanted to join it, even though I had been in Egypt just one month before. It took me thirty-six hours to get from Hawaii to Cairo. I was very proud to stand among the young people who started the revolution that made Tahrir Square an internationally known site. I have to say that the people I saw in Tahrir Square represented not only young people, but also multiple generations. I saw an old woman in a wheelchair, with her children and grandchildren around her. After ten years, it's sad to say that this hopeful revolution failed. But there is a lot to learn from it. I will never forget the chant in Tahrir Square: "Hold your head high, you are an Egyptian!"

I consider myself lucky to have the family I have and the good friends I've gotten to know in Egypt and in America. I owe a great deal to the many people who helped and encouraged me along this life's journey. I've been fortunate to be able to travel to many places in the world, including India, China, Japan, Yemen, Morocco, and Ethiopia. Even though I live on a small piece of America in the middle of the Pacific Ocean, very far from Egypt, Egypt will always be inside me. It's in my DNA.

———◆———

FIKRY ANDRAWES worked as an agronomist for the Egyptian government for five years before immigrating to the United States in 1970. After a few jobs, he went back to university and earned a PhD in chemistry. For several years, he worked at NASA before taking a job in the chemical industry. He is the author of numerous scientific articles in chemistry. Since his retirement in 2000, he has published many articles and several books in Arabic and English on topics relating to Egypt. He and his wife live in Hawaii.